WAY

SO-BWX-305

THE
National
JOBLINE
Directory

THE
National
JOBLINE
Directory

**Over 2,000 companies, Government
Agencies, and other Organizations
that Post Job Openings by Phone**

by
ROBERT SCHMIDT

BOB ADAMS, INC.
Holbrook, Massachusetts

Published by Bob Adams, Inc.
260 Center Street, Holbrook, MA 02343

ISBN: 1-55850-385-4

Printed in the United States of America.

J   I   H   G   F   E   D   C   B   A

Library of Congress Cataloging-in-Publication Data
Schmidt, Robert (Robert Vernon)
    The national job line directory: over 2,000 companies, government agencies, and other organizations that
post job openings by phone / Robert Schmidt.
    p.   cm.
    ISBN 1-55850-385-4
    1. Job hotlines—United States—Directories. 2. Job vacancies—United States—Directories.
    3. Job hunting—United States—Directories. 4. Civil services—United States—Directories.
    5. Americans—Employment—Directories. I. Title.
HF5382.75.U5S296   1994
331.12'8'02573—dc20   94-15482
                                                                   CIP

This publication is designed to provide accurate and authoritative information with regard to the subject
matter covered. It is sold with the understanding that the publisher is not engaged in rendering legal,
accounting, or other professional advice. If legal advice or other expert assistance is required, the services of
a competent professional person should be sought.
— From a *Declaration of Principles* jointly adopted by a Committee of the American Bar Association and
                                                a Committee of Publishers and Associations

Cover design: Berg Design

This book is available at quantity discounts for bulk purchases.
For information, call 1-800-872-5627.

Contents

Introduction

THE HIDDEN JOB MARKET

The typical job-seeker looks through the classified ads, scans the postings at the unemployment office, and asks a few friends if they know of anything. The person may uncover and apply for about one job a week.

The typical job-seeker is not very successful.

Nancy Hause, Director of the Career Center at Occidental College, says fewer than 50% of job openings are ever publicized. For whatever reason (the cost, the hassle), employers rely on internal advertisements and referrals to find qualified candidates. The average job-seeker never hears of these jobs.

But many organizations do list open positions for their employees, and often for outsiders, by means of an automated phone system. By simply calling up and pressing a few buttons, job-seekers can tap into the vast, unpublicized market of jobs.

Until now, no source has listed the thousands of phone numbers available to the job-seeker. Thus, the need for the *National Jobline Directory*.

HOW TO FIND A JOB

"People find jobs through networking," says Hause, "and these jobs are not necessarily advertised at all." For these opportunities, friends, relatives, co-workers, and other associates are the best source of information. The aspiring job-seeker, therefore, should network as much as possible.

But how feasible is this, realistically? How many of us can devote a full day to networking and other job-seeking strategies? We all have limitations of one sort or another: family duties, transportation problems, school conflicts, medical woes, legal hassles, and so forth.

Yet those who rely on traditional sources are in for trouble. According to Hause, for instance, "the smallest number of jobs are placed through the classifieds." Each listing in the Sunday want ads may invite up to 500 responses in today's economy. Imagine one's chances of landing such a job. Once again, the *National Jobline Directory* helps resolve the job-hunting dilemma. Job-seekers can call in the privacy of their homes at any hour of the day (e.g., after the kids are asleep). Too, the *Directory* offers help for those who, for whatever reason, are reluctant to call contacts directly for information. These people can tap into a job source many job-seekers don't know about, giving them the advantage.

WHAT THE RESEARCH SHOWS

Not surprisingly, the information in the *National Jobline Directory* reflects several well-known trends.

First, we found the majority of joblines in the West and South, following the long-term migration of jobs to the so-called Sunbelt. Or perhaps the use of progressive techniques such as joblines to locate desirable employees has led to the migration. We don't pretend to know.

The *Directory* also reflects the trend toward a service- and information-based economy. The majority of joblines are in government, colleges and universities, hotels, banks, and hospitals. Few jobs seem to be available in assembly lines or smokestack factories.

Unfortunately, the joblines are also a good indicator of the state of the economy. When times are lean, as they have been in recent years, organizations cut staffs and budgets. The result is that some recorded messages will say a place has a hiring freeze or is not hiring for other reasons.

This may be disappointing, but if you have your heart set on working for a place, call the jobline regularly. You'll be the first to know when the organization resumes hiring.

Talking to representatives in the organizations or industries you're interested in, as well as calling their joblines, should be part of your job-hunting strategy. Our research showed that many employers, including those that don't have joblines, are willing to discuss their needs.

You need only call an organization and ask for Personnel, Human Resources, or Employment. When you get a live representative, ask if the place is hiring, or say what kind of work you're interested in. The Personnel people generally will be glad to help you; a few will talk your ear off about the possibilities.

Most states have a Department of Personnel or Administration, which handles hiring for state jobs, and a Job Service or Employment Security Commission, which maintains lists of private employers with openings. These lists may be too voluminous to place on joblines, but they are printed in bulletins and stored in databases. In some states you can use a computer system to access job lists across the country. Contact your local employment office and ask to use these resources.

HOW TO USE THIS DIRECTORY

How should you approach a job-hunting campaign with the *National Jobline Directory*? First, decide what you want to do and where you want to do it. Are you interested in all jobs? Degreed or nondegreed? Salaried or hourly? Many phone systems will ask you to make choices, so be prepared.

Do you want to stay in the same geographic area or relocate? Either way, the *Directory's* geographic organization will help you. Even though the *Directory* pinpoints a location for each organization, the associated jobline may list openings throughout the state or nation. A jobline usually covers the entire region in which an organization operates.

Do you want to work in a particular industry or field? Consult the Industry index, which is sorted by industry. If you can't find your field of choice, keep in mind that cities need computer programmers, schools need lawyers, and S&Ls need writers. The job you want may be where you least expect it.

Decide which organizations you want to call and develop a plan, such as making a set number of calls once a week. Most of the phone messages are updated only this often, so calling more frequently is pointless.

Because the joblines are automated systems, for the most part, you can call the numbers in this book any time. We recommend you do so late at night (after 11:00 p.m.), in the early morning (before 8:00 a.m.), or on weekends. That way, if you're making a long distance or local zone call, you'll get the lowest phone rates.

For numbers with just an extension listed (e.g., x811), press the given number (811) when prompted. You may be required to press a '1' before the number, or a '#'.

For numbers for which you have to ask for an operator's assistance, you'll have to wait for business hours, of course. These are typically 8:00 or 8:30 to 4:30 or 5:00. This applies to any number in the *Directory* with the "Ask for" instruction. (Note that hotels and hospitals generally have operators on duty around the clock.)

If the phone rings repeatedly, is busy, or doesn't ring at all, try again later. Often job-seekers will hit these joblines heavily during the day—another advantage of calling during off-hours. Occasionally machines and systems break down, so if the phone rings, beeps, or is busy, even in the middle of the night, try the main number provided. Ask a Personnel or Human Resource person if the jobline is available.

If you're hearing-impaired, fear not. There's a good chance an organization will have a separate TTD line with job information. Joblines in areas with large Latino populations may have Spanish-language alternatives. If the jobline itself doesn't say so, call and ask.

A few joblines don't list jobs but only tell you where the organization posts jobs, when and how to apply for them, or where to send a resume. We've tried not to include joblines in this book unless they provide actual job listings. In a small number of cases, we felt a jobline's information was so useful we decided to include it anyway even though it didn't list jobs.

If a jobline advises you to send in a resume to be kept on file, take the suggestion with a grain of salt. Though most organizations say they will keep your resume active for six months or a year, we advise against sending a resume unless it's directed to a specific job opening or individual. A blanket mailing wastes your time and money and probably won't lead to anything.

To contact one of the organizations in the *Directory*, call the main number or write to the Personnel Department at the address given. The *Directory* lists the number and address of Personnel if possible, or of the headquarters or main office otherwise.

TECHNICAL NOTES

To insure its accuracy, the *National Jobline Directory* has been updated to reflect all area code changes planned for 1994. These are:

Area code 215 (Philadelphia area) = 215, 610
Area code 919 (eastern North Carolina) = 919, 910
Area code 313 (Detroit area) = 313, 810

If you happen to employ this book before an area code has changed, simply use the old code. The phone companies will accept both area codes for a six-month grace period, after which the old code will no longer work.

OTHER RESOURCES

Many job-seekers will want more help than this book can provide. Nancy Hause and other experts recommend the following resources:

What Color Is Your Parachute? by Richard Nelson Bolles (Ten Speed Press).
The Professional's Job Finder by Daniel Lauber (Planning Communications).
The Complete Job Search Handbook: All the Skills You Need to Get Any Job and Have a Good Time Doing It by Howard E. Figler (Henry Holt & Co., Inc.).
The Right Place at the Right Time: Finding a Job in the 1990s by Robert Wegmann and Robert Chapman (Ten Speed Press).
The JobBank series (Bob Adams, Inc.).
The Overnight Resume by Donald Asher (Ten Speed Press).
Employment Weekly (newspaper).

WE NEED YOUR INPUT

We'd like to apologize if any of the listings are incorrect. Inevitably, organizations move, merge, or go out of business; names, phone numbers, and area codes change. As soon as this book is published, it's bound to be out of date.

Therefore, we solicit your help in improving our product. Please let us know if you know a jobline not listed in this book, or if an existing jobline is changed or discontinued. We'll reward each person who sends a valid new jobline number, or a change to an existing number, with a coupon for 50% off the price on this or future editions of the *National Jobline Directory*. The person also will receive a special list of joblines not published in this book. The same applies if an organization changes its name, address, or phone number, or if any of our information is wrong. No matter how small the detail, we want to know. Let us know and you'll receive the discount coupon and bonus list.

We appreciate your correspondence on any matter concerning the *National Jobline Directory*. Did the *Directory* help you find a job? We'd love to hear your experiences. How can we make the book better? Please direct all questions, comments, and criticisms to the author at the address listed below.

Robert Schmidt
c/o Bob Adams, Inc.
260 Center Street, Holbrook, MA 02343

START A JOBLINE

Finally, we'd like to urge all organizations—companies, governments, nonprofit associations, colleges and universities, and the rest—to set up joblines if they haven't already. The benefits are manifold:

1. An organization will locate more qualified candidates for those hard-to-fill jobs. More candidates means it can be more selective and obtain a better-qualified work force.
2. An organization can relieve the burden on its human resources staff, freeing workers for other tasks. Some companies have already realized the advantages of putting frequently-asked questions and answers on tape.
3. If every opening were listed publicly our economy would work perfectly, but, sadly, this is not the case. Unemployment and underemployment continue to bedevil us. An organization that helps correct this gains goodwill and status with customers, which adds to the bottom line.

Some organizations are too large to list every open job, but even the biggest company or government body, one with thousands of openings, can give some information over the phone. Is the organization hiring at all? If so, which divisions or departments? How does one contact them? What types of jobs is it hiring for? What procedures will help the applicant get a foot in the door?

If an organization does wish to set up a jobline, here are a few guidelines gleaned from our vast experience at listening to lengthy messages:

1. Use a system where a caller can push a button at any time.
2. Don't belabor the how-to-push-buttons instructions (most people have used such systems before).
3. Put the actual job listings up front; leave the application and equal opportunity information till the end. (Always assume callers are paying long distance rates.)
4. Include the official name and address (both physical and mailing) of the organization at some point.
5. Consider options for the hearing-impaired and speakers of foreign languages.
6. Always give an option to speak to an operator, or a number to call for further information (or for help when the system malfunctions).
7. Check the phone system at least weekly, even if the message remains the same. Machines do break down regularly.

Do your part . . . help make the economy go . . . start a jobline!

Alphabetical Listing of Joblines

Abbott Laboratories
1 Abbott Park Road, Abbott Park, IL 60064
Produces pharmaceutical preparations, hair products
    and toiletries, and diagnostic supplies.
(708) 937-6100
Jobline: (708) 938-6295

ACTION
1100 Vermont Avenue NW, Washington, DC 20525
Mobilizes Americans for voluntary service in programs
    that help meet basic human needs.
(202) 606-5263
Jobline: (202) 606-5039

Ada County
650 W. Main Street, Boise, ID 83702
Provides county services such as courts, motor vehicle
    registration, and social services.
(208) 364-2330
Jobline: (208) 364-2562

Ada County Sheriff's Department
7200 Barrister Drive, Boise, ID 83704
Provides sheriff's programs and services.
(208) 377-6708
Jobline: (208) 377-6707

Adam's Mark Houston
2900 Briarpark Drive at Westheimer Road, Houston, TX
    77042
604-room hotel.
(713) 978-7400
Jobline: (713) 735-2775

Adam's Mark Philadelphia
City Avenue and Monument Road, Philadelphia, PA
    19131
515-room hotel.
(215) 581-5000
Jobline: (215) 581-5074

Adams County
450 S. 4th Avenue, Brighton, CO 80601
Provides county services such as sheriffs, courts, motor
    vehicle registration, and social services.
(303) 654-6070
Jobline: (303) 654-6075

Addison (city)
5300 Belt Line Road, Addison, TX 75240
Provides municipal services such as police, firefighting,
    libraries, parks, and public works.
(214) 450-2817
Jobline: (214) 450-2815

Adolph Coors Co.
12th and Ford Streets, Golden, CO 80401
Produces beer and malt liquors, coated paperboard,
    porcelain electric supplies, and metal cans.
(303) 279-6565
Jobline: (303) 277-2450

Airborne Freight Corp.
P.O. Box 662, Seattle, WA 98111
Provides air courier services, package and letter
    delivery, and freight forwarding.
(800) 426-2323
Jobline: (800) 426-2323, x4815.

**Alabama (state) Industrial Relations Department
Employment Service Division**
Downtown Office
3440 3rd Avenue S., Birmingham, AL 35222
Seeks workers for private employers.
(205) 254-1300
Jobline: (205) 254-1389

Aladdin Hotel & Casino
3667 Las Vegas Boulevard South, Las Vegas, NV
    89109
1,095-room hotel.
(702) 736-0111
Jobline: (702) 736-0190

Alameda (city)
Santa Clara Avenue and Oak, Alameda, CA 94501
Provides municipal services such as police, firefighting,
    libraries, parks, and public works.
(510) 748-4521
Jobline: (510) 748-4635

Alamo Community College District
811 W. Houston Street, San Antonio, TX 78207
Includes Palo Alto College, St. Philip's College, and San
    Antonio College.
(210) 220-1601
Jobline: (210) 220-1600

Alaska (state)
P.O. Box 110201, Juneau, AK 99811
Provides state services such as conservation,
    education, highways, prisons, and welfare.
(907) 465-4430
Jobline: (907) 465-8910

701 E. Tudor Road, Anchorage, AK 99503
Provides state services such as conservation,
    education, highways, prisons, and welfare.
(907) 269-4800
Jobline: (907) 563-0200

Alaska (state) Department of Labor Employment Service
3301 Eagle Street, Room 101, P.O. Box 107024, Anchorage, AK 99510
Seeks workers for private employers.
Jobline: (907) 269-4725
Sales, service, and restaurant jobs.

Jobline: (907) 269-4730
Craft and trade jobs.

Jobline: (907) 269-4735
Part-time jobs.

Jobline: (907) 269-4740
Professional, technical, and clerical jobs.

Jobline: (907) 269-4750
Jobs for youths.

Jobline: (907) 269-4770
Seafood industry jobs.

Jobline: (907) 269-4865
Comprehensive information on employers and employment conditions in Alaska.

877 Commercial Drive, Wasilla, AK 99654
Seeks workers for private employers in the Matanuska/Susitna area.
(907) 376-2407
Jobline: (907) 376-8860

675 7th Avenue, P.O. Box 71010
Fairbanks, AK 99701
Seeks workers for private employers.
(907) 451-2871
Jobline: (907) 451-2875
Daily job list.

Alaska Air Group Inc.
19300 Pacific Highway South, P.O. Box 68947, Seattle, WA 98168
Provides scheduled air passenger transportation.
(206) 431-7040
Jobline: (206) 433-3230

Albertson's Inc.
250 Parkcenter Boulevard, Boise, ID 83726
Owns and operates chain supermarkets, superstores, and drug stores.
(208) 385-6200
Jobline: (208) 385-6422

Albuquerque (city)
400 Marquette Avenue NW, Albuquerque, NM 87102
Provides municipal services such as police, firefighting, libraries, parks, and public works.
(505) 768-3705
Jobline: (505) 768-4636

Alcon Surgical Inc.
6201 South Freeway, Fort Worth, TX 76134-2001
Manufactures pharmaceutical products, surgical instruments, and ophthalmic goods.
(817) 293-0450
Jobline: (714) 753-6585, press 1.

Alexandria (city)
301 King Street, Alexandria, VA 22314
Provides municipal services such as police, firefighting, libraries, parks, and public works.
(703) 838-4745
Jobline: (703) 838-4422

Allen County
City-County Building, 2nd Floor, 1 E. Main Street, Fort Wayne, IN 46802
Provides county services such as sheriffs, courts, motor vehicle registration, and social services.
(219) 428-7217
Jobline: (219) 428-7510

Alliant Health System
315 E. Broadway, Louisville, KY 40201
Owns or operates not-for-profit hospitals with more than 2,600 beds in three states.
(502) 629-6000
Jobline: (800) 789-5627

Amarillo (city)
509 E. 7th Avenue, Amarillo, TX 79101
Provides municipal services such as police, firefighting, libraries, parks, and public works.
(806) 378-4294
Jobline: (806) 378-4205

America West Airlines Inc.
4000 E. Sky Harbor Boulevard, Phoenix, AZ 85034
Provides scheduled air passenger transportation.
(602) 693-0800
Jobline: (602) 693-8650

American Family Mutual Insurance Co.
6000 American Parkway, Madison, WI 53783
Provides life, fire, marine, and casualty insurance, and other insurance and financial services.
(608) 249-2111
Jobline: (608) 242-4100, x34222.

American General Corp.
2929 Allen Parkway, Houston, TX 77019
Provides fire, life, health, and accident insurance, and other insurance and financial services.
(713) 522-1111
Jobline: (713) 831-3100

American Marketing Association
Southern California Chapter
18415 Dearborn Street, Northridge, CA 91325
Professional association of executives, managers, researchers, and others interested in marketing.
(818) 363-3917
Jobline: (818) 363-4127

American Medical International Inc.
8201 Preston Road, Suite 300, P.O. Box 25651, Dallas, TX 75225
Operates for-profit hospitals with more than 7,000 beds in 12 states.
(214) 360-6300
Jobline: (214) 360-6373

American Medical Laboratories Inc.
14225 Newbrook Drive, P.O. Box 10841, Chantilly, VA
   22021
Operates medical laboratories.
(703) 802-6900
Jobline: (703) 802-7282

American President Companies Ltd.
1111 Broadway, Oakland, CA 94607
Transports freight by deep-sea ship and by truck.
(510) 272-8000
Jobline: (510) 272-8082

American Red Cross
Los Angeles Chapter
2700 Wilshire Boulevard, Los Angeles, CA 90057
Serves members of the U.S. armed forces, aids
   disaster victims, and provides other services.
(213) 739-5200
Jobline: (213) 739-4596

American Savings of Florida FSB
17801 NW 2nd Avenue, Miami, FL 33169-5003
Operates federal savings and loan associations.
(305) 653-5353
Jobline: (305) 770-2019

American Stores Co.
709 E. South Temple, Salt Lake City, UT 84102
Operates combination food and drug stores,
   supermarkets, and super drug stores.
(801) 539-0112
Jobline: (800) 284-5560

American Telephone and Telegraph Co.
32 Avenue of the Americas, New York, NY 10013
Provides long distance and other telephone services,
   telephone sets and equipment, and computers.
(212) 387-5400
Jobline: (800) 562-7288
Jobs other than management.

Jobline: (800) 348-4313
Management jobs in the 13 Western states.

American University
Washington, DC 20016-8001
Medium-sized, church-affiliated, comprehensive
   institution with campuses in residential Washington.
(202) 885-1000
Jobline: (202) 885-2639

Ameritech Corp.
30 S. Wacker Drive, Chicago, IL 60606
Provides local, long distance, and other telephone
   services, telephone equipment, and directories.
(312) 750-5000
Jobline: (800) 808-5627
For callers in Illinois.

AMI Brookwood Medical Center
2010 Brookwood Medical Center Drive, Birmingham, AL
   35209
For-profit hospital with more than 500 beds.
(205) 877-1000
Jobline: (205) 877-1910

Amoco Corp.
200 E. Randolph Drive, Chicago, IL 60601
Produces crude oil, natural gas, gasolines, motor oils,
   diesel and jet fuels, and other products.
(312) 856-6111
Jobline: (312) 856-5551

AMR Corp.
P.O. Box 619616, Dallas/Fort Worth Airport, TX 75261
Provides scheduled air passenger and cargo
   transportation and data processing services.
(817) 963-1234
Jobline: (817) 963-1234

Jobline: (817) 963-1110
Corporate jobs.

Anaheim (city)
200 S. Anaheim Boulevard, Anaheim, CA 92805
Provides municipal services such as police, firefighting,
   libraries, parks, and public works.
(714) 254-5111
Jobline: (714) 254-5197

Anaheim Hilton & Towers
777 Convention Way, Anaheim, CA 92802
1,600-room hotel near Disneyland.
(714) 750-4321
Jobline: (714) 740-4319

Anchor Savings Bank
1420 Broadway, Hewlett, NY 11557
Operates federal savings banks and mortgage bankers.
(516) 596-3900
Jobline: (800) 932-2995

Anchorage (city)
632 W. 6th Avenue, Room 720, P.O. Box 196650,
   Anchorage, AK 99519-6650
Provides municipal services such as police, firefighting,
   libraries, parks, and public works.
(907) 343-4452
Jobline: (907) 343-4451

Anchorage Hilton
500 W. 3rd Avenue, Anchorage, AK 99501
600-room hotel.
(907) 272-7411
Jobline: (907) 265-7124

Anheuser-Busch Companies Inc.
1 Busch Place, Saint Louis, MO 63118
Produces beer and near beer, breads and dough
   products, and metal cans, and operates theme parks.
(314) 577-2000
Jobline: (314) 577-2392

Anne Arundel County
44 Calvert Street, Annapolis, MD 21401
Provides county services such as sheriffs, courts, motor
   vehicle registration, and social services.
(410) 222-1721
Jobline: (410) 222-1170

Anoka County
Government Center, 2100 3rd Avenue, Anoka, MN
    55303
Provides county services such as sheriffs, courts, motor
    vehicle registration, and social services.
(612) 323-5525
Jobline: (612) 422-7498

Antioch (city)
3rd and H Streets, P.O. Box 130, Antioch, CA 94509
Provides municipal services such as police, firefighting,
    libraries, parks, and public works.
(510) 779-7020
Jobline: (510) 779-7022

Appalachian State University
Boone, NC 28608
Medium-sized, public university with two campuses in
    Boone, west of Winston-Salem.
(704) 262-2179
Jobline: (704) 262-6488

Applied Magnetics Corp.
75 Robin Hill Road, Goleta, CA 93117
Manufactures computer magnetic storage devices.
(805) 683-5353
Jobline: (805) 683-5353, ask for x6003.

Arapahoe County
5334 S. Prince Street, Littleton, CO 80120
Provides county services such as sheriffs, courts, motor
    vehicle registration, and social services.
(303) 795-4482
Jobline: (303) 795-4480

Arizona (state)
1831 W. Jefferson Street, Phoenix, AZ 85003
Provides state services such as conservation,
    education, highways, prisons, and welfare.
(602) 542-5216
Jobline: (602) 542-4966

400 W. Congress Street, Room 139, Tucson, AZ 85701
Provides state services such as conservation,
    education, highways, prisons, and welfare.
(602) 628-6590
Jobline: (602) 792-2853

Arizona (state) Department of Economic Security
Job Service
397 S. Malpais Lane, #9, Flagstaff, AZ 86001
Seeks workers for private and public employers in the
    Flagstaff/Sedona/Page area.
(602) 779-4513
Jobline: (602) 526-1800, x1410.

Arizona (state) Department of Public Safety
2102 W. Encanto Boulevard, Phoenix, AZ 85009
Provides highway patrol programs and services.
(602) 223-2291
Jobline: (602) 223-2148

Arizona State University
Tempe, AZ 85287
Large, public, comprehensive institution near downtown
    Tempe.
(602) 965-9011
Jobline: (602) 965-5627

Arizona State University, West
4701 W. Thunderbird Road, Phoenix, AZ 85069-7100
New Arizona State University campus in northwest
    Phoenix.
(602) 543-3308
Jobline: (602) 543-5627

Arkansas (state) Department of Computer Services
1 Capitol Mall, P.O. Box 3155, Little Rock, AR 72203
Computer services for Arkansas state government.
(501) 682-5780
Jobline: (501) 682-9500

Arkansas (state) Department of Finance and Administration
1515 W. 7th Street, Room 605, P.O. Box 2485, Little
    Rock, AR 72203
Financial and administrative services for Arkansas state
    government.
(501) 324-9063
Jobline: (501) 682-5627

Arkansas (state) Game and Fish Commission
2 Natural Resources Drive, Little Rock, AR 72205
Manages and conserves game and fish resources.
(501) 223-6317
Jobline: (501) 377-6600

Arlington (city)
501 W. Main Street, Arlington, TX 76010
Provides municipal services such as police, firefighting,
    libraries, parks, and public works.
(817) 459-6868
Jobline: (817) 265-7938

Arlington County
2100 Clarendon Boulevard, Suite 511, Arlington, VA
    22201
Provides county services such as sheriffs, courts, motor
    vehicle registration, and social services.
(703) 358-3500
Jobline: (703) 358-3363

Armstrong World Industries Inc.
P.O. Box 3001, Lancaster, PA 17604
Manufactures floor coverings, other tile and board
    products, and living room and bedroom furniture.
(717) 397-0611
Jobline: (717) 396-3441
Production jobs.

Arvada (city)
8101 Ralston Road, Arvada, CO 80002
Provides municipal services such as police, firefighting,
    libraries, parks, and public works.
(303) 431-3089
Jobline: (303) 431-3008, x453.

Ashland Oil Inc.
P.O. Box 391, Ashland, KY 41114
Refines, transports, and markets petroleum and
    petroleum products, and operates other businesses.
(606) 329-3333
Jobline: (606) 329-4328

AST Research Inc.
16215 Alton Parkway, Irvine, CA 92718
Manufacturers PCs, computer storage devices, graphic
   displays, and other computer equipment.
(714) 727-4141
Jobline: (714) 727-4141, ask for job hotline.

Atlanta (city)
68 Mitchell Street SW, Atlanta, GA 30303
Provides municipal services such as police, firefighting,
   libraries, parks, and public works.
(404) 330-6369
Jobline: (404) 330-6456

Atlanta Airport Hilton & Towers
1031 Virginia Avenue, Atlanta, GA 30354
501-room hotel near Atlanta/Hartsfield International
   Airport.
(404) 767-9000
Jobline: (404) 559-6781

Atlanta Hilton & Towers
225 Courtland Street, Atlanta, GA 30303
1,224-room hotel.
(404) 659-2000
Jobline: (404) 221-6807

Atlanta Renaissance Hotel
4736 Best Road, Atlanta, GA 30337
496-room hotel near Atlanta/Hartsfield International
   Airport.
(404) 762-7676
Jobline: (404) 762-7676, ask for job hotline.

Atlanta Renaissance Hotel
590 W. Peachtree Street NW, Atlanta, GA 30308
504-room hotel.
(404) 881-6000
Jobline: (404) 881-6000, ask for job hotline.

Atlas Hotels Inc.
500 Hotel Circle North, San Diego, CA 92108
Operates Town & Country Hotel, a 1,000-room hotel.
(619) 291-7131
Jobline: (619) 299-2254

Auburn (city)
City Hall, 25 W. Main Street, Auburn, WA 98001
Provides municipal services such as police, firefighting,
   libraries, parks, and public works.
(206) 931-3040
Jobline: (206) 931-3077

Auburn University
Auburn University, AL 36849
Medium-sized, public, multipurpose, land-grant
   university in Auburn.
(205) 844-4000
Jobline: (205) 844-4336

Auburn University at Montgomery
Montgomery, AL 36117-3596
Medium-sized, public institution near downtown
   Montgomery.
(205) 244-3000
Jobline: (205) 244-3218

Aurora (city)
1470 S. Havana Street, Aurora, CO 80012
Provides municipal services such as police, firefighting,
   libraries, parks, and public works.
(303) 695-7225
Jobline: (303) 695-7222

Austin (city)
206 E. 9th Street, Austin, TX 78701
Provides municipal services such as police, firefighting,
   libraries, parks, and public works.
(512) 499-3301
Jobline: (512) 499-3201
Jobs for Austin city employees.

Jobline: (512) 499-3202
Professional jobs.

Jobline: (512) 499-3203
Clerical jobs.

Jobline: (512) 499-3204
Technical maintenance jobs.

Austin Community College
Austin, TX 78714
Large, district-supported, 2-year college in Austin.
(512) 483-7572
Jobline: (512) 483-7648

Avery Dennison Corp.
150 N. Orange Grove Boulevard, Pasadena, CA 91103
Manufacturers adhesive papers, labels, and tapes,
   gummed and coated papers, and other products.
(818) 304-2000
Jobline: (800) 456-2751

Avis Inc.
900 Old Country Road, Garden City, NY 11530
Operates and franchises car rental and other
   automotive services.
(516) 222-3000
Jobline: (516) 222-3399

Bahia Hotel and Catamaran Resort Hotel
998 W. Mission Bay Drive, San Diego, CA 92109
325- and 315-room hotels.
(619) 488-0551
Jobline: (619) 539-7733

Bainbridge School District
8489 Madison Avenue NE, Bainbridge Island, WA 98110
Five-school district in Bainbridge Island.
(206) 842-4714
Jobline: (206) 842-2920

Baldwin Park (city)
14403 E. Pacific Avenue, Baldwin Park, CA 91706
Provides municipal services such as police, firefighting,
   libraries, parks, and public works.
(818) 813-5207
Jobline: (818) 813-5206

Ball State University
Muncie, IN 47306
Medium-sized, public, comprehensive university in
  residential Muncie.
(317) 285-8300
Jobline: (317) 285-8565, press 1.

Bally's Park Palace Casino Hotel & Tower and Grand Casino Hotel
Park Place and Boardwalk, Atlantic City, NJ 08401
1,272- and 518-room hotels.
(609) 340-2000
Jobline: (609) 340-2211

Baltimore (city)
111 N. Calvert Street, Baltimore, MD 21202
Provides municipal services such as police, firefighting,
  libraries, parks, and public works.
(410) 396-3860
Jobline: (410) 576-9675

Baltimore County
308 Allegheny Avenue, Towson, MD 21204
Provides county services such as sheriffs, courts, motor
  vehicle registration, and social services.
(410) 887-3135
Jobline: (410) 887-5627

Baltimore County Public Schools
6901 N. Charles Street, Towson, MD 21204
148-school district in the Baltimore area.
(410) 887-4191
Jobline: (410) 887-4080

Baltimore Marriott Hunt Valley Inn
245 Showan Road, Hunt Valley, MD 21031
392-room hotel near Baltimore.
(410) 785-7000
Jobline: (410) 637-5574

Baltimore Marriott Inner Harbor
Pratt and Eutaw Streets, Baltimore, MD 21201
525-room hotel.
(410) 962-0202
Jobline: (410) 962-0202, ask for x2127.

Banc One Corp.
100 E. Broad Street, Columbus, OH 43271
Bank holding company that operates national and state
  commercial banks.
(614) 248-5944
Jobline: (614) 248-0779

Bank of America Arizona
1825 E. Buckeye Road, P.O. Box 16290, Phoenix, AZ
  85011
Operates state commercial banks.
(602) 597-5000
Jobline: (602) 594-2500

Bank of America Nevada
4101 E. Charleston Boulevard, P.O. Box 98600, Las
  Vegas, NV 89193-8600
Operates state commercial banks.
(800) 288-3162
Jobline: (800) 288-3162, ask for job hotline.

Bank of America Oregon
121 SW Morrison Street, Portland, OR 97204
Operates state commercial banks.
(800) 756-2222
Jobline: (503) 275-1390

Bank of America Texas NA
1925 W. John Carpenter Freeway, Irving, TX 75063
Operates national commercial banks.
(214) 444-5555
Jobline: (214) 444-6970

Bank of Boston Connecticut
81 W. Main Street, Waterbury, CT 06702
Operates state commercial banks.
(203) 574-7000
Jobline: (203) 574-7109

Bank of Boston Corp.
100 Federal Street, Boston, MA 02210
Bank holding company that operates national and state
  commercial banks and other banking businesses.
(617) 434-2200
Jobline: (617) 434-0165

Bank of California NA
550 S. Hope Street, Los Angeles, CA 90071
Operates national commercial banks.
(213) 243-3320
Jobline: (213) 243-3333
Includes jobs throughout California.

400 California Street, San Francisco, CA 94104
(415) 765-0400
Jobline: (415) 765-3535

Bank of Oklahoma NA
1 Williams Center, P.O. Box 2300, Tulsa, OK 74192
Operates national commercial banks, mortgage
  bankers, and other banking businesses.
(918) 588-6000
Jobline: (918) 588-6828

Bank One Akron NA
50 S. Main Street, Akron, OH 44309
Operates national commercial banks.
(800) 477-2265
Jobline: (216) 972-1810

Bank One Arizona NA
241 N. Central Avenue, P.O. Box 71, Phoenix, AZ 85001
Operates national commercial banks.
(602) 221-2900
Jobline: (602) 221-2441

Bank One Columbus NA
100 E. Broad Street, Columbus, OH 43271
Operates national commercial banks.
(614) 248-5800
Jobline: (614) 248-0779

Bank One Dayton NA
P.O. Box 1103, Dayton, OH 45401
Operates national commercial banks.
(513) 449-8600
Jobline: (513) 449-7446

Bank One Lexington NA
201 E. Main Street, Lexington, KY 40507
Operates national commercial banks.
(606) 231-1000
Jobline: (606) 231-2760

Bank One Milwaukee NA
111 E. Wisconsin Avenue, Milwaukee, WI 53202
Operates national commercial banks.
(414) 765-3000
Jobline: (414) 765-2677

Bank One Texas NA
1717 Main Street, P.O. Box 655415, Dallas, TX
75265-5415
Operates national commercial banks.
(214) 290-3687
Jobline: (214) 290-3637
Jobs in the Dallas area.

1301 S. Bowen Road, Arlington, TX 76013
(817) 548-3061
Jobline: (817) 459-9910
Jobs in the Arlington area.

500 Throckmorton Street, P.O. Box 2050, Fort Worth,
TX 76113
(817) 884-4192
Jobline: (817) 884-6709
Jobs in the Fort Worth area.

Processing Center
1900 L. Don Dodson Drive, Bedford, TX 76021
Processes checks and performs other central
operations.
(817) 884-6509
Jobline: (817) 884-6761

Bankers Trust New York Corp.
280 Park Avenue, New York, NY 10017
Bank holding company that operates national & state
commercial banks and other banking businesses.
(212) 250-2500
Jobline: (212) 250-9955

Baptist Hospital of Miami
8900 N. Kendall Drive, Miami, FL 33176
Not-for-profit hospital with more than 400 beds.
(305) 596-1960
Jobline: (305) 598-5999

Baptist Hospitals & Health Systems Inc.
2224 W. Northern Avenue, Phoenix, AZ 85021
Operates four not-for-profit hospitals with more than
800 beds in the Phoenix area.
(602) 864-1184
Jobline: (602) 246-5627

Barnett Bank of Pinellas County
4800 140th Avenue North, Clearwater, FL 34662
Operates state commercial banks.
(813) 535-0711
Jobline: (813) 539-9300

Barnett Banks Inc.
50 N. Laura Street, P.O. Box 40789, Jacksonville, FL
32203-0789
Bank holding company that operates national and state
commercial banks and other banking businesses.
(904) 791-7720
Jobline: (904) 464-2426, press 1.

Barnett Banks of South Florida NA
701 Brickell Avenue, Miami, FL 33131
Operates national commercial banks.
(305) 350-7100
Jobline: (305) 374-4473

Barnett Banks of Southwest Florida
240 S. Pineapple Avenue, P.O. Box 1478, Sarasota, FL
34230
Operates state commercial banks.
(813) 951-4800
Jobline: (813) 951-4753

Barnett Banks of Tampa NA
P.O. Box 30014, Tampa, FL 33630
Operates national commercial banks.
(813) 225-8111
Jobline: (813) 225-8761

Baton Rouge (city)
103 France Street, Baton Rouge, LA 70802
Provides municipal services such as police, firefighting,
libraries, parks, and public works.
(504) 389-4981
Jobline: (504) 389-4980

Battle Ground Public Schools
204 W. Main Street, Battle Ground, WA 98604
16-school district in Battle Ground.
(206) 687-6534
Jobline: (206) 256-5385
Classified and certificated jobs.

Bausch and Lomb Inc.
1 Lincoln First Square, Rochester, NY 14601
Manufacturers contact lenses, glasses, magnifiers,
pharmaceutical and other optical products.
(716) 338-6000
Jobline: (716) 338-8265

Baxter HealthCare Corp.
Hyland Division, 550 N. Brand Boulevard, Glendale, CA
91203
Develops, manufactures, and distributes biological and
biopharmaceutical products and therapies.
(818) 956-2300
Jobline: (818) 507-8394, press 1, then 3.

Baxter International Inc.
1 Baxter Parkway, Deerfield, IL 60015-4625
Manufactures medical instruments, pharmaceutical
products, and other medical supplies and equipment.
(708) 948-2000
Jobline: (800) 322-9837

Baylor University
Waco, TX 76798
Medium-sized, church-affiliated university in residential
    Waco.
(817) 755-1011
Jobline: (817) 755-3675

Beaumont (city)
P.O. Box 3827, Beaumont, TX 77704
Provides municipal services such as police, firefighting,
    libraries, parks, and public works.
(409) 880-3777
Jobline: (409) 838-5627

Beaverton (city)
4755 SW Griffith Drive, Beaverton, OR 97005
Provides municipal services such as police, firefighting,
    libraries, parks, and public works.
(503) 526-2200
Jobline: (503) 526-2299

Beaverton School District No. 48J
P.O. Box 200, Beaverton, OR 97075
38-school district in Beaverton.
(503) 591-4330
Jobline: (503) 591-4600

Bechtel Group Inc.
P.O. Box 193965, San Francisco, CA 94119
Provides civil engineering, industrial plant construction,
    and project management services.
(415) 768-1234
Jobline: (415) 768-4448

Bell Atlantic Corp.
1600 Market Street, Philadelphia, PA 19103
Provides local and other telephone services, data
    processing equipment repair, and other services.
(215) 963-6000
Jobline: (800) 967-5422

BellSouth Corp.
1155 Peachtree Street NE, Atlanta, GA 30367-6000
Provides local, long distance, and other telephone
    services, telephone equipment, and directories.
(404) 249-2000
Jobline: (404) 329-9455

Benton County
Law Enforcement Building, 2nd Floor, 180 NW 5th
    Street, Corvallis, OR 97330
Provides county services such as sheriffs, courts, motor
    vehicle registration, and social services.
(503) 757-6802
Jobline: (503) 757-6755

Bergen Brunswig Corp.
4000 W. Metropolitan Drive, Orange, CA 92668-3502
Distributes pharmaceuticals and other health care
    products wholesale.
(714) 385-4000
Jobline: (714) 385-4473

Berkeley (city)
2180 Milvia Street, Berkeley, CA 94704
Provides municipal services such as police, firefighting,
    libraries, parks, and public works.
(510) 644-6460
Jobline: (510) 644-6122

Bernalillo County
City-County Government Center, 10th Floor, 1 Civic
    Plaza NW, Albuquerque, NM 87102
Provides county services such as sheriffs, courts, motor
    vehicle registration, and social services.
(505) 768-4010
Jobline: (505) 768-4887, press 1.

Bethel College
Saint Paul, MN 55112-6999
Small, church-affiliated, liberal arts college near St. Paul.
(612) 638-6400
Jobline: (612) 635-8633

Bethel School District
516 E. 176th Street, Spanaway, WA 98387
26-school district in Spanaway.
(206) 536-7272
Jobline: (206) 536-7270

Beverly Hilton
9876 Wilshire Boulevard, Beverly Hills, CA 90210
325-room hotel in the Los Angeles area.
(310) 276-2251
Jobline: (310) 285-1340

Bexar County
Courthouse, Suite 201, 100 Dolorosa, San Antonio, TX
    78205
Provides county services such as sheriffs, courts, motor
    vehicle registration, and social services.
(210) 220-2545
Jobline: (210) 270-6333

Biltmore Hotel
506 S. Grand Avenue, Los Angeles, CA 90071
700-room hotel.
(213) 624-1011
Jobline: (213) 612-1585

Biola University
La Mirada, CA 90639
Small, university with a religious orientation in La
    Mirada, near Los Angeles.
(310) 903-6000
Jobline: (310) 903-4767

Black Hills State University
Spearfish, SD 57799
Small, public university in Spearfish, 47 miles northwest
    of Rapid City.
(605) 642-6011
Jobline: (605) 642-6511, press 1.

Bloomsburg University of Pennsylvania
Bloomsburg, PA 17815
Medium-sized, public, multipurpose university in
    Bloomsburg.
(717) 389-4000
Jobline: (717) 389-2093

Blue Cross of California Inc.
21555 Oxnard Street, Woodland Hills, CA 91367
Provides group hospitalization plans.
(818) 703-2345
Jobline: (818) 703-3181

Blue Springs (city)
903 Main Street, Blue Springs, MO 64015
Provides municipal services such as police, firefighting, libraries, parks, and public works.
(816) 228-0138
Jobline: (816) 228-0290

Boatmen's Bancshares Inc.
800 Market Street, Saint Louis, MO 63101
Bank holding company that operates national and state commercial banks.
(314) 466-7720
Jobline: (314) 466-4473

Boatmen's First National Bank of Kansas City
14 W. 10th Street, P.O. Box 419038, Kansas City, MO 64183
Operates state commercial banks.
(816) 221-2800
Jobline: (816) 691-7000

Boeing Co.
7755 E. Marginal Way South, Seattle, WA 98108-4002
Manufactures aircraft, guided missiles, space vehicles, computer software, and other products.
(206) 655-2121
Jobline: (206) 965-3111

Boise (city)
601 W. Idaho Street, Boise, ID 83702
Provides municipal services such as police, firefighting, libraries, parks, and public works.
(208) 384-3850
Jobline: (208) 384-3855

Boise Cascade Corp.
1 Jefferson Square, Boise, ID 83728
Manufactures uncoated and newsprint paper, stationery and office supplies, wood, and other products.
(208) 384-6161
Jobline: (208) 384-4900

Bonaventure Resort & Spa
250 Racquet Club Road, Fort Lauderdale, FL 33326
500-room hotel.
(305) 389-3300
Jobline: (305) 389-0185

Boston Park Plaza Hotel & Towers
64 Arlington Street at Park Plaza, Boston, MA 02117
977-room hotel.
(617) 426-2000
Jobline: (617) 457-2452

Boulder (city)
1101 Arapahoe Avenue, Boulder, CO 80302
Provides municipal services such as police, firefighting, libraries, parks, and public works.
(303) 441-3070
Jobline: (303) 441-3434

Boulder City (city)
401 California Avenue, Boulder City, NV 89005
Provides municipal services such as police, firefighting, libraries, parks, and public works.
(702) 293-9202
Jobline: (702) 293-9430

Boulder County
2040 14th Street, Boulder, CO 80304
Provides county services such as sheriffs, courts, motor vehicle registration, and social services.
(303) 441-3508
Jobline: (303) 441-4555

Bowling Green State University
Bowling Green, OH 43403
Medium-sized, public university in Bowling Green, 23 miles south of Toledo.
(419) 372-2531
Jobline: (419) 372-8522
Administrative staff jobs.

Jobline: (419) 372-8669
Classified jobs.

Brandeis University
Waltham, MA 02254-9110
Small, private, liberal arts university in Waltham, 10 miles west of Boston.
(617) 736-2000
Jobline: (617) 736-5627

Brea (city)
1 Civic Center Circle, Brea, CA 92621
Provides municipal services such as police, firefighting, libraries, parks, and public works.
(714) 671-4447
Jobline: (714) 671-4420

Brevard Community College
Cocoa, FL 32922
Medium-sized, state-supported, 2-year college in Cocoa.
(407) 632-1111
Jobline: (407) 632-1111, x2561.

Brigham Young University
Provo, UT 84602
Large, church-affiliated university in Provo, 45 miles from Salt Lake City.
(801) 378-4636
Jobline: (801) 378-4357

Brinker International Inc.
6820 Lyndon B. Johnson Freeway, Suite 200, Dallas, TX 75240
Operates and franchises restaurants and related bars.
(214) 980-9917
Jobline: (214) 770-9463

Broadmoor
1 Lake Circle, Colorado Springs, CO 80906
550-room hotel.
(719) 598-7656
Jobline: (719) 577-5858

Broomfield (city)
6 Garden Center, Broomfield, CO 80020
Provides municipal services such as police, firefighting,
  libraries, parks, and public works.
(303) 469-3301
Jobline: (303) 438-6475

Broward Community College
Fort Lauderdale, FL 33301
Large, state-supported, 2-year college.
(305) 761-7464
Jobline: (305) 761-7503

Broward County
115 S. Andrews Avenue, Fort Lauderdale, FL 33301
Provides county services such as sheriffs, courts, motor
  vehicle registration, and social services.
(305) 357-7585
Jobline: (305) 357-6450

Brown Group Inc.
8400 Maryland Avenue, Saint Louis, MO 63105
Manufactures and sells dress, athletic, casual, and
  children's shoes, and piece goods and notions.
(314) 854-4000
Jobline: (314) 854-2434

Brown University
Providence, RI 02912
Medium-sized, private, liberal arts university in
  Providence, south of Boston.
(401) 863-1000
Jobline: (401) 863-9675

Bucknell University
Lewisburg, PA 17837
Small, private university in Lewisburg, 60 miles from
  Harrisburg.
(717) 523-1271
Jobline: (717) 524-1635

Buena Park (city)
6650 Beach Boulevard, Buena Park, CA 90621
Provides municipal services such as police, firefighting,
  libraries, parks, and public works.
(714) 562-3515
Jobline: (714) 562-3519

Buena Vista Palace at Walt Disney World
1900 Buena Vista Drive, Walt Disney World, FL 32830
1,028-room hotel in the Orlando area.
(407) 827-3333
Jobline: (407) 827-3255

Burbank (city)
275 E. Olive Avenue, Burbank, CA 91502
Provides municipal services such as police, firefighting,
  libraries, parks, and public works.
(818) 953-9721
Jobline: (818) 953-9724

Burbank Airport Hilton & Convention Center
2500 Hollywood Way, Burbank, CA 91501
500-room hotel in the Los Angeles area.
(818) 843-6000
Jobline: (818) 840-6471

Bureau of Broadcasting
330 Independence Avenue SW, Washington, DC 20547
Produces and broadcasts Voice of America and other
  radio programs for overseas audiences.
(202) 619-3117
Jobline: (202) 619-0909

Burlingame (city)
501 Primrose Road, Burlingame, CA 94010
Provides municipal services such as police, firefighting,
  libraries, parks, and public works.
(415) 696-7206
Jobline: (415) 737-1238

Burlington (city)
135 Church Street, Burlington, VT 05401
Provides municipal services such as police, firefighting,
  libraries, parks, and public works.
(802) 865-7145
Jobline: (802) 865-7147

Burlington Air Express Inc.
18200 Von Karman Avenue, Irvine, CA 92715
Provides freight forwarding, customhouse brokers, and
  flying charter services.
(714) 752-4000
Jobline: (714) 752-1212, x4210.

Burnsville (city)
100 Civic Center Parkway, Burnsville, MN 55337
Provides municipal services such as police, firefighting,
  libraries, parks, and public works.
(612) 895-4470
Jobline: (612) 895-4475

Butler University
Indianapolis, IN 46208
Small, private university in residential Indianapolis.
(317) 283-8000
Jobline: (317) 283-9984
Call after 5 p.m. or on weekends.

Butte County
25 County Center Drive, Oroville, CA 95965
Provides county services such as sheriffs, courts, motor
  vehicle registration, and social services.
(916) 538-7651
Jobline: (916) 538-7653

Caesars Atlantic City Hotel Casino
2100 Pacific Avenue, Atlantic City, NJ 08401
645-room hotel.
(609) 348-4411
Jobline: (609) 343-2660

Caesars Palace
3570 Las Vegas Boulevard South, Las Vegas, NV
  89109
1,748-room hotel.
(800) 634-6001
Jobline: (702) 731-7386

CalFed Inc.
5700 Wilshire Boulevard, Los Angeles, CA 90036
Operates federal savings banks and an insurance
  agency.
(213) 932-4506
Jobline: (818) 312-6078

California (state)
801 Capitol Mall, Sacramento, CA 95814
Provides state services such as conservation,
    education, highways, prisons, and welfare.
(916) 653-1705
Jobline: (213) 620-6450
For callers in the Los Angeles area.

Jobline: (619) 237-6163
For callers in the San Diego area.

Jobline: (916) 445-0538
For callers in the Sacramento area.

California (state) Conservation Department
801 K Street, Sacramento, CA 95814
Provides conservation programs and services.
(916) 322-7685
Jobline: (916) 327-2672

California (state) Corrections Department
1515 S St., Sacramento, CA 95814
Provides correctional programs and services.
(916) 445-7682
Jobline: (800) 622-9675

California (state) Department of Health Services
744 P Street, Sacramento, CA 95814
Provides health programs and services.
(916) 657-0373
Jobline: (916) 657-0141
Legal, medical, scientific, fiscal management, and staff
    services jobs.

Jobline: (916) 657-2976
Clerical, supervisory, and trade jobs.

California (state) Department of Transportation
District 2
1657 Riverside Drive, Redding, CA 96001
Provides transportation programs and services.
(916) 225-3426
Jobline: (916) 225-3000

District 4
111 Grand Avenue, Oakland, CA 94612
(510) 286-5830
Jobline: (510) 286-6354
Includes jobs in Berkeley, Oakland, Alameda, and San
    Leandro.

District 7
120 S. Spring Street, Los Angeles, CA 90012
(213) 897-3656
Jobline: (213) 897-3653

California (state) Education Department
720 Capitol Mall, Sacramento, CA 95814
Provides educational programs and services.
(916) 657-3139
Jobline: (916) 657-3821

California (state) Employment Development Department
50 S. King Road, San Jose, CA 95116
Seeks workers for private employers.
(408) 928-1350
Jobline: (408) 928-1308

409 K Street, Eureka, CA 95501
(707) 445-6660
Jobline: (707) 444-2222

1401 S. H Street, Bakersfield, CA 93304
(805) 395-2500
Jobline: (805) 325-5627

California (state) Energy Commission
1516 9th Street, Sacramento, CA 95814
Provides energy programs and services.
(916) 654-4309
Jobline: (916) 654-4316

California (state) Food and Agriculture Department
1220 N Street, Sacramento, CA 95814
Provides food and agricultural programs and services.
(916) 654-0790
Jobline: (916) 654-0441

California (state) Franchise Tax Board
9645 Butterfield Way, P.O. Box 550, Sacramento, CA
    95812-0550
Collects and processes state income taxes and other
    state revenues.
(916) 369-3649
Jobline: (916) 369-3624
Seasonal clerk jobs.

Jobline: (916) 369-3626
Jobs other than seasonal clerk.

California (state) Highway Patrol
Golden Gate Division
1551 Benecia Road, Vallejo, CA 94951
Provides highway patrol programs and services.
(707) 648-4180
Jobline: (707) 648-4195

California (state) Lottery
600 N. 10th Street, Sacramento, CA 95814
Provides lottery programs and services.
(916) 324-9974
Jobline: (916) 322-0023

California (state) Motor Vehicles Department
2570 24th Street, Sacramento, CA 94232-3150
Provides motor vehicle programs and services.
(916) 657-6477
Jobline: (916) 657-7713

California (state) Parks and Recreation Department
1416 9th Street, Sacramento, CA 95814
Provides parks and recreational programs and services.
(916) 653-6644
Jobline: (916) 653-9903

California (state) Social Services Department
744 P Street, Room 1516, MS 15-58, Sacramento, CA 95814
Provides social programs and services.
(916) 657-1762
Jobline: (916) 657-1696

California Institute of Technology
Pasadena, CA 91125
Small, private university and research center in residential Pasadena.
(818) 356-6811
Jobline: (818) 796-2229

California Polytechnic State University, San Luis Obispo
San Luis Obispo, CA 93407
Medium-sized, public university in San Luis Obispo.
(805) 756-0111
Jobline: (805) 756-1533

California State Polytechnic University, Pomona
Pomona, CA 91768-4019
Medium-sized, public university in Pomona, 30 miles east of Los Angeles.
(909) 869-7659
Jobline: (909) 869-2100

California State University, Chico
Chico, CA 95929
Medium-sized, public, multipurpose university in the Sierra foothills.
(916) 898-6116
Jobline: (916) 898-6888

California State University, Dominguez Hills
Carson, CA 90747
Medium-sized, public, comprehensive university near Los Angeles.
(310) 516-3300
Jobline: (310) 516-3840

California State University, Fresno
Fresno, CA 93740
Medium-sized, public, comprehensive university with a campus and a university farm near Fresno.
(209) 278-4240
Jobline: (209) 278-2360

California State University, Fullerton
Fullerton, CA 92634
Medium-sized, public university in Fullerton, 35 miles from Los Angeles.
(714) 773-2011
Jobline: (714) 773-3385

California State University, Hayward
Hayward, CA 94542
Medium-sized, public university in Hayward, near San Francisco.
(510) 881-3000
Jobline: (510) 881-7474

California State University, Long Beach
Long Beach, CA 90840
Large, public, comprehensive university in Long Beach.
(310) 985-4111
Jobline: (310) 985-5491

California State University, Los Angeles
Los Angeles, CA 90032
Medium-sized, public, comprehensive university in Los Angeles.
(213) 343-3000
Jobline: (213) 343-3678

California State University, Northridge
Northridge, CA 91330
Large, public university in the San Fernando Valley, north of Los Angeles.
(818) 885-1200
Jobline: (818) 885-2087

California State University, Sacramento
Sacramento, CA 95819
Large, public university in Sacramento, along the American River.
(916) 278-6011
Jobline: (916) 278-6704

California State University, San Bernardino
San Bernardino, CA 92407
Medium-sized, public university at the foot of the San Bernardino Mountains.
(909) 880-5000
Jobline: (909) 880-5139

California State University, Stanislaus
Turlock, CA 95380
Small, public university midway between San Francisco and the Sierra Nevadas.
(209) 667-3122
Jobline: (209) 667-3354

Callaway Gardens
U.S. Route 27, Pine Mountain, GA 31822
800-room hotel.
(800) 282-8181
Jobline: (706) 663-5012

Cameron University
Lawton, OK 73505
Small, public, multipurpose university in Lawton, 90 miles from Oklahoma City.
(405) 581-2200
Jobline: (405) 581-2501

Camino Real Paso del Norte
101 S. El Paso Street, El Paso, TX 79901
375-room hotel.
(915) 534-3000
Jobline: (915) 534-3067

Capital Cities/ABC Inc.
4151 Prospect Avenue, Los Angeles, CA 90027
Operates TV and radio stations, provides warehousing services, and owns advertising agencies.
(310) 557-7777
Jobline: (310) 557-4222

Capitol Hilton
16th and K Streets NW, Washington, DC 20036
541-room hotel.
(202) 393-1000
Jobline: (202) 639-5745

Capitol-EMI Music Inc.
1750 N. Vine Street, Hollywood, CA 90028
Produces pre-recorded CDs and tapes.
(213) 462-6252
Jobline: (213) 871-5763

Captain Cook Hotel
5th Avenue and K Street, Anchorage, AK 99501
600-room hotel.
(907) 276-6000
Jobline: (907) 276-6000, ask for x3833.

Carlsbad (city)
1200 Carlsbad Village Drive, Carlsbad, CA 92008
Provides municipal services such as police, firefighting,
   libraries, parks, and public works.
(619) 434-2852
Jobline: (619) 434-2940

Carnegie Mellon University
Pittsburgh, PA 15213
Medium-sized, private university five miles from
   downtown Pittsburgh.
(412) 268-2000
Jobline: (412) 268-8545

Carnival Cruise Lines Inc.
3655 NW 87th Avenue, Miami, FL 33178-2418
Operates cruise ships and casino hotels, sightseeing
   tour companies, and bus charter services.
(305) 599-2600
Jobline: (305) 599-2600

Carson City (city)
2621 Northgate Lane, Suite 6, Carson City, NV 89706
Provides municipal services such as police, firefighting,
   libraries, parks, and public works.
(702) 887-2103
Jobline: (702) 887-2240

Carver County
600 E. 4th Street, P.O. Box 15, Chaska, MN 55318
Provides county services such as sheriffs, courts, motor
   vehicle registration, and social services.
(612) 361-1525
Jobline: (612) 361-1522

Cary (city)
P.O. Box 1147, Cary, NC 27512-1147
Provides municipal services such as police, firefighting,
   libraries, parks, and public works.
(919) 469-4070
Jobline: (919) 460-4905

Case Western Reserve University
Cleveland, OH 44106
Medium-sized, private, comprehensive university near
   downtown Cleveland.
(216) 368-2000
Jobline: (216) 368-4500

Catholic University of America
Washington, DC 20064
Medium-sized, church-affiliated institution in residential
   Washington.
(202) 319-5000
Jobline: (202) 319-5263

CCH Computax Inc.
21250 Hawthorne Boulevard, Torrance, CA 90503
Provides tax return software and computerized filing
   services for professional tax preparers.
(310) 543-6200
Jobline: (310) 543-8100

Central and South West Corp.
1616 Woodall Rodgers Parkway, P.O. Box 660164,
   Dallas, TX 75266-0164
Generates, transmits, and distributes electric power.
(214) 777-1000
Jobline: (214) 777-1877

Central Intelligence Agency
Washington, DC 20505
Collects, evaluates, and disseminates information
   abroad needed to safeguard national security.
(703) 482-1100
Jobline: (703) 482-0677
Call (800) 562-7242 outside the Mid-Atlantic region.

Central Kitsap School District
9210 Silverdale Way NW, P.O. Box 8, Silverdale, WA
   93838
18-school district in Silverdale.
(206) 692-3118
Jobline: (206) 698-3470

Central Michigan University
Mount Pleasant, MI 48859
Small, public university in Mount Pleasant, 60 miles
   west of Saginaw.
(517) 774-4000
Jobline: (517) 774-7195

Central Missouri State University
Warrensburg, MO 64093
Medium-sized, public, multipurpose university in
   Warrensburg.
(816) 543-4111
Jobline: (816) 543-8300

Central Piedmont Community College
Charlotte, NC 28235
Medium-sized, state- and locally-supported, 2-year
   college in Charlotte.
(704) 342-6631
Jobline: (704) 342-6400

Central Washington University
Ellensburg, WA 98926
Medium-sized, public university in Ellinsburg, 110 miles
   southeast of Seattle.
(509) 963-1111
Jobline: (509) 963-1562

Century Plaza Hotel & Towers
2025 Avenue of the Stars, Los Angeles, CA 90067
1,072-room hotel.
(310) 277-2000
Jobline: (310) 551-3390

Cerritos College
11110 E. Alondra Boulevard, Norwalk, CA 90650
Medium-sized, state- and locally-supported, 2-year
 college in Norwalk.
(310) 860-2451
Jobline: (310) 467-5042

Certified Grocers of California Limited
2601 S. Eastern Avenue, Los Angeles, CA 90040-1401
Distributes groceries, bakery products, dried and
 canned food, pasta, rice, and other merchandise.
(213) 726-2601
Jobline: (213) 726-2601, press 3.

Cessna Aircraft Co.
6330 W. Southwest Boulevard, Wichita, KS 67215
Manufacturers airplanes, especially light airplanes.
(316) 941-6000
Jobline: (316) 941-6155

Chaffey College
5885 Haven Avenue, Rancho Cucamonga, CA
 91701-3002
Medium-sized, district-supported, 2-year college in
 Rancho Cucamonga.
(909) 987-1737
Jobline: (909) 941-2750

Chandler (city)
25 S. Arizona Place, Suite 201, Chandler, AZ 85224
Provides municipal services such as police, firefighting,
 libraries, parks, and public works.
(602) 786-2290
Jobline: (602) 786-2294

Charleston (city)
701 E. Bay Street, Charleston, SC 29403
Provides municipal services such as police, firefighting,
 libraries, parks, and public works.
(803) 724-7388
Jobline: (803) 720-3907

Charleston County
2 Court House Square, Charleston, SC 29401
Provides county services such as sheriffs, courts, motor
 vehicle registration, and social services.
(803) 723-6717
Jobline: (803) 724-0694

Charlotte (city and county)
City Hall, 600 E. Trade Street, Charlotte, NC 28202
Provides government services such as police,
 firefighting, libraries, parks, and public works.
(704) 336-2287
Jobline: (704) 336-3968

Charter Medical Corp.
577 Mulberry Street, P.O. Box 209, Macon, GA 31298
Operates for-profit hospitals with more than 7,000 beds
 in 25 states.
(912) 742-1161
Jobline: (800) 633-2415

Chase Manhattan Bank NA
1 Lincoln First Square, Rochester, NY 14643
Operates national commercial banks.
(716) 258-5000
Jobline: (716) 258-5000, ask for job hotline.

Chase Manhattan Corp.
1 Chase Manhattan Plaza, New York, NY 10081
Bank holding company that operates national
 commercial banks and other banking businesses.
(212) 552-2222
Jobline: (718) 242-7537

Chatham County
124 Bull Street, Savannah, GA 31401
Provides county services such as sheriffs, courts, motor
 vehicle registration, and social services.
(912) 652-7925
Jobline: (912) 652-7931

Chesapeake (city)
306 Cedar Road, P.O. Box 15225, Chesapeake, VA
 23328
Provides municipal services such as police, firefighting,
 libraries, parks, and public works.
(804) 547-6492
Jobline: (804) 547-6416

Chevron Corp.
225 Bush Street, San Francisco, CA 94104
Produces gasoline and other petroleum products,
 agricultural chemicals, and other products.
(415) 894-7700
Jobline: (415) 894-2552

Chicago (city)
121 N. La Salle Street, Chicago, IL 60602
Provides municipal services such as police, firefighting,
 libraries, parks, and public works.
(312) 744-4976
Jobline: (312) 744-1369

Chicago Hilton & Towers
720 S. Michigan Avenue, Chicago, IL 60605
1,543-room hotel.
(312) 922-4400
Jobline: (312) 922-4400, ask for job hotline.

Children's Hospital of Orange County
455 S. Main Street, Orange, CA 92668
Not-for-profit hospital with more than 100 beds.
(714) 997-3000
Jobline: (714) 532-8500

Chino (city)
13220 Central Avenue, Chino, CA 91710
Provides municipal services such as police, firefighting,
 libraries, parks, and public works.
(909) 591-9807
Jobline: (909) 591-9808

Chula Vista (city)
276 4th Avenue, Chula Vista, CA 91910
Provides municipal services such as police, firefighting,
 libraries, parks, and public works.
(619) 691-5096
Jobline: (619) 691-5095

Cincinnati (city)
801 Plum Street, Cincinnati, OH 45202
Provides municipal services such as police, firefighting,
 libraries, parks, and public works.
(513) 352-4000
Jobline: (513) 352-2489

Cincinnati Bell Inc.
201 E. 4th Street, Cincinnati, OH 45202
Provides local, long distance, and other telephone
   services, computer software, and other services.
(513) 397-9900
Jobline: (513) 397-9900
Management jobs.
Ask for job hotline for management.

Circuit City Stores Inc.
9950 Mayland Drive, Richmond, VA 23233
Operates stores that sell TV sets, VCRs, radios, and
   electric appliances.
(804) 527-4000
Jobline: (804) 527-4094

Circus Circus Enterprises Inc.
2880 Las Vegas Boulevard South, Las Vegas, NV
   89109
Operates the Circus Circus Hotel & Casino, a
   2,913-room hotel.
(702) 734-0410
Jobline: (702) 794-3732

Citibank NA
399 Park Avenue, New York, NY 10022
Operates national commercial banks and other banking
   businesses.
(212) 559-1000
Jobline: (718) 248-7072

Clackamas County
904 Main Street, Oregon City, OR 97045
Provides county services such as sheriffs, courts, motor
   vehicle registration, and social services.
(503) 655-8459
Jobline: (503) 655-8894

Claremont (city)
207 Harvard Avenue, Claremont, CA 91711
Provides municipal services such as police, firefighting,
   libraries, parks, and public works.
(909) 399-5450
Jobline: (909) 399-5351

Claremont Colleges
Claremont, CA 91711
Includes Pomona, Claremont McKenna, Scripps,
   Harvey Mudd, and Pitzer Colleges.
(909) 621-8000
Jobline: (909) 621-9443
Graduate School and University Center jobs.

Claremont McKenna College
Claremont, CA 91711
Small, private, liberal arts college at the foot of the San
   Gabriel Mountains.
(909) 621-8000
Jobline: (909) 621-8491

Claridge Casino & Hotel
Indiana Avenue and Boardwalk, Atlantic City, NJ 08401
504-room hotel.
(609) 340-3434
Jobline: (609) 340-3604

Clarion Hotel New Orleans
1500 Canal Street, New Orleans, LA 70112
759-room hotel in downtown New Orleans.
(504) 522-4500
Jobline: (504) 522-4500, ask for job hotline.

Clarion University of Pennsylvania
Clarion, PA 16214
Medium-sized, public university 85 miles northeast of
   Pittsburgh.
(814) 226-2000
Jobline: (814) 226-2045

Clark Atlanta University
Atlanta, GA 30314
Small, private university one mile west of downtown
   Atlanta.
(404) 880-8000
Jobline: (404) 880-8368

Clark County
225 Bridger Avenue, 9th Floor, Las Vegas, NV 89101
Provides county services such as sheriffs, courts, motor
   vehicle registration, and social services.
(702) 455-4565
Jobline: (702) 455-3174

Clark County
1013 Franklin Street, Vancouver, WA 98660
Provides county services such as sheriffs, courts, motor
   vehicle registration, and social services.
(206) 699-2456
Jobline: (206) 737-6018

Clayton County
7994 N. McDonough Street, Jonesboro, GA 30236
Provides county services such as sheriffs, courts, motor
   vehicle registration, and social services.
(404) 477-3239
Jobline: (404) 473-5800

Clemson University
Clemson, SC 29634-4024
Medium-sized, public university in Clemson, 27 miles
   southwest of Greenville.
(803) 656-3311
Jobline: (803) 656-2228

Clermont County
76 S. Riverside Drive, 3rd Floor, Batavia, OH 45103
Provides county services such as sheriffs, courts, motor
   vehicle registration, and social services.
(513) 732-7464
Jobline: (513) 732-7853

Cleveland (city)
City Hall, Room 121, 601 Lakeside Avenue, Cleveland,
   OH 44114
Provides municipal services such as police, firefighting,
   libraries, parks, and public works.
(216) 664-2493
Jobline: (216) 664-2420

Cleveland State University
Cleveland, OH 44115
Medium-sized, public university in downtown Cleveland.
(216) 687-2000
Jobline: (216) 687-9300

Clorox Co.
1221 Broadway Avenue, Oakland, CA 94612
Produces household bleach, cleaning products,
    specialty food products, and other consumer goods.
(510) 271-7000
Jobline: (510) 271-7625

Clover Park School District
10903 Gravelly Lake Drive SW, Tacoma, WA 98499
28-school district in Tacoma.
(206) 589-7433
Jobline: (206) 589-7436
Classified and certificated jobs.

Clovis (city)
1033 5th Street, Clovis, CA 93612
Provides municipal services such as police, firefighting,
    libraries, parks, and public works.
(209) 297-2328
Jobline: (209) 297-2329

Clubcorp International
3030 Lyndon B. Johnson Freeway, Dallas, TX 75234
Operates lodgings for membership organizations.
(214) 243-6191
Jobline: (214) 888-7599

Coast Community College District
1370 Adams Avenue, Costa Mesa, CA 92626
Includes Coastline Community College, Golden West
    College, and Orange Coast College.
(714) 432-5898
Jobline: (714) 432-5526
Certificated jobs.

Jobline: (714) 432-5586
Classified jobs.

Coast Federal Bank
1000 Wilshire Boulevard, Los Angeles, CA 90017
Operates federal savings banks and other investment
    and insurance businesses.
(213) 362-2000
Jobline: (818) 366-8730

Coastal Corp.
9 E. Greenway Plaza, Houston, TX 77046
Produces natural gas and other petroleum products,
    agricultural chemicals, and coal.
(713) 877-1400
Jobline: (713) 877-6978

Cobb County
100 Cherokee Street, Suite 350, Marietta, GA
    30090-9679
Provides county services such as sheriffs, courts, motor
    vehicle registration, and social services.
(404) 528-2535
Jobline: (404) 528-2555

Coca Cola Bottling Co.
1334 S. Central Avenue, Los Angeles, CA 90021-2210
Bottles and distributes soft drinks and carbonated
    waters.
(213) 746-5555
Jobline: (213) 746-5555, x4444.

College of Charleston
Charleston, SC 29424
Medium-sized, public liberal arts institution in central
    Charleston.
(803) 953-5500
Jobline: (803) 953-5419

College of DuPage
Glen Ellyn, IL 60137
Large, state- and locally-supported 2-year college in
    Glen Ellyn.
(708) 858-2800
Jobline: (708) 858-2800, ask for x2796.

College of Saint Rose
Albany, NY 12203
Small, independent, liberal arts college in residential
    Albany.
(518) 454-5111
Jobline: (518) 458-5475

College of William and Mary in Virginia
Williamsburg, VA 23185
Medium-sized, public university in Williamsburg, 15
    miles from Newport News.
(804) 221-4000
Jobline: (804) 221-3167

Colorado (state) Department of Education
State Library, 201 E. Colfax Avenue, Suite 309, Denver,
    CO 80203-1704
Provides library programs and services.
(303) 866-6900
Jobline: (303) 866-6741
Jobs in public and private libraries throughout Colorado.

Colorado (state) Department of Natural Resources
Division of Wildlife
6060 Broadway, Denver, CO 80216
Manages and conserves wildlife resources.
(303) 866-2667
Jobline: (303) 291-7527

Colorado (state) Department of Transportation
4201 E. Arkansas Avenue, Denver, CO 80222
Provides transportation programs and services.
(303) 757-9216
Jobline: (303) 757-9623

Colorado College
Colorado Springs, CO 80903
Small, private, liberal arts college in Colorado Springs,
    south of Denver.
(719) 389-6000
Jobline: (719) 389-6888

Colorado National Bank of Denver
918 17th Street, Denver, CO 80202
Operates national commercial banks.
(303) 585-5000
Jobline: (303) 585-8600

Columbia (city)
1737 Main Street, Columbia, SC 29201
Provides municipal services such as police, firefighting,
    libraries, parks, and public works.
(803) 733-8268
Jobline: (803) 733-8478

Columbia University
Columbia College, New York, NY 10027
Small, private institution in residential Manhattan.
(212) 854-1754
Jobline: (212) 854-5804, ask for information line.

Columbus (city)
50 W. Gay Street, Room 600, Columbus, OH 43215
Provides municipal services such as police, firefighting,
    libraries, parks, and public works.
(614) 645-8300
Jobline: (614) 645-7667

Columbus Bank and Trust Co.
1148 Broadway, P.O. Box 120, Columbus, GA 31902
Bank holding company that operates national and state
    commercial banks.
(706) 649-2311
Jobline: (706) 649-4758

Columbus Consolidated Government (city and county)
Government Center West Wing, 100 10th Street,
    Columbus, GA 31993
Provides government services such as police,
    firefighting, libraries, parks, and public works.
(706) 571-4740
Jobline: (706) 571-4738

Columbus State Community College
Columbus, OH 43216
Medium-sized, state-supported, 2-year college in
    Columbus.
(800) 621-6407
Jobline: (800) 621-6407, ask for x5454.

Comdata Holdings Corp.
5301 Maryland Way, Brentwood, TN 37027
Owns Comdata Networks Inc., which operates an
    electronic funds transfer network.
(615) 370-7000
Jobline: (615) 370-7747

Comerica Bank Texas
1601 Elm Street, Dallas, TX 75201
Operates state commercial banks.
(214) 841-1400
Jobline: (214) 969-6177

Comerica Inc.
1 Detroit Center, 500 Woodward Avenue, Detroit, MI
    48226
Bank holding company that operates state commercial
    banks.
(313) 222-3300
Jobline: (313) 222-6266

Commerce (city)
2535 Commerce Way, Commerce, CA 90040
Provides municipal services such as police, firefighting,
    libraries, parks, and public works.
(213) 722-4805
Jobline: (213) 887-4415

Commerce Bank of Kansas City NA
1000 Walnut Street, Kansas City, MO 64106
Operates national commercial banks.
(816) 234-2000
Jobline: (816) 234-2139

Commerce Bank of Saint Louis NA
8000 Forsyth Boulevard, Clayton, MO 63105
Operates national commercial banks.
(314) 726-2255
Jobline: (314) 746-7382

Commerce City (city)
5291 E. 60th Avenue, Commerce City, CO 80022
Provides municipal services such as police, firefighting,
    libraries, parks, and public works.
(303) 289-3624
Jobline: (303) 289-3618

Commercial National Bank
333 Texas Street, P.O. Box 21119, Shreveport, LA 71152
Operates national commercial banks.
(318) 429-1000
Jobline: (318) 429-1803

Commodity Futures Trading Commission
2033 K Street NW, Washington, DC 20581
Studies and regulates futures trading to promote
    economic growth and ensure the market's integrity.
(202) 254-6387
Jobline: (202) 254-3346

ConAgra Inc.
1 ConAgra Drive, Omaha, NE 68102-1826
Produces flour and grain products, canned goods, and
    cooking oils; operates meat and poultry plants.
(402) 595-4000
Jobline: (402) 595-4499

Concord (city)
1957 Parkside Drive, Concord, CA 94519
Provides municipal services such as police, firefighting,
    libraries, parks, and public works.
(510) 671-3308
Jobline: (510) 671-3151

Connecticut College
New London, CT 06320-4196
Small, private, liberal arts institution two miles from
    downtown New London.
(203) 447-1911
Jobline: (203) 439-2069

Consolidated Rail Corp.
2 Commerce Square, 2001 Market Street, Philadelphia,
    PA 19101
Operates line-haul railroads.
(215) 209-2000
Jobline: (609) 231-2165

Continental Airlines Holdings Inc.
P.O. Box 4330, Houston, TX 77210-4330
Provides scheduled air passenger transportation.
(713) 834-5302
Jobline: (713) 834-5300

Continental Bank
1500 Market Street, Philadelphia, PA 19102
Operates state commercial banks.
(215) 564-7000
Jobline: (215) 564-7678

Contra Costa Community College District
500 Court Street, Martinez, CA 94553
Includes Contra Costa College, Diablo Valley College,
    and Los Medanos College.
(510) 229-1000
Jobline: (510) 229-1000, x200.

Contra Costa County
651 Pine Street, 2nd Floor, Martinez, CA 94553
Provides county services such as sheriffs, courts, motor
    vehicle registration, and social services.
(510) 646-4047
Jobline: (510) 646-4046

Copley Plaza
138 St. James Avenue, Boston, MA 02116
370-room hotel.
(617) 267-5300
Jobline: (617) 421-9478

CoreStates Bank NA
1500 Market Street, Philadelphia, PA 19101
Operates national commercial banks.
(215) 973-3100
Jobline: (215) 973-4556

Corning Inc.
Houghton Park, Corning, NY 14831
Manufactures glass and glass products including
    tableware, cooking utensils, and ophthalmic glass.
(607) 974-9000
Jobline: (607) 974-2393

Corporation for Public Broadcasting
1111 16th Street NW, Washington, DC 20036
Promotes and finances the growth and development of
    noncommercial radio and television.
(202) 955-5100
Jobline: (202) 393-1045

Corpus Christi (city)
City Hall, 2nd Floor, 1201 Leopard Street, Corpus
    Christi, TX 78401
Provides municipal services such as police, firefighting,
    libraries, parks, and public works.
(512) 880-3300
Jobline: (512) 880-3333

Corvallis (city)
501 SW Madison Avenue, Corvallis, OR 97333
Provides municipal services such as police, firefighting,
    libraries, parks, and public works.
(503) 757-6902
Jobline: (503) 757-6955

Costa Mesa (city)
P.O. Box 1200, Costa Mesa, CA 92627-1200
Provides municipal services such as police, firefighting,
    libraries, parks, and public works.
(714) 754-5350
Jobline: (714) 754-5070

Countrywide Mortgage Investments Inc.
155 N. Lake Avenue, Pasadena, CA 91109
Operates real estate investment trusts.
(818) 304-8400
Jobline: (818) 304-5925

Covina (city)
125 E. College Street, Covina, CA 91723
Provides municipal services such as police, firefighting,
    libraries, parks, and public works.
(818) 858-7221
Jobline: (818) 858-7225

Creighton University
Omaha, NE 68178
Small, church-affiliated university on the northwest edge
    of downtown Omaha.
(402) 280-2700
Jobline: (402) 280-2943

Crestar Bank
919 E. Main Street, Richmond, VA 23219-4625
Operates state commercial banks and other banking
    businesses.
(804) 782-5000
Jobline: (804) 270-8572

Cubic Corp.
9333 Balboa Avenue, San Diego, CA 92123-1515
Manufactures flight simulators, elevators, fare registers,
    and communications and other equipment.
(619) 277-6780
Jobline: (619) 277-6780, ask for x3300 (may beep
    before message).

Culver City (city)
4095 Overland Avenue, Culver City, CA 90232
Provides municipal services such as police, firefighting,
    libraries, parks, and public works.
(310) 202-5750
Jobline: (310) 202-5751

Cuna Mutual Insurance Group
5910 Mineral Point Road, Madison, WI 53705
Provides life, accident, and health insurance.
(608) 238-5851
Jobline: (800) 562-2862

Cuyahoga County
1219 Ontario Avenue, 4th Floor, Cleveland, OH 44113
Provides county services such as sheriffs, courts, motor
    vehicle registration, and social services.
(216) 443-7694
Jobline: (216) 443-2039

Dade County
140 W. Flagler Street, Miami, FL 33130
Provides county services such as sheriffs, courts, motor
    vehicle registration, and social services.
(305) 375-2683
Jobline: (305) 375-1871

Dade County Fire Department
6000 SW 87th Avenue, Miami, FL 33173
Provides firefighting programs and services.
(305) 596-8591
Jobline: (305) 596-8645

Dakota County
1590 W. Highway 55, Hastings, MN 55033
Provides county services such as sheriffs, courts, motor
vehicle registration, and social services.
(612) 438-4418
Jobline: (612) 438-4473

Dallas (city)
1500 Marilla Street, Dallas, TX 75201
Provides municipal services such as police, firefighting,
libraries, parks, and public works.
(214) 670-3552
Jobline: (214) 670-3552, press 3552, then 4, then 1.

Dallas County
501 Main Street, Dallas, TX 75202
Provides county services such as sheriffs, courts, motor
vehicle registration, and social services.
(214) 653-7637
Jobline: (214) 653-7637, press 1.

Dallas County Community College District
701 Elm Street, Dallas, TX 75202
Includes Eastfield, El Centro, North Lake, Richland, and
Brookhaven Colleges.
(214) 746-2149
Jobline: (214) 746-2438

Daly City (city)
240 92nd Street, Daly City, CA 94105
Provides municipal services such as police, firefighting,
libraries, parks, and public works.
(415) 991-8028
Jobline: (415) 991-8028
Call after office hours.

Dane County
City-County Building, Room 418, 210 Martin Luther
King Jr. Boulevard, Madison, WI 53710
Provides county services such as sheriffs, courts, motor
vehicle registration, and social services.
(608) 266-4125
Jobline: (608) 266-4123

Daniel Freeman Memorial Hospital
333 N. Prarie Avenue, Inglewood, CA 90301
Not-for-profit hospital with more than 300 beds.
(310) 674-7050
Jobline: (310) 419-8373
Jobs other than nursing.

Jobline: (310) 419-8377
Nursing jobs.

Dartmouth College
Hanover, NH 03755
Medium-sized, private college in Hanover, 130 miles
northwest of Boston.
(603) 646-1110
Jobline: (603) 646-3328

Dauphin Deposit Bank and Trust Co.
P.O. Box 2961, Harrisburg, PA 17105
Operates state commercial banks.
(717) 255-2121
Jobline: (717) 255-2121, ask for x3275.

Davis (city)
23 Russell Boulevard, Davis, CA 95616
Provides municipal services such as police, firefighting,
libraries, parks, and public works.
(916) 757-5644
Jobline: (916) 757-5645

Davis County
Courthouse, 28 E. State, Farmington, UT 84025
Provides county services such as sheriffs, courts, motor
vehicle registration, and social services.
(801) 451-3415
Jobline: (801) 451-3484

Dayton (city)
City Hall, 101 W. 3rd Street, Dayton, OH 45402
Provides municipal services such as police, firefighting,
libraries, parks, and public works.
(513) 443-3700
Jobline: (513) 443-3719

Dayton Hudson Corp.
777 Nicollett Mall, Minneapolis, MN 55402
Operates department stores & upscale discount stores.
(612) 370-6948
Jobline: (612) 375-2200, ask for job hotline.

De Soto (city)
211 E. Pleasant Run Road, De Soto, TX 75115
Provides municipal services such as police, firefighting,
libraries, parks, and public works.
(214) 230-9638
Jobline: (214) 230-9698

Deaconess Hospital of Cleveland
4229 Pearl Road, Cleveland, OH 44109
Not-for-profit hospital with more than 200 beds.
(216) 459-6300
Jobline: (216) 459-6560

Dekalb County
1300 Commerce Drive, 1st Floor, Decatur, GA 30030
Provides county services such as sheriffs, courts, motor
vehicle registration, and social services.
(404) 371-2332
Jobline: (404) 371-2331

Delaware (state) Employment and Training Department
3301 Lancaster Pike, Wilmington, DE 19805
Seeks workers for private employers.
(302) 577-2755
Jobline: (302) 577-2750

P.O. Box 616, Dover, DE 19903
(302) 739-5473
Jobline: (302) 739-4434

Delaware (state) Employment and Training Department (cont.)
P.O. Box 548, Georgetown, DE 19947
(302) 856-5230
Jobline: (302) 856-5625

Deluxe Corp.
1080 W. County Road F, Shoreview, MN 55126
Produces checkbooks and other business forms; provides funds transfer and other financial services.
(612) 483-7111
Jobline: (612) 481-4100

Denver (city and county)
110 16th Street, Denver, CO 80202-5206
Provides government services such as police, firefighting, libraries, parks, and public works.
(303) 640-2151
Jobline: (303) 640-1234

Denver (city and county) New Airport Employment Office
1391 N. Speer Boulevard, Suite 500, Denver, CO 80204
Coordinates construction and administration jobs for Denver's new airport.
(303) 899-4030
Jobline: (800) 866-3382
For callers in Colorado.

Denver Convention Complex
700 14th Street, Denver, CO 80202
Provides and manages facilities for exhibits and events.
(303) 640-8000
Jobline: (303) 640-8119

Denver Museum of Natural History
2001 Colorado Boulevard, Denver, CO 80205
Presents exhibits and programs on natural history.
(303) 370-6425
Jobline: (303) 370-6437

Denver Regional Council of Governments
2048 W. 26th Avenue, Suite 200B, Denver, CO 80211
Provides programs and services to governments in the Denver region.
(303) 455-1000
Jobline: (303) 480-6714
Police and firefighting jobs.

DePaul University
Chicago, IL 60604
Medium-sized, private, church-affiliated university with a main campus near downtown Chicago.
(312) 341-8000
Jobline: (312) 362-6803

Des Moines (city)
400 E. 1st Street, Des Moines, IA 50309
Provides municipal services such as police, firefighting, libraries, parks, and public works.
(515) 283-4213
Jobline: (515) 283-4115

Detroit (city)
316 City County Building, 2 Woodward Avenue, Detroit, MI 48226
Provides municipal services such as police, firefighting, libraries, parks, and public works.
(313) 224-3700
Jobline: (313) 224-6928

Detroit Edison Co.
2000 2nd Avenue, Detroit, MI 48226-1203
Generates, transmits, and distributes electric power, and provides other energy-related services.
(313) 237-8000
Jobline: (313) 237-6600

Diamond Shamrock Inc.
P.O. Box 696000, San Antonio, TX 78269
Refines and transports petroleum, and markets gasoline and consumer goods through retail outlets.
(210) 641-6800
Jobline: (210) 641-2387

Disneyland International
1313 S. Harbor Boulevard, Anaheim, CA 92802
Operates amusement park owned by Walt Disney Co.
(714) 999-4000
Jobline: (714) 999-4343
Entertainment jobs.

Casting Center
Stadium Towers, 1st Floor, 2400 E. Katella Avenue, Anaheim, CA 92806
Handles casting for seasonal positions at Disneyland.
Jobline: (714) 999-4407

Doctors Hospital
5815 Airline Drive, Houston, TX 77076
For-profit hospital with more than 100 beds.
(713) 695-6041
Jobline: (713) 696-4488

Dominion First Union Bank of Virginia
7711 Plantation Road, Roanoke, VA 24019
Operates national commercial banks.
(703) 563-7000
Jobline: (703) 563-7907

Doral Ocean Beach Resort
4833 Collins Avenue, Miami Beach, FL 33140
420-room hotel.
(305) 532-3600
Jobline: (305) 535-2055

Doral Resort & Country Club
4400 NW 87th Avenue, Miami, FL 33178
650-room hotel.
(305) 592-2000
Jobline: (305) 591-6424

Doubletree Hotel
835 Airport Road, San Francisco, CA 94010
293-room hotel near San Francisco International Airport.
(415) 344-5500
Jobline: (415) 348-4247

Doubletree Hotel
100 The City Drive South, Orange, CA 92668
454-room hotel near Disneyland.
(714) 634-4500
Jobline: (714) 634-4500, ask for x4470.

Doubletree Hotel
215 W. South Temple, Salt Lake City, UT 84101
381-room hotel.
(801) 531-7500
Jobline: (801) 531-7500, ask for x3050.

Doubletree Hotel at Concourse
7 Concourse Parkway, Atlanta, GA 30328
370-room hotel.
(404) 395-3900
Jobline: (404) 395-3900, ask for job hotline.

Doubletree Hotel at Lincoln Centre
5410 Lyndon B. Johnson Freeway, Dallas, TX 75240
500-room hotel.
(214) 934-8400
Jobline: (214) 701-5279

Doubletree Hotel Austin
6505 N. IH-35, Austin, TX 78752
350-room hotel.
(512) 454-3737
Jobline: (512) 454-4107

Doubletree Hotel Pasadena
191 N. Los Robles Avenue, Pasadena, CA 91101
350-room hotel.
(818) 792-2727
Jobline: (818) 792-2727, ask for job hotline.

Doubletree Hotel Post Oak Galleria
2001 Post Oak Boulevard, Houston, TX 77056
450-room hotel.
(713) 961-9300
Jobline: (713) 961-9300, ask for job hotline.

Doubletree Marina del Rey
4100 Admiralty Way, Marina del Rey, CA 90292
300-room hotel near Los Angeles International Airport.
(310) 301-3000
Jobline: (310) 301-3000, ask for x3050.

Doubletree Philadelphia
Broad Street at Locust Street, Philadelphia, PA 19107
431-room hotel.
(215) 893-1600
Jobline: (215) 893-1600, ask for x3340.

Douglas County
101 3rd Street, Castle Rock, CO 80104
Provides county services such as sheriffs, courts, motor
vehicle registration, and social services.
(303) 660-7427
Jobline: (303) 660-7420

Douglas County
8460 Courthouse Square East, Douglasville, GA 30134
Provides county services such as sheriffs, courts, motor
vehicle registration, and social services.
(404) 920-7264
Jobline: (404) 920-7363

Douglas County
1819 Farnam Street, Room 505, Omaha, NE 68183
Provides county services such as sheriffs, courts, motor
vehicle registration, and social services.
(402) 444-6188
Jobline: (402) 444-6270

Douglas County
Douglas County Courthouse, 1036 SE Douglas
Avenue, Roseburg, OR 97470
Provides county services such as sheriffs, courts, motor
vehicle registration, and social services.
(503) 440-4405
Jobline: (503) 440-6291

Dow Chemical Co.
2030 Willard H. Dow Center, Midland, MI 48674
Manufactures plastics, industrial and agricultural
chemicals, metals, and other products.
(517) 636-1000
Jobline: (517) 636-6100

Downey Savings and Loan Association
3501 Jamboree Road, Newport Beach, CA 92660
Operates federal savings banks.
(714) 854-3100
Jobline: (714) 509-4310

Drake City Center
140 E. Walton Place, Chicago, IL 60611
535-room hotel.
(312) 787-2200
Jobline: (312) 787-2200, ask for x4236.

Drake University
Des Moines, IA 50311
Medium-sized, private university in Des Moines.
(515) 271-2011
Jobline: (515) 271-4144

Drew University
Madison, NJ 07940
Small, private university in Madison, 27 miles south of
New York City.
(201) 408-3000
Jobline: (201) 408-5555

Drexel University
Philadelphia, PA 19104
Medium-sized, private university in West Philadelphia.
(215) 895-2000
Jobline: (215) 895-2562

Duke Power Co.
422 S. Church Street, Charlotte, NC 28242-0001
Generates, transmits, and distributes electric power,
and develops land and timber tracts.
(704) 373-4011
Jobline: (800) 726-6736

Duke University
Durham, NC 27706
Medium-sized, church-affiliated university in residential
Durham.
(919) 684-2323
Jobline: (919) 684-8895
Administrative and professional jobs.

Duke University (cont.)
Jobline: (919) 684-8896
Clerical jobs.

Jobline: (919) 684-8897
Technical and paraprofessional jobs.

Jobline: (919) 684-8898
Skilled crafts and service jobs.

Jobline: (919) 684-8899
Daily updates of the job hotline.

Duracell International Inc.
Berkshire Industrial Park, Bethel, CT 06801
Manufactures storage batteries.
(203) 796-4000
Jobline: (203) 796-4650, press 2.

E.I. du Pont de Nemours and Company Inc.
1007 Market Street, Wilmington, DE 19898
Extracts, refines, and markets petroleum, petroleum
    products, and coal, and produces other products.
(302) 774-1000
Jobline: (302) 992-6349

East Stroudsburg University of Pennsylvania
East Stroudsburg, PA 18301
Medium-sized, public university in the foothills of the
    Pocono Mountains.
(717) 424-3211
Jobline: (717) 424-3280

Eastern Michigan University
Ypsilanti, MI 48197
Medium-sized, public, multipurpose university in
    Ypsilanti, near Ann Arbor.
(313) 487-1849
Jobline: (313) 487-2462

Eastern Montana College
Billings, MT 59101
Small, public college in Billings.
(406) 657-2011
Jobline: (406) 657-2116

Eastern New Mexico University
Portales, NM 88130
Small, public, comprehensive university in Portales,
    southeast of Albuquerque.
(505) 562-1011
Jobline: (505) 562-2411

Eastern Washington University
Cheney, WA 99004
Medium-sized, public, multipurpose university in
    Cheney, near Spokane.
(509) 359-6200
Jobline: (509) 359-6200, x4390.

Eastman Kodak Co.
343 State Street, Rochester, NY 14650
Manufactures film, cameras, pharmaceutical
    preparations, chemicals, resins, and other products.
(716) 724-4000
Jobline: (716) 724-4609

Eaton County
1045 Independence, Charlotte, MI 48813
Provides county services such as sheriffs, courts, motor
    vehicle registration, and social services.
(517) 485-6444
Jobline: (517) 543-2452

Edmond (city)
P.O. Box 2970, Edmond, OK 73083
Provides municipal services such as police, firefighting,
    libraries, parks, and public works.
(405) 359-4685
Jobline: (405) 840-8000, x9421.

Edmonds School District
20420 68th Avenue W., Lynnwood, WA 98036
38-school district in Lynnwood.
(206) 670-7020
Jobline: (206) 670-7021

El Cajon (city)
200 E. Main Street, El Cajon, CA 92020
Provides municipal services such as police, firefighting,
    libraries, parks, and public works.
(619) 441-1736
Jobline: (619) 441-1671

El Dorado County
2850 Fairlane Court, Placerville, CA 95667
Provides county services such as sheriffs, courts, motor
    vehicle registration, and social services.
(916) 621-5565
Jobline: (916) 621-5579

El Monte (city)
11333 Valley Boulevard, El Monte, CA 91731
Provides municipal services such as police, firefighting,
    libraries, parks, and public works.
(818) 580-2040
Jobline: (818) 580-2041

El Paso (city)
2 Civic Center Plaza, El Paso, TX 79901
Provides municipal services such as police, firefighting,
    libraries, parks, and public works.
(915) 541-4504
Jobline: (915) 541-4094

El Paso County
27 E. Vermijo Avenue, Colorado Springs, CO 80903
Provides county services such as sheriffs, courts, motor
    vehicle registration, and social services.
(719) 520-7401
Jobline: (719) 520-7400

El Paso County
El Paso County Courthouse, Room 302, 500 E. San
    Antonio Avenue, El Paso, TX 79901
Provides county services such as sheriffs, courts, motor
    vehicle registration, and social services.
(915) 546-2218
Jobline: (915) 546-2039

El Paso County Social Services Department
105 N. Spruce Street, Colorado Springs, CO 80905
Provides social programs and services.
(719) 444-5661
Jobline: (719) 444-5663

Electronics and Space Corp.
8100 W. Florissant Avenue, Saint Louis, MO 63136
Manufactures defense systems and equipment.
(314) 553-3334
Jobline: (314) 553-2485

Eli Lilly and Co.
Lilly Corporate Center, Indianapolis, IN 46285
Produces pharmaceuticals, electromedical equipment,
    and other medical and agricultural products.
(317) 276-2000
Jobline: (317) 276-7472

Elk Grove Unified School District
8820 Elk Grove Boulevard, Sacramento, CA 95624
34-school district in Sacramento.
(916) 686-5085
Jobline: (916) 686-7781
Classified jobs.

Elon College
Elon College, NC 27244
Small, church-affiliated, liberal arts college west of the
    Research Triangle.
(910) 584-9711
Jobline: (910) 584-2255

Emerson College
Boston, MA 02116
Small, private college with an urban campus in Boston's
    historic Back Bay.
(617) 578-8500
Jobline: (617) 578-8578

Encinitas (city)
505 S. Vulcan Avenue, Encinitas, CA 92024
Provides municipal services such as police, firefighting,
    libraries, parks, and public works.
(619) 633-2727
Jobline: (619) 633-2726

Englewood (city)
3400 S. Elati Street, Englewood, CO 80111
Provides municipal services such as police, firefighting,
    libraries, parks, and public works.
(303) 762-2370
Jobline: (303) 762-2304

Enoch Pratt Free Library
400 Cathedral Street, Baltimore, MD 21201
Provides library programs and services.
(410) 396-5394
Jobline: (410) 396-5353, press 1.

Enron Corp.
1400 Smith Street, Houston, TX 77002-7337
Produces natural gas and petroleum, and provides
    other energy-related products and services.
(713) 853-6161
Jobline: (713) 853-5884

Environmental Protection Agency
401 M Street SW, Washington, DC 20460
Seeks to control and abate pollution to protect and
    enhance the U.S. environment.
(202) 260-3144
Jobline: (202) 260-5055

Region 4
345 Courtland Street NE, Atlanta, GA 30308
(404) 347-3486
Jobline: (800) 833-8130

Region 4 (satellite office)
79 P.W. Alexander Dr., Mail Drop 29, Research Triangle
    Park, NC 27711
(919) 541-3071
Jobline: (919) 541-3014

Region 5
77 W. Jackson Boulevard, 4th Floor, Chicago, IL 60604
(312) 353-2000
Jobline: (312) 353-2026

Region 6
1445 Ross Avenue at 1 Fountain Plaza, Dallas, TX
    75202
(214) 655-6444
Jobline: (214) 655-6560

Region 7
726 Minnesota Avenue, Kansas City, KS 66101
(913) 551-7041
Jobline: (913) 551-7068

Region 8
999 18th Street, Denver, CO 80202
(303) 293-1487
Jobline: (303) 293-1564

Region 9
75 Hawthorne Street, San Francisco, CA 94105
(415) 744-1500
Jobline: (415) 744-1111

Andrew Breidenbach Center
26 W. Martin Luther King Drive, Cincinnati, OH 45268
Laboratory that conducts water research for the EPA.
(513) 569-7812
Jobline: (513) 569-7840

Equifax Inc.
1600 Peachtree Street NW, Atlanta, GA 30309
Provides information-based services and systems for
    consumer-initiated financial transactions.
(404) 885-8000
Jobline: (404) 885-8550

Escondido (city)
201 N. Broadway, Escondido, CA 92025
Provides municipal services such as police, firefighting,
    libraries, parks, and public works.
(619) 741-4641
Jobline: (619) 432-4585

Ethicon Inc.
U.S. Highway 22, Somerville, NJ 08876
Manufactures sutures, ligatures, and surgical stapling
    devices.
(908) 218-0707
Jobline: (800) 642-9534

Eugene (city)
777 Pearl Street, Eugene, OR 97401
Provides municipal services such as police, firefighting,
libraries, parks, and public works.
(503) 687-5061
Jobline: (503) 687-5060

Eugene (city) Water and Electric Board
500 E. 4th Avenue, Eugene, OR 97401
Provides water and electric services.
(503) 484-2411
Jobline: (503) 484-3769

Eugene School District No. 4J
200 N. Monroe Street, Eugene, OR 97402
44-school district in Eugene.
(503) 687-3247
Jobline: (503) 687-3344

Euless (city)
201 N. Ector Drive, Euless, TX 76039
Provides municipal services such as police, firefighting,
libraries, parks, and public works.
(817) 685-1450
Jobline: (817) 685-1456

Eureka (city)
531 K Street, Eureka, CA 95501
Provides municipal services such as police, firefighting,
libraries, parks, and public works.
(707) 441-4124
Jobline: (707) 441-4134

Everett (city)
3002 Wetmore Avenue, Everett, WA 98201
Provides municipal services such as police, firefighting,
libraries, parks, and public works.
(206) 259-8767
Jobline: (206) 259-8768

Everett School District
4730 Colby Avenue, Everett, WA 98203
26-school district in Everett.
(206) 339-4245
Jobline: (206) 259-2935
Classified and certificated jobs.

Evergreen School District
13905 NE 28th Avenue, Vancouver, WA 98686
25-school district in Vancouver.
(206) 256-6011
Jobline: (206) 254-7403
Classified and certificated jobs.

Evergreen State College
Olympia, WA 98505
Small, public college on Puget Sound.
(206) 866-6000
Jobline: (206) 866-6000, x6361.

Executive Office of the President
The White House, 1600 Pennsylvania Avenue NW,
Washington, DC 20500
Includes the White House staff and the President's
various policy-making offices and councils.
(202) 456-1414
Jobline: (202) 395-5892

Export-Import Bank
811 Vermont Avenue NW, Washington, DC 20571
Facilitates and aids in financing the export of U.S.
goods and services.
(202) 566-8834
Jobline: (202) 377-6396

Fairbanks North Star Borough
809 Pioneer Road, Fairbanks, AK 99707
Provides county services such as sheriffs, courts, motor
vehicle registration, and social services.
(907) 459-1202
Jobline: (907) 459-1206

Fairfax (city)
10455 Armstrong Street, Fairfax, VA 22030
Provides municipal services such as police, firefighting,
libraries, parks, and public works.
(703) 385-7850
Jobline: (703) 385-7861

Fairfax County
12000 Government Center Parkway, Fairfax, VA 22030
Provides county services such as sheriffs, courts, motor
vehicle registration, and social services.
(703) 324-3303
Jobline: (703) 324-5627, press 1, then 2.

Fairfield (city)
1000 Webster, Fairfield, CA 94533
Provides municipal services such as police, firefighting,
libraries, parks, and public works.
(707) 428-7394
Jobline: (707) 428-7396

Fairmont Hotel
170 S. Market Street, San Jose, CA 95113
541-room hotel.
(408) 998-1900
Jobline: (408) 998-1900, ask for job hotline.

Fairmont Hotel
Nob Hill, San Francisco, CA 94108
600-room hotel.
Jobline: (415) 772-5000
(415) 772-5139

Fairmont Hotel
University Place, 123 Baronne Street, New Orleans, LA
70140
750-room hotel.
(504) 529-7111
Jobline: (504) 529-7111, ask for job hotline.

Fairmont Hotel Dallas Arts District
1717 N. Akard Street, Dallas, TX 75201
550-room hotel.
(214) 720-2020
Jobline: (214) 720-5311

Falls Church (city)
300 Park Avenue, Falls Church, VA 22046
Provides municipal services such as police, firefighting,
libraries, parks, and public works.
(703) 241-5025
Jobline: (703) 241-5163

Far West Federal Savings Bank
421 SW 6th Avenue, Portland, OR 97204
Operates federal savings banks.
(503) 224-4444
Jobline: (503) 323-6467

Farmers Branch (city)
13000 William Dodson Parkway, Farmers Branch, TX 75234
Provides municipal services such as police, firefighting, libraries, parks, and public works.
(214) 919-2556
Jobline: (214) 919-2559

Farmland Industries Inc.
3315 N. Oak Trafficway, Kansas City, MO 64116
Produces petroleum products, fertilizers, feed and other farm supplies, and other products.
(816) 459-6000
Jobline: (816) 459-5056

Fayette County
140 W. Stonewall Avenue, Fayetteville, GA 30214
Provides county services such as sheriffs, courts, motor vehicle registration, and social services.
(404) 461-6041
Jobline: (404) 461-6041, ask for x110.

Federal Communications Commission
1919 M Street NW, Washington, DC 20554
Regulates interstate and foreign communications by radio, television, wire, satellite, and cable.
(202) 632-1107
Jobline: (202) 632-0101

Federal Deposit Insurance Corp.
550 17th Street NW, Washington, DC 20429
Protects the money supply by providing insurance coverage for bank deposits.
(202) 393-8400
Jobline: (800) 695-8052

Federal Emergency Management Agency
500 C Street SW, Washington, DC 20472
Responsible for federal emergency preparedness, mitigation, and response activities.
(202) 646-3962
Jobline: (202) 646-3244

Federal Express Corp.
2005 Corporate Avenue, Memphis, TN 38132
Provides air package, letter, and parcel delivery and other transportation services.
(901) 369-3600
Jobline: (901) 535-9555
Hub jobs.

Jobline: (901) 797-6830
Corporate jobs.

Southern California District
800 Newport Center Drive, Newport Beach, CA 92660
(714) 729-0336
Jobline: (714) 729-0330

Los Angeles Metro District
Jobline: (818) 753-5552

Federal Reserve Bank of Atlanta
104 Marietta Street NW, Atlanta, GA 30303-2706
Implements general monetary, credit, and operating policies for the Federal Reserve System.
(404) 521-8500
Jobline: (404) 521-8767

Federal Reserve Bank of Miami
9100 NW 36th Street, Miami, FL 33178
Implements general monetary, credit, and operating policies for the Federal Reserve System.
(305) 471-6434
Jobline: (305) 471-6480

Federal Reserve Bank of San Francisco
P.O. Box 7702, San Francisco, CA 94120
Implements general monetary, credit, and operating policies for the Federal Reserve System.
(415) 974-2000
Jobline: (415) 974-3330

Federal Reserve System
Board of Governors
20th Street and Constitution Avenue NW, Washington, DC 20551
Determines general monetary, credit, and operating policies for the Federal Reserve System.
(202) 452-3000
Jobline: (202) 452-3038

Federal Trade Commission
Pennsylvania Avenue at 6th Street NW, Washington, DC 20580
Seeks to maintain free and fair competition as the guiding force of the American economic system.
(202) 326-2222
Jobline: (202) 326-2020

Federal Way (city)
33530 1st Way South, Federal Way, WA 98003
Provides municipal services such as police, firefighting, libraries, parks, and public works.
(206) 661-4083
Jobline: (206) 661-4089

Federal Way School District
31405 18th Avenue South, Federal Way, WA 98003
33-school district in Federal Way.
(206) 941-0100
Jobline: (206) 941-2058
Certificated jobs.

Jobline: (206) 941-2273
Classified jobs.

Ferris State University
Big Rapids, MI 49307
Medium-sized, public university in Big Rapids, 50 miles from Grand Rapids.
(616) 592-2000
Jobline: (616) 592-5627

Fifth Third Bank
38 Fountain Square Plaza, Cincinnati, OH 45263
Operates state commercial banks.
(513) 579-5300
Jobline: (513) 579-5627

Fifth Third Bank of Toledo NA
606 Madison Avenue, Toledo, OH 43604
Operates national commercial banks.
(419) 259-7890
Jobline: (419) 259-7694

First American Corp.
500 Metroplex Drive, Nashville, TN 37211-7115
Bank holding company that operates First American
   National Bank, a national commercial bank.
(615) 748-2000
Jobline: (615) 781-7400

First Commercial Corp.
400 W. Capitol Avenue, P.O. Box 1471, Little Rock, AR
   72203
Bank holding company that operates national and state
   commercial banks.
(501) 371-7000
Jobline: (501) 371-3310

First Hawaiian Bank
165 S. King Street, Honolulu, HI 96847
Operates state commercial banks.
(808) 525-7000
Jobline: (808) 525-5627

First Interstate Bank NA
530 Broadway, San Diego, CA 92101
Operates national commercial banks.
(619) 557-2200
Jobline: (619) 557-3069
Includes jobs in the Inland Empire area.

First Interstate Bank of Arizona NA
First Interstate Bank Plaza, 100 W. Washington Street,
   Phoenix, AZ 85072
Operates national commercial banks.
(602) 528-6000
Jobline: (602) 528-1199

First Interstate Bank of Denver NA
633 17th Street, Denver, CO 80270
Operates national commercial banks.
(303) 293-2211
Jobline: (303) 293-5777

First Interstate Bank of Nevada NA
P.O. Box 11007, Reno, NV 89520
Operates national commercial banks.
(702) 784-3000
Jobline: (702) 334-5666

First Interstate Bank of Oregon NA
1300 SW 5th Avenue, P.O. Box 3131, Portland, OR
   97208
Operates national commercial banks and foreign
   banking businesses.
(503) 225-2111
Jobline: (503) 340-8888

First Interstate Bank of Texas NA
801 Travis Street, Houston, TX 77002
Operates national commercial banks.
(713) 224-6611
Jobline: (713) 250-7356

First Interstate Bank of Utah NA
180 S. Main Street, Salt Lake City, UT 84101
Operates national commercial banks.
(801) 350-7000
Jobline: (801) 350-7070

First Interstate Bank of Washington NA
P.O. Box 160, Seattle, WA 98111
Operates national commercial banks.
(206) 292-3111
Jobline: (206) 292-3551

First National Bank of Anchorage
425 G Street, P.O. Box 100720
Anchorage, AK 99510-0720
Operates national commercial banks.
(907) 265-3436
Jobline: (907) 265-3027

First National Bank of Boston
100 Federal Street, Boston, MA 02110
Operates national commercial banks.
(617) 434-2200
Jobline: (617) 434-0165

First National Bank of Commerce
210 Baronne Street, New Orleans, LA 70112
Operates national commercial banks.
(504) 561-1371
Jobline: (504) 582-7500

First National Bank of Maryland
25 S. Charles Street, Baltimore, MD 21201
Operates national commercial banks.
(410) 244-4000
Jobline: (410) 347-6562
Call (800) 424-4864 outside the Baltimore area.

First Security Bank of Idaho NA
119 N. 9th Street, P.O. Box 7069, Boise, ID 83730
Operates national commercial banks.
(208) 338-4000
Jobline: (208) 393-2453

First Security Bank of Utah NA
79 S. Main Street, Salt Lake City, UT 84111
Operates national commercial banks.
(801) 350-6000
Jobline: (801) 246-1885

First Tennessee Bank NA
300 Court Street, P.O. Box 84, Memphis, TN
   38101-8416
Operates national commercial banks and provides data
   processing, real estate, and other services.
(901) 523-4444
Jobline: (901) 523-5033
Professional and managerial jobs.

Jobline: (901) 523-5056
Full-time jobs.

Jobline: (901) 523-5090
Part-time jobs.

First Union National Bank of Florida
200 S. Biscayne Boulevard, Miami, FL 33131
Operates national commercial banks.
(305) 375-7500
Jobline: (305) 467-5292

225 Water Street, Jacksonville, FL 32202
(904) 361-2265
Jobline: (904) 361-6971

First Union National Bank of Georgia
999 Peachtree Street, P.O. Box 740074, Atlanta, GA
  30374
Operates national commercial banks.
(404) 827-7100
Jobline: (404) 827-7150

First Union National Bank of Tennessee
150 4th Avenue North, Nashville, TN 37219
Operates national commercial banks.
(615) 251-9200
Jobline: (615) 251-9238

First Union National Bank of Virginia
1751 Pinnacoe Drive, McLean, VA 22102
Operates national commercial banks.
(703) 821-7777
Jobline: (703) 903-7777

Firstar Corp.
777 E. Wisconsin Avenue, Milwaukee, WI 53202
Bank holding company that operates national and state
  commercial banks.
(414) 765-4321
Jobline: (414) 765-5627

FirsTier Bank NA Lincoln
233 S. 13th Street, Lincoln, NE 68501
Operates national commercial banks.
(402) 434-1231
Jobline: (402) 434-1426

FirsTier Bank NA Omaha
1700 Farnam Street, Omaha, NE 68102
Operates national commercial banks.
(402) 348-6000
Jobline: (402) 348-6400

Flamingo Hilton Reno
255 N. Sierra Street, Reno, NV 89501
604-room hotel.
(702) 322-1111
Jobline: (702) 785-7006

Fleet Bank
1 Clinton Square, P.O. Box 4821, Syracuse, NY 13221
Operates national commercial banks.
(315) 426-4100
Jobline: (315) 798-2680

Fleet Bank of Maine
P.O. Box 1280, Portland, ME 04104
Operates state commercial banks.
(207) 874-5000
Jobline: (207) 874-5000
Ask for job hotline.
Call (800) 499-5627 in Maine.

Fleetwood Enterprises Inc.
3125 Myers Street, P.O. Box 7638, Riverside, CA 92513
Manufactures prefabricated wood and metal buildings,
  motor homes, and travel trailers and campers.
(909) 351-3500
Jobline: (909) 788-5627

Florida (state) Agency for Health Care Administration
Fort Knox Executive Office Building, 2727 Mahan Drive,
  Tallahassee, FL 32308
Insures access to affordable, quality health care.
(904) 922-8435
Jobline: (904) 488-8356

Florida (state) Attorney
1350 NW 12th Avenue, Miami, FL 33136
Investigates and prosecutes cases.
(305) 547-0540
Jobline: (305) 547-0533

Florida (state) court system
Supreme Court Building, Duval Street, Tallahassee, FL
  32399-1900
Provides judicial programs and services.
(904) 487-0778
Jobline: (904) 488-2556

Florida (state) Department of Agriculture and Consumer Services
408 Mayo Building, Tallahassee, FL 32399-0800
Provides agricultural and consumer programs and
  services.
(904) 487-2785
Jobline: (904) 487-2474

Florida (state) Department of Business and Professional Regulation
Northwood Centre, 1940 N. Monroe Street,
  Tallahassee, FL 32399-0750
Regulates businesses and professions.
(904) 488-7506
Jobline: (904) 488-4874

Florida (state) Department of Commerce
402 Collins Building, Tallahassee, FL 32399-2000
Provides commerce programs and services.
(904) 487-2431
Jobline: (904) 488-0869

Florida (state) Department of Community Affairs
152 Rhyne Building, 2740 Centerview Drive,
  Tallahassee, FL 32399-2100
Provides community programs and services.
(904) 487-4627
Jobline: (904) 488-4776

Florida (state) Department of Corrections
Region 1
4610 Highway 90 East, Marianna, FL 32446
Provides correctional programs and services.
(904) 482-9533
Jobline: (904) 482-3531

Florida (state) Department of Corrections (cont.)
Region 2
P.O. Box 147007, Gainesville, FL 32614-7007
(904) 336-2035
Jobline: (904) 334-1722

Region 3
400 W. Robinson Street, Suite N-909, Orlando, FL
32801
(407) 423-6125
Jobline: (407) 423-6600

Region 4
3810 Inverrary Boulevard, Lauderhill, FL 33319
(305) 497-3300
Jobline: (305) 497-3398

Region 5
5422 W. Bay Center Drive, Tampa, FL 33609
(813) 871-7230
Jobline: (813) 871-7142

Florida (state) Department of Education
101 Florida Education Center, 325 W. Gaines Street,
Tallahassee, FL 32399-0400
Provides educational programs and services.
(904) 488-8652
Jobline: (904) 487-2367

**Florida (state) Department of Environmental
Protection**
353 Douglas Building, 3900 Commonwealth Boulevard,
Tallahassee, FL 32399-3000
Provides environmental protection programs and
services.
(904) 488-0450
Jobline: (904) 487-0436

**Florida (state) Department of Health and
Rehabilitative Services**
Headquarters
223 Building 3, Winewood Office Complex, 1317
Winewood Boulevard, Tallahassee, FL 32399-0700
Provides health and rehabilitative programs and
services.
(904) 488-2840
Jobline: (904) 488-2255

District 1
P.O. Box 8420, 160 Governmental Center, Pensacola,
FL 32505-2949
(904) 444-8180
Jobline: (904) 444-8037

District 2
215-A Cedars Executive Center, 2639 N. Monroe
Street, Tallahassee, FL 32399-2949
(904) 487-2800
Jobline: (904) 488-0831

District 3
1000 NE 16th Avenue, Building J, Gainesville, FL 32601
(904) 955-5074
Jobline: (904) 955-5190

District 4 and District 12
5920 Arlington Expressway, Jacksonville, FL 32211
(904) 723-2177
Jobline: (904) 723-2024

District 5
11351 Ulmerton Road, Largo, FL 34648
(813) 588-6630
Jobline: (813) 588-6628

District 6
4000 W. Dr. Martin Luther King Jr. Boulevard, Tampa,
FL 33614
(813) 871-7345
Jobline: (813) 877-8349

District 7
400 W. Robinson Street, Suite 725, Orlando, FL 32801
(407) 423-6196
Jobline: (407) 423-6207

District 9
111 Georgia Avenue, Suite 104, West Palm Beach, FL
33401
(407) 837-5091
Jobline: (407) 837-5014

District 10
201 W. Broward Boulevard, Fort Lauderdale, FL
33301-1885
(305) 467-4240
Jobline: (305) 467-4279

District 11
401 NW 2nd Avenue, Room 821, Miami, FL 33128
(305) 377-5205
Jobline: (305) 377-5747

**Florida (state) Department of Highway Safety
and Motor Vehicles**
Neil Kirkman Building, Room A428, 2900 Apalachee
Parkway, Tallahassee, FL 32399-0525
Provides highway safety and motor vehicle programs
and services.
(904) 488-3014
Jobline: (904) 487-3669

Florida (state) Department of Insurance
112 Larson Building, Tallahassee, FL 32399-0300
Regulates insurance.
(904) 922-3182
Jobline: (904) 487-2644

**Florida (state) Department of Labor and
Employment Security**
209 Hartman Building, 2012 Capital Circle SE,
Tallahassee, FL 32399-2166
Provides labor and employment security programs and
services.
(904) 487-2960
Jobline: (904) 487-5627

Florida (state) Department of Law Enforcement
2331 Phillips Road, P.O. Box 1489, Tallahassee, FL
32399-2166
Provides law enforcement programs and services.
(904) 488-4814
Jobline: (904) 488-0797

Florida (state) Department of Management Services
Koger Executive Center, 2737 Centerview Drive,
Tallahassee, FL 32399-0950
Provides management services for the Florida state
government.
(904) 488-2707
Jobline: (904) 487-3988

Florida (state) Department of Revenue
118 Carlton Building, 501 S. Calhoun Street,
Tallahassee, FL 32399-0100
Collects and processes state income taxes and other
state revenues.
(904) 488-2635
Jobline: (904) 488-3895

Florida (state) Department of State
1902 Capitol Building, Tallahassee, FL 32399-0252
Manages elections, library services, cultural affairs,
corporate filings, and other functions.
(904) 488-1177
Jobline: (904) 488-1179

Division of Library and Information Services
500 S. Bronough Street, Tallahassee, FL 32399-0250
Provides library and information programs and services.
(904) 487-2651
Jobline: (904) 488-5232

Florida (state) Department of Transportation
Haydon Burns Building, Room 588, 605 Suwannee
Street, Tallahassee, FL 32399-0450
Provides transportation programs and services.
(904) 488-6816
Jobline: (904) 922-9867

District 6
1000 NW 111th Avenue, Miami, FL 33172
(305) 470-5120
Jobline: (305) 470-5128

Florida (state) Game and Fresh Water Fish Commission
106 Bryant Building, 620 S. Meridian Street,
Tallahassee, FL 32399-1600
Manages and conserves game and fresh water fish
resources.
(904) 488-6411
Jobline: (904) 488-5805

Florida (state) Lottery
250 Marriott Drive, Tallahassee, FL 32399-4014
Provides lottery programs and services.
(904) 487-7721
Jobline: (904) 487-7731

Florida Agricultural and Mechanical University
211 Foote-Hilyer Building, Tallahassee, FL 32307
Medium-sized, public university in Tallahassee.
(904) 599-3000
Jobline: (904) 561-2436

Florida Atlantic University
500 NW 20th Street, Boca Raton, FL 33431-0991
Medium-sized, public, multipurpose university with a
main campus in Boca Raton.
(407) 367-3000
Jobline: (407) 367-3506

Florida Hospital Medical Center
601 E. Rollins Street, Orlando, FL 32803
Operates four not-for-profit hospitals with more than
1,200 beds in the Orlando area.
(407) 896-6611
Jobline: (407) 331-8000, x 6125.
Clerical jobs.

Florida Institute of Technology
Melbourne, FL 32901
Small, private institution in Melbourne, 60 miles
southeast of Orlando.
(407) 768-8000
Jobline: (407) 768-8000, press 93, then 5.

Florida International University
107 Avenue SW 8th Street, Miami, FL 33199
Medium-sized, public university 10 miles from
downtown Miami.
(305) 348-2000
Jobline: (305) 348-2500

Florida State University
216 W.M. Johnston Building, Tallahassee, FL
32306-1009
Large, public, comprehensive university within a mile of
downtown Tallahassee.
(904) 644-2525
Jobline: (904) 644-6066

Fluor Daniel Inc.
3333 Michelson Drive, Irvine, CA 92730-0001
Provides building construction consulting and
decontamination services.
(714) 975-2000
Jobline: (714) 975-5253

Fontainebleau Hilton Resort
4441 Collins Avenue, Miami Beach, FL 33140
1,206-room hotel.
(305) 538-2000
Jobline: (305) 538-2000, ask for x43723.

Fontana (city)
8353 Sierra Avenue, Fontana, CA 92335
Provides municipal services such as police, firefighting,
libraries, parks, and public works.
(909) 350-7650
Jobline: (909) 350-7652

Food Lion Inc.
P.O. Box 1330, Salisbury, NC 28145-1330
Operates supermarkets.
(704) 633-8250
Jobline: (704) 633-8250, x2144.

Foothill-De Anza Community College District
12345 El Monte Road, Los Altos Hills, CA 94022-4599
Includes Foothill College and De Anza College.
(415) 949-7363
Jobline: (415) 949-6218

Forsyth County
Hall of Justice, 200 N. Main Street, Winston Salem, NC 27101
Provides county services such as sheriffs, courts, motor vehicle registration, and social services.
(910) 727-2851
Jobline: (910) 631-6333

Fort Wayne (city)
City-County Building, 3rd Floor, 1 E. Main Street, Fort Wayne, IN 46802
Provides municipal services such as police, firefighting, libraries, parks, and public works.
(219) 427-1180
Jobline: (219) 427-1186

Fort Wayne National Bank Inc.
110 W. Berry Street, Fort Wayne, IN 46802-2304
Operates national commercial banks.
(219) 426-0555
Jobline: (219) 461-6200

Fort Worth (city)
City Hall, Municipal Building, 1000 Throckmorton Street, Fort Worth, TX 76102
Provides municipal services such as police, firefighting, libraries, parks, and public works.
(817) 871-7750
Jobline: (817) 871-7760

Fountain Valley (city)
10200 Slater Avenue, Fountain Valley, CA 92708
Provides municipal services such as police, firefighting, libraries, parks, and public works.
(714) 965-4400
Jobline: (714) 965-4409

Four Seasons Hotel
300 S. Doheny Drive, Los Angeles, CA 90048
285-room hotel.
(310) 273-2222
Jobline: (310) 276-0822

Four Seasons Hotel Houston
1300 Lamar Street, Houston, TX 77010
399-room hotel.
(713) 650-1300
Jobline: (713) 650-3437

Four Seasons Hotel Newport Beach
690 Newport Center Drive, Newport Beach, CA 92660
284-room hotel in the Orange County coastal area.
(714) 759-0808
Jobline: (714) 854-9675

Four Seasons Olympic Hotel
411 University Street, Seattle, WA 98101
450-room hotel.
(206) 621-1700
Jobline: (206) 682-9164

Franklin Pierce School District
315 S. 129th Street, Tacoma, WA 98444
14-school district in Tacoma.
(206) 537-0211
Jobline: (206) 535-8829

Fred Meyer Inc.
3800 SE 22nd Avenue, Portland, OR 97202-2918
Operates variety stores.
(503) 232-8844
Jobline: (800) 401-5627

Freightliner Corp.
4747 N. Channel Avenue, Portland, OR 97217
Assembles truck tractors for highway use, and provides motor vehicle parts and accessories.
(503) 735-8000
Jobline: (503) 735-7091
Factory jobs.

Jobline: (503) 735-8657
Corporate jobs.

Fremont (city)
Administration Center
39100 Liberty Street at Capitol Avenue, Fremont, CA 94538
Provides municipal services such as police, firefighting, libraries, parks, and public works.
(510) 494-4660
Jobline: (510) 494-4669

Fresno (city)
2600 Fresno Street, 1st Floor, Fresno, CA 93721
Provides municipal services such as police, firefighting, libraries, parks, and public works.
(209) 498-1574
Jobline: (209) 498-1573

Fresno County
2220 Tulare Street, 14th Floor, Fresno, CA 93721
Provides county services such as sheriffs, courts, motor vehicle registration, and social services.
(209) 488-3364
Jobline: (209) 488-3017

Frito-Lay Inc.
9535 Archibald Avenue, Rancho Cucamonga, CA 91730
Produces potato and corn chips, cookies and crackers, and other snack food.
(909) 948-3600
Jobline: (909) 948-3622

Frost National Bank
100 W. Houston Street, San Antonio, TX 78205
Operates national commercial banks and commercial and industrial buildings.
(210) 220-4011
Jobline: (210) 220-5627

Fullerton (city)
303 W. Commonwealth Avenue, Fullerton, CA 92632
Provides municipal services such as police, firefighting, libraries, parks, and public works.
(714) 738-6360
Jobline: (714) 738-6378

Fulton County
Fulton County Government Center, Suite 4035, 141
 Pryor Street SW, Atlanta, GA 30303
Provides county services such as sheriffs, courts, motor
 vehicle registration, and social services.
(404) 730-6720
Jobline: (404) 730-5627

Gannett Company Inc.
1100 Wilson Boulevard, Arlington, VA 22234
Publishes newspapers, operates TV and radio stations,
 and provides other media services.
(703) 284-6000
Jobline: (703) 284-6054

Gap Inc.
1 Harrison Street, San Francisco, CA 94105
Operates family clothing stores.
(415) 952-4400
Jobline: (415) 737-4495

Garden Grove (city)
11391 Acacia Parkway, Garden Grove, CA 92640
Provides municipal services such as police, firefighting,
 libraries, parks, and public works.
(714) 741-5000
Jobline: (714) 741-5016

Gardena (city)
1700 W. 162nd Street, Room 108, Gardena, CA 90247
Provides municipal services such as police, firefighting,
 libraries, parks, and public works.
(310) 217-9574
Jobline: (310) 217-9515

Gates Corp.
900 S. Broadway, P.O. Box 5887, Denver, CO 80217
Manufactures molded rubber products, storage
 batteries, and automotive parts and accessories.
(303) 744-1911
Jobline: (303) 744-5900

Gaylord Entertainment Co.
Broadcast Division
2806 Opryland Drive, Nashville, TN 37214
Operates Country Music Television, Opryland Music
 Group, and other broadcast properties.
(615) 871-6776
Jobline: (615) 871-5920

GEICO Corp.
1 GEICO Plaza, Washington, DC 20076
Provides fire, marine, casualty, life, and other insurance.
(301) 986-3000
Jobline: (800) 434-2655

General Accounting Office
441 G Street NW, Washington, DC 20548
Examines all matters relating to the receipt and
 disbursement of public funds for Congress.
(202) 512-3000
Jobline: (202) 512-6092

General Mills Inc.
1 General Mills Boulevard, Minneapolis, MN 55426
Operates restaurants and produces breakfast cereals,
 flour mixes and doughs, and other products.
(612) 540-2311
Jobline: (612) 540-2334

General Services Administration
Region 4
75 Spring Street SW, Atlanta, GA 30303
Provides economical and efficient management of U.S.
 government property and records.
(404) 331-3200
Jobline: (404) 331-5102

Region 6
1500 E. Bannister Road, Kansas City, MO 64131
(816) 926-5194
Jobline: (816) 926-7804

Region 9
9 CPE, 525 Market Street, San Francisco, CA 94105
(415) 744-5055
Jobline: (800) 347-3378

George Mason University
Fairfax, VA 22030
Medium-sized, public university in Fairfax, 18 miles
 south of Washington, D.C.
(703) 993-1000
Jobline: (703) 993-8799

Georgetown University
Washington, DC 20057
Medium-sized, church-affiliated, liberal arts university in
 Washington.
(202) 687-5055
Jobline: (202) 687-2900
University and medical center jobs.

Jobline: (202) 784-2370
Nursing jobs.

Jobline: (202) 784-2683
Hospital jobs.

Georgia Institute of Technology
Atlanta, GA 30332
Medium-sized, public institute near downtown Atlanta.
(404) 894-2000
Jobline: (404) 894-4592

Georgia Southern University
Statesboro, GA 30460-8024
Medium-sized, public university in Statesboro, 50 miles
 northwest of Savannah.
(912) 681-5531
Jobline: (912) 681-0629

Georgia State University
Atlanta, GA 30303
Large, public university in Atlanta.
(404) 651-2000
Jobline: (404) 651-4270

Germantown Savings Bank
1 Belmont Avenue, Bala-Cynwyd, PA 19004
Operates state savings banks.
(610) 667-9300
Jobline: (610) 660-8451

Gilbert (city)
1025 S. Gilbert Road, Gilbert, AZ 85296
Provides municipal services such as police, firefighting,
  libraries, parks, and public works.
(602) 892-0800
Jobline: (602) 497-4950

Gillette Co.
3900 Prudential Tower, Boston, MA 02199-8001
Manufactures razors and razor blades, electric
  housewares and fans, food mixes, and other
  products.
(617) 421-7000
Jobline: (617) 421-7567

Glendale (city)
5850 W. Glendale Avenue, Glendale, AZ 85301
Provides municipal services such as police, firefighting,
  libraries, parks, and public works.
(602) 435-4121
Jobline: (602) 435-4402

Glendale (city)
613 E. Broadway, Room 100, Glendale, CA 91206
Provides municipal services such as police, firefighting,
  libraries, parks, and public works.
(818) 548-2100
Jobline: (818) 548-2127

Glendora (city)
116 E. Foothill Boulevard, Glendora, CA 91741
Provides municipal services such as police, firefighting,
  libraries, parks, and public works.
(818) 914-8203
Jobline: (818) 914-8206

Golden 1 Credit Union
P.O. Box 15966, Sacramento, CA 95852
Provides banking and other financial and consumer
  services.
(916) 732-2900
Jobline: (916) 732-2844

Gonzaga University
Spokane, WA 99258-0001
Small, church-affiliated university in residential Spokane.
(509) 484-6096
Jobline: (509) 484-6816

Grand Hyatt New York Park Avenue at Grand Central
Grand Central Station, New York, NY 10017
1,407-room hotel.
(212) 883-1234
Jobline: (212) 850-5942

Grand Hyatt San Francisco on Union Square
345 Stockton Street, San Francisco, CA 94108
693-room hotel.
(415) 398-1234
Jobline: (415) 398-1234, ask for job hotline.

Grand Hyatt Washington at Washington Center
1000 H Street NW, Washington, DC 20001
907-room hotel.
(202) 582-1234
Jobline: (202) 637-4946

Grand Prairie (city)
326 W. Main Street, Grand Prairie, TX 75050
Provides municipal services such as police, firefighting,
  libraries, parks, and public works.
(214) 660-8192
Jobline: (214) 660-8190

Grandview Hospital and Medical Center
405 W. Grand Avenue, Dayton, OH 45405
Not-for-profit hospital with more than 400 beds.
(513) 226-3200
Jobline: (513) 226-2675

Great Western Bank
9200 Oakdale Avenue, Chatsworth, CA 91311
Operates federal savings banks.
(818) 775-3411
Jobline: (800) 367-5545

Greenlefe Resort
3200 State Road 546, Haines City, FL 33844-9732
950-room hotel near Orlando.
(813) 422-7511
Jobline: (813) 421-5027

Greensboro (city)
300 W. Washington Street P.O. Box 3136, Greensboro,
  NC 27402-3136
Provides municipal services such as police, firefighting,
  libraries, parks, and public works.
(910) 373-2065
Jobline: (910) 373-2080

Gresham (city)
501 NE Hood Avenue, Suite 230, Gresham, OR 97030
Provides municipal services such as police, firefighting,
  libraries, parks, and public works.
(503) 669-2676
Jobline: (503) 669-2309

Grossmont-Cuyamaca Community College District
8800 Grossmont College Drive, El Cajon, CA 92020
Includes Grossmont College and Cuyamaca College.
(619) 465-1700
Jobline: (619) 589-7312, x8081.
Classified jobs.

Jobline: (619) 589-7312, x 8082.
Certificated jobs.

GTE California Inc.
10900 E. 183rd Street, Suite 397, Cerritos, CA
  90701-5346
Provides local and other telephone services, electronic
  equipment rental, and other services.
(310) 924-1142
Jobline: (800) 482-5627

GTE California Inc. (cont.)
730 Paseo Camarillo, P.O. Box 6000, Camarillo, CA 93011-6000
(805) 987-7600
Jobline: (800) 521-5749

675 E. Bonita Avenue, Pomona, CA 91767
(800) 483-4000
Jobline: (800) 852-8884

Guilford County
301 W. Market Street, Greensboro, NC 27401
Provides county services such as sheriffs, courts, motor vehicle registration, and social services.
(910) 373-3324
Jobline: (910) 373-3600

Hamilton County
County Administration Building, Room 101, 138 E. Court Street, Cincinnati, OH 45202
Provides county services such as sheriffs, courts, motor vehicle registration, and social services.
(513) 632-8841
Jobline: (513) 763-4900

Hamot Medical Center
201 State Street, Erie, PA 16550
Not-for-profit hospital with more than 500 beds.
(814) 870-6000
Jobline: (814) 877-5627

Hampton (city)
City Hall, 22 Lincoln Street, Hampton, VA 23669
Provides municipal services such as police, firefighting, libraries, parks, and public works.
(804) 727-6407
Jobline: (804) 727-6406

Hampton University
Hampton, VA 23368
Medium-sized, private university in Hampton, near Newport News.
(804) 727-5000
Jobline: (804) 727-5954

Handlery Union Square
351 Geary Street, San Francisco, CA 94102
377-room hotel.
(415) 781-7800
Jobline: (415) 781-7922, x159.

Hanna-Barbera Productions Inc.
3400 Cahuenga Boulevard, Hollywood, CA 90068
Produces animated and other films for theatrical release, TV, TV commercials, and industrial uses.
(213) 851-5000
Jobline: (213) 969-1262

Harcourt Brace and Co.
6277 Sea Harbor Drive, Orlando, FL 32821
Publishes textbooks, education materials, books, and trade journals and provides other services.
(407) 345-2000
Jobline: (407) 345-3060

Harford County
220 S. Main Stree, Bel Air, MD 21014
Provides county services such as sheriffs, courts, motor vehicle registration, and social services.
(410) 638-3201
Jobline: (410) 638-4473

Harnischfeger Corp.
4400 W. National Avenue, P.O. Box 310, Brookfield, WI 53201
Manufactures papermaking and pulp mill machinery, and construction tools and equipment.
(414) 671-4400
Jobline: (414) 671-7528

Harrah's Lake Tahoe Casino Hotel
P.O. Box 8, South Lake Tahoe, CA 89449
540-room hotel.
(702) 588-6611
Jobline: (702) 588-6611, ask for x2114.

Harrah's Las Vegas
3475 Las Vegas Boulevard, Las Vegas, NV 89109
1,725-room hotel.
(702) 369-5000
Jobline: (702) 369-5050

Harrah's Marina Hotel Casino
1725 Brigantine Boulevard, Atlantic City, NJ 08401
760-room hotel.
(609) 441-5000
Jobline: (609) 441-5681

Harris Trust and Savings Bank
P.O. Box 755, Chicago, IL 60690
Operates state commercial banks, manages real estate, and provides other financial services.
(312) 461-2121
Jobline: (312) 461-6900

Hartford (city) courts
75 Elm Street, Hartford, CT 06106
Adjudicates criminal and civil cases for Hartford.
(203) 722-5859
Jobline: (203) 566-1326

Harvey Hotel Dallas-Fort Worth
4545 W. John Carpenter Freeway, Irving, TX 75063
506-room hotel near Dallas-Fort Worth Int'l Airport.
(214) 929-4500
Jobline: (214) 929-4500, ask for x1736.

Harvey's Resort Hotel & Casino
P.O. Box 128, Stateline, NV 89449
540-room hotel.
(702) 588-2411
Jobline: (702) 588-2411, ask for x2085.

Hawaii (state)
830 Punchbowl Street, Honolulu, HI 96813
Provides state services such as conservation, education, highways, prisons, and welfare.
(808) 587-1077
Jobline: (808) 587-0977

Hayward (city)
25151 Clawiter Road, Hayward, CA 94545
Provides municipal services such as police, firefighting,
    libraries, parks, and public works.
(510) 293-8669
Jobline: (510) 293-5313

Health Net
P.O. Box 9103, Van Nuys, CA 91409
Operates health maintenance organizations.
(818) 719-6775
Jobline: (818) 593-7236

Hechinger Co.
1616 McCormick Drive, Landover, MD 20785
Operates home centers.
(301) 341-1000
Jobline: (301) 341-0526

Helena (city)
316 N. Park Avenue, Helena, MT 59623
Provides municipal services such as police, firefighting,
    libraries, parks, and public works.
(406) 447-8404
Jobline: (406) 447-8444

Henderson (city)
240 S. Water Street, Henderson, NV 89015
Provides municipal services such as police, firefighting,
    libraries, parks, and public works.
(702) 565-2070
Jobline: (702) 565-2318

Hennepin County
Hennepin County Government Center, 300 S. 6th
    Street, Minneapolis, MN 55487-0040
Provides county services such as sheriffs, courts, motor
    vehicle registration, and social services.
(612) 348-2163
Jobline: (612) 348-4698

Hercules (city)
111 Civic Drive, Hercules, CA 94547
Provides municipal services such as police, firefighting,
    libraries, parks, and public works.
(510) 799-8200
Jobline: (510) 799-8204

Hercules Inc.
1313 N. Market Street, Wilmington, DE 19894
Produces plastic materials and resins, papermaking
    chemicals, and other substances and products.
(302) 594-5000
Jobline: (302) 594-6122

Herndon (city)
200 Spring Street, Suite 132 P.O. Box 427, Herndon,
    VA 22070
Provides municipal services such as police, firefighting,
    libraries, parks, and public works.
(703) 435-6817
Jobline: (703) 481-3892

Hesperia (city)
15888 Main Street, Hesperia, CA 92345
Provides municipal services such as police, firefighting,
    libraries, parks, and public works.
(619) 947-1100
Jobline: (619) 261-3660

Hewlett-Packard Co.
3000 Hanover Street, Palo Alto, CA 94304-1112
Manufactures computers, calculators, printers, and
    other electronic computing and measuring devices.
(415) 857-1501
Jobline: (415) 857-2092
College recruiting.

16399 W. Bernardo Drive, San Diego, CA 92127-1801
Manufactures electrical and electronic equipment, and
    conducts commercial physical research.
(619) 487-4100
Jobline: (619) 592-8444

8000 Foothills Boulevard, Roseville, CA 95747-6502
Manufactures computers, measuring instruments,
    computer peripherals, and computer terminals.
(916) 786-8000
Jobline: (916) 786-6662

700 71st Avenue, Greeley, CO 80634-9776
Manufactures and repairs computers, calculators,
    printers, and other computer components.
(303) 350-4000
Jobline: (303) 350-4442, press 3.

1900 Garden of the Gods Road, Colorado Springs, CO
    80907-3423
Manufactures instruments to measure electricity.
(719) 590-1900
Jobline: (719) 590-2014

Boise Division
11311 Chinden Boulevard, Boise, ID 83714-1021
Manufactures keyboards, computers, and office
    machines.
(208) 323-6000
Jobline: (208) 396-5200

Colorado Networks Division
3404 E. Harmony Road, Fort Collins, CO 80525-9544
Develops and applies computer software.
(303) 229-3800
Jobline: (800) 228-1399, press 3.

Corvallis Division
1000 NE Circle Boulevard, Corvallis, OR 97330-4239
Manufactures hand-held calculators.
(503) 750-2000
Jobline: (503) 754-0919

Medical Products Group Division
3000 Minuteman Road, Andover, MA 01810-1099
Manufactures medical apparatus and supplies.
(508) 687-1501
Jobline: (508) 659-3012

Hewlett-Packard Co. (cont.)
Mid-America Sales Region
5201 Tollview Drive, Rolling Meadows, IL 60008-3700
Provides sales support for HP data processing,
  measuring, and testing equipment.
(708) 255-9800
Jobline: (708) 245-3909

Sonoma County area
1212 Valley House Drive, Rohnert Park, CA 94928-4902
Manufactures circuit test equipment, electric measuring
  instruments, computers, and other devices.
(707) 794-1212
Jobline: (707) 794-3918

Southern California area
1421 S. Manhattan Avenue, Fullerton, CA 92631-5221
Manufactures electronic and electrical equipment, and
  repairs electronic equipment.
(714) 999-6700
Jobline: (714) 758-5414

Spokane Division
24001 E. Mission Avenue, Spokane, WA 99220
Manufactures test equipment for electronic and electric
  measurement, and radio and TV equipment.
(509) 921-4001
Jobline: (509) 921-4888

Vancouver Division
18110 SE 34th Street, Camas, WA 98607-9410
Manufacturers Deskjet printers.
(206) 254-8110
Jobline: (206) 944-2493

Hialeah (city)
City Hall, 3rd Floor, 501 Palm Avenue, Hialeah, FL
  33010
Provides municipal services such as police, firefighting,
  libraries, parks, and public works.
(305) 883-8050
Jobline: (305) 883-8057

Hibernia National Bank
313 Carondelet Street, P.O. Box 61540
New Orleans, LA 70161
Operates national commercial banks.
(504) 586-5553
Jobline: (504) 586-5518

Highline School District
15675 Arbaum Boulevard SW, Seattle, WA 98166
37-school district in Seattle.
(206) 433-2281
Jobline: (206) 433-6339

Hillsborough Community College
Tampa, FL 33631
Medium-sized, state-supported, 2-year college in
  Tampa.
(813) 253-7004
Jobline: (813) 253-7185

Hilton O'Hare
P.O. Box 66414, Chicago, IL 60666
885-room hotel near Chicago O'Hare International
  Airport.
(312) 686-8000
Jobline: (312) 601-2800

Hilton Palacio del Rio
200 S. Alamo Street, San Antonio, TX 78205
482-room downtown hotel.
(210) 222-1400
Jobline: (210) 222-1400, ask for x377.

Holiday Inn Briley Parkway
2200 Elm Hill Park, Nashville, TN 37210
385-room hotel.
(615) 883-9770
Jobline: (615) 885-4491

Holiday Inn Crowne Plaza
1750 Rockville Pike, Rockville, MD 20852
315-room hotel near Washington, D.C.
(301) 468-1100
Jobline: (301) 230-6770

Holiday Inn Crowne Plaza
66 Hale Avenue, White Plains, NY 10601
400-room hotel in Westchester County near New York
  City.
(914) 682-0050
Jobline: (914) 682-0050, ask for x1537.

Holiday Inn Crowne Plaza
2222 W. Loop South, Houston, TX 77027
477-room hotel.
(713) 961-7272
Jobline: (713) 961-7272, ask for x2675.

Holiday Inn Crowne Plaza Metro Center
775 12th Street NW, Washington, DC 20005
456-room hotel.
(202) 737-2200
Jobline: (202) 737-2200, ask for x2031.

Holiday Inn Crowne Plaza Ravinia
4355 Ashford Dunwoody Road, Atlanta, GA 30346
492-room hotel.
(404) 395-7700
Jobline: (404) 395-7700, ask for x3054.

Holiday Inn Fisherman's Wharf
1300 Columbus Avenue, San Francisco, CA 94133
580-room hotel.
(415) 771-9000
Jobline: (415) 771-9000, ask for job hotline.

Holiday Inn Houston West Holidome
14703 Park Row, Houston, TX 77079
352-room hotel.
(713) 558-5580
Jobline: (713) 558-5580, ask for x2540.

Holiday Inn on the Bay Embarcadero
1355 N. Harbor Drive, San Diego, CA 92101
600-room hotel.
(619) 232-3861
Jobline: (619) 232-3861, press 0, then ask for job
  hotline.

Holiday Inn Union Square
480 Sutter Street at Powell Street, San Francisco, CA 94108
400-room hotel.
(415) 398-8900
Jobline: (415) 398-8900, ask for job hotline.

Hollywood (city)
2600 Hollywood Boulevard, Hollywood, FL 33020
Provides municipal services such as police, firefighting, libraries, parks, and public works.
(305) 921-3216
Jobline: (305) 921-3292

Home Depot Inc.
2727 Paces Ferry Road NW, Atlanta, GA 30339
Operates home centers.
(404) 433-8211
Jobline: (404) 433-8211

Home Shopping Network Inc.
2501 118th Avenue North, P.O. Box 9090, Clearwater, FL 34618-9090
Provides TV home shopping and catalog sales.
(813) 572-8585
Jobline: (813) 572-8585, x6117.

HomeFed Bank
5535 Morehouse Drive, San Diego, CA 92121
Operates federal savings banks.
(619) 699-8000
Jobline: (800) 552-3638

Honeywell Inc.
P.O. Box 524, Minneapolis, MN 55440
Manufactures building, industrial, and aerospace automation and control products and systems.
(612) 951-1000
Jobline: (612) 951-2914

Honolulu (city and county)
City Hall Annex, 550 S. King Street, Honolulu, HI 96813
Provides government services such as police, firefighting, libraries, parks, and public works.
(808) 527-5611
Jobline: (808) 523-4303

Hospital of the Good Samaritan
616 S. Witmer Street, Los Angeles, CA 90017
Not-for-profit hospital and nursing home-type unit with more than 300 beds.
(213) 977-2121
Jobline: (213) 977-2300

Hotel del Coronado
1500 Orange Avenue, Coronado, CA 92118
685-room hotel.
(619) 239-2200
Jobline: (619) 522-8158

Hotel Inter-Continental Chicago
525 N. Michigan Avenue, Chicago, IL 60611
517-room hotel.
(312) 944-0055
Jobline: (312) 321-8819

Hotel Inter-Continental New Orleans
444 St. Charles Avenue, New Orleans, LA 70130
481-room hotel.
(504) 525-5566
Jobline: (504) 525-5566, ask for job hotline.

Hotel Macklowe
145 W. 44th Street, New York, NY 10036
638-room hotel.
(212) 768-4400
Jobline: (212) 789-7600

Hotel Nikko at Beverly Hills
465 S. La Cienega Boulevard, Los Angeles, CA 90048
304-room hotel.
(310) 247-0700
Jobline: (310) 246-2074

Hotel Parker Meridien
118 W. 57th Street, New York, NY 10019
700-room hotel.
(212) 245-5000
Jobline: (212) 708-7351

Hotel Sofitel
223 Twin Dolphin Drive, San Francisco, CA 94065
324-room hotel near San Francisco International Airport.
(415) 598-9000
Jobline: (415) 598-9000, ask for job hotline.

Hotel Sofitel Ma Maison
8555 Beverly Boulevard, Los Angeles, CA 90048
311-room hotel.
(310) 278-5444
Jobline: (310) 278-5444, ask for x413.

Houston Community College System
320 Jackson Hill Street, Houston, TX 77007
Includes Central, Southeast, Southwest, Northeast, and Northwest Colleges and College Without Walls.
(713) 868-0709
Jobline: (713) 866-8369
Classified and clerical jobs.

Jobline: (713) 868-0711
Faculty jobs.

Houston Lighting and Power Co.
P.O. Box 1700, Houston, TX 77251
Generates, transmits, and distributes electric power.
(713) 228-9211
Jobline: (713) 238-5854

Houston Medallion
3000 N. Loop West, Houston, TX 77092
383-room hotel.
(713) 688-0100
Jobline: (713) 688-0100, ask for job hotline.

Houston Northwest Medical Center
710 FM 1960 West, Houston, TX 77090
For-profit hospital and nursing home-type unit with more than 400 beds.
(713) 440-1000
Jobline: (713) 440-6321

Howard County
3420 Court House Drive, Ellicott City, MD 21043
Provides county services such as sheriffs, courts, motor
  vehicle registration, and social services.
(410) 313-2033
Jobline: (410) 313-4460

Howard University
Washington, DC 20059
Medium-sized, private, comprehensive, historically
  black university with campuses in Washington.
(202) 806-6100
Jobline: (202) 806-7711

HTH Corp.
711 Keeaumoku Street, Suite 101, Honolulu, HI 96814
Manages the Pacific Beach, King Kamehameha's Kona
  Beach, and Pagoda Hotels and the Kaimana Villa.
(808) 949-5756
Jobline: (808) 921-6110

Humana Inc.
500 W. Main Street, Louisville, KY 40202
Operates health maintenance organizations and
  provides health insurance.
(502) 580-1000
Jobline: (502) 580-3450

Humboldt County
825 5th Street, Eureka, CA 95501
Provides county services such as sheriffs, courts, motor
  vehicle registration, and social services.
(707) 445-7315
Jobline: (707) 445-7366

Humboldt State University
Arcata, CA 95521
Medium-sized, public, comprehensive university in
  Arcata, in redwood country.
(707) 826-3011
Jobline: (707) 826-4500

Huntington Bank
Huntington Center, 41 S. High Street, Columbus, OH
  43215
Operates national commercial banks.
(614) 476-8300
Jobline: (614) 463-4305

Huntington Beach (city)
2000 Main Street, Huntington Beach, CA 92648
Provides municipal services such as police, firefighting,
  libraries, parks, and public works.
(714) 536-5491
Jobline: (714) 374-1570

Huntington Memorial Hospital
100 W. California Boulevard, P.O. Box 7013, Pasadena,
  CA 91109
Not-for-profit hospital and nursing home-type unit with
  more than 600 beds.
(818) 397-5000
Jobline: (818) 397-8504

Huntington Park (city)
6550 Miles Avenue, Huntington Park, CA 90255
Provides municipal services such as police, firefighting,
  libraries, parks, and public works.
(213) 584-6227
Jobline: (213) 584-6209

Huntsville (city)
P.O. Box 308, Huntsville, AL 35804
Provides municipal services such as police, firefighting,
  libraries, parks, and public works.
(205) 532-7332
Jobline: (205) 535-4942

Huntsville (city) Schools
P.O. Box 1256, Huntsville, AL 35807
Includes Huntville's schools except those in the
  Madison County School District.
(205) 532-4676
Jobline: (205) 532-4746
Includes jobs in the administrative offices and in
  schools.

Hyatt at Fisherman's Wharf
555 N. Point Street, San Francisco, CA 94133
313-room hotel.
(415) 563-1234
Jobline: (415) 563-1234, ask for job hotline.

Hyatt Hotels
200 S. Pine Avenue, Long Beach, CA 90802
Hotel chain that includes Hyatt Hotels in the Southern
  California area.
(310) 491-1234
Jobline: (310) 432-7690

Hyatt Islandia on San Diego Mission Bay
1441 Quivira Road, San Diego, CA 92109
423-room hotel.
(619) 224-1234
Jobline: (619) 221-4888

Hyatt Orlando/Neighbor to Walt Disney
6375 W. Irlo Bronson Memorial Highway, Orlando, FL
  34746
924-room hotel.
(407) 396-1234
Jobline: (407) 396-5001

Hyatt Regency Albuquerque
330 Tijeras Avenue NW, Albuquerque, NM 87102
395-room hotel.
(505) 842-1234
Jobline: (505) 766-6730

Hyatt Regency Atlanta in Peachtree Center
265 Peachtree Street NE, Atlanta, GA 30371
1,279-room hotel.
(404) 577-1234
Jobline: (404) 588-3746

Hyatt Regency Austin on Town Lake
208 Barton Springs Road, Austin, TX 78704
448-room hotel.
(512) 477-1234
Jobline: (512) 477-1234, ask for job hotline.

Hyatt Regency Baltimore Inner Harbor
300 Light Street, Baltimore, MD 21202
487-room hotel.
(410) 528-1234
Jobline: (410) 528-1234, ask for job hotline.

Hyatt Regency Bethesda
1 Bethesda Metro Center, Bethesda, MD 20814
380-room hotel near Washington, D.C.
(301) 657-1234
Jobline: (301) 657-1234, ask for job hotline.

Hyatt Regency Cambridge Overlooking Boston
575 Memorial Drive, Boston, MA 02139
469-room hotel.
(617) 492-1234
Jobline: (617) 492-1234, ask for job hotline.

Hyatt Regency Chicago in Illinois Center
151 E. Wacker Drive, Chicago, IL 60601
2,033-room hotel.
(312) 565-1234
Jobline: (312) 565-1234, ask for x6252.

Hyatt Regency Crown Center Kansas City
2345 McGee Street, Kansas City, MO 64108
731-room hotel.
(816) 421-1234
Jobline: (816) 283-4473

Hyatt Regency Crystal City-National Airport
2799 Jefferson Davis Highway, Arlington, VA 22202
685-room hotel near Washington, D.C.
(703) 418-1234
Jobline: (703) 418-7228

Hyatt Regency Dallas at Reunion
300 Reunion Boulevard, Dallas, TX 75207
945-room hotel.
(214) 651-1234
Jobline: (214) 712-7018

Hyatt Regency Dallas-Fort Worth International Airport
P.O. Box 619014, Dallas-Fort Worth Airport, TX 75261
1,400-room hotel near Dallas-Fort Worth International Airport.
(214) 453-1234
Jobline: (214) 615-6809

Hyatt Regency Grand Cypress Resort
1 Grand Cypress Boulevard, Orlando, FL 32836
750-room hotel.
(407) 239-1234
Jobline: (407) 239-3899

Hyatt Regency Greenwich
1800 E. Putnam Avenue, Greenwich, CT 06870
353-room hotel.
(203) 637-1234
Jobline: (203) 637-1234, ask for job hotline.

Hyatt Regency Houston Center of Downtown
1200 Louisiana Avenue, Houston, TX 77002
959-room hotel.
(713) 654-1234
Jobline: (713) 646-6912

Hyatt Regency Irvine Near SNA Airport
17900 Jamboree Boulevard, Irvine, CA 92714
536-room hotel in the Orange County coastal area.
(714) 975-1234
Jobline: (714) 863-1818

Hyatt Regency La Jolla at Aventine
3777 La Jolla Village Drive, San Diego, CA 92122
400-room hotel.
(619) 552-1234
Jobline: (619) 552-6058

Hyatt Regency Lake Tahoe Resort & Casino
Lakeshore and Country Club Drives, Incline Village, NV 89450
458-room hotel.
(702) 831-1111
Jobline: (702) 832-3274

Hyatt Regency Los Angeles at Broadway Place
711 S. Hope Street, Los Angeles, CA 90017
484-room hotel.
(213) 683-1234
Jobline: (213) 683-1234, ask for x3139.

Hyatt Regency Minneapolis Nicollet Mall
1300 Nicollet Mall, Minneapolis, MN 55403
534-room hotel.
(612) 370-1234
Jobline: (612) 370-1202

Hyatt Regency Monterey Hotel/Conference Center
1 Old Golf Course Road, Monterey, CA 93940
575-room hotel.
(408) 372-1234
Jobline: (408) 372-1234, ask for x4051.

Hyatt Regency New Orleans at Superdome
Poydras and Loyola Avenues, New Orleans, LA 70140
1,193-room hotel.
(504) 561-1234
Jobline: (504) 561-1234, ask for job hotline.

Hyatt Regency Orlando International Airport
9673 Tradeport Drive, Orlando, FL 32827
443-room hotel.
(407) 825-1234
Jobline: (407) 825-1342

Hyatt Regency Phoenix at Civic Plaza
122 N. 2nd Street, Phoenix, AZ 85004
711-room hotel.
(602) 252-1234
Jobline: (602) 252-1234, ask for x3154.

Hyatt Regency Sacramento at Capitol Park
1209 L Street, Sacramento, CA 95814
500-room hotel.
(916) 443-1234
Jobline: (916) 441-3111

Hyatt Regency San Antonio on the Riverwalk
123 Losoya Street, San Antonio, TX 78205
632-room hotel.
(210) 222-1234
Jobline: (210) 531-2396

Hyatt Regency San Diego
1 Market Place, San Diego, CA 92101
875-room hotel.
(619) 232-1234
Jobline: (619) 687-6000

Hyatt Regency San Francisco Airport
1333 Bayshore Highway, Burlingame, CA 94010
791-room hotel near San Francisco International Airport.
(415) 347-1234
Jobline: (415) 696-2625

Hyatt Regency San Francisco in Embarcadero Center
5 Embarcadero Center, San Francisco, CA 94111
803-room hotel.
(415) 788-1234
Jobline: (415) 788-1234, ask for x6624.

Hyatt Regency Savannah Riverfront
2 W. Bay Street, Savannah, GA 31401
346-room hotel.
(912) 354-8560
Jobline: (912) 944-3647

Hyatt Regency Tampa at Tampa City Center
2 Tampa City Center, Tampa, FL 33602
517-room hotel.
(813) 225-1234
Jobline: (813) 225-1234, ask for job hotline.

Hyatt Regency Tech Center Denver
7800 E. Tufts Avenue, Denver, CO 80906
450-room hotel.
(303) 779-1234
Jobline: (303) 779-1234, ask for job hotline.

Hyatt Regency Washington on Capitol Hill
400 New Jersey Avenue NW, Washington, DC 20001
834-room hotel.
(202) 737-1234
Jobline: (202) 942-1586

Hyatt Regency Westshore at Tampa International
6200 Courtney Campbell Causeway, Tampa, FL 33607
445-room hotel.
(813) 874-1234
Jobline: (813) 287-0666

Hyatt Regency Woodfield Schaumburg
1800 E. Golf Road, Schaumburg, IL 60173
478-room hotel.
(708) 605-1234
Jobline: (708) 605-1234, ask for job hotline.

Hyatt San Jose at San Jose Airport
1740 N. 1st Street, San Jose, CA 95112
474-room hotel.
(408) 993-1234
Jobline: (408) 993-1234, ask for job hotline.

Idaho (state)
700 W. State Street, Boise, ID 83702
Provides state services such as conservation,
   education, highways, prisons, and welfare.
(208) 334-2263
Jobline: (208) 334-2568

Idaho (state) Department of Employment
317 Main Street, Boise, ID 83702
Seeks workers for private and public employers.
(208) 334-6201
Jobline: (208) 334-6457

Illinois (state)
100 W. Randolph Street, 3rd Floor, Chicago, IL 60601
Provides state services such as conservation,
   education, highways, prisons, and welfare.
(312) 814-2390
Jobline: (312) 814-2390

Illinois Institute of Technology
Chicago, IL 60616
Small, private institute near downtown Chicago.
(312) 567-3000
Jobline: (312) 567-5703

Imperial County
940 W. Main Street, El Centro, CA 92243
Provides county services such as sheriffs, courts, motor
   vehicle registration, and social services.
(619) 339-4488
Jobline: (619) 339-4577

Imperial Palace Hotel
3535 Las Vegas Boulevard South, Las Vegas, NV
   89109
2,700-room hotel.
(702) 731-3311
Jobline: (702) 794-3191

INB National Bank
1 Indiana Square, Indianapolis, IN 46266
Operates national commercial banks.
(317) 266-6000
Jobline: (317) 266-7788

Independence (city)
223 N. Memorial Drive, 3rd Floor, Independence, MO
   64050
Provides municipal services such as police, firefighting,
   libraries, parks, and public works.
(816) 325-7390
Jobline: (816) 325-7394

Indiana State University
Terre Haute, IN 477809
Medium-sized, public university in Terre Haute, 60 miles
   from Indianapolis.
(812) 237-6311
Jobline: (812) 237-4122

Indiana University at South Bend
South Bend, IN 46634
Small, public, comprehensive institution east of
   downtown South Bend.
(219) 237-4111
Jobline: (219) 237-4182

Indiana University Bloomington
Bloomington, IN 47401
Large, public, comprehensive institution in Bloomington.
(812) 332-0211
Jobline: (812) 855-9102

Indiana University-Purdue University at Fort Wayne
Fort Wayne, IN 46805-1499
Small, public, multipurpose university in Fort Wayne.
(219) 481-6812
Jobline: (219) 481-6971

Indiana University-Purdue University at Indianapolis
Indianapolis, IN 46202
Medium-sized, public, comprehensive university with an
urban campus in Indianapolis.
(317) 264-4595
Jobline: (317) 274-2255

Ingham County
5303 S. Cedar Street, Lansing, MI 48911
Provides county services such as sheriffs, courts, motor
vehicle registration, and social services.
(517) 887-4328
Jobline: (517) 887-4329

Inglewood (city)
1 Manchester Boulevard, Inglewood, CA 90301
Provides municipal services such as police, firefighting,
libraries, parks, and public works.
(310) 412-5460
Jobline: (310) 412-8888

Inova Health Systems Inc.
8001 Braddock Road, Springfield, VA 22151
Operates three not-for-profit hospitals with more than
1,000 beds in the northern Virginia area.
(703) 321-4200
Jobline: (800) 854-6682
Includes jobs in the corporate office.

Intel Corp.
P.O. Box 58065, Santa Clara, CA 95052
Manufactures microprocessors, microcommunication
components and systems, and semiconductor
memory.
(408) 765-8080
Jobline: (408) 765-3981

Intelligent Electronics Inc.
411 Eagleview Boulevard, Exton, PA 19341
Produces computers, peripherals, and software, and
franchises computer and software stores.
(610) 458-5500
Jobline: (610) 458-6793

Intermountain Health Care Inc.
36 S. State Street, Salt Lake City, UT 84111
Owns or operates not-for-profit hospitals with more than
2,100 beds in three states.
(801) 533-8282
Jobline: (801) 533-3654

International MultiFoods Corp.
Multifoods Tower, Minneapolis, MN 55402
Produces consumer foods and animal feeds, and
operates flour mills and fast food franchises.
(612) 340-3300
Jobline: (612) 340-3923

Intrust Bank NA
105 N. Main Street, P.O. Box 1, Wichita, KS 67201
Operates national commercial banks.
(316) 383-1111
Jobline: (316) 383-1155

Iowa (state)
Grimes Office Building, E. 14th Street at Grand Avenue,
Des Moines, IA 5031-0150
Provides state services such as conservation,
education, highways, prisons, and welfare.
(515) 281-3087
Jobline: (515) 281-5820

Iowa (state) Workforce Center
800 7th Street SE, Cedar Rapids, IA 52406
Seeks workers for private and public employers.
(319) 365-9474
Jobline: (319) 365-9474, press 2, then 2.

Iowa State University
Ames, IA 50011
Large, public, land-grant university in Ames, 30 miles
north of Des Moines.
(515) 294-4111
Jobline: (515) 294-0146

Irvine (city)
P.O. Box 19575, Irvine, CA 92713
Provides municipal services such as police, firefighting,
libraries, parks, and public works.
(714) 724-6005
Jobline: (714) 724-6096

ITT Corp.
1330 Avenue of the Americas, New York, NY 10019
Provides insurance, consumer and business financing,
and local and long distance telephone services.
(212) 258-1000
Jobline: (212) 258-1768

Jack Eckerd Corp.
8333 Bryan Dairy Road, Largo, FL 34647
Operates drug stores, optical goods stores, film
processing labs, and other businesses.
(813) 399-6000
Jobline: (813) 399-6443

Jackson (city)
218 S. President Street, Jackson, MS 39201
Provides municipal services such as police, firefighting,
libraries, parks, and public works.
(601) 960-1053
Jobline: (601) 960-1003

Jackson County
415 E. 12th Street, Kansas City, MO 64106
Provides county services such as sheriffs, courts, motor
vehicle registration, and social services.
(816) 881-3135
Jobline: (816) 881-3134

Jackson County Circuit Court
415 E. 12th Street, Kansas City, MO 64106
Adjudicates cases for Jackson County.
(816) 881-3559
Jobline: (816) 881-3470

Jackson-Madison County General Hospital
708 W. Forest Avenue, Jackson, TN 38301
County hospital with more than 600 beds.
(901) 423-3544
Jobline: (901) 425-6759

Jacksonville (city)
220 E. Bay Street, Room 113, Jacksonville, FL 32202
Provides municipal services such as police, firefighting,
     libraries, parks, and public works.
(904) 630-1111
Jobline: (904) 630-1144

Jacksonville (city) Port Authority
2831 Talleyrand Avenue, Jacksonville, FL 32206
Manages the commercial activities of the port of
     Jacksonville.
(904) 630-3069
Jobline: (904) 630-3095

Jacksonville State University
Jacksonville, AL 36265
Medium-sized, public, multipurpose university in
     Jacksonville.
(205) 782-5781
Jobline: (205) 782-5578

James Madison University
Harrisonburg, VA 22807
Medium-sized, public university in Harrisonburg.
(703) 568-6211
Jobline: (703) 568-3561

JC Penney Co.
6501 Legacy Drive, P.O. Box 10001, Dallas, TX 75301
Operates department and drug stores, and offers
     catalog sales and insurance services.
(214) 591-1000
Jobline: (214) 431-2300

Jefferson County
180 19th Street, Golden, CO 80401
Provides county services such as sheriffs, courts, motor
     vehicle registration, and social services.
(303) 271-8400
Jobline: (303) 271-8401

Jefferson County
517 Court Place, Room 301, Louisville, KY 40202
Provides county services such as sheriffs, courts, motor
     vehicle registration, and social services.
(502) 574-6151
Jobline: (502) 574-6182

Jefferson County
1001 Pearl Street, Beaumont, TX 77704
Provides county services such as sheriffs, courts, motor
     vehicle registration, and social services.
(409) 835-8400
Jobline: (409) 839-2384

Jefferson County Board of Education
801 6th Avenue South, Birmingham, AL 35233
Oversees Jefferson County's schools.
(205) 325-5607
Jobline: (205) 325-5107

Johns Hopkins University
Baltimore, MD 21218
Small, private university in residential Baltimore.
(410) 516-8000
Jobline: (410) 516-8022

Johnson and Johnson Inc.
1 Johnson and Johnson Plaza, New Brunswick, NJ
     08933
Manufactures hygiene products, pharmaceutical
     preparations, and surgical and other medical
     products.
(908) 524-0400
Jobline: (908) 524-2086

Johnson County
Administration Building, 111 S. Cherry Street, Olathe,
     KS 66061-3441
Provides county services such as sheriffs, courts, motor
     vehicle registration, and social services.
(913) 782-7770
Jobline: (913) 780-2929

JR Simplot Co.
P.O. Box 27, Boise, ID 83707
Produces frozen and dehydrated potato products,
     fertilizers, prepared feeds, and livestock.
(208) 336-2110
Jobline: (208) 384-8002
Food division jobs.

Jobline: (208) 389-7510
For jobs in divisions other than food.

JW Marriott at Lenox
3300 Lenox Road NE, Atlanta, GA 30326
371-room hotel.
(404) 262-3344
Jobline: (404) 262-3344, ask for job hotline.

JW Marriott Westheimer by the Galleria
5150 Westheimer Road, Houston, TX 77056
494-room hotel.
(713) 961-1500
Jobline: (713) 961-1500, ask for x6143.

Kaiser Foundation Health Plan Inc.
1 Kaiser Plaza, Oakland, CA 94612
Provides hospital and medical service plans.
(510) 271-5910
Jobline: (510) 271-6888

Kaiser Foundation Hospital
4867 Sunset Boulevard, Los Angeles, CA 90027
Not-for-profit hospital and nursing home-type unit with
     more than 600 beds.
(213) 667-8100
Jobline: (213) 667-6966

6041 Cadillac Avenue, Los Angeles, CA 90034
Not-for-profit hospital with more than 200 beds.
(213) 857-2000
Jobline: (213) 857-2615

25825 S. Vermont Avenue, Harbor City, CA 90710
Not-for-profit hospital with more than 200 beds.
(310) 325-5111
Jobline: (310) 517-3620

Kaiser Permanente
Regional Offices
393 E. Walnut Street, Pasadena, CA 91101-5103
Operates health maintenance organizations.
(818) 405-3279
Jobline: (818) 405-3280

Kanawha County Board of Education
200 Elizabeth Street, Charleston, WV 25311
Oversees Kanawha County's schools.
(304) 348-7712
Jobline: (304) 348-6193
Includes jobs in the administrative offices and in
   schools.

Kansas (state)
Landon State Office Building, Room 951 South, 9th and
   Jackson Streets, Topeka, KS 66612
Provides state services such as conservation,
   education, highways, prisons, and welfare.
(913) 296-4278
Jobline: (913) 296-2208

Kansas City (city)
701 N. 7th Street, Kansas City, KS 66105
Provides municipal services such as police, firefighting,
   libraries, parks, and public works.
(913) 573-5660
Jobline: (913) 573-5688

Kansas City (city)
414 E. 12th Street, Kansas City, MO 64106
Provides municipal services such as police, firefighting,
   libraries, parks, and public works.
(816) 274-2326
Jobline: (816) 274-1127

Kansas State University
Manhattan, KS 66506
Large, public, comprehensive, land-grant institution in
   northern Manhattan.
(913) 532-6250
Jobline: (913) 532-6271

KCET-TV
4401 Sunset Boulevard, Los Angeles, CA 90027
Nonprofit TV station affiliated with PBS that broadcasts
   in the public interest.
(213) 953-5240
Jobline: (213) 953-5236

Kennesaw State College
Marietta, GA 30061
Medium-sized, public, liberal arts college in Marietta, 25
   miles from Atlanta.
(404) 423-6000
Jobline: (404) 423-6031

Kent (city)
220 4th Avenue South, Kent, WA 98032
Provides municipal services such as libraries, parks,
   and public works.
(206) 859-3328
Jobline: (206) 859-3375

Kent (city) Civil Service Commission
220 S. 4th Avenue, Kent, WA 98032-5895
Administers exams for police, correctional, and
   firefighting positions.
(206) 859-6833
Jobline: (206) 859-2876

Kent School District
12033 SE 256th Street, Kent, WA 98031
33-school district in Kent.
(206) 859-7209
Jobline: (206) 859-7508
Classified jobs.

Kent State University
Kent, OH 44242
Large, public, comprehensive university in Kent,
   northeast of Akron.
(216) 672-2121
Jobline: (216) 672-2103

Kern County
1115 Truxton Avenue, Bakersfield, CA 93301
Provides county services such as sheriffs, courts, motor
   vehicle registration, and social services.
(805) 861-2195
Jobline: (805) 861-3712

Key Bank of Maine
1 Canal Plaza, Portland, ME 04112
Operates state commercial banks.
(207) 623-7000
Jobline: (207) 623-7000, ask for job hotline.

Key Bank of Oregon
1211 SW 5th Avenue, Portland, OR 97204
Operates state commercial banks.
(503) 790-7500
Jobline: (503) 598-3573

Key Bank of Utah
50 S. Main Street, Salt Lake City, UT 84144
Operates state commercial banks.
(801) 535-1000
Jobline: (801) 535-1117

Key Bank of Washington
1119 Pacific Avenue, Mail Stop 0250, P.O. Box 11500,
   Tacoma, WA 98411-5500
Operates state commercial banks.
(206) 593-3600
Jobline: (800) 677-6150

Key Services Corp.
17 Corporate Woods Boulevard, Albany, NY 12211
Provides data processing and bank operations services.
(518) 436-2000
Jobline: (518) 436-2533

King County
King County Administration Building, Room 450, 500
   4th Avenue, Seattle, WA 98104
Provides county services such as sheriffs, courts, motor
   vehicle registration, and social services.
(206) 296-7340
Jobline: (206) 296-5209

King County Metropolitan Services
Exchange Building, 4th Floor, 821 2nd Avenue, Seattle, WA 98104
Transit authority and water treatment provider for Seattle and King County.
(206) 684-2100
Jobline: (206) 684-1313

Kitsap County
614 Division Street, Port Orchard, WA 98366
Provides county services such as sheriffs, courts, motor vehicle registration, and social services.
(206) 876-7185
Jobline: (206) 876-7169

Klamath County
403 Pine Street, Klamath Falls, OR 97601
Provides county services such as sheriffs, courts, motor vehicle registration, and social services.
(503) 883-4296
Jobline: (503) 883-4188

KNBC-TV
3000 W. Alameda Avenue, Burbank, CA 91523
TV station affiliated with NBC.
(818) 840-4444
Jobline: (818) 840-4397

Knoxville (city)
City and County Building, 400 W. Main Avenue, Knoxville, TN 37902
Provides municipal services such as police, firefighting, libraries, parks, and public works.
(615) 521-2106
Jobline: (615) 521-2562

Kutztown University
Kutztown, PA 19530
Medium-sized, public university in Kutztown, between Reading and Allentown.
(610) 683-4000
Jobline: (610) 683-4130

L.A. Gear Inc.
4221 Redwood Avenue, Los Angeles, CA 90066
Manufactures athletic, children's, and men's and women's shoes.
(310) 822-1995
Jobline: (310) 822-1995, ask for x5800.

Lacey (city)
420 College Street SE, Lacey, WA 98503
Provides municipal services such as police, firefighting, libraries, parks, and public works.
(206) 491-3214
Jobline: (206) 491-3213

Laguna Hills (city)
25201 Paseo de Alicia, Laguna Hills, CA 92653
Provides municipal services such as police, firefighting, libraries, parks, and public works.
(714) 707-2620
Jobline: (714) 707-2628

Lake Oswego (city)
380 A Avenue, Lake Oswego, OR 97034
Provides municipal services such as police, firefighting, libraries, parks, and public works.
(503) 635-0220
Jobline: (503) 635-0256

Lake Oswego School District No. 7J
2455 SW Country Club Road, Lake Oswego, OR 97034
13-school district in Lake Oswego.
(503) 636-7691
Jobline: (503) 635-0342

Lakewood (city)
445 S. Allison Parkway, Lakewood, CO 80226
Provides municipal services such as police, firefighting, libraries, parks, and public works.
(303) 987-7700
Jobline: (303) 987-7777

Lamar University
Beaumont, TX 77710
Medium-sized, public, multipurpose university in Beaumont.
(409) 880-8345
Jobline: (409) 880-8371

Lancaster (city)
44933 N. Fern Avenue, Lancaster, CA 93534
Provides municipal services such as police, firefighting, libraries, parks, and public works.
(805) 723-6000
Jobline: (805) 723-6200

Land O'Lakes Inc.
P.O. Box 116, Minneapolis, MN 55440
Produces dairy products, animal feeds, farm supplies, fertilizers, and agricultural chemicals.
(612) 481-2222
Jobline: (612) 481-2250

Landmark Medical Center
Woonsocket and Fogarty Units
115 Cass Avenue, Woonsocket, RI 02895
Not-for-profit hospital with more than 200 beds.
(401) 769-4100
Jobline: (401) 769-4100, x2379.

Lane County
125 E. 8th Street, Eugene, OR 97401
Provides county services such as sheriffs, courts, motor vehicle registration, and social services.
(503) 687-4171
Jobline: (503) 687-4473, press 1.

Las Vegas (city)
416 N. 7th Street, Las Vegas, NV 89101
Provides municipal services such as police, firefighting, libraries, parks, and public works.
(702) 229-6315
Jobline: (702) 229-6346

Le Meridien Newport Beach
4500 MacArthur Boulevard, Newport Beach, CA 92660
435-room hotel in the Orange County coastal area.
(714) 476-2001
Jobline: (714) 955-5656

Lehigh County
Lehigh County Court House, 455 W. Hamilton Street
Allentown, PA 18101
Provides county services such as sheriffs, courts, motor
vehicle registration, and social services.
(610) 820-3130
Jobline: (610) 820-3386

Lehigh University
Bethlehem, PA 18015-3035
Medium-sized, private university in Bethlehem, 60 miles
from Philadelphia.
(610) 758-3000
Jobline: (610) 758-5627

Leon County
301 S. Monroe Street, Tallahassee, FL 32301
Provides county services such as sheriffs, courts, motor
vehicle registration, and social services.
(904) 487-2220
Jobline: (904) 922-4944

Levi Strauss Associates Inc.
1155 Battery Street, San Francisco, CA 94111
Manufactures jeans, slacks, skirts, T-shirts, and jackets.
(415) 544-6000
Jobline: (415) 544-7828

Lewis and Clark College
Portland, OR 97219
Small, church-affiliated college six miles from downtown
Portland.
(503) 244-6161
Jobline: (503) 768-7840

Lexington County
316 S. Lake Drive, Lexington, SC 29072
Provides county services such as sheriffs, courts, motor
vehicle registration, and social services.
(803) 359-8225
Jobline: (803) 359-8562

Liberty National Bank and Trust Company of Louisville
P.O. Box 32500, Louisville, KY 40232
Operates national commercial banks and other
investment, insurance, and other financial
businesses.
(502) 566-2000
Jobline: (502) 566-1629

Liberty National Bank and Trust Company of Tulsa
P.O. Box 1, Tulsa, OK 74193
Operates national commercial banks.
(918) 586-1000
Jobline: (918) 586-5818

Library of Congress
101 Independence Avenue SE, Washington, DC 20540
National library of the United States, with many
extensive collections for research purposes.
(202) 707-5000
Jobline: (202) 707-4315

Lincoln (city) and Lancaster County
555 S. 10th Street, Lincoln, NE 68508
Provides government services such as police,
firefighting, libraries, parks, and public works.
(402) 441-7596
Jobline: (402) 441-7736

Linn-Benton Community College
Albany, OR 97321
Medium-sized, state- and locally-supported, 2-year
college in Albany.
(503) 967-6106
Jobline: (503) 926-8800

Little Rock (city)
500 W. Markham Street, Little Rock, AR 72201
Provides municipal services such as police, firefighting,
libraries, parks, and public works.
(501) 371-4405
Jobline: (501) 371-4505

Little Rock (city) Water Works
P.O. Box 1789, Little Rock, AR 72203
Manages water supply and delivery systems.
(501) 377-1238
Jobline: (501) 377-7919

Littleton (city)
2255 W. Berry Avenue, Littleton, CO 80120
Provides municipal services such as police, firefighting,
libraries, parks, and public works.
(303) 795-3857
Jobline: (303) 795-3858

Livermore (city)
1052 S. Livermore Avenue, Livermore, CA 94550
Provides municipal services such as police, firefighting,
libraries, parks, and public works.
(510) 373-5110
Jobline: (510) 866-3799

Lodi (city)
221 W. Pine Street, Lodi, CA 95240
Provides municipal services such as police, firefighting,
libraries, parks, and public works.
(209) 333-6704
Jobline: (209) 333-6705

Loew's Anatole Dallas
2201 Stemmons Freeway, Dallas, TX 75207
1,620-room hotel.
(214) 748-1200
Jobline: (214) 761-7333

Loew's Coronado Bay Resort
4000 Coronado Bay, San Diego, CA 92118
440-room hotel.
(619) 424-4000
Jobline: (619) 424-4480

Loew's Santa Monica Beach Hotel
1700 Ocean Avenue, Santa Monica, CA 90401
350-room hotel in the Los Angeles area.
(310) 458-6700
Jobline: (310) 576-3121

Loew's Vanderbilt Plaza Hotel
2100 W. End Avenue, Nashville, TN 37203
340-room hotel.
(615) 320-1700
Jobline: (615) 321-1908

Long Beach (city)
333 W. Ocean Boulevard, Long Beach, CA 90802
Provides municipal services such as police, firefighting,
    libraries, parks, and public works.
(310) 570-6308
Jobline: (310) 570-6201

Long Beach City College
4901 E. Carson Street, Long Beach, CA 90808
Large, state-supported, 2-year college in Long Beach.
(310) 420-4111
Jobline: (310) 420-4050

Long Beach Hilton
2 World Trade Center, Long Beach, CA 90831
398-room hotel.
(310) 983-3400
Jobline: (310) 983-3445

Long Beach Memorial Medical Center
2801 Atlantic Avenue, P.O. Box 1428, Long Beach, CA
    90801
Not-for-profit hospital with more than 700 beds.
(310) 933-2000
Jobline: (310) 933-2482

Long Beach Press-Telegram
604 Pine Avenue, Long Beach, CA 90844
Publishes newspapers.
(310) 435-1161
Jobline: (310) 435-1161, x6239.

Long Beach Renaissance
111 E. Ocean Boulevard, Long Beach, CA 90804
380-room hotel.
(310) 437-5900
Jobline: (310) 499-2518

Long Island Marriott Hotel
101 James Doolittle Boulevard, Uniondale, NY 11553
620-room hotel near New York City.
(516) 794-3800
Jobline: (516) 794-3800, ask for x6669.

Los Angeles (city) City Attorney
200 N. Main Street, Los Angeles, CA 90012
Provides attorney services for L. A. city government.
(213) 847-9242
Jobline: (213) 847-9424

Los Angeles Airport Hilton & Towers
5711 W. Century Boulevard, Los Angeles, CA 90045
1,279-room hotel near Los Angeles International Airport.
(310) 410-4000
Jobline: (310) 410-6111

Los Angeles Community College District
617 W. 7th Street, Los Angeles, CA 90017-3896
Includes Los Angeles Valley College, Los Angeles
    Pierce College, and seven other community colleges.
(213) 628-7788
Jobline: (213) 891-2099

Los Angeles County Department of Public Works
900 S. Fremont Avenue, Alhambra, CA 91803
Provides public works programs and services.
(818) 458-4098
Jobline: (818) 458-3926

Los Angeles County Metropolitan Transportation Authority
818 W. 7th Street, Los Angeles, CA 90017
Manages public transportation in the Los Angeles area.
(213) 623-1194
Jobline: (213) 972-6217

Los Angeles County Office of Education
9300 E. Imperial Highway, Downey, CA 90242
Provides programs such as special education and
    juvenile court education to local school districts.
(310) 922-6111
Jobline: (310) 803-8408

Los Angeles County Superior Court
111 N. Hill Street, Los Angeles, CA 90012
Adjudicates civil cases for Los Angeles County.
(213) 974-5444
Jobline: (213) 974-5357

Los Angeles County-University of Southern California Medical Center
1200 N. State Street, Los Angeles, CA 90033
County hospital with four facilities and more than 1,400
    beds.
(213) 725-5039
Jobline: (213) 725-5083

Los Angeles Gay and Lesbian Community Services Center
1625 N. Hudson Avenue, West Hollywood, CA 90028
Provides essential human services and sponsors
    community activities for gays and lesbians.
(213) 993-7480
Jobline: (213) 993-7687

Los Angeles Hilton & Towers
930 Wilshire Boulevard, Los Angeles, CA 90017
900-room hotel.
(213) 629-4321
Jobline: (213) 612-3990

Los Angeles Times
Times Mirror Square, Los Angeles, CA 90053
Publishes newspapers.
(213) 237-5000
Jobline: (213) 237-5406
Secretarial and clerical jobs.

Jobline: (213) 237-5407
Production, entry-level, journey-level, and general jobs.

Jobline: (213) 237-5408
Professional, managerial, technical, and sales jobs.

Los Gatos (city)
110 E. Main Street, Los Gatos, CA 95032
Provides municipal services such as police, firefighting,
    libraries, parks, and public works.
(408) 354-6829
Jobline: (408) 354-6838

Los Rios Community College District
1919 Spanos Court, Sacramento, CA 95825
Includes American River College, Cosumnes River
    College, and Sacramento City College.
(916) 568-3112
Jobline: (916) 568-3011

Loudoun County
748 Miller Drive SW, Suite F-1, Leesburg, VA 22075
Provides county services such as sheriffs, courts, motor
    vehicle registration, and social services.
(703) 478-8410
Jobline: (703) 777-0536

**Louisiana State University and Agricultural and
Mechanical College**
Baton Rouge, LA 70803-2750
Large, public, comprehensive, land-grant university in
    Baton Rouge.
(504) 388-3202
Jobline: (504) 388-1101
Classified jobs.
Jobline: (504) 388-1201
Unclassified and academic jobs.

Louisville (city)
609 W. Jefferson Street, Louisville, KY 40202
Provides municipal services such as police, firefighting,
    libraries, parks, and public works.
(502) 574-3565
Jobline: (502) 574-3355

Loyola College
Baltimore, MD 21210
Medium-sized, church-affiliated, liberal arts college in
    residential Baltimore.
(410) 323-1010
Jobline: (410) 617-5037

Loyola Marymount University
Los Angeles, CA 90045
Small, church-affiliated university in residential Los
    Angeles.
(310) 642-2700
Jobline: (310) 338-4488

Loyola University
New Orleans, LA 70118
Small, church-affiliated university in residential New
    Orleans.
(504) 865-2011
Jobline: (504) 865-3400

Loyola University, Chicago
Chicago, IL 60611
Medium-sized, church-affiliated university in residential
    Chicago.
(312) 274-3000
Jobline: (312) 508-3400

Lubbock (city)
P.O. Box 2000, Lubbock, TX 79457
Provides municipal services such as police, firefighting,
    libraries, parks, and public works.
(806) 767-2311
Jobline: (806) 762-2444

Lyondell Petrochemical Co.
1221 McKinney Street, Houston, TX 77010
Produces organic chemicals, gasoline, oils, and fuels.
(713) 652-7200
Jobline: (713) 652-4562

M and I Data Services Inc.
4900 Brown Deer Road, Milwaukee, WI 53223-2422
Provides data processing services for Marshall and
    Ilsley Corp.'s banking operations.
(414) 765-7801
Jobline: (414) 357-5627

Macalester College
Saint Paul, MN 55105
Small, church-affiliated, liberal arts college in residential
    St. Paul.
(612) 696-6000
Jobline: (612) 696-6400

Macon (city)
P.O. Box 247, Macon, GA 31298
Provides municipal services such as police, firefighting,
    libraries, parks, and public works.
(912) 751-2721
Jobline: (912) 751-2733

Madison (city)
City-County Building, Room 501, 210 Martin Luther
    King Jr. Boulevard, Madison, WI 53710
Provides municipal services such as police, firefighting,
    libraries, parks, and public works.
(608) 266-4615
Jobline: (608) 266-6500

Madison County
100 Northside Square, Huntsville, AL 35801
Provides county services such as sheriffs, courts, motor
    vehicle registration, and social services.
(205) 532-3614
Jobline: (205) 532-6906

Madison County Board of Education
P.O. Box 226, Huntsville, AL 35804
Oversees Madison County's schools.
(205) 532-3522
Jobline: (205) 532-2851

Manor Care Inc.
10750 Columbia Pike, Silver Spring, MD 20901
Operates health care facilities, hotels, and nursing
    homes.
(301) 681-9400
Jobline: (800) 348-2041

Manteca Unified School District
2901 E. Louise Avenue, Lathrop, CA 95330
17-school district in Lathrop.
(209) 825-3230
Jobline: (209) 825-3233
Classified jobs.

Mapco Inc.
1800 S. Baltimore Avenue, Tulsa, OK 74119
Provides oil and gas production and marketing,
    petroleum products, and bituminous coal.
(918) 581-1800
Jobline: (918) 586-7178

Maricopa County
301 W. Jefferson Street, Phoenix, AZ 85003
Provides county services such as sheriffs, courts, motor
vehicle registration, and social services.
(602) 506-3236
Jobline: (602) 506-3329

Maricopa County Community College District
2411 W. 14th Street, Tempe, AZ 85281
Includes Mesa and Glendale Community Colleges,
Phoenix College, and seven other community
colleges.
(602) 731-8000
Jobline: (602) 731-8444

Marietta (city)
P.O. Box 609, Marietta, GA 30061
Provides municipal services such as police, firefighting,
libraries, parks, and public works.
(404) 528-0587
Jobline: (404) 528-0593
Includes jobs with the Board of Lights and Water.

Marin Community College
College Avenue, Kentfield, CA 94904
Medium-sized, state- and locally-supported, 2-year
college in Kentfield.
(415) 485-9411
Jobline: (415) 485-9693

Marin County
3501 Civic Center Drive, San Rafael, CA 94903
Provides county services such as sheriffs, courts, motor
vehicle registration, and social services.
(415) 499-6104
Jobline: (415) 472-2999

Marion County
100 High Street NE, Salem, OR 97301
Provides county services such as sheriffs, courts, motor
vehicle registration, and social services.
(503) 588-5165
Jobline: (503) 588-5589

Marquette University
Milwaukee, WI 53233
Medium-sized, church-affiliated university near
downtown Milwaukee.
(414) 288-7700
Jobline: (414) 288-7000

Marriott Anaheim
700 W. Convention Way, Anaheim, CA 92802
1,039-room hotel near Disneyland.
(714) 750-8000
Jobline: (714) 748-2482

Marriott at Sawgrass
Highway A1A South, Ponte Vedra Beach, FL 32082
550-room beachfront hotel near Jacksonville.
(904) 285-7777
Jobline: (904) 285-7777, ask for x6738.

Marriott at the Capitol
701 E. 11th Street, Austin, TX 78701
365-room hotel.
(512) 478-1111
Jobline: (512) 478-1111, ask for job hotline.

Marriott Berkeley Marina
200 Marina Boulevard, Berkeley, CA 94710
375-room hotel.
(510) 548-7920
Jobline: (510) 548-7920, ask for x741.

Marriott Biscayne Bay
1633 N. Bayshore Drive, Miami, FL 33132
605-room hotel.
(305) 374-3900
Jobline: (305) 536-6320

Marriott Boston Copley Place
110 Huntington Avenue, Boston, MA 02116
1,139-room hotel.
(617) 236-5800
Jobline: (617) 578-0686

Marriott Boston Long Wharf
296 State Street, Boston, MA 02109
400-room hotel.
(617) 227-0800
Jobline: (617) 227-0800, ask for x6968.

Marriott Cambridge
2 Cambridge Center, Cambridge, MA 02142
431-room hotel near Boston.
(617) 494-6600
Jobline: (617) 494-6600, ask for x6625.

Marriott Chicago Downtown
540 N. Michigan Avenue, Chicago, IL 60611
1,200-room hotel.
(312) 836-0100
Jobline: (312) 245-6909

Marriott City Center
1701 California Street, Denver, CO 80202
612-room hotel.
(303) 297-1300
Jobline: (303) 291-3644

Marriott City Center
30 S. 7th Street, Minneapolis, MN 55403
584-room hotel.
(612) 349-4000
Jobline: (612) 349-4077

Marriott Corp.
1 Marriott Drive, Washington, DC 20058
Operates and franchises hotels and restaurants, and
provides contract food and other services.
(301) 380-9000
Jobline: (301) 380-1202
Corporate jobs.

Marriott Hotel
18000 Von Karman Avenue, Irvine, CA 92715
502-room hotel in the Orange County coastal area.
(714) 553-0100
Jobline: (714) 724-3681

Marriott Hotel
700 Grand Avenue, Des Moines, IA 50309
416-room hotel.
(515) 245-5500
Jobline: (515) 245-5544

Marriott Hotel & Marina
333 W. Harbor Drive, San Diego, CA 92101-7700
1,355-room hotel.
(619) 234-1500
Jobline: (619) 230-8901

Marriott Hotel & Tennis Club
900 Newport Center Drive, Newport Beach, CA 92660
615-room hotel in the Orange County coastal area.
(714) 640-4000
Jobline: (714) 640-4000, ask for job hotline.

Marriott Hotel Albuquerque
2101 Louisiana Boulevard NE, Albuquerque, NM 87110
413-room hotel.
(505) 881-6800
Jobline: (505) 881-6800, ask for x6012.

Marriott Hotel Bloomington
2020 E. 79th Street, Minneapolis, MN 55425
479-room hotel four miles from the airport.
(612) 854-7441
Jobline: (612) 854-3809

Marriott Hotel Denver SE
I-25 at Hampden Avenue, Denver, CO 80222
595-room hotel.
(303) 758-7000
Jobline: (303) 782-3214

Marriott Hotel Newton
2345 Commonwealth Avenue, Newton, MA 02166
434-room hotel near Boston.
(617) 969-1000
Jobline: (617) 969-1000, ask for x8528.

Marriott Hotel Portland
1401 SW Front Avenue, Portland, OR 97201
503-room hotel.
(503) 226-7600
Jobline: (503) 499-6334

Marriott Hotel Riverwalk
711 E. River Walk Street, San Antonio, TX 78205
502-room downtown hotel.
(210) 224-4555
Jobline: (210) 299-6518

Marriott Hotel Torrance
3635 Fashion Way, Torrance, CA 90503-4897
487-room hotel.
(310) 316-3636
Jobline: (310) 316-3636, ask for job hotline.

Marriott Hotels
Charlotte area
100 W. Trade Street, Charlotte, NC 28202
Hotel chain that includes six Marriott hotels in the
    Charlotte, North Carolina area.
(704) 333-9000
Jobline: (704) 551-8000

Marriott Hotels
Washington D.C. and Virginia area
1 Marriott Drive, Washington, DC 20058
Hotel chain of 11 Marriott hotels in the D.C. area.
(301) 380-9000
Jobline: (703) 461-6100

Marriott La Jolla
4240 La Jolla Village Drive, La Jolla, CA 92037
360-room hotel.
(619) 587-1414
Jobline: (619) 552-8578

Marriott Los Angeles Airport
5855 W. Century Boulevard, Los Angeles, CA 90045
1,012-room hotel near Los Angeles International Airport.
(310) 641-5700
Jobline: (310) 337-5327

Marriott Marina del Rey
13480 Maxella Avenue, Marina del Rey, CA 90291
283-room hotel near Los Angeles International Airport.
(310) 822-8555
Jobline: (310) 822-8555, ask for x6199.

Marriott Marquis
265 Peachtree Center Avenue, Atlanta, GA 30303
1,674-room hotel.
(404) 521-0000
Jobline: (404) 586-6240

Marriott Marquis New York
1535 Broadway, New York, NY 10036
1,877-room hotel.
(212) 398-1900
Jobline: (212) 704-8959

Marriott Medical Center
6580 Fannin Street, Houston, TX 77030
389-room hotel.
(713) 796-0080
Jobline: (713) 796-2218

Marriott Mission Valley
8757 Rio San Diego Drive, San Diego, CA 92108
350-room hotel.
(619) 692-3800
Jobline: (619) 692-3800, ask for x44.

Marriott Orlando
8001 International Drive, Orlando, FL 32819
1,076-room hotel.
(407) 351-2420
Jobline: (407) 351-2420, ask for x7722.

Marriott Orlando Airport
7499 Augusta National Drive, Orlando, FL 32822
484-room hotel.
(407) 851-9000
Jobline: (407) 851-9000, ask for x5201.

Marriott Overland Park
10800 Metcalf Avenue, Overland Park, KS 66210
397-room hotel.
(913) 451-8000
Jobline: (913) 451-0259

Marriott Pavillion Hotel
1 Broadway, Saint Louis, MO 63102
671-room hotel in downtown St. Louis.
(314) 421-1776
Jobline: (314) 259-3381

Marriott Richmond
500 E. Broad Street, Richmond, VA 23219
400-room hotel.
(804) 643-3400
Jobline: (804) 643-3400, ask for job hotline.

Marriott River Center
101 Bowie Street, San Antonio, TX 78205
1,000-room hotel.
(210) 223-1000
Jobline: (210) 554-6289

Marriott Salt Lake City
75 S. West Temple, Salt Lake City, UT 84101
516-room hotel in the center of town.
(801) 531-0800
Jobline: (801) 537-6050

Marriott San Francisco Airport
1800 Old Bayshore Highway, Burlingame, CA 94010
684-room hotel near San Francisco International Airport.
(415) 692-9100
Jobline: (415) 692-9100, ask for job hotline.

Marriott Warner Center
21850 Oxnard Street, Woodland Hills, CA 91367
473-room hotel in the Los Angeles area.
(818) 887-4800
Jobline: (818) 887-4800, ask for job hotline.

Marriott's Orlando World Center
8701 World Center Drive, Orlando, FL 32821
1,503-room hotel.
(407) 239-4200
Jobline: (407) 238-8822

Marriott's Tan-Tar-A-Resort
Osage Beach, MO 65065
930-room hotel on the Lake of the Ozarks.
(314) 348-3131
Jobline: (314) 348-8429

Marriott's Wind Watch Hotel & Golf
1717 Vanderbilt Motor Parkway, Hauppauge, NY 11788
362-room hotel.
(516) 232-9800
Jobline: (516) 232-9800, ask for x379.

Marshall and Ilsley Corp.
770 N. Water Street, Milwaukee, WI 53202
Bank holding company that operates state commercial
    banks.
(414) 765-7801
Jobline: (414) 765-8300

Marshall University
Huntington, WV 25755-2020
Medium-sized, public university in Huntington, 50 miles
    west of Charleston.
(304) 696-3170
Jobline: (304) 696-3644

Martinez (city)
525 Henrietta, Martinez, CA 94553
Provides municipal services such as police, firefighting,
    libraries, parks, and public works.
(510) 372-3522
Jobline: (510) 372-3513

Mary Washington College
Fredericksburg, VA 22401-5358
Small, public, liberal arts college in Fredericksburg,
    south of Arlington.
(703) 899-4100
Jobline: (703) 899-4624
Call after 5 p.m. or on weekends.

Maryland (state)
Saratoga State Center, 311 W. Saratoga Street,
    Baltimore, MD 21201
Provides state services such as conservation,
    education, highways, prisons, and welfare.
(410) 333-0988
Jobline: (410) 333-7510

Marysville School District
4220 80th Street NE, Marysville, WA 98270
14-school district in Marysville.
(206) 653-0809
Jobline: (206) 653-0807
Classified and certificated jobs.

Massachusetts (state)
1 Ashburton Place, Boston, MA 02108
Provides state services such as conservation,
    education, highways, prisons, and welfare.
(617) 727-8370
Jobline: (617) 727-9244
Civil service jobs.

Massachusetts Water Resources Authority
Charlestown Navy Yard, 100 1st Avenue
Boston, MA 02129
Provides water and sewer services to governments in
    the region.
(617) 242-6000
Jobline: (617) 241-6400

Mattel Inc.
333 Continental Boulevard, El Segundo, CA 90245
Manufactures games, toys, children's vehicles, dolls,
    and stuffed animals.
(310) 524-2000
Jobline: (310) 524-3535

Mayflower Group Inc.
9998 N. Michigan Road, Carmel, IN 46032
Provides trucking, contract moving, freight forwarding,
    and warehousing and storage services.
(317) 875-1469
Jobline: (317) 875-1599

MCA Inc.
MCA/Universal City Studios
100 Universal City Plaza, Universal City, CA 91608
Motion picture-oriented theme park in the Los Angeles
    area.
(818) 777-1000
Jobline: (818) 777-5627

McCaw Communication Co.
5400 Carillon Point, Kirkland, WA 98033
Provides cellular and paging services, operates TV
    stations, and publishes magazines.
(206) 827-4500
Jobline: (206) 828-8484

McCormick and Co.
18 Loveton Circle, P.O. Box 6000
Sparks, MD 21152-6000
Produces spices, seasonings, gravy and sauce mixes,
flavoring extracts, and other food products.
(410) 771-7301
Jobline: (410) 527-6969

McDonnell Douglas Corp.
P.O. Box 516, Saint Louis, MO 63166
Manufactures aircraft, missiles, and space vehicles,
and provides other products and services.
(314) 232-0232
Jobline: (314) 232-4222

MCI Communications Corp.
1133 19th Street NW, Washington, DC 20036
Provides local and long distance telephone services.
(202) 872-1600
Jobline: (800) 234-5627
Multinational accounts jobs.

Jobline: (800) 289-0128
Strategy and technology jobs.

Jobline: (800) 695-2380
Systems engineering jobs.

Jobline: (800) 777-6063
Corporate jobs.

Jobline: (800) 888-2413
MCI International jobs.

2400 N. Glenville Drive, Richardson, TX 75082
(214) 918-3695
Jobline: (800) 456-5243
Network services jobs.

McKesson Corp.
1 Post Street, San Francisco, CA 94104
Produces pharmaceuticals, toiletries, sundries, medical
equipment and supplies, and other products.
(415) 983-8300
Jobline: (415) 983-8409
Professional, clerical, and secretarial jobs.

Jobline: (415) 983-8784
Computer professional jobs.

McLean Hilton at Tysons Corner
7920 Jones Branch Boulevard, McLean, VA 22102
457-room hotel near Washington, D.C.
(703) 847-5000
Jobline: (703) 761-5155

Mead School District
N. 12508 Freya Street, Mead, WA 99021
11-school district in Mead.
(509) 468-3007
Jobline: (509) 468-3193

Medical Center of Independence
17203 E. 23rd Street, Independence, MO 64057
Not-for-profit hospital with more than 100 beds.
(816) 373-2300
Jobline: (816) 373-7373, x170.

Mellon PSFS
Mellon Independence Center, 7th and Market Streets,
Philadelphia, PA 19101-7899
Operates national commercial banks.
(215) 553-3000
Jobline: (215) 553-3213

Memorial Medical Center of Jacksonville
3625 University Boulevard South, Jacksonville, FL
32216
Not-for-profit hospital with more than 300 beds.
(904) 399-6111
Jobline: (904) 399-6702

Memphis (city)
125 N. Main Street, Memphis, TN 38103
Provides municipal services such as police, firefighting,
libraries, parks, and public works.
(901) 576-6571
Jobline: (901) 576-6548

Memphis (city) Light Gas and Water Division
245 S. Main Street, Memphis, TN 38103
Provides electricity, gas, and water services.
(901) 544-6549
Jobline: (901) 528-4241

Mendocino County
175 S. School Street Courthouse Annex, Ukiah, CA
95482
Provides county services such as sheriffs, courts, motor
vehicle registration, and social services.
(707) 463-4261
Jobline: (707) 463-5424

Merced County
2222 M Street, Merced, CA 95340
Provides county services such as sheriffs, courts, motor
vehicle registration, and social services.
(209) 385-7682
Jobline: (209) 385-7516

Mercer Island (city)
City Hall, 9611 SE 36th Street, Mercer Island, WA 98040
Provides municipal services such as police, firefighting,
libraries, parks, and public works.
(206) 236-5300
Jobline: (206) 236-5326

Mercer Island School District
4160 86th Avenue SE, Mercer Island, WA 98040
Six-school district in Mercer Island.
(206) 236-3318
Jobline: (206) 236-3302

Merck and Co.
P.O. Box 2000, Rahway, NJ 07065
Produces pharmaceutical preparations, drugs,
biological products, chemicals, and other products.
(908) 594-4000
Jobline: (908) 423-7820

Mercy Hospital Medical Center
6th Street and University Avenue, Des Moines, IA 50314
Not-for-profit hospital and nursing home-type unit with
more than 500 beds.
(515) 247-3121
Jobline: (515) 247-3105

Meridian Bancorp Inc.
P.O. Box 1102, Reading, PA 19603
Bank holding company that operates state commercial
banks and other financial businesses.
(610) 655-3008
Jobline: (800) 321-5627

Merit Systems Protection Board
1120 Vermont Avenue NW, Washington, DC 20419
Protects the integrity of Federal merit systems and the
rights of Federal employees working in them.
(202) 653-5916
Jobline: (202) 254-8013

Merrimack College
North Andover, MA 01845
Small, church-affiliated, liberal arts college 25 miles
north of Boston.
(508) 837-5000
Jobline: (508) 837-5315

Merv Griffin's Resorts Casino Hotel
Boardwalk and N. Carolina Avenue, Atlantic City, NJ
08404
700-room oceanfront hotel.
(609) 340-6300
Jobline: (609) 340-6297

Mesa (city)
P.O. Box 1466, Mesa, AZ 85211-1466
Provides municipal services such as police, firefighting,
libraries, parks, and public works.
(602) 644-2365
Jobline: (602) 644-2759

Mesquite (city)
1515 N. Galloway Avenue, Mesquite, TX 75149
Provides municipal services such as police, firefighting,
libraries, parks, and public works.
(214) 216-6218
Jobline: (214) 216-6484

Methodist Hospital of Southern California
300 W. Huntington Drive, Arcadia, CA 91107
Not-for-profit hospital and nursing home-type unit with
more than 300 beds.
(818) 574-3607
Jobline: (818) 574-3760

Metpath Inc.
1 Malcolm Avenue, Teterboro, NJ 07608
Performs clinical laboratory testing.
(201) 393-5000
Jobline: (201) 393-6161

Metpath of Michigan
4444 Giddings Road, Auburn Hills, MI 48326
Operates medical laboratories.
(810) 373-9120
Jobline: (810) 373-9120, x355.

Metropolitan Life Insurance Co.
1 Madison Avenue, New York, NY 10010
Provides life, accident, and health insurance, and other
insurance and business services.
(212) 578-2211
Jobline: (212) 578-4111

Metropolitan Park District of Tacoma
4702 S. 19th Street, Tacoma, WA 98405
Provides park and recreational programs and services.
(206) 305-1003
Jobline: (206) 305-1009

Metropolitan Service District
600 NE Grand Avenue, Portland, OR 97232
Provides solid waste, recycling, land use and other
services for governments in the Portland area.
(503) 797-1700
Jobline: (503) 797-1777

Metropolitan State College of Denver
Denver, CO 80217-3362
Medium-sized, public, comprehensive institution in
downtown Denver.
(303) 556-2953
Jobline: (303) 556-8430
Includes jobs at the U. of Colorado at Denver and the
Comm. College of Denver.

**Metropolitan Water District of Southern
California**
1111 W. Sunset Boulevard, Los Angeles, CA 90012
Provides water services for Southern California.
(213) 250-6000
Jobline: (800) 540-6311

Miami (city)
300 Biscayne Boulevard Way, Miami, FL 33131
Provides municipal services such as police, firefighting,
libraries, parks, and public works.
(305) 579-2411
Jobline: (305) 579-2400

Miami Herald Publishing Inc.
1 Herald Plaza, Miami, FL 33132
Publishes newspapers.
(305) 350-2111
Jobline: (305) 376-2880

Jobline: (305) 376-8959
Subscription-selling jobs.

Miami University
Oxford, OH 45056
Medium-sized, state-assisted institution in southwestern
Ohio.
(513) 529-1809
Jobline: (513) 529-6400

Miami-Dade Community College
Kendall and Homestead Campuses
11011 SW 104th Street, Miami, FL 33176
Large, state- and locally-supported, 2-year colleges.
(305) 237-2051
Jobline: (305) 237-0965
Administrative and staff jobs.

Jobline: (305) 237-2925
Faculty jobs.

Medical Center Campus
950 NW 20th Street, Miami, FL 33127
(305) 237-3036
Jobline: (305) 237-0985
Administrative and staff jobs.

Miami-Dade Community College (cont.)
Jobline: (305) 237-2945
Faculty jobs.

Mitchell Wolfson Campus
300 NE 2nd Avenue, Miami, FL 33132
(305) 237-3036
Jobline: (305) 237-0975
Administrative and staff jobs.

Jobline: (305) 237-2935
Faculty jobs.

North Campus
11380 NW 27th Avenue, Miami, FL 33167
(305) 237-2051
Jobline: (305) 237-0955
Administrative and staff jobs.

Jobline: (305) 237-2915
Faculty jobs.

Michigan (state) Department of Corrections
206 E. Michigan Avenue, Lansing, MI 48933
Provides correctional programs and services.
(517) 373-4121
Jobline: (517) 373-4246

Michigan (state) Public Health Department
3423 N. Logan Street, P.O. Box 30195, Lansing, MI
    48409
Provides public health programs and services.
(517) 335-8790
Jobline: (517) 335-8797

Michigan National Bank
27777 Inkster Road, P.O. Box 9065
Farmington Hills, MI 48333-9065
Operates national commercial banks.
(810) 473-3000
Jobline: (810) 473-4328

Michigan State University
East Lansing, MI 48824-1046
Large, public, comprehensive, land-grant university in
    East Lansing.
(517) 355-1855
Jobline: (517) 355-9518

Michigan Technological University
Houghton, MI 49931
Medium-sized, public university on Portage Lake in
    Houghton, on Michigan's Upper Peninsula.
(906) 487-1885
Jobline: (906) 487-2895

Micro Technology Inc.
5065 E. Hunter Avenue, Anaheim, CA 92807
Manufactures computer disk drives, computers,
    peripherals, and software.
(714) 970-0300
Jobline: (714) 970-0300, ask for x5050.

Middlebury College
Middlebury, VT 05753
Small, private college on a hill overlooking the village of
    Middlebury and Lake Champlain.
(802) 388-3711
Jobline: (802) 388-3711, press 5627, then 5627#, then #.
Off-campus jobs.

Midlantic National Bank
499 Thornall Street, Edison, NJ 08818
Operates national commercial banks.
(908) 321-8000
Jobline: (908) 321-2562

Midwest City (city)
100 N. Midwest Boulevard, Midwest City, OK 73110
Provides municipal services such as police, firefighting,
    libraries, parks, and public works.
(405) 739-1234
Jobline: (405) 739-1236

Milford Memorial Hospital
Clarke Avenue, P.O. Box 199, Milford, DE 19963
Not-for-profit hospital with more than 100 beds.
(302) 422-3311
Jobline: (302) 424-5519

Milpitas (city)
455 E. Calaveras Boulevard, Milpitas, CA 95035
Provides municipal services such as police, firefighting,
    libraries, parks, and public works.
(408) 942-2321
Jobline: (408) 262-5146

Milwaukee (city)
200 E. Wells Street, Milwaukee, WI 53202
Provides municipal services such as police, firefighting,
    libraries, parks, and public works.
(414) 286-3751
Jobline: (414) 286-5555

Milwaukee County
901 N. 9th Street, Milwaukee, WI 53233
Provides county services such as sheriffs, courts, motor
    vehicle registration, and social services.
(414) 278-4143
Jobline: (414) 278-5321

Minneapolis (city)
Public Health Center Building, 312 3rd Avenue South,
    Minneapolis, MN 55415
Provides municipal services such as police, firefighting,
    libraries, parks, and public works.
(612) 673-2282
Jobline: (612) 673-2666
Open jobs.

Jobline: (612) 673-2999
Promotional jobs.

Minneapolis Cityline
3415 University Avenue West, Saint Paul, MN 55114
Provides information on a variety of topics for the
    Minneapolis/St. Paul area.
(612) 642-4559
Jobline: (612) 645-6060, x 5628.
Professional and administrative jobs.

Minneapolis Cityline (cont.)
Jobline: (612) 645-6060, x 5629.
Financial and accounting jobs.

Jobline: (612) 645-6060, x 5630.
Sales and marketing jobs.

Jobline: (612) 645-6060, x 5631.
Computers and technical engineering jobs.

Jobline: (612) 645-6060, x 5632.
Office support and clerical jobs.

Jobline: (612) 645-6060, x 5633.
Secretarial typing jobs.

Jobline: (612) 645-6060, x5634.
Word processing jobs.

Jobline: (612) 645-6060, x5635.
Health care jobs.

Jobline: (612) 645-6060, x5636.
Industrial, construction, and labor jobs.

Jobline: (612) 645-6060, x5637.
Driving and transportation jobs.

Jobline: (612) 645-6060, x5638.
Restaurant and food service jobs.

Jobline: (612) 645-6060, x5639.
Miscellaneous jobs.

Jobline: (612) 645-6060, x5640.
Part-time and seasonal jobs.

Jobline: (612) 645-6060, x5641.
Temporary jobs.

Minnesota (state)
200 Centennial Building, 658 Cedar Street,
    Minneapolis, MN 55416
Provides state services such as conservation,
    education, highways, prisons, and welfare.
(612) 296-6700
Jobline: (612) 296-2616

Mirage
3400 Las Vegas Boulevard South, Las Vegas, NV
    89109
3,044-room hotel.
(702) 791-7111
Jobline: (702) 791-7111, ask for job hotline.

Miramar Sheraton Hotel
101 Wilshire Boulevard, Santa Monica, CA 90401
305-room hotel in the Los Angeles area.
(310) 576-7777
Jobline: (310) 319-3145

Mission Federal Credit Union
P.O. Box 919023, San Diego, CA 92191
Provides banking and other financial and consumer
    services.
(619) 546-2000
Jobline: (619) 546-2010

Mississippi State University
Mississippi State, MS 39762
Medium-sized, public, comprehensive university in
    Starkville, 65 miles north of Meridian.
(601) 325-2323
Jobline: (601) 325-4132

Mobil Corp.
3225 Gallows Road, Fairfax, VA 22037
Extracts, refines, transports, and markets petroleum
    and petroleum products.
(703) 846-3000
Jobline: (703) 846-2777
Corporate jobs.

Jobline: (703) 849-6005
Marketing jobs.

Mobile County school board
P.O. Box 1327, Mobile, AL 36633
Oversees Mobile County's schools.
(205) 690-8077
Jobline: (205) 690-8394

Modesto (city)
801 11th Street, Modesto, CA 95354
Provides municipal services such as police, firefighting,
    libraries, parks, and public works.
(209) 577-5402
Jobline: (209) 577-5498

Monroe County
5100 W. College Road, Key West, FL 33040
Provides county services such as sheriffs, courts, motor
    vehicle registration, and social services.
(305) 292-4557
Jobline: (305) 292-4457

Montana State University
Bozeman, MT 59717
Medium-sized, public, comprehensive university in
    Bozeman.
(406) 994-0211
Jobline: (406) 994-3343

Montebello (city)
1600 W. Beverly Boulevard, Montebello, CA 90640
Provides municipal services such as police, firefighting,
    libraries, parks, and public works.
(213) 887-1377
Jobline: (213) 887-1380

Monterey (city)
399 Madison, Monterey, CA 93940
Provides municipal services such as police, firefighting,
    libraries, parks, and public works.
(408) 646-3765
Jobline: (408) 646-3751

Monterey County
240 Church Street, Room 218, Salinas, CA 93901
Provides county services such as sheriffs, courts, motor
    vehicle registration, and social services.
(408) 647-7716
Jobline: (408) 647-7726

Monterey Marriott
350 Calle Principal, Monterey, CA 93940
350-room hotel.
(408) 694-4234
Jobline: (408) 647-4066

Montgomery (city and county)
103 N. Perry Street, P.O. Box 1111, Montgomery, AL
  36101-1111
Provides government services such as police,
  firefighting, libraries, parks, and public works.
(205) 241-2675
Jobline: (205) 241-2217

Montgomery College
51 Mannakee Street, Rockville, MD 20850
Large, state- and locally-supported, 2-year college with
  three campuses near Washington, D.C.
(301) 279-5353
Jobline: (301) 279-5373
Staff jobs.

Jobline: (301) 279-5374
Faculty jobs.

Montgomery County
451 W. 3rd Street, Dayton, OH 45402
Provides county services such as sheriffs, courts, motor
  vehicle registration, and social services.
(513) 225-4018
Jobline: (513) 225-6128

Morehead State University
Morehead, KY 40351
Medium-sized, public, comprehensive institution in
  Morehead, 60 miles from Lexington.
(606) 783-2221
Jobline: (606) 783-2101

Morgan Hill (city)
17555 Peak Avenue, Morgan Hill, CA 95037
Provides municipal services such as police, firefighting,
  libraries, parks, and public works.
(408) 779-7271
Jobline: (408) 779-7276

Morton Electronic Materials
2631 Michelle Drive, Tustin, CA 92680
Manufactures photo resists, solder masks, specialty
  inks and coatings, and other products.
(714) 730-4200
Jobline: (714) 730-4200, ask for x5020.

Motorola Inc.
1303 E. Algonquin Road, Schaumburg, IL 60196
Manufactures radio and TV communications equipment,
  semiconductors, and electronic products.
(708) 576-5000
Jobline: (708) 576-2551

Mount Holyoke College
South Hadley, MA 01075-1497
Small, liberal arts college for women in the Connecticut
  River Valley.
(413) 538-2000
Jobline: (413) 538-2024

Mountain View (city)
500 Castro Street, Mountain View, CA 94041
Provides municipal services such as police, firefighting,
  libraries, parks, and public works.
(415) 903-6309
Jobline: (415) 903-6310

Multnomah County
Portland Building, Room 1430, 1120 SW 5th Avenue,
  Portland, OR 97204
Provides county services such as sheriffs, courts, motor
  vehicle registration, and social services.
(503) 248-5015
Jobline: (503) 248-5035

Multnomah Education Service District
11611 NE Ainsworth Circle, Portland, OR 97220
Provides special education programs for school districts
  in the Portland area.
(503) 255-1841
Jobline: (503) 257-1510

Munson Medical Center
1105 6th Street, Traverse City, MI 49684
Not-for-profit hospital with more than 300 beds.
(616) 922-9000
Jobline: (616) 935-7390

Murray (city)
5025 S. State Street, Murray, UT 84157
Provides municipal services such as police, firefighting,
  libraries, parks, and public works.
(801) 264-2656
Jobline: (801) 264-2525, press 2.

Mutual of Omaha Insurance Co.
Mutual of Omaha Plaza, 3301 Dodge Street, Omaha,
  NE 68175
Provides life and other types of insurance.
(402) 342-7600
Jobline: (402) 978-2040

Napa (city)
955 School Street, Napa, CA 94559
Provides municipal services such as police, firefighting,
  libraries, parks, and public works.
(707) 257-9505
Jobline: (707) 257-9542

Napa County
1195 3rd Street, Room 303, Napa, CA 94559
Provides county services such as sheriffs, courts, motor
  vehicle registration, and social services.
(707) 253-4303
Jobline: (707) 253-4808

Nashville (city) and Davidson County
214 Stahlman Building, 211 Union Street, Nashville, TN
  37201
Provides municipal services such as police, firefighting,
  libraries, parks, and public works.
(615) 862-6640
Jobline: (615) 862-6660

Nashville Airport Marriott
I-40 and Briley Parkway at Elm Hill Park, Nashville, TN
   37210
399-room hotel.
(615) 889-9300
Jobline: (615) 872-2952

National Aeronautics and Space Administration
Ames Research Center
Mail Stop 241-6, Moffett Field, CA 94035-1000
Manages a diverse program of research and
   development in support of the U.S.'s aerospace
   efforts.
(415) 604-5610
Jobline: (415) 604-8000

Goddard Space Flight Center
Building 1, Room 160, Greenbelt, MD 20771
Conducts development and flight operations for
   Earth-orbital spacecraft and experiments.
(301) 286-7918
Jobline: (301) 286-5326

National Bank of Alaska
301 W. Northern Lights Boulevard, Anchorage, AK
   99503
Operates national commercial banks.
(907) 276-1132
Jobline: (907) 265-2197

National City (city)
1245 National City Boulevard, National City, CA 91320
Provides municipal services such as police, firefighting,
   libraries, parks, and public works.
(619) 336-4300
Jobline: (619) 336-4306

National City Bank, Columbus
155 E. Broad Street, Columbus, OH 43251
Operates national commercial banks.
(614) 463-7100
Jobline: (614) 463-6736

National City Bank, Indiana
1 Merchants Plaza, Indianapolis, IN 46255
Operates national commercial banks.
(317) 267-7000
Jobline: (317) 267-7700

National City Bank, Kentucky
101 S. 5th Street, P.O. Box 36000, Louisville, KY 40233
Operates national commercial banks.
(502) 581-4200
Jobline: (502) 581-5627
Exempt jobs.

Jobline: (502) 581-7678
Non-exempt jobs.

National Processing Center
31 Durrett Lane, Louisville, KY 40217
Processes checks and performs other central
   operations.
(502) 364-2000
Jobline: (502) 364-2381

National City Bank, Northeast
1 Cascade Plaza, Akron, OH 44308
Operates national commercial banks.
(216) 375-8300
Jobline: (216) 375-8685

National City Bank, Northwest
405 Madison Avenue, P.O. Box 1688, Toledo, OH 43603
Operates national commercial banks.
(419) 259-7700
Jobline: (419) 259-6710

National Endowment for the Arts
1100 Pennsylvania Avenue NW, Washington, DC 20506
Fosters, nurtures, and sustains artistic excellence in the
   U.S. through a series of grants.
(202) 682-5400
Jobline: (202) 682-5799

National Endowment for the Humanities
1100 Pennsylvania Avenue NW, Washington, DC 20506
Supports research, education, and public programs in
   the humanities through a series of grants.
(202) 606-8438
Jobline: (202) 606-8281

National Medical Enterprises Inc.
2700 Colorado Avenue, Santa Monica, CA 90404
Owns and operates acute care hospitals, psychiatric
   facilities, and related health care businesses.
(310) 998-8000
Jobline: (310) 998-8500

National Railroad Passenger Corp. (Amtrak)
60 Massachusetts Avenue NE, Washington, DC 20002
Operates line-haul railroads.
(202) 906-3000
Jobline: (202) 906-3866

National Renewable Energy Laboratory
1617 Cole Boulevard, Golden, CO 80401
Contracts with the U.S. Department of Energy to
   conduct research on all aspects of renewable energy.
(303) 231-1000
Jobline: (303) 628-4650

National Science Foundation
1800 G Street NW, Washington, DC 20550
Promotes the progress of science and engineering
   through research and educational programs.
(202) 357-7602
Jobline: (202) 357-7735

NationsBank of Florida NA
400 N. Ashley Street, Tampa, FL 33602
Operates national commercial banks.
(813) 224-5151
Jobline: (813) 224-5921

NationsBank of Georgia NA
600 Peachtree Street, Atlanta, GA 30303
Operates national commercial banks.
(404) 581-2121
Jobline: (404) 491-4530

NationsBank of Maryland NA
6610 Rockledge Drive, Bethesda, MD 20817
Operates national commercial banks.
(301) 270-5000
Jobline: (301) 897-0547

NationsBank of Tennessee NA
1 NationsBank Plaza, Nashville, TN 37239
Operates national commercial banks.
(615) 749-3333
Jobline: (615) 749-3900

NationsBank of Texas NA
901 Main Street, Dallas, TX 75202
Operates national commercial banks.
(214) 508-6262
Jobline: (214) 712-2103

NationsBank of Virginia NA
1 Commercial Place, Norfolk, VA 23510
Operates national commercial banks.
(804) 446-3726
Jobline: (804) 441-4451

Nationwide Mutual Insurance Co.
1 Nationwide Plaza, Columbus, OH 43216
Provides various types of insurance, operates radio and
    TV stations, and develops land.
(614) 249-7111
Jobline: (614) 249-5725

Navy Federal Credit Union
P.O. Box 3000, Merrifield, VA 22119
Provides banking & other financial and consumer services.
(703) 255-8000
Jobline: (703) 255-8800

Nebraska (state)
301 Centennial Mall South, Lincoln, NE 68508
Provides state services such as conservation,
    education, highways, prisons, and welfare.
(402) 471-2075
Jobline: (402) 471-2200

Nebraska (state) Job Service
1010 N Street, Lincoln, NE 68508
Seeks workers for private employers.
(402) 471-2275
Jobline: (402) 471-3607
Part-time and temporary jobs.

Neutrogena Corp.
5760 W. 96th Street, Los Angeles, CA 90045
Produces cosmetics, hair preparations, face creams,
    and other skin care products.
(310) 642-1150
Jobline: (310) 216-5238

Nevada (state)
2501 E. Sahara Avenue, Las Vegas, NV 89104
Provides state services such as conservation,
    education, highways, prisons, and welfare.
(702) 486-4017
Jobline: (702) 486-4020

209 E. Musser Street, Carson City, NV 89701
(702) 687-4050
Jobline: (702) 687-4160

Nevada County
950 Maidu Avenue, Nevada City, CA 95959
Provides county services such as sheriffs, courts, motor
    vehicle registration, and social services.
(916) 265-1225
Jobline: (916) 265-1366

Nevada Power Co.
6226 W. Sahara Avenue, Las Vegas, NV 89102
Generates, transmits, and distributes electric power.
(702) 367-5212
Jobline: (702) 367-5200

New Haven (city)
200 Orange Street, New Haven, CT 06510
Provides municipal services such as police, firefighting,
    libraries, parks, and public works.
(203) 787-6488
Jobline: (203) 787-8265

New Jersey (state) Corrections Department
CN 860, Trenton, NJ 08625
Provides correctional programs and services.
(609) 633-0477
Jobline: (609) 633-0496

New Jersey (state) Personnel Department
44 S. Clinton Avenue, Trenton, NJ 08609
Administers exams for state and local positions.
(201) 648-2565
Jobline: (609) 292-8668, press 2.
Police and firefighting jobs.

New Mexico State University
Las Cruces, NM 88003
Medium-sized, public, multipurpose institution with a
    main campus in Las Cruces, north of El Paso.
(505) 646-0111
Jobline: (505) 646-1900

New York Hilton & Towers
1335 Avenue of the Americas, New York, NY 10019
2,042-room hotel.
(212) 586-7000
Jobline: (212) 586-7000, ask for x5719.

Newport News (city)
2400 Washington Avenue, Newport News, VA 23607
Provides municipal services such as police, firefighting,
    libraries, parks, and public works.
(804) 247-8444
Jobline: (804) 928-9281, press 1.

Newsday Inc.
235 Pinelawn Road, Melville, NY 11747
Publishes newspapers.
(516) 454-2020
Jobline: (516) 843-2076
Telemarketing jobs on Long Island.
Recording asks for name, address, etc.

Jobline: (718) 575-2498
Telemarketing jobs in Queens.
Recording asks for name, address, etc.

Nichols Institute
33608 Ortega Highway, San Juan Capistrano, CA 92690-6130
Provides diagnostic and substance abuse testing, and manufactures diagnostic test kits.
(714) 728-4000
Jobline: (714) 728-4526

Nike Inc.
1 Bowerman Drive, Beaverton, OR 97005
Manufactures athletic shoes, athletic suits, shorts, and other clothing.
(503) 671-6453
Jobline: (503) 644-4224

Norfolk (city)
City Hall Building, 4th Floor, 810 Union Street, Norfolk, VA 25301
Provides municipal services such as police, firefighting, libraries, parks, and public works.
(804) 441-2391
Jobline: (804) 627-8768

Norfolk State University
Norfolk, VA 23504
Medium-sized, public, comprehensive university in Norfolk.
(804) 683-8600
Jobline: (804) 683-8184

Norfolk Waterside Marriott
235 E. Main Street, Norfolk, VA 23510
405-room hotel.
(804) 627-4200
Jobline: (804) 628-6491

Norman (city)
201-C W. Gray Street, Norman, OK 73069
Provides municipal services such as police, firefighting, libraries, parks, and public works.
(405) 366-5482
Jobline: (405) 366-5321

North Carolina (state) Office of the Controller
3700 Wake Forest Road, Raleigh, NC 27609
Provides financial and information services for the North Carolina state government.
(919) 981-5004
Jobline: (919) 715-5627

North Carolina State University
Raleigh, NC 27695-7103
Large, public, comprehensive institution in Raleigh.
(919) 515-2011
Jobline: (919) 515-3737, press 2.

North Colorado Medical Center
1801 16th Street, Greeley, CO 80631
Not-for-profit hospital with more than 200 beds.
(303) 352-4121
Jobline: (303) 350-6397
Nursing jobs.

Jobline: (303) 350-6565
Jobs other than nursing.

North Dakota (state) Job Service
216 N. 2nd Street, Bismarck, ND 58502
Seeks workers for private and public employers.
(701) 221-5047
Jobline: (701) 221-5049

North Dakota State University
Fargo, ND 58105
Medium-sized, public, comprehensive institution with a main campus in Fargo.
(701) 237-8525
Jobline: (701) 237-8273
Current part-time jobs in the community.
Ask for tape 3008.

Secretarial jobs.
Ask for tape 3021.

Trade, technical, and food service jobs.
Ask for tape 3022.

Professional research jobs.
Ask for tape 3023.

Professional jobs other than research.
Ask for tape 3024.

North Harris Montgomery Community College District
250 Sam Houston Parkway, Houston, TX 77060
Includes North Harris College and Tomball College.
(713) 591-3500
Jobline: (713) 591-3534

North Island Federal Credit Union
P.O. Box 85833, San Diego, CA 92186
Provides banking and other financial and consumer services.
(619) 656-6525
Jobline: (619) 656-6525, press 1, then 4.

North Las Vegas (city)
220 Civic Center Drive, North Las Vegas, NV 89030
Provides municipal services such as police, firefighting, libraries, parks, and public works.
(702) 649-0257
Jobline: (702) 642-9266

North Miami (city)
776 NE 125th Street, North Miami, FL 33161
Provides municipal services such as police, firefighting, libraries, parks, and public works.
(305) 893-6511
Jobline: (305) 895-8095

North Miami Beach (city)
17011 NE 19th Avenue, North Miami Beach, FL 33162
Provides municipal services such as police, firefighting, libraries, parks, and public works.
(305) 948-2918
Jobline: (305) 947-7581, x37.

North Orange County Community College District
1000 N. Lemon Street, Fullerton, CA 92634
Includes Cypress College and Fullerton College.
(714) 871-4030
Jobline: (714) 870-7371

Northeastern University
Boston, MA 02115
Small, private, multipurpose institution with a main
  campus near Boston's Back Bay.
(617) 373-2000
Jobline: (617) 373-5373

Northern Arizona University
Flagstaff, AZ 86011
Medium-sized, public institution.
(602) 523-9011
Jobline: (602) 523-5627

Northern Illinois University
DeKalb, IL 60115
Large, public institution with a main campus in DeKalb,
  65 miles west of Chicago.
(815) 753-1000
Jobline: (815) 753-1051

Northern Kentucky University
Highland Heights, KY 41076
Medium-sized, public university seven miles southeast
  of Cincinnati.
(606) 572-5100
Jobline: (606) 572-5201

Northern Virginia Community College
Annandale, VA 22003
Large, state-supported, 2-year college in Annandale.
(703) 323-3328
Jobline: (703) 323-3444

Northglenn (city)
11701 Community Center Drive, Northglenn, CO 80233
Provides municipal services such as police, firefighting,
  libraries, parks, and public works.
(303) 450-8732
Jobline: (303) 450-8789

Norwest Bank Arizona NA
3300 N. Central Avenue, Phoenix, AZ 85012
Operates national commercial banks.
(602) 248-2223
Jobline: (602) 248-1283

Norwest Bank Denver NA
1740 Broadway, Denver, CO 80274
Operates national commercial banks.
(303) 861-8811
Jobline: (303) 863-5627

Norwest Bank Fort Wayne NA
P.O. Box 960, Fort Wayne, IN 46801
Operates national commercial banks.
(219) 461-6000
Jobline: (219) 461-6318

Norwest Corp.
6th Street and Marquette Avenue, Minneapolis, MN
  55479
Bank holding company that operates national and state
  commercial banks and other banking businesses.
(612) 667-1234
Jobline: (612) 667-5627

Nueces County
901 Leopard Street, Suite 306, Corpus Christi, TX
  78401
Provides county services such as sheriffs, courts, motor
  vehicle registration, and social services.
(512) 888-0208
Jobline: (512) 888-0563

NYNEX Corp.
335 Madison Avenue, New York, NY 10017
Provides local and other telephone services, directories,
  equipment financing, and other services.
(212) 370-7400
Jobline: (212) 395-2800

Oakland (city)
505 14th Street, Oakland, CA 94612
Provides municipal services such as police, firefighting,
  libraries, parks, and public works.
(510) 238-3307
Jobline: (510) 238-3111

Oakland University
Rochester, MI 48309
Medium-sized, public institution between Pontiac and
  Rochester, near Detroit.
(810) 370-2100
Jobline: (810) 370-4500

Occidental College
1600 Campus Road, Los Angeles, CA 90041
Small, private, liberal arts college in residential Los
  Angeles.
(213) 259-2613
Jobline: (213) 259-2615

Oceanside (city)
300 N. Hill Street, Oceanside, CA 92054
Provides municipal services such as police, firefighting,
  libraries, parks, and public works.
(619) 966-4485
Jobline: (619) 966-4499

Office of Personnel Management
Career America Connection
4685 Log Cabin Drive, Macon, GA 31298
Provides Federal employment information, including the
  complete Federal Job Opportunities List.
(912) 744-2092
Jobline: (912) 757-3000
Includes jobs nationwide.

Federal Job Information Center
222 W. 7th Avenue, #22, Room 156, Anchorage, AK
  99513-7572
(907) 271-5821
Jobline: (907) 271-5821
Includes jobs in Alaska.

Office of Personnel Management (cont.)
Federal Job Information Center
Century Plaza Building, Room 1415 3225 N. Central
    Avenue, Phoenix, AZ 85012
(602) 640-4800
Jobline: (602) 640-4800
Includes jobs in Arizona.

Federal Job Information Center
211 Main Street, 2nd Floor, Room 235, P.O. Box 7405,
    San Francisco, CA 94120
(415) 744-7237
Jobline: (415) 744-5627
Includes jobs in the San Francisco area of California.

Federal Job Information Center
Federal Building, Suite 4218, 880 Front Street, San
    Diego, CA 92101-8821
(619) 557-6165
Jobline: (619) 557-6165
Includes jobs in the San Diego area of California.

Federal Job Information Center
9650 Flair Drive, Suite 100A, El Monte, CA 91731
(818) 575-6510
Jobline: (818) 575-6510
Includes jobs in the Los Angeles area of California and
    part of Nevada.

Federal Job Information Center
1029 J Street, Room 202, Sacramento, CA 95814
(916) 551-1464
Jobline: (916) 551-1464
Includes jobs in the Sacramento area of California and
    part of Nevada.

Federal Job Information Center
12345 W. Alameda Parkway, P.O. Box 25167,
    Lakewood, CO 80225
(303) 969-7055
Jobline: (303) 969-7055
Includes jobs in Colorado.

Jobline: (303) 969-7052
Includes jobs in Montana and Wyoming.

Jobline: (303) 969-7053
Includes jobs in Utah.

Federal Job Information Center
1900 E Street NW, Room 1416, Washington, DC 20415
(202) 606-2424
Jobline: (202) 606-2700, press 1, then 2, then 406.
Includes jobs in the DC metropolitan area.

Federal Job Information Center
Richard B. Russell Federal Building, Room 940A, 75
    Spring Street SW, Atlanta, GA 30303
(404) 331-3459
Jobline: (404) 331-4315
Includes jobs in Georgia.

Federal Job Information Center
Federal Building, Room 5316, 300 Ala Moana
    Boulevard, Honolulu, HI 96850
(808) 541-2791
Jobline: (808) 541-2791
Includes jobs on Oahu.

Jobline: (808) 541-2784
Includes jobs on neighbor islands, Guam, and the
    Pacific territories.

Federal Job Information Center
175 W. Jackson Boulevard, Room 530, Chicago, IL
    60604
(312) 353-2901
Jobline: (312) 353-6192
Includes jobs in most of Illinois and part of Iowa.

Jobline: (312) 353-6189
Includes jobs in part of Wisconsin.

Federal Job Information Center
One-Twenty Building, Room 101, 120 S. Market Street,
    Wichita KS 67202
(816) 426-7820
Jobline: (816) 426-7820
Includes jobs in most of Kansas.

Federal Job Information Center
300 W. Pratt Street, Room 101, Baltimore, MD 21201
(410) 962-3822
Jobline: (410) 962-3822
Includes jobs in most of Maryland.

Federal Job Information Center
Thomas P. O'Neill, Jr. Federal Building, 10 Causeway
    Street, Boston, MA 02222-1031
(617) 565-5900
Jobline: (617) 565-5900
Includes jobs in the six New England states.

Federal Job Information Center
477 Michigan Avenue, Room 565, Detroit, MI 48226
(313) 226-6950
Jobline: (313) 226-6950
Includes jobs in Michigan and parts of Indiana, Ohio,
    and Kentucky.

Federal Job Information Center
Bishop Henry Whipple Federal Building, Room 501, 1
    Federal Drive, Fort Snelling, Twin Cities, MN 55111
(612) 725-3430
Jobline: (612) 725-3430
Includes jobs in Minnesota, North Dakota, South
    Dakota, and part of Wisconsin.

Federal Job Information Center
400 Old Post Office Building, 815 Olive Street, Saint
    Louis, MO 63101
(314) 539-2285
Jobline: (314) 539-2285
Includes jobs in the St. Louis area of Missouri and part
    of Illinois.

Office of Personnel Management (cont.)
Federal Job Information Center
Federal Building, Room 134, 601 E. 12th Street,
Kansas City, MO 64106
(816) 426-5705
Jobline: (816) 426-5702
Includes jobs in parts of Missouri, Iowa, and Kansas.

Jobline: (816) 426-7819
Includes jobs in Nebraska.

Federal Job Information Center
505 Marquette Avenue, Suite 910, Albuquerque, NM
87102
(505) 766-2906
Jobline: (505) 766-5583
Includes jobs in New Mexico.

Federal Job Information Center
Jacob K. Javits Federal Building, Room 120, 26
Federal Plaza
New York, NY 10278
(212) 264-0422
Jobline: (212) 264-0422
Includes jobs in the New York City area of New York.

Federal Job Information Center
100 S. Clinton Street, P.O. Box 7257, Syracuse, NY
13260
(315) 423-5660
Jobline: (315) 423-5660
Includes jobs in the Syracuse area of New York.

Federal Job Information Center
4407 Bland Road, Suite 202, Raleigh, NC 27609-6296
(919) 790-2822
Jobline: (919) 790-2822
Includes jobs in North Carolina and South Carolina.

Federal Job Information Center
Federal Building, Room 506, 200 W. 2nd Street,
Dayton, OH 45402
(513) 225-2720
Jobline: (513) 225-2720
Includes jobs in West Virginia and parts of Ohio and
Kentucky.

Federal Job Information Center
Federal Building, Room 376, 1220 SW 3rd Avenue,
Portland, OR 97204
Provides federal employment information, including part
of the federal job opportunities list.
(503) 326-3141
Jobline: (503) 326-3141
Includes jobs in Oregon.

Federal Job Information Center
U.S. Federal Building, Room 340, 150 Carlos Avenue,
San Juan, PR 00918-1710
(809) 766-5242
Jobline: (809) 766-5242
Includes jobs in Puerto Rico.

Jobline: (809) 774-8790
Includes jobs in the Virgin Islands.

Federal Job Information Center
8610 Broadway, Room 305, San Antonio, TX 78217
(210) 805-2423
Jobline: (210) 805-2406
Includes jobs in the San Antonio area of Texas.

Jobline: (210) 805-2402
Includes jobs in Oklahoma, Arkansas, Louisiana, and
parts of Texas.

Federal Job Information Center
1100 Commerce Street, Room 6B10, Dallas, TX 75242
(214) 767-8227
Jobline: (214) 767-8035
Includes jobs in the Dallas area of Texas.

Federal Job Information Center
Federal Building, Room 110, 915 2nd Avenue, Seattle,
WA 98174
(206) 220-6400
Jobline: (206) 220-6400
Includes jobs in Washington and Idaho.

Ohio (state) Environmental Protection Agency
1800 Watermark Drive, Columbus, OH 43215
Provides environmental protection programs & services.
(614) 644-2100
Jobline: (614) 644-2102

Ohio State University, Columbus
Columbus, OH 43210
Large, major, comprehensive state university with a
main campus in Columbus.
(614) 292-6446
Jobline: (614) 292-1212

Ohio University
Athena, OH 45701
Medium-sized, public, comprehensive institution in
Athens, 75 miles southeast of Columbus.
(614) 593-1000
Jobline: (614) 593-4080

Oklahoma City (city)
201 Channing Square, Oklahoma City, OK 73102
Provides municipal services such as police, firefighting,
libraries, parks, and public works.
(405) 297-2530
Jobline: (405) 297-2419

Oklahoma State University
Stillwater, OK 74078
Medium-sized, public, comprehensive institution in
Stillwater, in north-central Oklahoma.
(405) 744-5000
Jobline: (405) 744-7692

Old Dominion University
Norfolk, VA 23529-0050
Medium-sized, university with an urban campus near
central Norfolk.
(804) 683-3000
Jobline: (804) 683-3066
Clerical jobs.

Jobline: (804) 683-4011
Administrative, professional, technical, service, trade,
and other jobs.

Olympia (city)
900 Plum Street SE, Olympia, WA 98501
Provides municipal services such as police, firefighting,
    libraries, parks, and public works.
(206) 753-8442
Jobline: (206) 753-8383

Omaha (city)
1819 Farnam Street, Room 506, Omaha, NE 68183
Provides municipal services such as police, firefighting,
    libraries, parks, and public works.
(402) 444-5300
Jobline: (402) 444-5302

Omni Charlotte
222 E. 3rd Street, Charlotte, NC 28202
410-room hotel.
(704) 377-6664
Jobline: (704) 377-6664, ask for x4333.

Omni Houston Hotel
4 Riverway Drive, Houston, TX 77056
381-room hotel.
(713) 871-8181
Jobline: (713) 624-4823

Omni Inner Harbor Hotel
101 W. Fayette Street, Baltimore, MD 21201
702-room hotel.
(410) 752-1100
Jobline: (410) 385-6442

Omni International Hotel
1601 Biscayne Boulevard, Miami, FL 33132
550-room hotel.
(305) 374-0000
Jobline: (305) 374-8065

Omni Parker House
Tremont and School Streets, Boston, MA 02108
535-room hotel.
(617) 227-8600
Jobline: (617) 725-1623

Omni Shoreham Hotel
2500 Calvert Street NW, Washington, DC 20008
770-room hotel.
(202) 234-0700
Jobline: (202) 483-1119

Ontario (city)
303 E. B Street, Ontario, CA 91764
Provides municipal services such as police, firefighting,
    libraries, parks, and public works.
(909) 391-0669
Jobline: (909) 391-2580

Orange (city)
300 E. Chapman Avenue, Orange, CA 92666
Provides municipal services such as police, firefighting,
    libraries, parks, and public works.
(714) 744-7255
Jobline: (714) 744-7262

Orange County
10 Civic Center Plaza, Santa Ana, CA 92701
Provides county services such as sheriffs, courts, motor
    vehicle registration, and social services.
(714) 834-2828
Jobline: (714) 834-5627

Orange County Register
625 Grand Avenue, P.O. Box 11626, Santa Ana, CA
    92711
Publishes newspapers.
(714) 835-1234
Jobline: (714) 664-5099

Orange Park Medical Center
2001 Kingsley Avenue, Orange Park, FL 32073
For-profit hospital with more than 200 beds.
(904) 276-8500
Jobline: (904) 276-8562

Oregon (state)
605 Cottage Street SE, Salem, OR 97301
Provides state services such as conservation,
    education, highways, prisons, and welfare.
(503) 373-1199
Jobline: (503) 378-8344

**Oregon (state) Department of Environmental
Quality**
811 SW 6th Avenue, Portland, OR 97204
Provides environmental protection programs and
    services.
(503) 229-5696
Jobline: (503) 229-5785

Oregon (state) Employment Division
119 NE 4th Street, P.O. Box 10, Newport, OR 97365
Seeks workers for private employers.
(503) 265-8891
Jobline: (503) 265-5627

818 Commercial Avenue, 4th Floor, P.O. Box 805,
    Astoria, OR 97103
Seeks workers for private employers.
(503) 325-4821
Jobline: (503) 325-7856

2510 Oakmont Way, Eugene, OR 97401
Seeks workers for private employers.
(503) 686-7601
Jobline: (503) 686-7652

Oregon City School District No. 62
1417 12th Street, Oregon City, OR 97045
14-school district in Oregon City.
(503) 656-4283
Jobline: (503) 657-2465

Oregon State University
Corvallis, OR 97331
Medium-sized, comprehensive state university in
    Corvallis, south of Salem.
(503) 737-0123
Jobline: (503) 737-0554

Ortho Diagnostic Systems Inc.
1001 U.S. Route 202, Raritan, NJ 08869-0606
Produces in vitro and in vivo diagnostic substances.
(908) 218-8000
Jobline: (908) 218-8808

Ortho McNeil Pharmaceutical Corp.
U.S. Route 202, P.O. Box 300, Raritan, NJ 08869-0602
Produces pharmaceutical preparations.
(908) 218-6000
Jobline: (908) 218-6200

Oryx Energy Co.
13155 Noel Road, Dallas, TX 75240
Provides oil and gas exploration, production,
acquisition, and marketing.
(214) 715-4000
Jobline: (214) 715-8200, press 3.

Overseas Private Investment Corp.
1615 M Street NW, Washington, DC 20527
Assists U.S. investors in making profitable investments
in developing countries.
(202) 336-8400
Jobline: (202) 336-8682

Owen Healthcare Inc.
9800 Centre Parkway, Houston, TX 77036
Manages hospital pharmacies and materials, and
provides home health care.
(713) 777-8173
Jobline: (713) 777-8173, ask for x5627.

Oxnard (city)
300 W. 3rd Street, Oxnard, CA 93030
Provides municipal services such as police, firefighting,
libraries, parks, and public works.
(805) 385-7590
Jobline: (805) 385-7580

PACCAR Inc.
777 106th Avenue NE, Bellevue, WA 98004
Assembles trucks, provides motor vehicle parts and
accessories, and manufactures winches and pumps.
(206) 455-7400
Jobline: (206) 637-5011

Pacific Bell
33 New Montgomery Street, Suite 1100, San Francisco,
CA 94105
Provides local, long distance, and other telephone
services.
(415) 542-8926
Jobline: (415) 542-0817
Nonsalaried jobs.
Call (800) 924-5627 in California.

Jobline: (800) 255-7571
Technical and professional jobs.

Pacific Bell Directory
3470 Wilshire Boulevard, Los Angeles, CA 90010
Publishes telephone directories.
(800) 248-2800
Jobline: (800) 559-7442

Pacific Gas and Electric Co.
201 Mission Street, San Francisco, CA 94105
Produces, transmits, and distributes electric power and
natural gas, and develops land.
(415) 973-7000
Jobline: (415) 973-5200

Pacific Lutheran University
Tacoma, WA 98447
Small, church-affiliated university in Parkland, a suburb
of Tacoma.
(206) 531-6900
Jobline: (206) 535-8598

PacifiCorp
920 SW 6th Avenue, Portland, OR 97204
Produces electricity, petroleum, and natural gas, and
conducts surface mining for various ores.
(503) 464-5100
Jobline: (503) 464-6848

Palace Station
2411 W. Sahara Avenue, Las Vegas, NV 89102
1,030-room hotel.
(702) 367-2411
Jobline: (702) 253-2950

Palm Beach Community College
Lake Worth, FL 33461
Medium-sized, state-supported, 2-year college in Lake
Worth, near Miami.
(407) 439-8000
Jobline: (407) 439-8232

Palmdale (city)
38246 Sierra Highway, Palmdale, CA 93550
Provides municipal services such as police, firefighting,
libraries, parks, and public works.
(805) 267-5400
Jobline: (805) 267-5627

Palmer House Hilton Hotel
17 E. Monroe Street at State Street , Chicago, IL 60603
1,694-room hotel.
(312) 726-7500
Jobline: (312) 726-7500, ask for job hotline.

Palo Alto (city)
Civic Center, 250 Hamilton Avenue, Palo Alto, CA 94301
Provides municipal services such as police, firefighting,
libraries, parks, and public works.
(415) 329-2376
Jobline: (415) 329-2222

Palomar College
1140 W. Mission Road, San Marcos, CA 92069-1487
Large, state- and locally-supported, 2-year college in
San Marcos.
(619) 744-1150
Jobline: (619) 744-1150, x2199.

Pan Pacific
400 W. Broadway, San Diego, CA 92101-3580
436-room hotel.
(619) 239-4500
Jobline: (619) 338-3659

Pan Pacific Hotel San Francisco
500 Post Street, San Francisco, CA 94102
330-room hotel.
(415) 771-8600
Jobline: (415) 929-2011

Paramount (city)
16400 Colorado Avenue, Paramount, CA 90723
Provides municipal services such as police, firefighting,
  libraries, parks, and public works.
(310) 220-2027
Jobline: (310) 220-2080, press 8005.

Paramount Pictures Corp.
5555 Melrose Avenue, Los Angeles, CA 90038
Produces and distributes motion pictures, TV films, and
  video tapes.
(213) 956-5065
Jobline: (213) 956-5216

Parc Oakland
1001 Broadway, Oakland, CA 94607
488-room hotel.
(510) 541-4000
Jobline: (510) 451-4000, ask for x6072.

Park Hyatt San Francisco
333 Battery and Clay Streets, San Francisco, CA 94111
360-room hotel.
(415) 392-1234
Jobline: (415) 392-1234, ask for x2916.

Parkway Regional Medical Center
160 NW 170th Street, North Miami Beach, FL 33169
For-profit hospital with more than 300 beds.
(305) 651-1100
Jobline: (305) 651-1100, ask for job hotline.

Pasadena (city)
100 N. Garfield Avenue, Pasadena, CA 91104
Provides municipal services such as police, firefighting,
  libraries, parks, and public works.
(818) 405-4366
Jobline: (818) 405-4600

Pasadena City College
1570 E. Colorado Boulevard, Pasadena, CA 91106
Large, district-supported, 2-year college in Pasadena,
  near Los Angeles.
(818) 585-7388
Jobline: (818) 585-7257

Pasadena Hilton
150 S. Los Robles Avenue, Pasadena, CA 91101
291-room hotel in the Los Angeles area.
(818) 577-1000
Jobline: (818) 577-1000, ask for job hotline.

Peabody Orlando
9801 International Drive, Orlando, FL 32819
891-room hotel.
(407) 352-4000
Jobline: (407) 352-6481

Peace Corps
1990 K Street NW, Washington, DC 20526
Promotes world peace, friendship, and understanding
  between the American people and others.
(202) 606-3886
Jobline: (202) 606-3214

Pembroke Pines (city)
10100 Pines Boulevard, Pembroke Pines, FL 33026
Provides municipal services such as police, firefighting,
  libraries, parks, and public works.
(305) 431-4566
Jobline: (305) 437-1108

Pembroke State University
Pembroke, NC 28372
Small, institution in Pembroke, in south-central North
  Carolina.
(910) 521-6000
Jobline: (910) 521-6532

Pennington County
315 St. Joseph Street, Rapid City, SD 57701
Provides county services such as sheriffs, courts, motor
  vehicle registration, and social services.
(605) 394-2153
Jobline: (605) 394-8090

Pennsylvania State University
University Park, PA 16802
Large, public university with a main campus near State
  College, 70 miles northwest of Harrisburg.
(814) 865-4700
Jobline: (814) 865-5627

Pennzoil Co.
P.O. Box 2967, Houston, TX 77252
Extracts, refines, transports, and markets petroleum
  and petroleum products.
(713) 546-4000
Jobline: (713) 546-6630, press 1.

Pension Benefit Guarantee Corp.
202 K Street NW, Washington, DC 20006
Guarantees payment of pension benefits in
  private-sector pension plans.
(202) 326-4110
Jobline: (202) 326-4111

Peoria (city)
8401 W. Monroe Street, Peoria, AZ 85345
Provides municipal services such as police, firefighting,
  libraries, parks, and public works.
(602) 412-7100
Jobline: (602) 412-7105

Peoria County
324 Main Street, Room 501, Peoria, IL 61602
Provides county services such as sheriffs, courts, motor
  vehicle registration, and social services.
(309) 672-6947
Jobline: (309) 672-6943

Pepperdine University
Malibu, CA 90263
Small, independent university in Malibu, north of Los
Angeles.
(310) 456-4000
Jobline: (310) 456-4776
Off-campus jobs.

Peralta Community College System
333 E. 8th Street, Oakland, CA 94606
Includes Laney College, Merritt College, College of
Alameda, and Vista College.
(510) 466-7200
Jobline: (510) 466-7223

Personal Products Co.
Van Liew Avenue, Milltown, NJ 08850
Manufactures sanitary paper products.
(908) 524-0400
Jobline: (908) 524-0257

Pfizer Inc.
235 E. 42nd Street, New York, NY 10017
Produces drugs, surgical supplies, electromedical
equipment, perfumes, and other products.
(212) 573-2323
Jobline: (212) 573-3000

Phelps Dodge Corp.
2600 N. Central Avenue, Phoenix, AZ 85004
Mines and processes copper ore, and manufactures
motor vehicle wheels and rims.
(602) 234-8100
Jobline: (602) 234-8281

Philadelphia Electric Co.
2301 Market Street, Philadelphia, PA 19101
Generates, transmits, and distributes electric power,
and distributes natural gas.
(215) 841-4000
Jobline: (215) 841-4340

Phillips Petroleum Co.
7th Street and Keeler Avenue, Bartlesville, OK 74004
Extracts, refines, transports, and markets petroleum
and petroleum products.
(918) 661-6600
Jobline: (918) 661-5547

Phoenician
6000 E. Camelback Road, Scottsdale, AZ 85251
580-room hotel.
(602) 941-8200
Jobline: (602) 941-8200, ask for x1033.

Phoenix (city)
135 N. 2nd Avenue, Phoenix, AZ 85004
Provides municipal services such as libraries, parks,
and public works.
(602) 262-6605
Jobline: (602) 252-5627
All jobs but police and firefighting.

Jobline: (602) 262-7356
Police and firefighting jobs.

Pico Rivera (city)
6615 S. Passons Boulevard, Pico Rivera, CA 90660
Provides municipal services such as police, firefighting,
libraries, parks, and public works.
(310) 801-4379
Jobline: (310) 801-4387

Pier 66 Resort and Marina
2301 SE 17 Street Causeway, Fort Lauderdale, FL
33316
388-room hotel.
(305) 776-5121
Jobline: (305) 728-3583

Pierce College
Tacoma, WA 98498
Medium-sized, state-supported, 2-year college in
Tacoma, near Seattle.
(206) 964-6623
Jobline: (206) 964-7341

Pierce County
615 S. 9th Street, #200, Tacoma, WA 98405
Provides county services such as sheriffs, courts, motor
vehicle registration, and social services.
(206) 591-7480
Jobline: (206) 591-7466

Pima Community College District
4909 E. Broadway, Tucson, AZ 85709
Includes the East, West, Downtown, Desert Vista, and
Community Campuses.
(602) 748-4624
Jobline: (602) 748-4623

Pima County
150 W. Congress Street, Tucson, AZ 85701
Provides county services such as sheriffs, courts, motor
vehicle registration, and social services.
(602) 740-8176
Jobline: (602) 740-3530

Pinellas Park (city)
5141 78th Avenue North, Pinellas Park, FL 34665
Provides municipal services such as police, firefighting,
libraries, parks, and public works.
(813) 541-0803
Jobline: (813) 541-0703

Pioneer Electronics USA Inc.
2265 E. 220th Street, Long Beach, CA 90801-1639
Manufactures electric appliances, stereo components,
and TV and radio sets.
(310) 835-6177
Jobline: (310) 835-6177, ask for job hotline, then
press 2.

Pittsburgh (city)
City-County Building, 4th Floor, 414 Grant Street,
Pittsburgh, PA 15219
Provides municipal services such as police, firefighting,
libraries, parks, and public works.
(412) 255-2710
Jobline: (412) 255-2388

Placer County
175 Fulweiler Avenue, Auburn, CA 95603
Provides county services such as sheriffs, courts, motor
   vehicle registration, and social services.
(916) 889-4060
Jobline: (916) 889-4070

Pleasant Hill (city)
100 Gregory Lane, Pleasant Hill, CA 94523
Provides municipal services such as police, firefighting,
   libraries, parks, and public works.
(510) 671-5220
Jobline: (510) 671-5255

Pleasant Valley Hospital
2309 Antonio Avenue, Camarillo, CA 93010
Not-for-profit hospital with more than 100 beds.
(805) 389-5626
Jobline: (805) 389-5198

Pleasanton (city)
123 Main Street, Pleasanton, CA 94566
Provides municipal services such as police, firefighting,
   libraries, parks, and public works.
(510) 484-8012
Jobline: (510) 484-8356

PNC Bank
P.O. Box 7648, Philadelphia, PA 19101
Operates national commercial banks.
(215) 585-5000
Jobline: (800) 762-5627
Includes jobs throughout the Philadelphia area.

Pointe Hilton at Squaw Peak
7677 N. 16th Street, Phoenix, AZ 85020
576-room hotel.
(602) 997-2626
Jobline: (602) 861-9505

Pointe Hilton on South Mountain
7777 S. Pointe Parkway, Phoenix, AZ 85044
638-room hotel.
(602) 438-9000
Jobline: (602) 438-9303

Pomona (city)
505 S. Garey Avenue, Pomona, CA 91766
Provides municipal services such as police, firefighting,
   libraries, parks, and public works.
(909) 620-2291
Jobline: (909) 620-2290

Pomona College
Claremont, CA 91711-6312
Small, private, liberal arts college at the foot of the San
   Gabriel Mountains.
(909) 621-8000
Jobline: (909) 621-8477

Port of Seattle
Pier 69, 2711 Alaskan Way, Seattle, WA 98121
Manages the commercial activities of the port of Seattle.
(206) 728-3286
Jobline: (206) 728-3290

Portland (city)
1220 SW 5th Avenue, Room 170, Portland, OR 97204
Provides municipal services such as police, firefighting,
   libraries, parks, and public works.
(503) 823-4352
Jobline: (503) 823-4573

Portland Community College
Portland, OR 97219
Large, state- and locally-supported, 2-year college in
   Portland.
(503) 244-6111
Jobline: (503) 273-2826

Portland Hilton
921 SW 6th Avenue, Portland, OR 97204
455-room hotel.
(503) 226-1611
Jobline: (503) 220-2560

Portland School District No. 1J
501 N. Dixon Street, Portland, OR 97227
100-school district in Portland.
(503) 331-3545
Jobline: (503) 331-3102

Portsmouth (city)
City Hall, 2nd Floor, 801 Crawford Street, Portsmouth,
   VA 23704
Provides municipal services such as libraries, parks,
   and public works.
(804) 393-8622
Jobline: (804) 398-0682, x100.
Professional and technical jobs.

Jobline: (804) 398-0682, x102.
Clerical and labor trade jobs.

Jobline: (804) 398-0682, x245.
Police and firefighting jobs.

Poway (city)
13325 Civic Center Drive, Poway, CA 92064
Provides municipal services such as police, firefighting,
   libraries, parks, and public works.
(619) 679-4234
Jobline: (619) 679-4300

PPG Industries Inc.
1 PPG Place, Pittsburgh, PA 15272
Manufactures glass products, coatings and resins,
   electromedical apparatus, and other products.
(412) 434-3131
Jobline: (412) 434-2002

Premier Bank NA
P.O. Box 3399, Baton Rouge, LA 70821
Operates national commercial banks.
(504) 332-4011
Jobline: (504) 332-3512

Prescott (city)
201 S. Cortez Street P.O. Box 2059, Prescott, AZ 86302
Provides municipal services such as police, firefighting,
   libraries, parks, and public works.
(602) 776-6216
Jobline: (602) 776-6280

Primerit Bank
3300 W. Sahara Avenue, Las Vegas, NV 89102
Operates federal savings banks.
(702) 362-5555
Jobline: (702) 226-0466

Princeton University
Princeton, NJ 08544
Small, Ivy League university in Princeton, northeast of
    Trenton.
(609) 258-3000
Jobline: (609) 258-6130

Principal Mutual Life Insurance Co.
Principal Financial Group Division
711 High Street, Des Moines, IA 50392-0001
Provides life, accident, and health insurance, insurance
    adjusting, and other financial services.
(515) 247-5111
Jobline: (800) 525-2593

Proctor and Gamble Co.
1 Proctor and Gamble Plaza, Cincinnati, OH 45202
Produces soaps, detergents, deodorants, cleansers,
    hair products, cosmetics, and other products.
(513) 983-1100
Jobline: (513) 983-2125
Nondegreed jobs.

Jobline: (513) 983-7494
Degreed jobs.

Promus Companies Inc.
1023 Cherry Road, Memphis, TN 38117
Operates and franchises resort hotels and casinos.
(901) 762-8600
Jobline: (901) 748-7626

Provident Bank of Maryland
7210 Ambassador Road, Baltimore, MD 21244
Operates state commercial banks.
(410) 281-7000
Jobline: (410) 281-7263

Prudential Insurance Company of America
751 Broad Street, Newark, NJ 07102
Provides life, accident, and health insurance, annuities,
    and other financial products and services.
(201) 877-6000
Jobline: (201) 802-8494

Public Service Company of Colorado
550 15th Street, Denver, CO 80202
Produces electricity, gas, and steam heat.
(303) 571-7511
Jobline: (303) 571-7563

Public Utilities Commission of Ohio
180 E. Broad Street, Columbus, OH 43215
Regulates utility and transportation industries.
(614) 466-7330
Jobline: (614) 644-5656

Purdue University
West Lafayette, IN 47907
Large, public, comprehensive institution with a main
    campus in West Lafayette, on the Wabash River.
(317) 494-4600
Jobline: (317) 494-6957
Technical jobs.

Jobline: (317) 494-7417
Administrative jobs.

Jobline: (317) 494-7418
Clerical jobs.

Jobline: (317) 494-7419
Service jobs.

Putnam County Board of Education
P.O. Box 47, Winfield, WV 25213
Oversees Putnam County's schools.
(304) 586-0500
Jobline: (304) 586-0555
Includes jobs in the administrative offices and in
    schools.

Quaker Oats Co.
321 N. Clark Street, Chicago, IL 60610
Produces cereals, flour mixes and doughs, pasta,
    syrups, chili, pet food, and other food products.
(312) 222-7111
Jobline: (312) 222-7744

Radford University
Radford, VA 24142
Medium-sized, public, comprehensive institution in
    Radford, 40 miles southwest of Roanoke.
(703) 831-5000
Jobline: (703) 831-5825

Radisson Hotel Denver
1550 Court Place, Denver, CO 80202
740-room hotel.
(303) 893-3333
Jobline: (303) 893-0642

Radisson Hotel South
7800 Normandale Boulevard, Minneapolis, MN 55435
575-room hotel.
(612) 835-7800
Jobline: (612) 835-7800, ask for x6416.

Radisson Plaza Fort Worth
815 Main Street, Fort Worth, TX 76102
517-room hotel.
(817) 870-2100
Jobline: (817) 870-2100, ask for x1362.

Radisson Plaza Hotel
1500 Town Cente, Southfield, MI 48075
385-room hotel near Detroit.
(810) 827-4000
Jobline: (810) 827-4000, ask for personnel, then ask for
    job hotline.

Radisson Plaza Hotel & Golf Course
1400 Parkview Avenue, Manhattan Beach, CA 90266
380-room hotel near Los Angeles International Airport.
(310) 546-7511
Jobline: (310) 546-9933

Radisson Plaza Hotel at Mark Center
5000 Seminary Road, Alexandria, VA 22311
500-room hotel near Washington, D.C.
(703) 845-1010
Jobline: (703) 845-7654

Radisson Pontchartrain Hotel
2 Washington Boulevard, Detroit, MI 48226
451-room hotel.
(313) 965-0200
Jobline: (313) 965-0200, ask for x3853.

Raleigh (city)
Municipal Complex, P.O. Box 590, Raleigh, NC 27602
Provides municipal services such as police, firefighting,
   libraries, parks, and public works.
(919) 890-3315
Jobline: (919) 890-3305

Ralston Purina Co.
Checkerboard Square, Saint Louis, MO 63134
Produces pet foods, livestock feeds, batteries, cereals,
   bakery products, and other goods.
(314) 982-1000
Jobline: (314) 982-2962

Ramada Astrodome
2100 S. Braeswood Boulevard, Houston, TX 77030
339-room hotel.
(713) 797-9000
Jobline: (713) 797-9000, ask for job hotline.

Ramada Hotel Tyson's
7801 Leesburg Pike, Falls Church, VA 22043
404-room hotel near Washington, D.C.
(703) 893-1340
Jobline: (703) 821-3161

Ramada Renaissance Hotel
701 E. Campbell Road, Richardson, TX 75081
342-room hotel near Dallas.
(214) 231-9600
Jobline: (214) 231-9600, ask for x2096.

Ramada Renaissance Washington Tech World
999 9th Street NW, Washington, DC 20001
801-room hotel.
(202) 898-9000
Jobline: (202) 682-3456

Ramsey County
50 W. Kellogg Boulevard, Saint Paul, MN 55102
Provides county services such as sheriffs, courts, motor
   vehicle registration, and social services.
(612) 266-2700
Jobline: (612) 266-2666

Rancho Santiago College
17th Street at Bristol Street, Santa Ana, CA 92706
Large, state-supported, 2-year college in Santa Ana,
   near Los Angeles.
(714) 564-6000
Jobline: (714) 564-6499

Rapid City (city)
300 6th Street, Rapid City, SD 57701
Provides municipal services such as police, firefighting,
   libraries, parks, and public works.
(605) 394-4136
Jobline: (605) 394-5329

Red Lion Hotel Bellevue
300 112th Avenue SE, Bellevue, WA 98004
355-room hotel.
(206) 455-1300
Jobline: (206) 455-1300, ask for job hotline.

Red Lion Hotel Los Angeles Airport
6161 Centinela Avenue, Culver City, CA 90230
365-room hotel near Los Angeles Int'l Airport.
(310) 649-1776
Jobline: (310) 649-1776, ask for job hotline.

Red Lion Hotel Omaha
1616 Dodge Street, Omaha, NE 68102
414-room hotel.
(402) 346-7600
Jobline: (402) 346-1250

Red Lion Hotel San Diego
7450 Hazard Center Drive, San Diego, CA 92108
300-room hotel.
(619) 297-5466
Jobline: (619) 688-4004

Red Lion Hotel San Jose
2050 Gateway Place, San Jose, CA 95110
507-room hotel.
(408) 453-4000
Jobline: (408) 437-2118

Red Lion Hotel SeaTac
18740 Pacific Highway South, Seattle, WA 98188
850-room hotel near Seattle-Tacoma International Airport.
(206) 246-8600
Jobline: (206) 246-8600, ask for job hotline.

Red Lion Hotel/Riverside
2900 Chinden Boulevard, Boise, ID 83714
308-room hotel.
(208) 343-1871
Jobline: (208) 386-9254

Red Lion Hotel/Salt Lake
255 S. West Temple, Salt Lake City, UT 84101
502-room hotel.
(801) 328-2000
Jobline: (801) 328-7082

Red Lion Hotels
1000 NE Multnomah Street, Portland, OR 97232
Hotel chain that includes seven Red Lion hotels in the
   Portland, Oregon area.
(503) 281-6111
Jobline: (503) 978-4515

Red Lion Sacramento Inn
1401 Arden Way, Sacramento, CA 95815
404-room hotel.
(916) 922-8041
Jobline: (916) 922-8041, ask for job hotline.

Redding (city)
760 Parkview Avenue, Redding, CA 96001
Provides municipal services such as police, firefighting,
    libraries, parks, and public works.
(916) 225-4065
Jobline: (916) 225-4069

Redlands (city)
1270 W. Park Avenue, Redlands, CA 92373
Provides municipal services such as police, firefighting,
    libraries, parks, and public works.
(909) 798-7514
Jobline: (909) 798-7645

Redondo Beach (city)
415 Diamond Street, Redondo Beach, CA 90277
Provides municipal services such as police, firefighting,
    libraries, parks, and public works.
(310) 318-0659
Jobline: (310) 318-0660

Redwood City (city)
900 Veterans Boulevard, #500, Redwood City, CA
    94063
Provides municipal services such as police, firefighting,
    libraries, parks, and public works.
(415) 780-7281
Jobline: (415) 364-4425

Regent Beverly Wilshire
9500 Wilshire Boulevard, Beverly Hills, CA 90212
301-room hotel in the Los Angeles area.
(310) 275-5200
Jobline: (310) 288-0803

Regional Medical Center
877 Jefferson Avenue, Memphis, TN 38103
Not-for-profit hospital with more than 400 beds.
(901) 575-7100
Jobline: (901) 575-8432

Registry Resort
475 Seagate Drive, Naples, FL 33940
474-room hotel.
(813) 597-3232
Jobline: (813) 597-6859

Renaissance Hotel Los Angeles
9620 Airport Boulevard, Los Angeles, CA 90045
505-room hotel near Los Angeles International Airport.
(310) 337-2800
Jobline: (310) 337-4646

Reno (city)
P.O. Box 1900, Reno, NV 89505
Provides municipal services such as police, firefighting,
    libraries, parks, and public works.
(702) 334-2285
Jobline: (702) 334-2287

Reno Hilton
2500 E. 2nd Street, Reno, NV 89595
2,001-room hotel between the airport and downtown
    Las Vegas.
(702) 789-2000
Jobline: (702) 789-2223

Renton (city)
City Hall, 200 Mill Avenue South, Renton, WA 98055
Provides municipal services such as police, firefighting,
    libraries, parks, and public works.
(206) 235-2556
Jobline: (206) 235-2514

Renton School District
435 Main Avenue South, Renton, WA 98055
25-school district in Renton.
(206) 235-2385
Jobline: (206) 235-5826
Classified and certificated jobs.

Republic National Bank of Miami
10 NW 42nd Avenue, Miami, FL 33126
Operates national commercial banks.
(305) 441-7300
Jobline: (305) 250-5051

Rialto (city)
150 S. Palm Avenue, Rialto, CA 92376
Provides municipal services such as police, firefighting,
    libraries, parks, and public works.
(909) 820-2540
Jobline: (909) 820-2640

Rice University
Houston, TX 77251
Small, private university three miles from downtown
    Houston.
(713) 527-8101
Jobline: (713) 527-6080

Richardson (city)
411 W. Arapaho Road, Richardson, TX 75080
Provides municipal services such as police, firefighting,
    libraries, parks, and public works.
(214) 238-4150
Jobline: (214) 238-4151

Richland (city)
505 Swift Boulevard, Richland, WA 99352
Provides municipal services such as police, firefighting,
    libraries, parks, and public works.
(509) 943-7391
Jobline: (509) 943-7399

Richland County
202 Hampton Street, Room 4047, P.O. Box 192
Columbia, SC 29202
Provides county services such as sheriffs, courts, motor
    vehicle registration, and social services.
(803) 748-4831
Jobline: (803) 748-4832

Richmond (city)
2600 Barrett Aven, Richmond, CA 94804
Provides municipal services such as police, firefighting, libraries, parks, and public works.
(510) 620-6602
Jobline: (510) 620-6610

Ritz-Carlton
160 E. Pearson Street, Chicago, IL 60611
431-room hotel.
(312) 266-1000
Jobline: (312) 266-1000, ask for job hotline.

Ritz-Carlton Kansas City
401 Ward Parkway, Kansas City, MO 64112
373-room hotel.
(816) 756-1500
Jobline: (816) 756-1500, ask for job hotline.

Ritz-Carlton Laguna Niguel
33533 Ritz-Carlton Drive, Dana Point, CA 92629
393-room hotel in the Orange County coastal area.
(714) 240-2000
Jobline: (714) 240-5037

Riverside (city)
4075 Main Street, Riverside, CA 92509
Provides municipal services such as police, firefighting, libraries, parks, and public works.
(909) 782-5808
Jobline: (909) 782-5492

Riverside County
46209 Oasis Street, Room 308, Indio, CA 92201
Provides county services such as sheriffs, courts, motor vehicle registration, and social services.
(619) 863-8327
Jobline: (619) 863-8970

4080 Lemon Street, Room 109, Riverside, CA 92501
Provides county services such as sheriffs, courts, motor vehicle registration, and social services.
(909) 275-3500
Jobline: (909) 275-3500, press 1.

Riverside Medical Center
350 N. Wall Street, Kankakee, IL 60901
Not-for-profit hospital with more than 300 beds.
(815) 933-1671
Jobline: (815) 937-7969

Roche Biomedical Laboratories Inc.
430 S. Spring Street, P.O. Box 2240, Burlington, NC 27216
Operates clinical laboratories that perform specimen testing.
(910) 229-1127
Jobline: (910) 229-1127, ask for x4900.
Administrative jobs.
Call (800) 222-7566 outside North Carolina.

Jobline: (910) 229-1127, ask for x3900.
Laboratory jobs.
Call (800) 222-7566 outside North Carolina.

Rockdale County
929 Court Street NE, Conyers, GA 30207
Provides county services such as sheriffs, courts, motor vehicle registration, and social services.
(404) 929-4030
Jobline: (404) 929-4157

Rohr Industries Inc.
P.O. Box 878, Chula Vista, CA 91912
Manufactures aircraft, guided missile, and space vehicle parts and equipment.
(619) 691-4111
Jobline: (619) 691-2601

Roseville (city)
311 Vernon Street, Roseville, CA 95678
Provides municipal services such as police, firefighting, libraries, parks, and public works.
(916) 774-5475
Jobline: (916) 782-8107

Rowan College of New Jersey
Glassboro, NJ 08028
Medium-sized, public, comprehensive college in Glassboro, east of Philadelphia.
(609) 863-5000
Jobline: (609) 863-5329
Off-campus jobs.

Royal Sonesta Hotel
300 Bourbon Street, New Orleans, LA 70140
500-room hotel.
(504) 586-0300
Jobline: (504) 553-2336

Rutgers, the State University of New Jersey
P.O. Box 2101, New Brunswick, NJ 08903-2101
Network of colleges and specialized schools with a main campus in New Brunswick.
(908) 932-3770
Jobline: (908) 445-2720
Administrative, professional, and supervisory jobs.

Jobline: (908) 445-3031
Service maintenance jobs.

Jobline: (908) 445-3045
Clerical, laboratory, and technical jobs.

Ryder System Inc.
3600 NW 82nd Avenue, Miami, FL 33166
Leases and rents trucks, and provides customized transportation, repair, and other services.
(305) 593-3726
Jobline: (305) 593-3066

S and A Restaurant Corp.
12404 Park Central Drive, Dallas, TX 75251
Operates restaurants.
(214) 404-5000
Jobline: (214) 404-5622

Sacramento (city)
921 10th Street, Room 101, Sacramento, CA 95814
Provides municipal services such as police, firefighting, libraries, parks, and public works.
(916) 264-5762
Jobline: (916) 443-9990

Sacramento County
710 J Street, Sacramento, CA 95814
Provides county services such as sheriffs, courts, motor
vehicle registration, and social services.
(916) 440-5593
Jobline: (916) 440-6771

Sacred Heart Medical Center
101 W. 8th Avenue, P.O. Box 2555
Spokane, WA 99220-2550
Not-for-profit hospital with more than 600 beds.
(509) 455-3131
Jobline: (509) 455-3192

Saddleback Community College District
28000 Marguerite Parkway, Mission Viejo, CA 92626
Includes Saddleback College and Irvine Valley College.
(714) 582-4840
Jobline: (714) 582-4469
Classified jobs.

Jobline: (714) 582-4852
Academic jobs.

SAFECO Corp.
SAFECO Plaza, Seattle, WA 98185
Provides property and other types of insurance, and
other investment and management services.
(206) 545-5000
Jobline: (206) 545-3233

Safeway Inc.
201 4th Street, Oakland, CA 94660
Operates chain supermarkets and superstores.
(510) 891-3000
Jobline: (800) 255-0812

Saint Anthony
300 E. Travis Street, San Antonio, TX 78205
350-room downtown hotel.
(210) 227-4392
Jobline: (210) 227-4392, ask for x112.

Saint David's Hospital
919 E. 32nd Street P.O. Box 4039, Austin, TX
78765-4039
Not-for-profit hospital with more than 300 beds.
(512) 476-7111
Jobline: (512) 397-4000

Saint Louis Community College
300 S. Broadway, Saint Louis, MO 63102
Includes St. Louis Community College at Florissant
Valley, at Forest Park, and at Meramec.
(314) 539-5204
Jobline: (314) 539-5200

Saint Louis County
41 S. Central Avenue, Saint Louis, MO 63105
Provides county services such as sheriffs, courts, motor
vehicle registration, and social services.
(314) 889-2429
Jobline: (314) 889-3665

Saint Louis University
Saint Louis, MO 63103
Medium-sized, Catholic institution with an urban
campus in St. Louis.
(314) 658-2311
Jobline: (314) 658-2265

Saint Luke's Medical Center
2900 W. Oklahoma Avenue, P.O. Box 2901
Milwaukee, WI 53201
Not-for-profit hospital with more than 500 beds.
(414) 649-6000
Jobline: (414) 649-6378

Saint Mary Medical Center
1050 Linden Avenue, P.O. Box 887, Long Beach, CA
90801
Not-for-profit hospital and nursing home-type unit with
more than 400 beds.
(310) 491-9000
Jobline: (310) 491-9014
Nursing jobs.

Jobline: (310) 491-9844
Professional and ancillary jobs.

Saint Mary's University
San Antonio, TX 78284-0400
Small, church-affiliated institution in San Antonio.
(210) 436-3011
Jobline: (210) 436-3343

Saint Paul (city)
230 City Hall Annex, 25 W. 4th Street, Saint Paul, MN
55110
Provides municipal services such as police, firefighting,
libraries, parks, and public works.
(612) 298-4221
Jobline: (612) 266-6502

Saint Petersburg (city)
175 5th Street North, Room 107, Saint Petersburg, FL
33701
Provides municipal services such as police, firefighting,
libraries, parks, and public works.
(813) 363-9233
Jobline: (813) 893-7033

Saint Vincent's Health Systems
1800 Barrs Street, P.O. Box 2982, Jacksonville, FL
32203-9954
Includes Saint Vincent's Medical Center and other
health services.
(904) 387-7307
Jobline: (904) 387-7363

Salem (city)
City Hall, 555 Liberty Street SE, Salem, OR 97301
Provides municipal services such as police, firefighting,
libraries, parks, and public works.
(503) 588-6162
Jobline: (503) 588-6162

Salem-Keizer School District No. 24J
1309 Ferry Street SE, Salem, OR 97301
48-school district in Salem.
(503) 399-3063
Jobline: (503) 399-3404
Classified jobs.

Salinas (city)
200 Lincoln Avenue, Salinas, CA 93901
Provides municipal services such as police, firefighting,
    libraries, parks, and public works.
(408) 758-7254
Jobline: (408) 758-7246

Salt Lake City (city)
451 S. State Street, Salt Lake City, UT 84111
Provides municipal services such as police, firefighting,
    libraries, parks, and public works.
(801) 535-7900
Jobline: (801) 535-6625

Salt Lake County
2001 S. State Street, Salt Lake City, UT 84115
Provides county services such as sheriffs, courts, motor
    vehicle registration, and social services.
(801) 468-2351
Jobline: (801) 468-2390

Sam Houston State University
Huntsville, TX 77341
Medium-sized, public, multipurpose institution in
    Huntsville, 70 miles northwest of Houston.
(409) 294-1111
Jobline: (409) 294-1067

San Antonio (city)
115 Plaza de Armas, San Antonio, TX 78205
Provides municipal services such as police, firefighting,
    libraries, parks, and public works.
(210) 299-8108
Jobline: (210) 299-7280

San Antonio (city) Water System
1001 E. Market Street, San Antonio, TX 78205
Provides water services.
(210) 704-7276
Jobline: (210) 704-7280

San Antonio Airport Hilton
611 NW Loop 410, San Antonio, TX 78216
374-room hotel.
(210) 340-6060
Jobline: (210) 340-6060, ask for job hotline.

San Bernardino (city)
300 N. D Street, San Bernardino, CA 92418
Provides municipal services such as police, firefighting,
    libraries, parks, and public works.
(909) 384-5061
Jobline: (909) 384-5376

San Bernardino Community College District
633 N. E Street, San Bernardino, CA 92410-3080
Includes San Bernardino Valley College and Crafton
    Hills College.
(909) 884-2533
Jobline: (909) 384-0853

San Bernardino County
157 W. 5th Street, San Bernardino, CA 92401
Provides county services such as sheriffs, courts, motor
    vehicle registration, and social services.
(909) 387-8304
Jobline: (909) 387-5611

San Clemente (city)
100 Avenida Presidio, San Clemente, CA 92672
Provides municipal services such as police, firefighting,
    libraries, parks, and public works.
(714) 361-8324
Jobline: (714) 361-8294

San Diego (city)
1200 3rd Avenue, San Diego, CA 92101
Provides municipal services such as police, firefighting,
    libraries, parks, and public works.
(619) 236-4000
Jobline: (619) 450-6210

San Diego Community College District
3375 Camino Del Rio South, Suite 330, San Diego, CA
    92108
Includes San Diego Miramar College, San Diego Mesa
    College, and San Diego City College.
(800) 648-4023
Jobline: (619) 584-6580, press 6580.

San Diego County
1600 Pacific Highway, Room 207, San Diego, CA 92101
Provides county services such as sheriffs, courts, motor
    vehicle registration, and social services.
(619) 236-2191
Jobline: (619) 531-5764

San Diego Hilton Beach & Tennis Resort
1775 E. Mission Bay Drive, San Diego, CA 92109
354-room hotel.
(619) 276-4010
Jobline: (619) 275-8994

San Diego Mission Valley Hilton
901 Camino del Rio South, San Diego, CA 92108
358-room hotel.
(619) 543-9000
Jobline: (619) 543-9441

San Diego State University
San Diego, CA 92182-0771
Large, public university in San Diego.
(619) 594-5200
Jobline: (619) 594-5801
Clerical and secretarial jobs.

Jobline: (619) 594-5850
Technical, research, and physical plant jobs.

Jobline: (619) 594-5861
Administrative and professional jobs.

San Francisco (city and county)
44 Gough Street, San Francisco, CA 94103
Provides government services such as police,
    firefighting, libraries, parks, and public works.
(415) 557-4800
Jobline: (415) 557-4888

San Francisco (city and county) Department of Public Health
Central Office
101 Grove Street, San Francisco, CA 94102
Provides public health programs and services.
(415) 554-2581
Jobline: (415) 206-5317

San Francisco Airport Hilton
International Airport, P.O. Box 8355, San Francisco, CA 94128
530-room hotel near San Francisco International Airport.
(415) 589-0770
Jobline: (415) 875-3071

San Francisco Community College District
33 Gough Street, San Francisco, CA 94103
Includes City College of San Francisco and San Francisco Community College Centers.
(415) 239-3000
Jobline: (415) 241-2349

San Francisco Hilton & Towers
1 Hilton Square, San Francisco, CA 94102
1,906-room hotel.
(415) 771-1400
Jobline: (415) 923-5068

San Francisco State University
San Francisco, CA 94132
Large, public university in San Francisco.
(415) 338-1111
Jobline: (415) 338-1871

San Francisco Unified School District
135 Van Ness Avenue, San Francisco, CA 94102
106-school district in San Francisco.
(415) 241-6025
Jobline: (415) 241-6162

San Joaquin County
24 S. Hunter Street, Room 106, Stockton, CA 95202
Provides county services such as sheriffs, courts, motor vehicle registration, and social services.
(209) 468-3370
Jobline: (209) 468-3377

San Joaquin County Department of Health Care Services
500 W. Hospital Road, French Camp, CA 95231
Provides public health programs and services.
(209) 468-6090
Jobline: (209) 468-6034

San Joaquin Delta College
5151 Pacific Avenue, Stockton, CA 95207
Medium-sized, district-supported, 2-year college in Stockton.
(209) 474-5151
Jobline: (209) 474-5627

San Jose (city)
801 N. 1st Street, San Jose, CA 95110
Provides municipal services such as police, firefighting, libraries, parks, and public works.
(408) 277-4205
Jobline: (408) 277-5627

San Jose Evergreen Community College District
4750 San Felipe Road, San Jose, CA 95135-1599
Includes San Jose City College and Evergreen Valley College.
(408) 274-6700
Jobline: (408) 223-6707

San Jose Hilton & Towers
300 Almaden Boulevard, San Jose, CA 95110
355-room hotel.
(408) 287-2100
Jobline: (408) 947-4458

San Jose State University
San Jose, CA 95192
Large, public, multipurpose institution in San Jose.
(408) 924-1000
Jobline: (408) 924-1000, press 2.

San Leandro (city)
835 E. 14th Street, San Leandro, CA 94577
Provides municipal services such as police, firefighting, libraries, parks, and public works.
(510) 577-3396
Jobline: (510) 577-3397

San Luis Obispo (city)
P.O. Box 8100, San Luis Obispo, CA 93403-8100
Provides municipal services such as police, firefighting, libraries, parks, and public works.
(805) 781-7250
Jobline: (805) 781-7153

San Luis Obispo County
1035 Palm Street, San Luis Obispo, CA 93408
Provides county services such as sheriffs, courts, motor vehicle registration, and social services.
(805) 781-5959
Jobline: (805) 781-5958

San Mateo (city)
330 W. 20th Avenue, San Mateo, CA 94403
Provides municipal services such as police, firefighting, libraries, parks, and public works.
(415) 377-3350
Jobline: (415) 377-4797, x424.

San Mateo County
County Office Building, 590 Hamilton Street, Redwood City, CA 94063
Provides county services such as sheriffs, courts, motor vehicle registration, and social services.
(415) 363-4343
Jobline: (415) 368-7214

San Mateo County Community College District
3401 CSM Drive, San Mateo, CA 94402
Includes Cañada College, College of San Mateo, and Skyline College.
(415) 574-6444
Jobline: (415) 574-6111

San Ramon (city)
2222 Camino Ramon, San Ramon, CA 94583
Provides municipal services such as police, firefighting, libraries, parks, and public works.
(510) 275-2240
Jobline: (510) 275-2338

Sands Hotel & Casino
Indiana Avenue and Brighton Park, Atlantic City, NJ
08401
500-room hotel.
(609) 441-4000
Jobline: (609) 441-4525

Sandy (city)
10000 S. Centennial Parkway, Sandy, UT 84070
Provides municipal services such as police, firefighting,
libraries, parks, and public works.
(801) 568-7151
Jobline: (801) 561-7009, x702.
Full-time jobs.

Jobline: (801) 561-7009, x703.
Part-time and seasonal jobs.

Santa Ana (city)
20 Civic Center Plaza, Santa Ana, CA 92701
Provides municipal services such as police, firefighting,
libraries, parks, and public works.
(714) 647-5340
Jobline: (714) 953-9675

Santa Barbara County
1226 Anacapa Street, Santa Barbara, CA 93101
Provides county services such as sheriffs, courts, motor
vehicle registration, and social services.
(805) 568-2800
Jobline: (805) 568-2820

Santa Clara (city)
1500 Warburton Avenue, Santa Clara, CA 95050
Provides municipal services such as police, firefighting,
libraries, parks, and public works.
(408) 984-5122
Jobline: (408) 984-3150

Santa Clara County
70 W. Hedding Street, San Jose, CA 95110
Provides county services such as sheriffs, courts, motor
vehicle registration, and social services.
(408) 299-2341
Jobline: (408) 299-2856

Santa Clara University
Santa Clara, CA 95053
Medium-sized, Catholic institution in Santa Clara, 46
miles south of San Francisco.
(408) 554-4764
Jobline: (408) 554-4030

Santa Clarita (city)
23920 W. Valencia Boulevard, Santa Clarita, CA 91355
Provides municipal services such as police, firefighting,
libraries, parks, and public works.
(805) 286-4180
Jobline: (805) 255-4392

Santa Cruz (city)
337 Locust Street, Santa Cruz, CA 95060
Provides municipal services such as police, firefighting,
libraries, parks, and public works.
(408) 429-3616
Jobline: (408) 429-3040

Santa Cruz County
701 Ocean Street, Room 310, Santa Cruz, CA 95060
Provides county services such as sheriffs, courts, motor
vehicle registration, and social services.
(408) 454-2600
Jobline: (408) 454-2151

Santa Monica (city)
1685 Main Street, Santa Monica, CA 90401
Provides municipal services such as police, firefighting,
libraries, parks, and public works.
(310) 458-8246
Jobline: (310) 458-8697

Santa Monica Community College
1900 Pico Boulevard, Santa Monica, CA 90405-1628
Large, state- and locally-supported, 2-year college.
(310) 450-5150
Jobline: (310) 450-5150, press 6.

Santa Rosa (city)
100 Santa Rosa Avenue, Santa Rosa, CA 95404
Provides municipal services such as police, firefighting,
libraries, parks, and public works.
(707) 543-3060
Jobline: (707) 543-3076

Santa Rosa Health Care Corp.
519 W. Houston Street, San Antonio, TX 78207
Operates four not-for-profit hospitals with more than
1,100 beds in the San Antonio area.
(210) 228-2011
Jobline: (210) 228-2343

Santa Rosa Junior College
1501 Mendocino Avenue, Santa Rosa, CA 95401-4395
Large, state- and locally-supported, 2-year college in
Santa Rosa.
(707) 527-4509
Jobline: (707) 527-4707

Sante Fe (city)
200 Lincoln Avenue, Santa Fe, NM 87501
Provides municipal services such as police, firefighting,
libraries, parks, and public works.
(505) 984-6597
Jobline: (505) 984-6742

Santee (city)
10765 Woodside Avenue, Santee, CA 92071
Provides municipal services such as police, firefighting,
libraries, parks, and public works.
(619) 258-4120
Jobline: (619) 258-4123

Sanwa Bank California
601 S. Figueroa Street, Los Angeles, CA 90017
Operates state commercial banks.
(213) 896-7000
Jobline: (213) 896-7214

Savannah (city)
132 E. Broughton Street, Savannah, GA 31401
Provides municipal services such as police, firefighting,
libraries, parks, and public works.
(912) 651-6484
Jobline: (912) 651-6488

Schnuck Markets Inc.
11420 Lackland Road, Saint Louis, MO 63146
Operates grocery stores, drug stores, restaurants, and
    video stores.
(314) 994-9900
Jobline: (314) 344-9292

Science Applications International Corp.
10260 Campus Point Drive, San Diego, CA 92121
Conducts commercial research in the applied sciences,
    and develops military software and systems.
(619) 546-6000
Jobline: (619) 535-7536

Scott County
Courthouse, Room 104, 428 S. Holmes Street,
    Shakopee, MN 55379
Provides county services such as sheriffs, courts, motor
    vehicle registration, and social services.
(612) 496-8103
Jobline: (612) 496-8598

Scott Paper Co.
Scott Plaza, Philadelphia, PA 19113
Manufactures sanitary, kitchen, and other paper
    products, and operates paper mills and sawmills.
(215) 522-5000
Jobline: (215) 522-5885

Scottsdale (city)
7575 E. Main Street, Suite 205, Scottsdale, AZ 85251
Provides municipal services such as police, firefighting,
    libraries, parks, and public works.
(602) 994-2491
Jobline: (602) 994-2395

Scottsdale Memorial Health Systems Inc.
3621 Wells Fargo Avenue, Scottsdale, AZ 85251
Operate two not-for-profit hospitals with more than 600
    beds in the Scottsdale area.
(602) 481-4327
Jobline: (602) 941-5221

Scottsdale Princess
7575 E. Princess Drive, Scottsdale, AZ 85255
600-room hotel.
(602) 585-2755
Jobline: (602) 585-2756

Scottsdale Unified School District No. 48
3811 N. 44th Street, Phoenix, AZ 85018
26-school district in Phoenix.
(602) 952-6173
Jobline: (602) 952-6296
Includes jobs in the district offices and in schools.

Sea World of Florida Inc.
7007 Sea World Drive, Orlando, FL 32821
Operates the Sea World amusement park.
(407) 363-2571
Jobline: (407) 363-2612

Seafirst Corp.
P.O. Box 3977, Seattle, WA 98124
Bank holding company that operates national
    commercial banks.
(206) 358-3000
Jobline: (206) 358-7523

Seagate Technology Inc.
920 Disc Drive, Scotts Valley, CA 95066
Manufactures hard disk drives for small computers.
(408) 438-6550
Jobline: (408) 439-5627

SeaTac (city)
City Hall, 19215 28th Avenue South, SeaTac, WA 98188
Provides municipal services such as police, firefighting,
    libraries, parks, and public works.
(206) 878-9219
Jobline: (206) 878-6190

Seattle (city)
Dexter Horton Building, 12th Floor, 710 2nd Avenue,
    Seattle, WA 98104
Provides municipal services such as libraries, parks,
    and public works.
(206) 684-7952
Jobline: (206) 684-7999

**Seattle (city) Public Safety Civil Service
Commission**
700 3rd Avenue, Suite 360, Seattle, WA 98104
Administers exams for police and firefighting positions.
(206) 386-1303
Jobline: (206) 386-1303

Seattle Center
305 Harrison Street, Seattle, WA 98109
Cultural complex that includes a science center,
    theaters, a sports arena, and an amusement park.
(206) 684-7221
Jobline: (206) 684-7218

Seattle Community College District
1500 Harvard Avenue, Seattle, WA 98122
Includes North Seattle, Seattle Central, and South
    Seattle Community Colleges.
(206) 587-4155
Jobline: (206) 587-5454

Seattle Marriott SeaTac Airport
3201 S. 176th Street, Seattle, WA 98188
459-room hotel near Seattle-Tacoma International
    Airport.
(206) 241-2000
Jobline: (206) 241-2421

Seattle Pacific University
Seattle, WA 98119
Small, evangelical Christian university in residential
    Seattle with a camp on Puget Sound.
(206) 281-2050
Jobline: (206) 281-2065, press 1.

Seattle School District
815 4th Avenue North, Room 140, Seattle, WA 98109
111-school district in Seattle.
(206) 298-7377
Jobline: (206) 298-7382

Seattle Sheraton Hotel & Towers
1400 6th Avenue, Seattle, WA 98101
840-room hotel.
(206) 621-9000
Jobline: (206) 287-5505

Seattle University
Seattle, WA 98122
Medium-sized, Catholic institution operated by Jesuits in Seattle.
(206) 296-6000
Jobline: (206) 296-6363

Sedgwick County
510 N. Main Street, Wichita, KS 67203
Provides county services such as sheriffs, courts, motor vehicle registration, and social services.
(316) 383-7178
Jobline: (316) 383-7633

Service Merchandise Company Inc.
7100 Service Merchandise Boulevard, Brentwood, TN 37027
Sells housewares, appliances, sporting goods, jewelry, and other products through catalog showrooms.
(615) 660-6000
Jobline: (615) 660-3199

ServiceMaster Limited Partnership
2300 Warrensville Road, 1 ServiceMaster Way
Downer's Grove, IL 60515
Provides management, custodial, pest control, lawn care, and other services to facilities.
(708) 964-1300
Jobline: (800) 999-6678, x4444.

Sharp Healthcare
3131 Berger Avenue, Suite 100, San Diego, CA 92123
Operates five not-for-profit hospitals with more than 1,400 beds in the San Diego area.
(619) 541-4000
Jobline: (619) 450-6241

Shasta County
1600 Court Street, Redding, CA 96001
Provides county services such as sheriffs, courts, motor vehicle registration, and social services.
(916) 225-5515
Jobline: (916) 225-5078

Shawnee County
200 SE 7th Street, Topeka, KS 66603
Provides county services such as sheriffs, courts, motor vehicle registration, and social services.
(913) 233-8200
Jobline: (913) 233-8200, x5627.

Shelby County
160 N. Main Street, Memphis, TN 38103
Provides county services such as sheriffs, courts, motor vehicle registration, and social services.
(901) 576-4342
Jobline: (901) 576-4434

Sheraton Atlanta Airport Hotel
1325 Virginia Avenue at I-85, Atlanta, GA 30344
365-room hotel near Atlanta/Hartsfield International Airport.
(404) 768-6660
Jobline: (404) 768-6660, ask for job hotline.

Sheraton Bal Harbour Resort
9701 Collins Avenue, Miami Beach, FL 33154
650-room hotel.
(305) 865-7511
Jobline: (305) 865-7511, ask for x3275.

Sheraton Chicago Hotel & Towers
301 E. North Water Street, Chicago, IL 60611
1,200-room hotel.
(312) 464-1000
Jobline: (312) 464-1000, ask for job hotline.

Sheraton Civic Center Hotel
2101 Civic Center Boulevard, Birmingham, AL 35203
771-room hotel.
(205) 324-5000
Jobline: (205) 307-3016

Sheraton Colony Square Hotel
188 14th Street NE, Atlanta, GA 30361
461-room hotel.
(404) 892-6000
Jobline: (404) 892-6000, ask for x470.

Sheraton Crown Hotel & Conference Center
15700 John F. Kennedy Boulevard, Houston, TX 77032
419-room hotel near Houston Intercontinental Airport.
(713) 442-5100
Jobline: (713) 442-5100, ask for x1710.

Sheraton Denver Tech Center Hotel
4900 DTC Parkway, Denver, CO 80237
623-room hotel.
(303) 779-1100
Jobline: (303) 779-1100, ask for x170.

Sheraton Grande
333 S. Figueroa Street, Los Angeles, CA 90071
469-room hotel in downtown Los Angeles.
(213) 617-1133
Jobline: (213) 617-6088

Sheraton Grande Torrey Pines
10950 N. Torrey Pines Road, La Jolla, CA 92037
400-room hotel.
(619) 558-1500
Jobline: (619) 558-8058

Sheraton Gunter Hotel
205 E. Houston Street, San Antonio, TX 78205
325-room hotel.
(210) 227-3241
Jobline: (210) 227-3241, ask for job hotline.

Sheraton Harbor Island Hotel
1380 Harbor Island Drive, San Diego, CA 92101-1092
700-room hotel.
(619) 291-2900
Jobline: (619) 692-2793

Sheraton Hartford
315 Trumbull Street , Hartford, CT 06130
382-room hotel.
(203) 728-5151
Jobline: (203) 240-7255

Sheraton Inner Harbor Hotel
300 S. Charles Street, Baltimore, MD 21201
339-room hotel.
(410) 962-8300
Jobline: (410) 347-1808

Sheraton Long Beach
333 E. Ocean Boulevard, Long Beach, CA 90802
460-room hotel.
(310) 436-3000
Jobline: (310) 499-2056

Sheraton New Orleans Hotel
500 Canal Street, New Orleans, LA 70130
1,100-room hotel.
(504) 525-2500
Jobline: (504) 525-2500, ask for job hotline.

Sheraton New York Hotel & Towers
811 7th Avenue, New York, NY 10019
1,759-room hotel.
(212) 581-1000
Jobline: (212) 581-3300, ask for job hotline.

Sheraton Park Central Hotel & Towers
12720 Merit Drive, Dallas, TX 75251
550-room hotel.
(214) 385-3000
Jobline: (214) 385-3000, ask for x6011.

Sheraton Premiere at Tyson's Corner
8661 Leesburg Pike, Vienna, VA 22182
455-room hotel near Washington, D.C.
(703) 448-1234
Jobline: (703) 506-2518

Sheraton Stamford Hotel
1 Stamford Place, Stamford, CT 06902
505-room hotel.
(203) 967-2222
Jobline: (203) 351-1897

Sheraton Tara Hotel & Resort Danvers
50 Ferncroft Road, Danvers, MA 01923
367-room hotel near Boston.
(508) 777-2500
Jobline: (508) 777-2500, ask for x7927.

Sheraton Tara Hotel Braintree
37 Forbes Road, Braintree, MA 02184
377-room hotel near Boston.
(617) 848-0600
Jobline: (617) 848-0600, ask for x2320.

Sheraton Tucson El Conquistador Resort
10000 N. Oracle Road, Tucson, AZ 85737
431-room hotel.
(602) 742-7000
Jobline: (602) 544-1240

Sheraton Washington
2660 Woodley Road NW, Washington, DC 20008
1,505-room hotel.
(202) 328-2000
Jobline: (202) 328-2000, ask for x5617.

Sheraton World Resort
10100 International Drive, Orlando, FL 32821
788-room hotel.
(407) 352-1100
Jobline: (407) 354-5057

Sheraton-Palace
2 New Montgomery Street, San Francisco, CA 94105
550-room hotel.
(415) 392-8600
Jobline: (415) 392-8600, ask for x6026.

Sherwin-Williams Co.
101 Prospect Avenue NW, Cleveland, OH 44115
Produces and sells paints, varnishes, lacquers, other
    painting supplies, and chemical products.
(216) 566-2000
Jobline: (216) 566-2120

Shreveport (city)
1237 Murphy Street, Room 103, Shreveport, LA 71130
Provides municipal services such as police, firefighting,
    libraries, parks, and public works.
(318) 673-5150
Jobline: (318) 226-3564

Sierra College
5000 Rocklin Road, Rocklin, CA 95677
Medium-sized, state-supported, 2-year college in
    Rocklin, near Sacramento.
(916) 781-0525
Jobline: (916) 781-0424

Signal Hill (city)
2175 Cherry Avenue, Signal Hill, CA 90806
Provides municipal services such as police, firefighting,
    libraries, parks, and public works.
(310) 989-7307
Jobline: (310) 989-7385

Signet Bank/Maryland
7 Saint Paul Street, Baltimore, MD 21202
Operates state commercial banks and leases and rents
    equipment.
(410) 332-5000
Jobline: (410) 332-5627

Sinai Hospital
6767 W. Outer Drive, Detroit, MI 48235
Not-for-profit hospital with more than 400 beds.
(313) 493-6162
Jobline: (313) 493-6161

Sizzler International Inc.
12655 W. Jefferson Boulevard, Los Angeles, CA 90066
Operates and franchises restaurants.
(310) 827-2300
Jobline: (310) 827-2300, x3634.

Smith College
Northampton, MA 01063
Small, liberal arts college for women in the Connecticut
    River Valley.
(413) 584-2700
Jobline: (413) 585-2278

Smithsonian Institution
1000 Jefferson Drive SW, Washington, DC 20560
Independent trust instrumentality of the U.S. that fosters
the increase and diffusion of knowledge.
(202) 287-3100
Jobline: (202) 287-3102

Snohomish County
Administration Building, 1st Floor, 3000 Rockefeller
Avenue, Mail Stop 503
Everett, WA 98201-4046
Provides county services such as sheriffs, courts, motor
vehicle registration, and social services.
(206) 388-3411
Jobline: (206) 388-3686

Society Bank NA
34 N. Main Street, Dayton, OH 45402
Operates national commercial banks.
(513) 226-6000
Jobline: (513) 226-6388

Society Corp.
Society Center, 127 Public Square, Cleveland, OH
44114
Bank holding company that operates national and state
commercial banks and other businesses.
(216) 689-3000
Jobline: (216) 689-5153

Society National Bank, Indiana
1 Plaza Place, 210 S. Michigan Street, South Bend, IN
46601
Operates national commercial banks.
(219) 237-5432
Jobline: (219) 239-4865

Solano County
580 Texas, Fairfield, CA 94533
Provides county services such as sheriffs, courts, motor
vehicle registration, and social services.
(707) 421-6170
Jobline: (707) 421-6174

Sonoma County
2550 Ventura Avenue, Santa Rosa, CA 95403
Provides county services such as sheriffs, courts, motor
vehicle registration, and social services.
(707) 527-2331
Jobline: (707) 527-2803

Sonoma County Office of Education
5340 Skylane Boulevard, Santa Rosa, CA 95403
Provides programs such as special education and ROP,
and administers court and county schools.
(707) 524-2678
Jobline: (707) 524-2680
Includes certificated and classified jobs.

Sonoma State University
Rohnert Park, CA 94928
Medium-sized, public university in Rohnert Park, north
of San Francisco.
(707) 664-2880
Jobline: (707) 664-2168

Sony Pictures Entertainment Inc.
10202 Washington Boulevard, Culver City, CA
90232-3119
Produces, distributes, and exhibits motion pictures and
TV programs.
(310) 280-8000
Jobline: (310) 280-4436, press1.
Includes jobs at Columbia Pictures TV, Tri-Star TV, and
Sony Pictures Studios. Press 1.

South Carolina (state)
2221 Devine Street, Room 100, Columbia, SC 29205
Provides state services such as conservation,
education, highways, prisons, and welfare.
(803) 734-9075
Jobline: (803) 734-9333
Professional jobs.

Jobline: (803) 734-9334
Clerical, technical, and skilled jobs.

South Carolina (state) Department of Corrections
4330 Broad River Road, Columbia, SC 29210
Provides correctional programs and services.
(803) 896-1649
Jobline: (803) 896-1201
Administrative and clerical jobs.

Jobline: (803) 896-1202
Trade and labor jobs.

Jobline: (803) 896-8524
Professional and technical jobs.

South Carolina (state) Department of Juvenile Justice
110 Centerview Drive, Room 349, Columbia, SC 29210
Provides juvenile justice programs and services.
(803) 737-4290
Jobline: (803) 737-4293

South Carolina (state) Department of Mental Health
2414 Bull Street, Columbia, SC 29201
Provides mental health programs and services.
(803) 734-7670
Jobline: (803) 734-7674

South Carolina (state) Educational Television Commission
1103 George Rogers Boulevard, Columbia, SC 29201
Broadcasts educational programs via radio and
television.
(803) 737-3249
Jobline: (803) 737-3320

South County Community College District
25555 Hesperian Boulevard, Hayward, CA 94545
Includes Chabot College and Las Positas College.
(510) 786-6600
Jobline: (510) 786-6966, press 1801.
Classified jobs.

Jobline: (510) 786-6966, press 1802.
Faculty and management jobs.

South Dakota (state)
500 E. Capitol Avenue, Pierre, SD 57501-5070
Provides state services such as conservation,
   education, highways, prisons, and welfare.
(605) 773-3148
Jobline: (605) 773-3326

South Kitsap School District
1962 Hoover Avenue SE, Port Orchard, WA 98366
17-school district in Port Orchard.
(206) 876-7306
Jobline: (206) 876-7389

South San Francisco (city)
400 Grand Avenue, South San Francisco, CA 94080
Provides municipal services such as police, firefighting,
   libraries, parks, and public works.
(415) 877-8522
Jobline: (415) 877-3976

Southern California Edison Co.
2244 Walnut Grove Avenue, Rosemead, CA 91770
Generates, transmits, and distributes electric power.
(818) 302-1212
Jobline: (818) 302-9850

Southern California Gas Co.
555 W. 5th Street, Los Angeles, CA 90013
Produces, transmits, and distributes natural gas.
(213) 244-1200
Jobline: (213) 244-1234

Southern Co.
64 Perimeter Center East, Atlanta, GA 30346
Generates, transmits, and distributes electric power.
(404) 393-0650
Jobline: (404) 668-3464

Southern Illinois University at Carbondale
Carbondale, IL 62901
Large, public, comprehensive institution in southern
   Illinois.
(618) 536-3369
Jobline: (618) 536-2116

Southern Illinois University at Edwardsville
Edwardsville, IL 62026-1001
Medium-sized, public, comprehensive institution near
   the Mississippi River.
(618) 692-2000
Jobline: (618) 692-2420

Southern Methodist University
Dallas, TX 75275
Medium-sized, private, church-affiliated institution north
   of downtown Dallas.
(214) 768-2000
Jobline: (214) 768-1111, press 2, then 1.

Southern New England Telecommunications Corp.
227 Church Street, New Haven, CT 06506
Provides local, long distance, and other telephone
   services, and other products and services.
(203) 771-2156
Jobline: (203) 771-5200, ask for job listings.
Call (800) 562-9008 in Connecticut.

Jobline: (800) 562-7006
Job bank (for callers in Connecticut).

Southern Ohio Medical Center
1248 Kinneys Lane, Portsmouth, OH 45662
Operates two not-for-profit hospitals with more than 300
   beds.
(614) 354-5000
Jobline: (614) 354-7644

Southland Corp.
2711 N. Haskell Avenue, Dallas, TX 75204
Operates and franchises chain convenience stores, and
   provides groceries and other food products.
(214) 828-7011
Jobline: (214) 841-6758

SouthTrust Bank of Georgia NA
34 Peachtree Street, Atlanta, GA 30303
Operates national commercial banks.
(404) 951-4000
Jobline: (404) 951-4010

Southwest Airlines Co.
2702 Love Field Drive, P.O. Box 36611, Dallas, TX
   75235
Provides scheduled air passenger and cargo
   transportation.
(214) 904-4000
Jobline: (214) 904-4803

Southwest Texas State University
San Marcos, TX 78666
Medium-sized, public, comprehensive university in San
   Marcos, northeast of San Antonio.
(512) 245-2111
Jobline: (512) 245-2619

Southwestern Bell Corp.
1 Bell Center, Saint Louis, MO 63101
Provides local, long distance, and other telephone
   services, and consults with public utilities.
(314) 235-9800
Jobline: (314) 235-9800, ask for job hotline.

Sparks (city)
431 Prater Way, Sparks, NV 89431
Provides municipal services such as police, firefighting,
   libraries, parks, and public works.
(702) 353-2345
Jobline: (702) 353-2444

Special Libraries Association
Southern California Chapter
1201 E. California Boulevard, Pasadena, CA 91106
Organization of information professionals who work in
   special libraries.
(818) 795-2145
Jobline: (818) 795-2145

Spelman College
Atlanta, GA 30314
Small, historically black, liberal arts college in west
   Atlanta.
(404) 681-3643
Jobline: (404) 223-5627

Spokane (city)
City Hall, 808 W. Spokane Falls Boulevard, Spokane, WA 99201
Provides municipal services such as police, firefighting, libraries, parks, and public works.
(509) 625-6363
Jobline: (509) 625-6161

Spokane School District
Administrative Center, 200 N. Bernard Street, Spokane, WA 99201
63-school district in Spokane.
(509) 353-5336
Jobline: (509) 353-5459
Classified jobs.

Jobline: (509) 353-7639
Certificated jobs.

Springfield (city)
Municipal Building, Room 215, Springfield, IL 62701
Provides municipal services such as police, firefighting, libraries, parks, and public works.
(217) 789-2446
Jobline: (217) 789-2440

Springfield (city)
City Hall, 225 5th Street, Springfield, OR 97477
Provides municipal services such as police, firefighting, libraries, parks, and public works.
(503) 726-3704
Jobline: (503) 726-3648

Springfield School District No. 19
525 Mill Street, Springfield, OR 97477
22-school district in Springfield.
(503) 726-3231
Jobline: (503) 726-3364

Stanford University
Stanford, CA 94305
Medium-sized, private university in Palo Alto, south of San Francisco.
(415) 723-2300
Jobline: (415) 725-5627

Stanford University
Hospital
300 Pasteur Road, Stanford, CA 94305
Not-for-profit hospital with more than 600 beds on the Stanford University campus.
(415) 723-4000
Jobline: (415) 723-5140

Stanislaus County
1100 H Street, Modesto, CA 95354-2379
Provides county services such as sheriffs, courts, motor vehicle registration, and social services.
(209) 525-6341
Jobline: (209) 525-4339

State Center Community College District
1525 E. Weldon Avenue
Fresno, CA 93704
Includes Fresno City College and Kings River Community College.
(209) 226-0720
Jobline: (209) 226-5129

State National Bank
221 N. Kansas Street P.O. Box 1072, El Paso, TX 79958
Operates national commercial banks.
(915) 532-9922
Jobline: (915) 546-4335

State University of New York at Albany
Albany, NY 12222
Medium-sized, university center in Albany.
(518) 442-3300
Jobline: (518) 442-3151

State University of New York at Stony Brook
Stony Brook, NY 11794
Medium-sized, university center on Long Island, 60 miles east of Manhattan.
(516) 689-6000
Jobline: (516) 632-9222

State University of New York at Stony Brook
Hospital
Stony Brook, NY 11794
Not-for-profit hospital affiliated with the State University of New York at Stony Brook.
(516) 689-6000
Jobline: (516) 444-7710

Stater Brothers
21700 Barton Road, Colton, CA 92324
Operates retail food supermarkets.
(909) 783-5000
Jobline: (909) 783-5031

Stephen F. Austin State University
Nacogdoches, TX 75962-3051
Medium-sized, university with a main campus, farm, and dairy in Nacogdoches.
(409) 568-2104
Jobline: (409) 568-3003

Stetson University
De Land, FL 32720
Small, private university with a main campus in De Land, north of Orlando.
(904) 822-7000
Jobline: (904) 822-7562

Stockton (city)
425 N. El Dorado Street, Stockton, CA 95202
Provides municipal services such as police, firefighting, libraries, parks, and public works.
(209) 937-8233
Jobline: (209) 937-8523

Stouffer Austin Hotel
9721 Arboretum Boulevard, Austin, TX 78759
478-room hotel.
(512) 343-2626
Jobline: (512) 343-2626, ask for x6310.

Stouffer Dallas Hotel
2222 Stemmons Freeway, Dallas, TX 75207
540-room hotel.
(214) 631-2222
Jobline: (214) 631-2222, ask for job hotline.

Stouffer Harborplace Hotel
202 E. Pratt Street, Baltimore, MD 21202
662-room hotel.
(410) 547-1200
Jobline: (410) 752-1920

Stouffer Madison Hotel
515 Madison Street , Seattle, WA 98104
553-room hotel.
(206) 583-0300
Jobline: (206) 583-0300, ask for x2923.

Stouffer Riviere Hotel
1 W. Wacker Drive, Chicago, IL 60601
565-room hotel.
(312) 372-7200
Jobline: (312) 372-2022

Stouffer Waverly Hotel
2450 Galleria Parkway, Atlanta, GA 30339
521-room hotel.
(404) 953-4500
Jobline: (404) 953-4500, ask for x4310.

Suffolk (city)
441 Market Street, Suffolk, VA 23434
Provides municipal services such as police, firefighting,
libraries, parks, and public works.
(804) 925-6447
Jobline: (804) 925-6435

Suffolk University
Boston, MA 02108
Small, private, nonresidential university in the Beacon
Hills section of Boston.
(617) 573-8000
Jobline: (617) 573-8055

SunBank NA
200 S. Orange Avenue, Orlando, FL 32801
Operates national commercial banks.
(407) 237-4141
Jobline: (407) 237-6878

SunBank of Tampa Bay
315 E. Madison Street, Tampa, FL 33602
Operates state commercial banks.
(813) 224-2121
Jobline: (813) 224-2001
Exempt jobs.

Jobline: (813) 224-2002
Non-exempt jobs.

SunBank/Miami NA
777 Brickell Avenue, Miami, FL 33131
Operates national commercial banks.
(305) 592-0800
Jobline: (305) 579-7001

SunBank/South Florida NA
501 E. Las Olas Boulevard, Fort Lauderdale, FL 33301
Operates national commercial banks.
(305) 467-5000
Jobline: (305) 765-7100

Sundstrand Corp.
4949 Harrison Avenue, P.O. Box 7003, Rockford, IL
61125
Manufactures electronic aircraft control systems,
measuring instruments, pumps, and other products.
(815) 226-6000
Jobline: (815) 226-6269, press 1.

SunHealth Corp.
13180 N. 103rd Street, P.O. Box 1278
Sun City, AZ 85372
Operates two not-for-profit hospitals with more than 400
beds in the Phoenix area.
(602) 977-7211
Jobline: (602) 974-7984

Sutter County
1160 Civic Center Boulevard, Yuba City, CA 95993
Provides county services such as sheriffs, courts, motor
vehicle registration, and social services.
(916) 741-7113
Jobline: (916) 671-1687

Swissotel Boston
1 Avenue de Lafayette, Boston, MA 02111
496-room hotel.
(617) 451-2600
Jobline: (617) 422-5425

Swissotel Chicago
323 E. Wacker Drive, Chicago, IL 60601
647-room hotel.
(312) 565-0565
Jobline: (312) 565-0565, ask for job hotline.

Syntex Laboratories
3401 Hillview Avenue, Palo Alto, CA 94304-1320
Produces pharmaceutical preparations.
(415) 855-5050
Jobline: (415) 852-1800

Syva Co.
3403 Yerba Buena Road, P.O. Box 49013
San Jose, CA 95161-9013
Produces in vitro and in vivo diagnostic substances.
(408) 239-2000
Jobline: (408) 239-2725

Tacoma (city)
747 Market Street, Tacoma, WA 98402
Provides municipal services such as police, firefighting,
libraries, parks, and public works.
(206) 591-5400
Jobline: (206) 591-5795

Tacoma School District
601 S. 8th Street, Tacoma, WA 98405
71-school district in Tacoma.
(206) 596-1250
Jobline: (206) 596-1265

Tallahassee (city)
300 S. Adams Street, Tallahassee, FL 32301
Provides municipal services such as police, firefighting,
libraries, parks, and public works.
(904) 891-8215
Jobline: (904) 891-8219

Tandy Corp.
1800 One Tandy Center, Fort Worth, TX 76102
Operates consumer electronics stores and
manufactures electronic parts and equipment.
(817) 390-3700
Jobline: (817) 390-2949

Tarleton State University
Stephenville, TX 76402
Medium-sized, public university in Stephenville, 65
miles from Fort Worth.
(817) 968-9000
Jobline: (817) 968-9750

Tarrant County Junior College
Fort Worth, TX 76102
Large, county-supported, 2-year college in Fort Worth.
(817) 336-7851
Jobline: (817) 335-6721

Tele-Communications Inc.
5619 DTC Parkway, Englewood, CO 80111
Provides cable and subscription TV services, and
operates motion picture theaters.
(303) 721-5500
Jobline: (303) 267-6650

Tempe (city)
140 E. 5th Street, Tempe, AZ 85281
Provides municipal services such as police, firefighting,
libraries, parks, and public works.
(602) 350-8276
Jobline: (602) 350-8217

Tenneco Inc.
1010 Milam Street, P.O. Box 2511, Houston, TX
77252-2511
Manufactures farm machinery and equipment,
construction equipment, and operates other
businesses.
(713) 757-2131
Jobline: (713) 757-4193

Texas (state)
Central Services Building, Suite 123, 1711 San Jacinto
Boulevard, Austin, TX 78701
Provides state services such as conservation,
education, highways, prisons, and welfare.
(512) 463-3434
Jobline: (512) 463-3433

Texas (state) Auditor
206 E. 9th Street, Austin, TX 78701
Provides auditing programs and services.
(512) 479-4800
Jobline: (512) 479-3055

Texas (state) Department of Insurance
333 Guadalupe Street, Mail Code 302-1A, Austin, TX
78701
Regulates insurance.
(512) 463-6169
Jobline: (512) 463-6170, press 1.

Texas (state) Department of Protective and Regulatory Services
3635 SE Military Drive, San Antonio, TX 78223
Manages child abuse cases, adoption services, foster
homes, and child care licensing.
(210) 337-3290
Jobline: (210) 337-3234

701 W. 51st Street, Austin, TX 78751
(512) 450-3038
Jobline: (512) 450-3600

1200 Golden Key Circle, 4th Floor, El Paso, TX 79925
(915) 599-3600
Jobline: (915) 599-3635

Texas (state) Department of Transportation
200 E. Riverside Drive, Room 218, Austin, TX 78704
Provides transportation programs and services.
(512) 416-2994
Jobline: (512) 416-3000

Texas (state) Higher Education Coordinating Board
Building 5, Room 120, 7745 Chevy Chase Drive,
Austin, TX 78711
Coordinates higher education programs and services.
(512) 483-6190
Jobline: (512) 483-6574

Texas (state) Library and Archives
1201 Brazos Street, Austin, TX 78701
Provides library development, information, archival, and
genealogical programs and services.
(512) 463-5465
Jobline: (512) 463-5470

Texas (state) Natural Resource Conservation Commission
12100 Park 35 Circle, Building A, P.O. Box 13087,
Austin, TX 78711-3087
Manages and conserves natural resources.
(512) 239-0104
Jobline: (512) 239-0100, press 1.

Texas (state) Rehabilitation Commission
4900 N. Lamar Boulevard, Austin, TX 78751
Provides rehabilitative programs and services.
(512) 483-4320
Jobline: (512) 483-4880

Texas A&I University
Kingsville, TX 78363
Small, public, comprehensive university with a main
campus in Kingsville.
(512) 595-2111
Jobline: (512) 595-3004

Texas A&M University, College Station
College Station, TX 77843
Large, public, comprehensive university in College
Station.
(409) 845-3211
Jobline: (409) 845-4444

Texas Christian University
Fort Worth, TX 76129
Medium-sized, church-affiliated university near
    downtown Fort Worth.
(817) 921-7000
Jobline: (817) 921-7791

Texas Commerce Bank Dallas NA
2200 Ross Avenue, P.O. Box 660197, Dallas, TX
    75266-0197
Operates national commercial banks.
(214) 922-2300
Jobline: (214) 922-2224

Texas Commerce Bank El Paso NA
P.O. Drawer 140, El Paso, TX 79980
Operates national commercial banks.
(915) 546-6500
Jobline: (915) 546-6540

Texas Commerce Bank Houston NA
712 Main Street, Houston, TX 77002
Operates national commercial banks.
(713) 236-4865
Jobline: (713) 216-4541

Texas Instruments Inc.
7839 Churchill Way, Dallas, TX 75251
Manufactures semiconductors, integrated circuits, and
    other industrial and electronic products.
(214) 995-2535
Jobline: (214) 995-6666
Non-exempt jobs.

Texas Southern University
Houston, TX 77004
Medium-sized, public, historically black university in
    Houston.
(713) 527-7521
Jobline: (713) 527-7011, ask for job hotline.

Texas Tech University
Lubbock, TX 79409
Large, public, multipurpose university in Lubbock.
(806) 742-2011
Jobline: (806) 742-2211

Texas Woman's University
Denton, TX 76204
Medium-sized, public, comprehensive university with a
    main campus in Denton.
(817) 898-2000
Jobline: (817) 898-3565

Thornton (city)
9500 Civic Center Drive, Thornton, CO 80229
Provides municipal services such as police, firefighting,
    libraries, parks, and public works.
(303) 538-7245
Jobline: (303) 538-7629, x342.

Thurston County
Building 4, Room 202, 921 Lakeridge Drive SW,
    Olympia, WA 98502
Provides county services such as sheriffs, courts, motor
    vehicle registration, and social services.
(206) 786-5498
Jobline: (206) 786-5499

Tigard (city)
13125 SW Hall Boulevard, Tigard, OR 97223
Provides municipal services such as police, firefighting,
    libraries, parks, and public works.
(503) 639-4171
Jobline: (503) 624-9471

Torrance (city)
3231 Torrance Boulevard, Torrance, CA 90503
Provides municipal services such as police, firefighting,
    libraries, parks, and public works.
(310) 618-2960
Jobline: (310) 618-2969

Torrance Memorial Medical Center
3330 Lomita Boulevard, Torrance, CA 90505
Not-for-profit hospital with more than 300 beds.
(310) 325-9110
Jobline: (310) 517-4790

Transamerica Life Companies
1150 S. Olive Street, Los Angeles, CA 90015
Provides life, accident, and health insurance, and
    pension and investment services.
(213) 742-5151
Jobline: (213) 741-7834

Travis County
314 W. 11th Street, Suite 100, Austin, TX 78767
Provides county services such as sheriffs, courts, motor
    vehicle registration, and social services.
(512) 473-9165
Jobline: (512) 473-9675

Tri-County Metropolitan Transportation District of Oregon
4012 SE 17th Avenue, Portland, OR 97202
Manages public transportation for Clackamas,
    Multnomah, and Washington Counties.
(503) 238-4841
Jobline: (503) 238-4840

Trinity University
San Antonio, TX 78212
Small, private university overlooking San Antonio from
    Trinity Hill.
(210) 736-7011
Jobline: (210) 736-7510

Tropworld Casino & Entertainment Resort
Brighton Park and Boardwalk, Atlantic City, NJ
    08401-6390
1,014-room hotel.
(609) 340-4398
Jobline: (609) 340-4261

Trump Plaza Hotel & Casino
Mississippi Avenue and Boardwalk, P.O. Box 988,
    Atlantic City, NJ 08401
556-room hotel.
(609) 441-6000
Jobline: (800) 677-5627

Trump Taj Mahal
1000 Boardwalk at Virginia Street, Atlantic City, NJ
08401
1,250-room hotel.
(609) 449-1000
Jobline: (609) 449-5627

Trump's Castle Casino Resort by the Bay
Huron Avenue and Brigantine Boulevard, Atlantic City,
NJ 08401
725-room hotel.
(609) 441-8428
Jobline: (609) 441-8464

Trust Company Bank
25 Park Place NE, P.O. Box 4418, Atlanta, GA 30302
Operates state commercial banks and other investment
businesses.
(404) 588-7711
Jobline: (404) 588-7251

Trustmark National Bank
248 E. Capitol Street, Jackson, MS 39201
Operates national commercial banks.
(601) 354-5111
Jobline: (601) 949-2337

Tucson (city)
110 E. Pennington Street, Tucson, AZ 85701
Provides municipal services such as police, firefighting,
libraries, parks, and public works.
(602) 791-4241
Jobline: (602) 791-5068

Tulane University
New Orleans, LA 70118
Medium-sized, private university in residential New
Orleans.
(504) 865-5000
Jobline: (504) 865-5627

Tulare County
2900 Burrel Avenue, Visalia, CA 93291
Provides county services such as sheriffs, courts, motor
vehicle registration, and social services.
(209) 733-6266
Jobline: (209) 733-6704
Beeps if no jobs available.

Tulsa (city)
200 Civic Center, Tulsa, OK 74103
Provides municipal services such as police, firefighting,
libraries, parks, and public works.
(918) 596-7427
Jobline: (918) 596-7444

Tulsa Junior College
Tulsa, OK 74135
Medium-sized, state-supported, 2-year college in Tulsa.
(918) 631-7000
Jobline: (918) 631-7854, press 1.

Tuolumne County
2 S. Green Street, Sonora, CA 95370
Provides county services such as sheriffs, courts, motor
vehicle registration, and social services.
(209) 533-5566
Jobline: (209) 533-5631

Twentieth Century-Fox Film Corp.
10201 W. Pico Boulevard, P.O. Box 900, Beverly Hills,
CA 90213
Produces and distributes motion pictures, TV films, and
video tapes.
(310) 277-2211
Jobline: (310) 203-1360

U.S. Bank Nevada
1 E. Liberty Street, Reno, NV 89501
Operates state commercial banks.
(702) 688-3555
Jobline: (800) 366-6698

U.S. Bank of Washington NA
1415 5th Avenue, P.O. Box 720, Seattle, WA 98111
Operates national commercial banks.
(206) 344-2300
Jobline: (206) 344-5656

UAL Corp.
1200 E. Algonquin Road, P.O. Box 66100, Chicago, IL
60666
Provides scheduled air passenger transportation.
(708) 952-4000
Jobline: (708) 952-4000, press 1.

Unicare Health Facilities Inc.
105 W. Michigan Street, Milwaukee, WI 53203
Operates long-term health care facilities.
(414) 271-9696
Jobline: (414) 347-4343
Corporate office jobs.

Jobline: (414) 347-4636
Field jobs.

Union Bank NA
350 California Street, San Francisco, CA 94104
Operates national commercial banks.
(415) 445-0332
Jobline: (415) 705-7013

530 B Street, San Diego, CA 92101
(619) 230-4383
Jobline: (619) 230-3371

Union Pacific Railroad Co.
1416 Dodge Street, Omaha, NE 68179
Operates line-haul railroads.
(402) 271-5000
Jobline: (402) 271-5000, press 7, then 1, then 3.

Union Planters National Bank
7130 Goodlett Farms Parkway, Cordova, TN 38018
Operates national commercial banks.
(901) 383-6000
Jobline: (901) 383-6663

United Parcel Service of America Inc.
400 Perimeter Center Terrace North, Atlanta, GA 30346
Transports and delivers parcels.
(404) 913-6000
Jobline: (404) 913-6800

United States Air Force Academy
Colorado Springs, CO 80840
Small, public service academy in Colorado Springs.
(719) 472-1818
Jobline: (719) 472-2222

United States Courts
Administrative Offices, Washington, DC 20544
Handles the nonjudicial, administrative business of the
United States Courts.
(202) 273-2777
Jobline: (202) 273-2760

United States Department of Agriculture
Agricultural Research Service
Beltsville, MD 20705
Applies research to solve problems relating to
agricultural resources, products, and conditions.
(202) 720-5626
Jobline: (301) 344-2288

Farmers Home Administration
1520 Market Street, Saint Louis, MO 63103
Provides credit for those in the rural U.S. unable to get
credit from other sources.
(314) 539-2403
Jobline: (314) 539-2830

Forest Service
P.O. Box 96060, Washington, DC 20090-6090
Manages the National Forest System's natural
resources for their continued use and protection.
(202) 720-8732
Jobline: (703) 235-5627

Forest Service
Tonto National Forest, 2324 E. McDowell Road,
Phoenix, AZ 85010
Manages the Tonto National Forest.
(602) 225-5384
Jobline: (602) 225-5382

Forest Service
Helena National Forest, 2880 Skyway Drive, Helena,
MT 59601
Manages the Helena National Forest.
(406) 449-5201
Jobline: (406) 449-5419

Forest Service
Siskiyou National Forest, 200 NE Greenfield Road, P.O.
Box 440, Grants Pass, OR 97526
Manages the Siskiyou National Forest.
(503) 471-6710
Jobline: (503) 471-6715
Firefighting jobs.

United States Department of the Air Force
The Pentagon
Washington, DC 20330-1000
Provides an aerial capability to preserve the peace and
security of the United States.
(703) 697-0580
Jobline: (703) 693-6550, press 1, then 1.
Civilian jobs.

Charleston Air Force Base
437 MSSQ/MSC, 101 E. Hill Boulevard, Building 503,
Charleston Air Force Base, SC 29404-5021
Supports the Air Force's mission to preserve the peace
and security of the United States.
(803) 566-4501
Jobline: (803) 566-4490
Civilian jobs.

Dobbins Air Reserve Base
94 STTG/DPC, 1315 Barracks Court, Building 802,
Atlanta, GA 30069-4916
(404) 421-4969
Jobline: (404) 421-4968
Civilian jobs.

McClellan Air Force Base
Sacramento, CA 95652
(916) 643-2111
Jobline: (916) 643-5911
Civilian jobs.

Tinker Air Force Base
3000 S. Douglas Boulevard, Tinker Air Force Base, OK
73150
(405) 732-7321
Jobline: (405) 739-3271
Civilian jobs.

United States Department of the Army
The Pentagon
Washington, DC 20310
Organizes, trains, and equips forces to defend the
peace and security of the United States.
(202) 545-6700
Jobline: (703) 695-2589
Civilian jobs.

Corps of Engineers
District Office, 700 W. Capitol Avenue, Little Rock, AR
72201
Manages and executes engineering, construction, and
real estate programs for the U.S. Army.
(501) 324-5656
Jobline: (501) 324-5660

Corps of Engineers
District Office, 1222 Spruce Street, Saint Louis, MO
63103
(314) 331-8536
Jobline: (314) 331-8550

Corps of Engineers
District Office, 4735 E. Marginal Way South, Seattle,
WA 98134
(206) 764-3742
Jobline: (206) 764-3739

Fort Benjamin Harrison
Indianapolis Center, DFAS-IN-HUJ, Mail Stop 54 8899
E. 56th Street, Indianapolis, IN 46249
Supports the Army's mission to preserve the peace and
security of the United States.
(317) 542-2401
Jobline: (317) 542-2454
Civilian jobs.

United States Department of the Army (cont.)
Fort Benning
Meloy Hall, Building 6, Fort Benning, GA 31905-5031
(706) 545-2470
Jobline: (706) 545-7084
Civilian jobs.

Fort Bliss and William Beaumont Army Medical Center
ATZC-CSR, Fort Bliss, TX 79916-5803
(915) 568-6232
Jobline: (915) 568-4755
Civilian jobs.

Fort Carson
1 Fort Carson, Colorado Springs, CO 80913
(719) 526-4524
Jobline: (719) 526-3307
Civilian jobs.

Peninsula Job Information Center
11824 Fishing Point Drive, Suite C, Newport News, VA
23606
Includes Ft. Eustis, Ft. Monroe, Ft. Story, Ft. Lee, and
DECA at Ft. Lee.
(804) 873-3142
Jobline: (804) 873-3160
Civilian jobs.

Rock Island Arsenal
Rock Island, IL 61299-5000
Manufactures howitzers and weapon prototypes.
(309) 782-1247
Jobline: (309) 782-2214
Civilian jobs.

United States Department of Commerce
14th Street, Washington, DC 20230
Serves and promotes the U.S.'s international trade,
economic growth, and technological advancement.
(202) 377-2000
Jobline: (202) 482-5138

Bureau of the Census
Washington, DC 20230
Collects, tabulates, and publishes statistical data about
the U.S. people and economy.
(301) 763-7470
Jobline: (301) 763-6064

Central Administrative Support Center
601 E. 12th Street, Kansas City, MO 64106
Serves and promotes the U.S.'s international trade,
economic growth, and technological advancement.
(816) 426-7468
Jobline: (816) 426-7463

National Institute of Standards and Technology
Gaithersburg, MD 20899
Science and engineering laboratory for measurement
technology and standards research.
(301) 975-2000
Jobline: (301) 926-4851

National Oceanic and Atmospheric Administration
Mountain Administrative Support Center, 325 Broadway
Street, Boulder, CO 80303
Studies, monitors, and predicts conditions in the
oceans, atmosphere, and space.
(303) 497-3000
Jobline: (303) 497-6332

National Oceanic and Atmospheric Administration
Eastern Administrative Support Center, 253 Monticello
Avenue, Norfolk, VA 23510-2314
(804) 441-6516
Jobline: (804) 441-3720

National Oceanic and Atmospheric Administration
Western Administrative Support Center, 7600 Sand
Point Way NE, Building 1, Seattle, WA 98115
Studies, monitors, and predicts conditions in the
oceans, atmosphere, and space.
(206) 526-6053
Jobline: (206) 526-6051
Jobs on board NOAA research vessels.

Jobline: (206) 526-6294
Continue listening while menu repeats.

Patent and Trademark Office
Washington, DC 20230
Seeks to promote the progress of the useful arts by
issuing patents and registering trademarks.
(703) 308-4357
Jobline: (703) 305-4221, press 1.

Defense Contract Audit Agency
Building 4, Cameron Station, Alexandria, VA 22304-6178
Provides all necessary contract audit functions for the
Department of Defense.
(703) 274-7328
Jobline: (703) 274-4068

Defense Intelligence Agency
The Pentagon
Washington, DC 20340-0001
Produces and disseminates military intelligence for
major components of the Department of Defense.
(703) 284-1321
Jobline: (703) 284-1110
Civilian jobs.
Call (800) 526-4629 outside the 703 area code.

Defense Logistics Agency
Defense Distribution Region Central, 2163 Airways
Boulevard, Memphis, TN 38114
Provides worldwide logistic support for the Department
of Defense and other organizations.
(901) 775-4934
Jobline: (901) 775-4933
Civilian jobs.

Defense Logistics Agency
Cameron Station, Alexandria, VA 22304-6100
(703) 274-6000
Jobline: (703) 274-7372

United States Department of Energy

1000 Independence Avenue SW, Washington, DC 20585
Coordinates and administers the energy functions of the federal government.
(202) 586-5000
Jobline: (202) 586-4333

Bonneville Power Administration
Puget Sound Area Office, 201 Queen Anne Avenue, Seattle, WA 98109
Markets electric power and energy from federal hydroelectric projects in the Pacific Northwest.
(206) 553-6053
Jobline: (206) 553-7564
Includes jobs in Portland and Vancouver areas.

Richland Field Office
825 Jadwin Avenue, P.O. Box 550, Richland, WA 99352
Coordinates and administers the energy functions of the federal government.
(509) 376-7395
Jobline: (800) 695-4363

Western Area Power Administration
1627 Cole Boulevard, Golden, CO 80401
Responsible for federal electric-power marketing and transmission functions in 15 western states.
(303) 275-1263
Jobline: (303) 275-1244

United States Department of Health and Human Services

200 Independence Avenue SW, Washington, DC 20201
Provides programs and services to maintain the health and welfare of the American people.
(202) 619-0257
Jobline: (202) 619-2560

Region 6
1200 Main Tower, Dallas, TX 75202
Promotes and supports Department of Health and Human Services programs and activities in the region.
(214) 767-3124
Jobline: (214) 767-3124, press 2.

Region 8
1961 Stout Street, Denver, CO 80294-3538
(303) 844-6391
Jobline: (303) 844-6329

Region 9
Federal Office Building, 50 United Nations Plaza, San Francisco, CA 94102
(415) 556-6746
Jobline: (415) 556-1088

Region 10
Blanchard Plaza Building, 2201 6th Avenue, Seattle, WA 98121
(206) 615-2030
Jobline: (206) 615-2036

Centers for Disease Control
1600 Clifton Road NE, Atlanta, GA 30333
Provides leadership and direction in the prevention and control of diseases.
(404) 639-3276
Jobline: (404) 332-4577

Food and Drug Administration
4B-41 Parklawn Building, 5600 Fishers Lane, Rockville, MD 20857
Protects the U.S. against impure and unsafe foods, drugs, and cosmetics.
(301) 443-2234
Jobline: (301) 443-1969

Health Resources and Services Administration
5600 Fishers Lane, Rockville, MD 20857
Provides the Public Health Service with leadership for general health services and resource issues.
(301) 443-5460
Jobline: (301) 443-1230

National Institutes of Health
9000 Rockville Pike, Bethesda, MD 20892
Seeks to improve the health of the American people.
(301) 496-4197
Jobline: (301) 496-2403, press 1.

Office of the Assistant Secretary for Health
5600 Fishers Lane, Rockville, MD 20857
Staff offices that help plan and direct the activities of the Public Health Service.
(301) 443-6900
Jobline: (301) 443-1986

Substance Abuse and Mental Health Services Administration
15C-12 Parklawn Building, 5600 Fishers Lane, Rockville, MD 20857
Promotes effective strategies for handling alcohol, drug, and mental health issues and problems.
(301) 443-4826
Jobline: (301) 443-2282

United States Department of Housing and Urban Development

451 7th Street SW, Washington, DC 20410
Concerned with the U.S.'s housing needs, fair housing opportunities, and community development.
(202) 708-0408
Jobline: (202) 708-3203

1405 Curtis Street, Denver, CO 80202
(303) 672-5259
Jobline: (303) 672-5263

United States Department of the Interior

1849 C Street NW, Washington, DC 20240
Manages most of the U.S.'s nationally owned public lands and natural resources.
(202) 208-3100
Jobline: (800) 336-4562

United States Department of the Interior (cont.)
Bureau of Indian Affairs
1849 C Street NW, Washington, DC 20240
Helps Native people manage their affairs under their
  trust relationship with the U.S.
(202) 208-2547
Jobline: (202) 208-2682

Bureau of Reclamation
Pacific Southwest Regional Office, 2800 Cottage Way,
  Sacramento, CA 95825
Responsible for providing water, generating
  hydroelectric power, regulating rivers, and other
  tasks.
(916) 978-5021
Jobline: (916) 978-4897

Bureau of Reclamation
Pacific Northwest Regional Office, 550 W. Fort Street,
  Boise, ID 83724
(208) 334-1221
Jobline: (208) 378-5144

Geological Survey
215 National Center, 12201 Sunrise Valley Drive
Reston, VA 22092
Assesses the U.S.'s natural resources, researches
  global change, and investigates natural hazards.
(703) 648-6131
Jobline: (703) 648-7676

Geological Survey
345 Middlefield Road, Menlo Park, CA 94025
(415) 329-4104
Jobline: (415) 329-4122

Geological Survey
Denver Federal Center, Building 25, Denver, CO 80225
(303) 236-5900
Jobline: (303) 236-5846

Geological Survey
75 Spring Street SW, Atlanta, GA 30303
(404) 331-5494
Jobline: (404) 448-5320

Geological Survey
1400 Independence Road, Rolla, MO 65401
(314) 341-0810
Jobline: (314) 341-0909

Minerals Management Service
1849 C Street NW, Washington, DC 20240
Manages the leasing and extraction of mineral
  resources from federal lands and waters.
(202) 208-3983
Jobline: (703) 787-1402

National Park Service
1849 C Street NW, Washington, DC 20240
Administers an extensive system of national parks,
  monuments, historic sites, and recreation areas.
(202) 619-7256
Jobline: (202) 619-7111

National Park Service
Western Regional Office, 600 Harrison Street, San
  Francisco, CA 94107
(415) 744-3888
Jobline: (415) 744-3884

National Park Service
Rocky Mountain Regional Office, 12795 W. Alameda
  Place, Lakewood, CO 80228
(303) 969-2772
Jobline: (303) 969-2010

National Park Service
Southeast Regional Office, 75 Spring Street SW,
  Atlanta, GA 30303
(404) 331-5714
Jobline: (404) 331-5189

National Park Service
North Atlantic Regional Office, 15 State Street, Boston,
  MA 02109
(617) 223-5101
Jobline: (617) 223-5200

National Park Service
Midwest Regional Office, 1709 Jackson Street, Omaha,
  NE 68102
(402) 221-3456
Jobline: (402) 221-3434

National Park Service
Pacific Northwest Regional Office, 83 S. King Street,
  Seattle, WA 98104
(206) 220-4053
Jobline: (206) 220-4053, press 1.

National Park Service
Golden Gate National Recreation Area, Fort Mason,
  Building 201, San Francisco, CA 94123
Manages the Golden Gate National Recreation Area.
(415) 556-2035
Jobline: (415) 556-1839

National Park Service
Olympic National Park, 600 E. Park, Port Angeles, WA
  98362
Manages the Olympic National Park.
(206) 452-0330
Jobline: (206) 452-0308

Office of the Secretary
1849 C Street NW, Washington, DC 20240
Directs and supervises all operations and activities of
  the Department of the Interior.
(202) 208-3100
Jobline: (800) 822-5463

United States Fish and Wildlife Service
1849 C Street NW, Washington, DC 20240
Conserves, protects, and enhances fish and wildlife and
  their habitats for the American people.
(202) 208-5634
Jobline: (703) 358-2120

United States Department of Justice
Bureau of Prisons
320 1st Street NW, Washington, DC 20534
Executes the will of the federal courts by providing
confinement services to committed offenders.
(202) 307-1304
Jobline: (800) 347-7744, press 1, then 1.

Immigration and Naturalization Service
425 I Street NW, Washington, DC 20536
Helps visitors and immigrants enter the U.S. legally and
prevents others from entering illegally.
(202) 514-2531
Jobline: (202) 514-4301

United States Marshals Service
600 Army Navy Drive, Arlington, VA 22202-4210
Secures federal courts, arrests and transports
suspects, and operates a witness protection program.
(202) 307-9000
Jobline: (202) 307-9400

United States Department of Labor
200 Constitution Avenue NW, Washington, DC 20210
Seeks to promote the welfare of wage earners and
improve their working conditions.
(202) 219-6677
Jobline: (202) 219-6646

United States Department of the Navy
Consolidated Civilian Personnel Office
Washington Navy Yard, Building 200, 11th and M Street
SE, Washington, DC 20374-5050
Seeks civilian workers for the U.S. Navy.
(202) 433-4931
Jobline: (202) 433-4930

Little Creek Amphibious Base and Oceana Naval Air
Station
487 E. C Street, Norfolk, VA 23511-3997
Prepares amphibious assault craft and aircraft for
deployment on ships in the U.S. Navy.
(804) 363-4432
Jobline: (804) 444-7541
Includes jobs at the Portsmouth Naval Medical Center.

Long Beach Naval Shipyard
300 Skipjack Road, Long Beach, CA 90822-5099
Builds and maintains ships for the U.S. Navy.
(310) 547-7217
Jobline: (310) 547-8277
Civilian jobs.

Naval Air Station
Patuxent River, MD 20670
Prepares aircraft for deployment on aircraft carriers in
the U.S. Navy.
(301) 826-3545
Jobline: (301) 826-4801
Civilian jobs.

Naval Medical Center
Code BLA, San Diego, CA 92134-5000
Provides medical services for the U.S. Navy.
(619) 532-9393
Jobline: (619) 532-9325
Civilian jobs.

Naval Weapon Station and Naval Warfare Assessment
Center
Seal Beach Boulevard and Bolsa Avenue, Seal Beach,
CA 90740
Stores and tests weapons and equipment for use by
the U.S. Navy.
(310) 594-7629
Jobline: (310) 594-7881
Military and civilian jobs.

Norfolk Naval Shipyard
Code 1117, Building 491, Portsmouth, VA 23709-5000
Builds and maintains ships for the U.S. Navy.
(804) 396-4052
Jobline: (804) 396-5657
Civilian jobs.

North Island Naval Air Station
Code 12210, P.O. Box 357041, San Diego, CA
92135-7041
Prepares aircraft for deployment on aircraft carriers in
the U.S. Navy.
(619) 545-1607
Jobline: (619) 545-1620
Civilian jobs.

United States Department of State
2201 C Street NW, Washington, DC 20520
Advises the President in the formulation and execution
of foreign policy.
(202) 647-6132
Jobline: (202) 647-7284

Foreign Service
2201 C Street NW, Washington, DC 20520
Conducts relations with foreign countries through
embassies and other establishments overseas.
(703) 875-7490
Jobline: (703) 875-7490

United States Department of the Treasury
Bureau of Alcohol, Tobacco and Firearms
1200 Pennsylvania Avenue NW, Washington, DC 20226
Administers laws covering the production, use, and
distribution of alcohol, tobacco, and firearms.
(202) 927-8610
Jobline: (202) 927-8423

Internal Revenue Service
Atlanta Service Center, 4800 Buford Highway,
Chamblee, GA 30341
Collects, processes, and stores national income tax
returns.
(404) 455-2381
Jobline: (404) 455-2455

Internal Revenue Service
Cincinnati Service Center, 200 W. 4th Street,
Covington, KY 41011
(606) 292-5686
Jobline: (606) 292-5304

Internal Revenue Service
Austin Service Center 3651, S. Interregional Highway
35, Austin, TX 78741
(512) 462-7601
Jobline: (512) 477-5627

United States Department of the Treasury (cont.)
Jobline: (512) 462-8115
Jobs for IRS employees.

Internal Revenue Service
Seattle District, 915 2nd Avenue, Seattle, WA 98104
Provides taxpayer assistance, personnel examinations,
and other services.
(206) 220-5725
Jobline: (206) 220-5757

United States Department of Transportation
400 7th Street SW, Washington, DC 20590
Establishes the U.S.'s overall transportation policy
through various administrations.
(202) 366-9392
Jobline: (202) 366-9397

Federal Aviation Administration
800 Independence Avenue SW, Washington, DC 20591
Regulates the manufacture, operation, and
maintenance of aircraft; certifies pilots and airports.
(202) 366-4000
Jobline: (202) 267-3229

Federal Aviation Administration
Northwest Mountain Regional Headquarters, 1601 Lind
Avenue SW, Renton, WA 98055
Regulates the manufacture, operation, and
maintenance of aircraft; certifies pilots and airports.
(206) 227-1727
Jobline: (206) 227-2014

United States Department of Veterans Affairs
Medical Center
5901 E. 7th Street, Long Beach, CA 90822
Hospital and nursing home-type unit with more than
400 beds for veterans of the U.S. armed forces.
(310) 494-5651
Jobline: (310) 494-5971

Medical Center
50 Irving Street NW, 05-A, Washington, DC 20422
Hospital and nursing home-type unit with more than
600 beds for veterans of the U.S. armed forces.
(202) 745-8204
Jobline: (202) 745-8000, press 1.

Medical Center
1201 NW 16th Street, Miami, FL 33125
Hospital and nursing home-type unit with more than
800 beds for veterans of the U.S. armed forces.
(305) 324-3155
Jobline: (305) 324-3154, press 3154.

Medical Center
Building 22, Room 326, 10000 Bay Pines Boulevard,
Bay Pines, FL 33504
Hospital and nursing home-type unit with more than
1,000 beds for veterans of the U.S. armed forces.
(813) 398-6661
Jobline: (813) 398-9493

Medical Center
3710 SW U.S. Veterans Hospital Road, P.O. Box 1034,
Portland, OR 97207
Hospital and nursing home-type unit with more than
2,100 beds for veterans of the U.S. armed forces.
(503) 273-5234
Jobline: (503) 273-5249
Includes jobs in the Portland and Vancouver divisions.

Medical Center
6010 W. Amarillo Boulevard, Amarillo, TX 79106
Hospital and nursing home-type unit with more than
200 beds for veterans of the U.S. armed forces.
(806) 354-7827
Jobline: (806) 354-7828

United States Information Agency
301 4th Street SW, Washington, DC 20547
Manages the U.S. Government's overseas information
and cultural programs.
(202) 619-4656
Jobline: (202) 619-4539

United States Marine Corps
The Pentagon
Washington, DC 20380-0001
Provides forces for seizing or defending advanced
naval bases, contributes to naval campaigns.
(703) 614-1046
Jobline: (703) 697-7474
Civilian jobs.

United States Naval Academy
Annapolis, MD 21402-5018
Small, public service academy in Annapolis, 30 miles
southeast of Baltimore.
(410) 293-6100
Jobline: (410) 293-3821

United States Senate
The Capitol
Washington, DC 20510
Wields legislative powers under the U.S. Constitution.
(202) 224-3121
Jobline: (202) 228-5627

Universities and Community Colleges of Nevada
Business Center North, Mail Stop 240, Reno, NV
89557-0055
Includes the University of Nevada, Reno and three
community colleges.
(702) 784-1110
Jobline: (702) 784-1464

University of Akron
Akron, OH 44325
Large, public, multipurpose institution near downtown
Akron.
(216) 972-7111
Jobline: (216) 972-7091

University of Alabama at Birmingham
Birmingham, AL 35294
Medium-sized, public university and medical center
complex near downtown Birmingham.
(205) 934-4011
Jobline: (205) 934-2611

University of Alabama in Huntsville
Huntsville, AL 35899
Small, public university with a main campus in northwest
  Huntsville and a medical campus downtown.
(205) 395-6120
Jobline: (205) 895-6105

University of Alabama, Tuscaloosa
Tuscaloosa, AL 35487-0132
Medium-sized, public institution in west central Alabama.
(205) 348-6010
Jobline: (205) 348-7780

University of Alaska Anchorage
Anchorage, AK 99508
Medium-sized, public, comprehensive institution near
  downtown Anchorage.
(907) 786-1800
Jobline: (907) 786-4887

University of Arizona
Tucson, AZ 85721-0007
Large, public institution in residential Tucson.
(602) 621-3237
Jobline: (602) 621-3087

University of Arkansas at Little Rock
Little Rock, AR 72204
Medium-sized, public institution in southwest Little Rock.
(501) 569-3000
Jobline: (501) 569-3038

University of Arkansas, Fayetteville
Fayetteville, AR 72701
Medium-sized, public, land-grant institution in the Ozark
  Mountains.
(501) 575-5200
Jobline: (501) 575-5627

University of California, Davis
Davis, CA 95616
Large, public university in Davis, 15 miles from
  Sacramento.
(916) 752-1011
Jobline: (916) 752-1760

University of California, Irvine
Medical Center
101 S. City Drive, Orange, CA 92668
Not-for-profit hospital with more than 400 beds affiliated
  with UC Irvine.
(714) 456-6011
Jobline: (714) 856-5850

University of California, Los Angeles
Medical Center
10833 Le Conte Avenue, Los Angeles, CA 90024
Not-for-profit hospital with more than 600 beds on the
  UCLA campus.
(310) 825-9111
Jobline: (310) 825-8320

University of California, San Diego
San Diego, CA 92093
Medium-sized, public university in La Jolla, 12 miles
  north of San Diego.
(619) 534-2230
Jobline: (619) 682-1000

University of California, Santa Barbara
Santa Barbara, CA 93106
Medium-sized, public university in Santa Barbara, north
  of Los Angeles.
(805) 893-8000
Jobline: (805) 893-3311

University of California, Santa Cruz
Santa Cruz, CA 95064
Medium-sized, public university in Santa Cruz,
  overlooking Monterey Bay.
(408) 459-0111
Jobline: (408) 459-2011, press 6.

University of Central Florida
Administration Building, Room 230, P.O. Box 160140,
  Orlando, FL 32816
Medium-sized, public university in Orlando.
(407) 823-2000
Jobline: (407) 823-2778

University of Central Oklahoma
Edmond, OK 73034
Medium-sized, public, liberal arts university in Edmond,
  12 miles from Oklahoma City.
(405) 341-2980
Jobline: (405) 341-2980, press 1, then 3089.

University of Colorado, Boulder
Boulder, CO 80309
Large, public, comprehensive university in Boulder,
  northwest of Denver.
(303) 492-1411
Jobline: (303) 492-5442

University of Connecticut
Storrs, CT 06268
Large, public, comprehensive university in Storrs,
  northeast of Hartford.
(203) 486-2000
Jobline: (203) 486-2466

University of Dayton
Dayton, OH 45469-0001
Medium-sized, church-affiliated institution in Dayton.
(513) 229-1000
Jobline: (513) 229-3377

University of Delaware
Newark, DE 19716
Medium-sized, private, state-assisted institution in
  Newark.
(302) 731-2000
Jobline: (302) 831-2100

University of Denver
Denver, CO 80208
Medium-sized, church-affiliated institution seven miles
  from downtown Denver.
(303) 871-2000
Jobline: (303) 871-3460

University of Florida
P.O. Box 115002, Gainesville, FL 32611-5002
Large, public, comprehensive university in Gainesville.
(904) 392-3261
Jobline: (904) 392-4631

University of Georgia
Athens, GA 30602
Large, public university in Athens, 80 miles east of
  Atlanta.
(706) 542-3000
Jobline: (706) 542-5720
Secretarial and clerical jobs.

Jobline: (706) 542-5769
Service, maintenance, and crafts jobs.

Jobline: (706) 542-5781
Professional and technical jobs.

Jobline: (706) 542-8722
Laboratory and research jobs.

University of Houston
Houston, TX 77204-2161
Large, public university three miles from downtown
  Houston.
(713) 743-1000
Jobline: (713) 743-5788

University of Houston, Downtown
Houston, TX 77002
Small, public university with a two-building campus at
  the edge of Houston's business district.
(713) 221-8000
Jobline: (713) 221-8609

University of Idaho
Moscow, ID 83843
Medium-sized, public, comprehensive, land-grant
  university in Moscow.
(208) 885-6111
Jobline: (208) 885-5702

University of Iowa
Iowa City, IA 52242
Large, public, comprehensive institution in Iowa City.
(319) 335-2656
Jobline: (319) 335-2684
Service and technical jobs.

Jobline: (319) 335-2685
Crafts and trade jobs.

Jobline: (319) 335-2686
Clerical and professional jobs.

University of Kansas
Lawrence, KS 66045
Large, public, comprehensive institution in residential
  Lawrence.
(913) 864-2700
Jobline: (913) 864-4623

University of Kentucky
Lexington, KY 40506
Medium-sized, public, comprehensive university in
  Lexington.
(606) 257-9000
Jobline: (606) 257-3841, press 200.

University of LaVerne
LaVerne, CA 91750
Small, church-affiliated university in LaVerne, 35 miles
  east of Los Angeles.
(909) 593-3511
Jobline: (909) 593-3511, press 1, then 6008.
Classified staff jobs.

Jobline: (909) 593-3511, press 1, then 6009.
Administrative and professional jobs.

Jobline: (909) 593-3511, press 1, then 6010.
Faculty jobs.

University of Louisville
Louisville, KY 40292
Medium-sized, public, comprehensive institution in
  Louisville.
(502) 852-6531
Jobline: (502) 852-5627

University of Maryland at College Park
College Park, MD 20742
Large, public institution in College Park, nine miles from
  Washington, D.C.
(301) 405-1000
Jobline: (301) 405-5677

University of Maryland Baltimore County
Baltimore, MD 21228
Provides county services such as sheriffs, courts, motor
  vehicle registration, and social services.
(410) 455-1000
Jobline: (410) 455-1100

University of Maryland Eastern Shore
Princess Anne, MD 21853
Small, public, multipurpose institution in Princess Anne,
  south of Salisbury.
(410) 651-2200
Jobline: (410) 651-6000

University of Miami
Coral Gables, FL 33124
Medium-sized, private, comprehensive institution with a
  main campus in suburban Miami.
(305) 284-2211
Jobline: (305) 284-6918

Jobline: (305) 547-6999
School of Medicine jobs.

University of Michigan, Ann Arbor
Ann Arbor, MI 48109-1316
Large, public, comprehensive institution in Ann Arbor,
  west of Detroit.
(313) 764-1817
Jobline: (313) 747-2375
Hospital jobs.

Jobline: (313) 764-7292
Campus jobs.

University of Michigan, Dearborn
Dearborn, MI 43128-1491
Small, public, comprehensive university in Dearborn.
(313) 593-5000
Jobline: (313) 593-5517

University of Minnesota, Duluth
Duluth, MN 55812
Medium-sized, public university in Duluth.
(218) 726-8000
Jobline: (218) 726-6506

University of Minnesota, Twin Cities
Minneapolis, MN 55455
Large, public university with a main campus in
   Minneapolis and another in St. Paul.
(612) 625-5000
Jobline: (612) 645-6060, x2500.

University of Mississippi
University, MS 38677
Medium-sized, public, comprehensive institution in
   Oxford, 75 miles south of Memphis.
(601) 232-7226
Jobline: (601) 232-7666

University of Missouri, Columbia
Columbia, MO 65211
Large, public, comprehensive institution in Columbia,
   west of St. Louis.
(314) 882-2121
Jobline: (314) 882-8800

University of Missouri, Kansas City
Kansas City, MO 64110
Medium-sized, public university in Kansas City.
(816) 235-1000
Jobline: (816) 235-1627

University of Missouri, Rolla
Rolla, MO 65401
Small, public university in Rolla, 95 miles southwest of
   St. Louis.
(314) 341-4111
Jobline: (314) 341-4242

University of Missouri, Saint Louis
Saint Louis, MO 63121
Medium-sized, public university in suburban West St.
   Louis.
(314) 553-5000
Jobline: (314) 553-5926

University of Montevallo
Montevallo, AL 35115-6000
Small, public institution in the town of Montevallo.
(205) 665-6000
Jobline: (205) 665-8050

University of Nebraska, Lincoln
Lincoln, NE 68588
Large, comprehensive institution with one campus in
   residential Lincoln and another downtown.
(402) 472-7211
Jobline: (402) 472-2303

University of Nebraska, Omaha
Omaha, NE 68182-0005
Medium-sized, public, comprehensive institution in
   residential Omaha.
(402) 554-2800
Jobline: (402) 554-2959

University of New Hampshire
Durham, NH 03824
Medium-sized, public, comprehensive institution in
   Durham, near the coastline.
(603) 862-1234
Jobline: (603) 862-4473

University of New Mexico
Albuquerque, NM 87131
Medium-sized, public, comprehensive institution in
   Albuquerque.
(505) 277-0111
Jobline: (505) 272-5627

University of North Carolina at Chapel Hill
Chapel Hill, NC 27514
Large, public university in Chapel Hill, west of Raleigh.
(919) 962-2211
Jobline: (919) 990-3000

University of North Carolina at Charlotte
Charlotte, NC 28223
Medium-sized, public university in Charlotte.
(704) 547-2000
Jobline: (704) 547-2075

University of North Carolina at Greensboro
Greensboro, NC 27412
Medium-sized, public, comprehensive university near
   downtown Greensboro.
(910) 334-5000
Jobline: (910) 334-5023

University of North Carolina at Wilmington
Wilmington, NC 28403
Medium-sized, public university in Wilmington, in
   southeast North Carolina near the Atlantic coast.
(910) 395-3000
Jobline: (910) 395-3791

University of North Texas
Denton, TX 76203-3797
Large, public, comprehensive university in Denton, 39
   miles from Dallas.
(817) 565-2000
Jobline: (817) 565-4070

University of Northern Iowa
Cedar Falls, IA 50614
Medium-sized, public, comprehensive institution in
   Cedar Falls, near Waterloo.
(319) 273-2311
Jobline: (319) 273-2421

University of Notre Dame
Notre Dame, IN 46556
Medium-sized, Catholic university.
(219) 631-5000
Jobline: (219) 631-4663

University of Oklahoma
Norman, OK 73019
Medium-sized, public, multipurpose institution with a
   main campus in Norman, near Oklahoma City.
(405) 325-1826
Jobline: (405) 325-2711
Student jobs.

University of Oklahoma (cont.)
Jobline: (405) 325-4343
Permanent jobs.

University of Pennsylvania
Philadelphia, PA 19104
Medium-sized, private, Ivy League university near
    downtown Philadelphia.
(215) 898-5000
Jobline: (215) 898-5627

University of Pittsburgh, Pittsburgh Campus
Pittsburgh, PA 15260
Medium-sized, state-related institution in the Oakland
    section of Pittsburgh.
(412) 624-4141
Jobline: (412) 624-8040

University of Portland
Portland, OR 97203-5798
Small, Catholic university in residential Portland.
(800) 227-4568
Jobline: (503) 283-7536
Jobs other than academic.

University of Redlands
Redlands, CA 92373-0999
Small, private, liberal arts university in Redlands, 65
    miles east of Los Angeles.
(909) 793-2121
Jobline: (909) 798-7482

University of Richmond
Richmond, VA 23173
Small, church-affiliated institution six miles from central
    Richmond.
(804) 289-8000
Jobline: (804) 287-6001

University of Saint Thomas
Saint Paul, MN 55105
Medium-sized, Catholic, diocesan institution between
    Minneapolis and St. Paul.
(612) 962-5000
Jobline: (612) 962-6520

University of San Diego
San Diego, CA 92110
Small, church-affiliated institution in San Diego.
(619) 260-4600
Jobline: (619) 260-4626

University of San Francisco
San Francisco, CA 94117-1080
Medium-sized, church-affiliated institution in San
    Francisco.
(415) 666-6292
Jobline: (415) 666-5600

University of South Carolina, Columbia
Columbia, SC 29208
Large, public institution in Columbia.
(803) 777-7000
Jobline: (803) 777-2100

University of South Florida
2172 Student Services Building, 4202 E. Fowler
    Avenue, Tampa, FL 33620
Medium-sized, public, multipurpose institution with a
    main campus near downtown Tampa.
(813) 974-2011
Jobline: (813) 974-2879

University of Southern California
Los Angeles, CA 90089-0911
Large, private university in Los Angeles.
(213) 743-2311
Jobline: (213) 740-4728

University of Tampa
Tampa, FL 33606
Small, private institution in central Tampa.
(813) 253-3333
Jobline: (813) 253-6254

University of Tennessee at Chattanooga
Chattanooga, TN 37403
Medium-sized, public, comprehensive institution near
    central Chattanooga.
(615) 755-4111
Jobline: (615) 755-4473

University of Tennessee at Knoxville
Knoxville, TN 37996
Medium-sized, public, comprehensive institution in
    Knoxville.
(615) 974-2184
Jobline: (615) 974-6644

University of Tennessee at Martin
Martin, TN 38238
Small, public institution in Martin, 125 miles northeast of
    Memphis.
(901) 587-7777
Jobline: (901) 587-7848

University of Texas at Arlington
Arlington, TX 76019
Medium-sized, public, comprehensive institution in
    Arlington.
(817) 273-2011
Jobline: (817) 273-3455

University of Texas at Austin
Austin, TX 78712-1159
Large, public, comprehensive institution with an urban
    campus in Austin.
(512) 471-3434
Jobline: (512) 471-4295

University of Texas at El Paso
El Paso, TX 79968
Medium-sized, public institution in El Paso.
(915) 747-5000
Jobline: (915) 747-8837

University of Texas at San Antonio
San Antonio, TX 78285
Medium-sized, public, comprehensive institution 16
    miles from San Antonio.
(210) 691-4011
Jobline: (210) 691-4650

University of the Pacific
Stockton, CA 95211
Small, private institution in Stockton, 85 miles east of
  San Francisco.
(209) 946-2124
Jobline: (209) 946-2621

University of Toledo
Toledo, OH 43606
Medium-sized, public institution in residential Toledo.
(419) 537-4242
Jobline: (419) 537-2020

University of Tulsa
Tulsa, OK 74104
Small, private institution with a main campus two miles
  from downtown Tulsa.
(918) 631-2000
Jobline: (918) 631-4000

University of Utah
Salt Lake City, UT 84112
Medium-sized, public institution in Salt Lake City.
(801) 581-7200
Jobline: (801) 581-5627

University of Vermont
Burlington, VT 05405-3596
Medium-sized, public, comprehensive institution in
  Burlington.
(802) 656-3480
Jobline: (802) 656-2248

University of Virginia
Charlottesville, VA 22903
Medium-sized, public institution in Charlottesville, 70
  miles from Richmond.
(804) 924-0311
Jobline: (804) 924-4400

University of Washington
Medical Center
Seattle, WA 98195
Not-for-profit hospital affiliated with the University of
  Washington.
(206) 543-2100
Jobline: (800) 685-4899

University of West Florida
Building 20 East, 11000 University Parkway, Pensacola,
  FL 32514
Small, public institution in residential Pensacola.
(904) 474-2000
Jobline: (904) 474-2842

University of Wisconsin, Milwaukee
Milwaukee, WI 53201
Medium-sized, public, multipurpose institution near
  downtown Milwaukee.
(414) 229-1122
Jobline: (414) 229-6629

University of Wisconsin, Stevens Point
Milwaukee, WI 54481
Medium-sized, public, multipurpose institution in
  Stevens Point.
(715) 346-2441
Jobline: (715) 346-2606, press 1.

University of Wyoming
Laramie, WY 82071
Medium-sized, public, multipurpose institution in
  Laramie, west of Cheyenne.
(307) 766-1121
Jobline: (307) 766-5602

University Park (city)
3800 University Boulevard, University Park, TX 75205
Provides municipal services such as police, firefighting,
  libraries, parks, and public works.
(214) 363-1644
Jobline: (214) 653-3175

Upjohn Co.
7000 Portage Road, Kalamazoo, MI 49001
Produces pharmaceuticals, agricultural products, and
  industrial chemicals.
(616) 323-4000
Jobline: (616) 329-5550

USAir Group Inc.
2345 Crystal Drive, Arlington, VA 22227
Provides scheduled air passenger and cargo
  transportation, aircraft servicing, and other services.
(703) 418-7000
Jobline: (703) 418-7499

Utah (state)
State Office Building, Room 2120, Capitol Hall, Salt
  Lake City, UT 84114
Provides state services such as conservation,
  education, highways, prisons, and welfare.
(801) 538-3025
Jobline: (801) 538-3118
Professional jobs.

Utah State University
Logan, UT 84322-1600
Medium-sized, public, comprehensive university in
  Logan, in northern Utah.
(801) 797-1000
Jobline: (801) 797-1819

Vacaville (city)
400 Boyd Street, Vacaville, CA 95688
Provides municipal services such as police, firefighting,
  libraries, parks, and public works.
(707) 449-5101
Jobline: (707) 449-5113

Vail Associates Inc.
P.O. Box 7, Vail, CO 81658
Owns and operates ski lifts, schools, and restaurants,
  and develops, sells, and leases real estate.
(303) 476-5601
Jobline: (303) 479-3068

Valencia Community College
Orlando, FL 32802
Medium-sized, state-supported, 2-year college in
  Orlando.
(407) 299-5000
Jobline: (407) 299-4943

Vallejo (city)
555 Santa Clara Street, Vallejo, CA 94590
Provides municipal services such as police, firefighting,
  libraries, parks, and public works.
(707) 648-4435
Jobline: (707) 648-4364

Vancouver (city)
1313 Main Street, P.O. Box 1995, Vancouver, WA
  98668-1995
Provides municipal services such as police, firefighting,
  libraries, parks, and public works.
(206) 696-8142
Jobline: (206) 696-8128

Vancouver School District
605 N. Devine Road, Vancouver, WA 98661
34-school district in Vancouver.
(206) 696-7127
Jobline: (206) 696-7023
Certificated jobs.

Vanderbilt University
Nashville, TN 37212-2099
Medium-sized, private university in the University City
  section of Nashville.
(615) 322-7311
Jobline: (615) 322-8383

Ventura (city)
501 Poli Street, Ventura, CA 93001
Provides municipal services such as police, firefighting,
  libraries, parks, and public works.
(805) 654-7853
Jobline: (805) 658-4777

Ventura County
800 S. Victoria Avenue, Ventura, CA 93003
Provides county services such as sheriffs, courts, motor
  vehicle registration, and social services.
(805) 654-2639
Jobline: (805) 654-2847

Ventura County Health Care Agency
800 S. Victoria Avenue, Ventura, CA 93003
Provides public health programs and services.
(805) 654-2639
Jobline: (805) 652-6696

Vermont (state)
110 State, Montpelier, VT 05602
Provides state services such as conservation,
  education, highways, prisons, and welfare.
(802) 828-3483
Jobline: (802) 828-3484

**Vermont (state) Employment and Training
Department**
Jobsline
Green Mountain Drive, P.O. Box 488, Montpelier, VT
  05602
Seeks workers for private employers.
(802) 828-4000
Jobline: (802) 828-3939
Call (800) 464-4473 in Vermont.

Viacom Productions Inc.
10 Universal City Plaza, Universal City, CA 91608
Produces TV films.
(818) 505-7500
Jobline: (818) 505-7581

Victorville (city)
14343 Civic Drive, Victorville, CA 92392
Provides municipal services such as police, firefighting,
  libraries, parks, and public works.
(619) 955-5048
Jobline: (619) 245-7499

Virginia Beach (city)
2396 Court Plaza Drive, Virginia Beach, VA 23456
Provides municipal services such as police, firefighting,
  libraries, parks, and public works.
(804) 427-4157
Jobline: (804) 427-3580, x815.
Currently-available jobs.

Jobline: (804) 427-3580, x800.
Miscellaneous part-time jobs

Jobline: (804) 427-3580, x801.
Clerical office support jobs

Jobline: (804) 427-3580, x802.
Management administrative jobs.

Jobline: (804) 427-3580, x803.
Mental health field jobs

Jobline: (804) 427-3580, x804.
MIS computer system jobs

Jobline: (804) 427-3580, x805.
Full-time parks and recreation jobs.

Jobline: (804) 427-3580, x806.
Part-time parks and recreation jobs.

Jobline: (804) 427-3580, x813.
Volunteer and intern jobs.

Jobline: (804) 427-3580, x807.
Professional and paraprofessional jobs.

Jobline: (804) 427-3580, x808.
Public safety jobs.

Jobline: (804) 427-3580, x809.
Service maintenance jobs.

Jobline: (804) 427-3580, x810.
Social services field jobs

Jobline: (804) 427-3580, x811.
Summer seasonal jobs

Jobline: (804) 427-3580, x812.
Technical skill craft jobs.

Virginia Commonwealth University
P.O. Box 980066, Richmond, VA 23298
Medium-sized, public university with academic and
  medical college campuses near downtown Richmond.
(804) 786-0557
Jobline: (804) 278-0266

Virginia Polytechnic Institute and State University
Blacksburg, VA 24061
Large, public, comprehensive university in Blacksburg,
  near Roanoke.
(703) 231-6000
Jobline: (703) 231-4649
Professional jobs.

Jobline: (703) 231-6160
Technical jobs.

Jobline: (703) 231-6176
Support jobs.

Jobline: (703) 231-6196
Clerical jobs.

Virginia State University
Petersburg, VA 23803
Small, public, comprehensive, historically black
  university in Petersburg.
(804) 524-5000
Jobline: (804) 524-5627

Visa International Service Association
3125 Clearview Way, San Mateo, CA 94402
Provides credit card services.
(415) 570-3200
Jobline: (415) 432-8299

Visalia (city)
810 W. Main Street, Visalia, CA 93291
Provides municipal services such as police, firefighting,
  libraries, parks, and public works.
(209) 738-3309
Jobline: (209) 730-7007

Vons Companies Inc.
618 Michillinda Avenue, P.O. Box 3338, Los Angeles,
  CA 91007
Operates chain supermarkets and drug stores.
(818) 821-7000
Jobline: (800) 283-8667

Vulcan Materials Co.
1 Metroplex Drive, Birmingham, AL 35209
Produces limestone, sand, other construction materials,
  and agricultural and industrial chemicals.
(205) 877-3000
Jobline: (205) 877-3986

Wachovia Bank of Georgia
P.O. Box 4148, Atlanta, GA 30302
Operates national commercial banks.
(404) 332-5000
Jobline: (404) 841-7050

Wachovia Corp.
301 N. Main Street, P.O. Box 3099, Winston Salem, NC
  27150
Bank holding company that operates national and state
  commercial banks and other banking businesses.
(910) 770-5000
Jobline: (910) 770-5520
Non-exempt jobs.

Wake County
800 County Office Building, 336 Fayetteville Street Mal,
  Raleigh, NC 27602
Provides county services such as sheriffs, courts, motor
  vehicle registration, and social services.
(919) 856-6090
Jobline: (919) 856-6115

Wake Forest University
Winston Salem, NC 27109
Small, church-affiliated university in Winston-Salem.
(910) 759-5201
Jobline: (910) 759-4448

Waldorf-Astoria
301 Park Avenue, New York, NY 10022
1,410-room hotel.
(212) 355-3000
Jobline: (212) 872-4717

Walnut Creek (city)
1666 N. Main Street, Walnut Creek, CA 94596
Provides municipal services such as police, firefighting,
  libraries, parks, and public works.
(510) 943-5815
Jobline: (510) 943-5817

Walt Disney Co.
500 S. Buena Vista Street, Burbank, CA 91521
Produces motion pictures and TV programs, operates
  amusement parks, and provides other services.
(818) 560-1000
Jobline: (818) 560-1811
Corporate jobs.

Walt Disney Consumer Products
500 S. Buena Vista Street, Burbank, CA 91521-6692
Develops and sells Disney products through various
  media and outlets.
(818) 567-5401
Jobline: (818) 567-5800

Walt Disney Film Entertainment
500 S. Buena Vista Street, Burbank, CA 91521
Produces and distributes motion pictures and TV
  programs.
(818) 560-6455
Jobline: (818) 560-6335
Film jobs.

Walt Disney Imagineering Inc.
1401 Flower Street, P.O. Box 25020, Glendale, CA
  91221-5020
Provides commercial and industrial design and
  architectural services, and builds custom structures.
(818) 544-6500
Jobline: (818) 544-5555

Walt Disney World Co.
P.O. Box 10000, Lake Buena Vista, FL 32830-1000
Operates amusement parks, hotels, and gift shops
    owned by Walt Disney Co.
(407) 824-2222
Jobline: (407) 345-5701
Entertainment jobs.

Walt Disney World Dolphin
1500 EPCOT Resorts Boulevard, Walt Disney World,
    FL 32830
1,510-room hotel in the Orlando area.
(407) 934-4000
Jobline: (407) 934-4200

Walt Disney World Swan
1200 EPCOT Resorts Boulevard, Walt Disney World,
    FL 32830
758-room hotel in the Orlando area.
(407) 934-3000
Jobline: (407) 934-1660

Washington (state)
600 Franklin Street SE, Olympia, WA 98501
Provides state services such as conservation,
    education, highways, prisons, and welfare.
(206) 753-5368
Jobline: (206) 464-7378
For callers in the Seattle area.

Jobline: (206) 586-0545
For callers in the Olympia area.

Jobline: (509) 456-2889
For callers in the Spokane area.

Washington (state) Department of Employment Security
Job Service
1530 Stevens Avenue, Walla Walla, WA 99362
Seeks workers for private employers.
(509) 527-4393
Jobline: (509) 527-4346

215 Bridge Street, Wenatchee, WA 98801
Seeks workers for private employers.
(509) 662-0413
Jobline: (509) 662-1811

Washington County
14900 N. 61st Street, Stillwater, MN 55082
Provides county services such as sheriffs, courts, motor
    vehicle registration, and social services.
(612) 430-6081
Jobline: (612) 430-6084

155 N. 1st Avenue, Suite 210, Hillsboro, OR 97124
Provides county services such as sheriffs, courts, motor
    vehicle registration, and social services.
(503) 648-8606
Jobline: (503) 648-8607

Washington Hilton & Towers
1919 Connecticut Avenue, Washington, DC 20009
1,123-room hotel.
(202) 483-3000
Jobline: (202) 797-5818

Washington Mutual Savings Bank
1201 3rd Avenue, Seattle, WA 98101
Operates federal and nonfederal savings banks.
(206) 461-2000
Jobline: (206) 461-8787

Washington Post Co.
1150 15th Street NW, Washington, DC 20071
Publishes newspapers and magazines and provides TV
    and cable TV broadcasting services.
(202) 334-6000
Jobline: (202) 334-5350

Washington State University
Pullman, WA 99164-1036
Medium-sized, public, comprehensive university in
    Pullman, south of Spokane.
(509) 335-3564
Jobline: (509) 335-7637

Washoe County
1001 E. 9th Street, Reno, NV 89520
Provides county services such as sheriffs, courts, motor
    vehicle registration, and social services.
(702) 328-2080
Jobline: (800) 473-2091

Waukesha County
515 W. Moreland Boulevard, Waukesha, WI 53188
Provides county services such as sheriffs, courts, motor
    vehicle registration, and social services.
(414) 548-7044
Jobline: (414) 548-7059

Wayne County
County Building, Room 107, 600 Randolph Street
Detroit, MI 48226
Provides county services such as sheriffs, courts, motor
    vehicle registration, and social services.
(313) 224-5933
Jobline: (313) 224-5900

Weirton Steel Corp.
400 Three Springs Drive, Weirton, WV 26062
Integrated primary steel producer that specializes in tin
    plate and flat rolled sheets.
(304) 797-2000
Jobline: (304) 797-4668

West Covina (city)
1440 W. Garvey Avenue, West Covina, CA 91790
Provides municipal services such as police, firefighting,
    libraries, parks, and public works.
(818) 814-8450
Jobline: (818) 814-8452

West Hollywood (city)
8611 Santa Monica Boulevard, West Hollywood, CA
    90069
Provides municipal services such as police, firefighting,
    libraries, parks, and public works.
(310) 854-7325
Jobline: (310) 854-7309

West Jordan (city)
8000 S. Redwood Road, West Jordan, UT 84088
Provides municipal services such as police, firefighting,
  libraries, parks, and public works.
(801) 569-5030
Jobline: (801) 569-5045

West One Bank Idaho NA
P.O. Box 8247, Boise, ID 83733
Operates national commercial banks.
(208) 383-7000
Jobline: (208) 383-5400

West Texas State University
Canyon, TX 79016
Small, public, comprehensive university with a main
  campus in Canyon, near Amarillo.
(806) 656-2000
Jobline: (806) 656-4636, press 4.

West Valley-Mission Community College District
14000 Fruitvale Avenue, Saratoga, CA 95070
Includes West Valley College and Mission College.
(408) 867-2200
Jobline: (408) 867-3240

West Virginia University
Morgantown, WV 26506-6009
Medium-sized, public, comprehensive institution with
  two campuses in Morgantown, near Pittsburgh.
(304) 293-0111
Jobline: (304) 293-7234
Call 4:45 p.m.-8:15 a.m. or weekends.

Westamerica Bancorporation
1108 5th Avenue, San Rafael, CA 94901
Operates national commercial banks, mortgage
  bankers, and other banking services.
(415) 257-8000
Jobline: (415) 382-6400

Western Digital Corp.
8105 Irvine Center Drive, Irvine, CA 92718
Manufactures computer disk drives, auxiliary storage
  units, semiconductors, and related devices.
(714) 932-5000
Jobline: (714) 932-5766

Western Michigan University
Kalamazoo, MI 49008
Large, public, comprehensive university in Kalamazoo,
  145 miles from Detroit.
(616) 387-1000
Jobline: (616) 387-3669

Western Washington University
Bellingham, WA 98225
Medium-sized, public, comprehensive university in
  Bellingham, near Vancouver.
(206) 650-3000
Jobline: (206) 650-3776

Westin Bonaventure
404 S. Figueroa Street, Los Angeles, CA 90071
1,474-room hotel.
(213) 624-1000
Jobline: (213) 612-4845

Westin Canal Place
100 Rue Iberville, New Orleans, LA 70130
438-room hotel.
(504) 566-7006
Jobline: (504) 553-5059

Westin Crown Center
1 Pershing Road, Kansas City, MO 64108
725-room hotel.
(816) 474-4400
Jobline: (816) 474-4400, ask for x4450.

Westin Galleria Hotel and Westin Oaks Hotel
5060 W. Alabama Street, Houston, TX 77056
485- and 406-room hotels.
(713) 960-8100
Jobline: (713) 960-6520

Westin Hotel at the San Francisco Airport
1 Old Bayshore Highway, Millbrae, CA 94030
388-room hotel near San Francisco International Airport.
(415) 692-3500
Jobline: (415) 872-8158

Westin Hotel Chicago
909 N. Michigan Avenue, Chicago, IL 60611
782-room hotel.
(312) 943-7200
Jobline: (312) 943-7200, ask for job hotline.

Westin Hotel Copley Place
10 Huntington Avenue, Boston, MA 02116
800-room hotel.
(617) 262-9600
Jobline: (617) 351-7337

Westin Hotel Indianapolis
50 S. Capitol Avenue, Indianapolis, IN 46204
573-room hotel.
(317) 262-8100
Jobline: (317) 231-3996

Westin Hotel Los Angeles Airport
5400 W. Century Boulevard, Los Angeles, CA 90045
750-room hotel near Los Angeles International Airport.
(310) 216-5858
Jobline: (310) 417-4538

Westin Hotel O'Hare
6100 River Road, Rosemont, IL 60018
558-room hotel near Chicago O'Hare International
  Airport.
(708) 698-6000
Jobline: (708) 698-6000, ask for job hotline.

Westin Hotel Seattle
1900 5th Avenue, Seattle, WA 98101
865-room hotel.
(206) 728-1000
Jobline: (206) 727-5766

Westin Hotel Tabor Center Denver
1672 Lawrence Street , Denver, CO 80202
420-room hotel.
(303) 572-9100
Jobline: (303) 572-9100, ask for job hotline.

Westin La Paloma
3800 E. Sunrise Drive, Tucson, AZ 85718
487-room hotel.
(800) 876-3683
Jobline: (602) 577-5850

Westin Peachtree Plaza
210 Peachtree Street NW, Atlanta, GA 30343-9986
1,074-room hotel.
(404) 659-1400
Jobline: (404) 659-1400, ask for x4044.

Westin Resort
2 Grasslawn Avenue, Hilton Head Island, SC 29928
410-room hotel.
(803) 681-4000
Jobline: (803) 681-4000, ask for job hotline.

Westin Saint Francis
335 Powell Street, San Francisco, CA 94102
1,200-room hotel.
(415) 397-7000
Jobline: (415) 397-7000, ask for x0666.

Westin South Coast Plaza
686 Anton Boulevard, Newport Beach, CA 92626-1988
392-room hotel in the Orange County coastal area.
(714) 540-2500
Jobline: (714) 540-2500, ask for job hotline.

Westminster (city)
4800 W. 92nd Avenue, Westminster, CO 80030
Provides municipal services such as police, firefighting,
  libraries, parks, and public works.
(303) 430-2400
Jobline: (303) 650-0115

Westmont College
Santa Barbara, CA 93108-1099
Small, religiously-oriented, liberal arts college in Santa
  Barbara.
(805) 565-6000
Jobline: (805) 565-6100

Westward Ho Hotel & Casino
2900 Las Vegas Boulevard South, Las Vegas, NV
  89109
800-room hotel.
(702) 731-2900
Jobline: (702) 731-6374

Whatcom County
316 Lottie Street, Bellingham, WA 98225
Provides county services such as sheriffs, courts, motor
  vehicle registration, and social services.
(206) 676-6802
Jobline: (206) 738-4550

Wheat Ridge (city)
7500 W. 29th Street, Wheat Ridge, CO 81008
Provides municipal services such as police, firefighting,
  libraries, parks, and public works.
(303) 235-2814
Jobline: (303) 234-5927

Wherehouse Entertainment
19701 Hamilton Avenue, Torrance, CA 90502
Provides pre-recorded music, videos, and related
  products.
(310) 538-2314
Jobline: (310) 538-2314, press 3.

White Memorial Medical Center
1720 Brooklyn Avenue, Los Angeles, CA 90033
Not-for-profit hospital and nursing home-type unit with
  more than 300 beds.
(213) 268-5000
Jobline: (213) 343-1323

Whitney National Bank
228 St. Charles Avenue, P.O. Box 61260
New Orleans, LA 70161
Operates national commercial banks.
(504) 586-7272
Jobline: (504) 586-3482

Whittier (city)
13230 E. Penn Street, Whittier, CA 90602
Provides municipal services such as police, firefighting,
  libraries, parks, and public works.
(310) 945-8200
Jobline: (310) 945-8226

Wichita (city)
455 Main Street, Wichita, KS 67202
Provides municipal services such as police, firefighting,
  libraries, parks, and public works.
(316) 268-4531
Jobline: (316) 268-4537

Wichita County
900 7th Street, Room 204, Wichita Falls, TX 76301
Provides county services such as sheriffs, courts, motor
  vehicle registration, and social services.
(817) 766-8108
Jobline: (817) 766-8129, press 129.

Willard Inter-Continental
1401 Pennsylvania Avenue, Washington, DC 20004
365-room hotel.
(202) 628-9100
Jobline: (202) 637-7445

Williams College
Williamstown, MA 01267
Small, private, liberal arts college in Williamstown, 140
  miles west of Boston.
(413) 597-3131
Jobline: (413) 597-2679

Wilmington Trust Co.
Rodney Square North, 1100 N. Market Street
Wilmington, DE 19890-0001
Operates state commercial banks.
(302) 651-1000
Jobline: (302) 427-4555

Winston Salem (city)
City Hall, 101 N. Main Street, Winston Salem, NC 27101
Provides municipal services such as police, firefighting,
  libraries, parks, and public works.
(910) 727-2895
Jobline: (910) 631-6496

Woodland (city)
300 1st Street, Woodland, CA 95695
Provides municipal services such as police, firefighting, libraries, parks, and public works.
(916) 661-5811
Jobline: (916) 661-5810

Worcester Polytechnic Institute
Worcester, MA 01609
Small, private, polytechnic institute in Worcester, 45 miles west of Boston.
(508) 831-5000
Jobline: (508) 831-5860

Worthen Banking Corp.
Worthen Banking Building, 200 W. Capitol Avenue, Little Rock, AR 72201
Bank holding company that operates national commercial banks, mortgage bankers, and other services.
(501) 378-1521
Jobline: (501) 377-1445

Wright State University
Dayton, OH 45435
Medium-sized, public, multipurpose university in Dayton.
(513) 873-3333
Jobline: (513) 873-4562

Wyndham Greenspoint
12400 Greenspoint Drive, Houston, TX 77060
472-room hotel.
(713) 875-2222
Jobline: (713) 875-4506

Yakima (city)
129 N. 2nd Street, Yakima, WA 98901
Provides municipal services such as police, firefighting, libraries, parks, and public works.
(509) 575-6090
Jobline: (509) 575-6089

Yakima School District
104 N. 4th Avenue, Yakima, WA 98902
27-school district in Yakima.
(509) 575-3228
Jobline: (509) 575-2988

Yavapai County
255 E. Gurley Street, Prescott, AZ 86301
Provides county services such as sheriffs, courts, motor vehicle registration, and social services.
(602) 771-3252
Jobline: (602) 771-3171

Yellow Freight System Inc.
10990 Roe Avenue, Overland Park, KS 66211
Provides trucking, automotive repair, and trailer repair services.
(913) 345-3000
Jobline: (913) 344-3900

Yolo County
625 Court Street, Woodland, CA 95695
Provides county services such as sheriffs, courts, motor vehicle registration, and social services.
(916) 666-8155
Jobline: (916) 666-8159

Yuba City (city)
1201 Civic Center Boulevard, Yuba City, CA 95993
Provides municipal services such as police, firefighting, libraries, parks, and public works.
(916) 741-4610
Jobline: (916) 741-4766

Yuba College
2088 N. Beale Road, Marysville, CA 95901
Medium-sized, state- and locally-supported, 2-year college in Marysville.
(916) 741-6705
Jobline: (916) 634-7733

Zale Corp.
901 W. Walnut Hill Lane, Irving, TX 75038
Operates retail jewelry stores and leased jewelry departments, and wholesales diamonds.
(214) 580-5408

Joblines by State

Alabama

Alabama (state) Industrial Relations Department
Employment Service Division
Birmingham, AL 35222, (205) 254-1389

AMI Brookwood Medical Center
Birmingham, AL 35209, (205) 877-1910

Auburn University
Auburn University, AL 36849, (205) 844-4336

Auburn University at Montgomery
Montgomery, AL 36117-3596, (205) 244-3218

Huntsville (city)
Huntsville, AL 35804, (205) 535-4942

Huntsville (city) Schools
Huntsville, AL 35807, (205) 532-4746

Jacksonville State University
Jacksonville, AL 36265, (205) 782-5578

Jefferson County Board of Education
Birmingham, AL 35233, (205) 325-5107

Madison County
Huntsville, AL 35801, (205) 532-6906

Madison County Board of Education
Huntsville, AL 35804, (205) 532-2851

Mobile County school board
Mobile, AL 36633, (205) 690-8394

Montgomery (city and county)
Montgomery, AL 36101-1111, (205) 241-2217

Sheraton Civic Center Hotel
Birmingham, AL 35203, (205) 307-3016

University of Alabama at Birmingham
Birmingham, AL 35294, (205) 934-2611

University of Alabama in Huntsville
Huntsville, AL 35899, (205) 895-6105

University of Alabama, Tuscaloosa
Tuscaloosa, AL 35487-0132, (205) 348-7780

University of Montevallo
Montevallo, AL 35115-6000, (205) 665-8050

Vulcan Materials Co.
Birmingham, AL 35209, (205) 877-3986

Alaska

Alaska (state)
Anchorage, AK 99503, (907) 563-0200
Juneau, AK 99811, (907) 465-8910

Alaska (state) Department of Labor
Employment Service
Anchorage, AK 99510, (907) 269-4865, (907)
  269-4730, (907) 269-4725, (907) 269-4740, (907)
  269-4750, (907) 269-4735, (907) 269-4770
Fairbanks, AK 99701, (907) 451-2875

Anchorage (city)
Anchorage, AK 99519-6650, (907) 343-4451

Anchorage Hilton
Anchorage, AK 99501, (907) 265-7124

Captain Cook Hotel
Anchorage, AK 99501, (907) 276-6000

Fairbanks North Star Borough
Fairbanks, AK 99707, (907) 459-1206

First National Bank of Anchorage
Anchorage, AK 99510-0720, (907) 265-3027

National Bank of Alaska
Anchorage, AK 99503, (907) 265-2197

Office of Personnel Management
Federal Job Information Center
Anchorage, AK 99513-7572, (907) 271-5821

University of Alaska Anchorage
Anchorage, AK 99508, (907) 786-4887

Arizona

America West Airlines Inc.
Phoenix, AZ 85034, (602) 693-8650

Arizona (state)
Phoenix, AZ 85003, (602) 542-4966
Tucson, AZ 85701, (602) 792-2853

Arizona (state) Department of Economic Security
Job Service
Flagstaff, AZ 86001, (602) 526-1800

Arizona (state) Department of Public Safety
Phoenix, AZ 85009, (602) 223-2148

Arizona State University
Tempe, AZ 85287, (602) 965-5627

Arizona State University, West
Phoenix, AZ 85069-7100, (602) 543-5627

Bank of America Arizona
Phoenix, AZ 85011, (602) 594-2500

Bank One Arizona NA
Phoenix, AZ 85001, (602) 221-2441

Baptist Hospitals & Health Systems Inc.
Phoenix, AZ 85021, (602) 246-5627

Chandler (city)
Chandler, AZ 85224, (602) 786-2294

First Interstate Bank of Arizona NA
Phoenix, AZ 85072, (602) 528-1199

Gilbert (city)
Gilbert, AZ 85296, (602) 497-4950

Glendale (city)
Glendale, AZ 85301, (602) 435-4402

Hilton & Towers Hotels & Resorts
Phoenix, AZ 85020, (602) 861-9505
Phoenix, AZ 85044, (602) 438-9303

Hyatt Regency Phoenix at Civic Plaza
Phoenix, AZ 85004, (602) 252-1234

Maricopa County
Phoenix, AZ 85003, (602) 506-3329

Maricopa County Community College District
Tempe, AZ 85281, (602) 731-8444

Mesa (city)
Mesa, AZ 85211-1466, (602) 644-2759

Northern Arizona University
Flagstaff, AZ 86011, (602) 523-5627

Norwest Bank Arizona NA
Phoenix, AZ 85012, (602) 248-1283

Office of Personnel Management
Federal Job Information Center
Phoenix, AZ 85012, (602) 640-4800

Peoria (city)
Peoria, AZ 85345, (602) 412-7105

Phelps Dodge Corp.
Phoenix, AZ 85004, (602) 234-8281

Phoenician
Scottsdale, AZ 85251, (602) 941-8200

Phoenix (city)
Phoenix, AZ 85004, (602) 252-5627, (602) 262-7356

Pima Community College District
Tucson, AZ 85709, (602) 748-4623

Pima County
Tucson, AZ 85701, (602) 740-3530

Prescott (city)
Prescott, AZ 86302, (602) 776-6280

Scottsdale (city)
Scottsdale, AZ 85251, (602) 994-2395

Scottsdale Memorial Health Systems Inc.
Scottsdale, AZ 85251, (602) 941-5221

Scottsdale Princess
Scottsdale, AZ 85255, (602) 585-2756

Scottsdale Unified School District No. 48
Phoenix, AZ 85018, (602) 952-6296

Sheraton Tucson El Conquistador Resort
Tucson, AZ 85737, (602) 544-1240

SunHealth Corp.
Sun City, AZ 85372, (602) 974-7984

Tempe (city)
Tempe, AZ 85281, (602) 350-8217

Tucson (city)
Tucson, AZ 85701, (602) 791-5068

United States Department of Agriculture
Forest Service
Phoenix, AZ 85010, (602) 225-5382

University of Arizona
Tucson, AZ 85721-0007, (602) 621-3087

Westin La Paloma
Tucson, AZ 85718, (602) 577-5850

Yavapai County
Prescott, AZ 86301, (602) 771-3171

Arkansas

Arkansas (state) Department of Computer Services
Little Rock, AR 72203, (501) 682-9500

Arkansas (state) Department of Finance and Administration
Little Rock, AR 72203, (501) 682-5627

Arkansas (state) Game and Fish Commission
Little Rock, AR 72205, (501) 377-6600

First Commercial Corp.
Little Rock, AR 72203, (501) 371-3310

Little Rock (city)
Little Rock, AR 72201, (501) 371-4505

Little Rock (city) Water Works
Little Rock, AR 72203, (501) 377-7919

United States Department of the Army
Corps of Engineers
Little Rock, AR 72201, (501) 324-5660

University of Arkansas at Little Rock
Little Rock, AR 72204, (501) 569-3038

University of Arkansas, Fayetteville
Fayetteville, AR 72701, (501) 575-5627

Worthen Banking Corp.
Little Rock, AR 72201, (501) 377-1445

California

Alameda (city)
Alameda, CA 94501, (510) 748-4635

Alcon Surgical Inc.
Fort Worth, TX 76134-2001, (714) 753-6585

American Marketing Association
Southern California Chapter
Northridge, CA 91325, (818) 363-4127

American President Companies Ltd.
Oakland, CA 94607, (510) 272-8082

American Red Cross
Los Angeles Chapter
Los Angeles, CA 90057, (213) 739-4596

Anaheim (city)
Anaheim, CA 92805, (714) 254-5197

Antioch (city)
Antioch, CA 94509, (510) 779-7022

Applied Magnetics Corp.
Goleta, CA 93117, (805) 683-5353

AST Research Inc.
Irvine, CA 92718, (714) 727-4141

Atlas Hotels Inc.
San Diego, CA 92108, (619) 299-2254

Avery Dennison Corp.
Pasadena, CA 91103, (800) 456-2751

Bahia Hotel and Catamaran Resort Hotel
San Diego, CA 92109, (619) 539-7733

Baldwin Park (city)
Baldwin Park, CA 91706, (818) 813-5206

Bank of California NA
Los Angeles, CA 90071, (213) 243-3333
San Francisco, CA 94104, (415) 765-3535

Baxter HealthCare Corp.
Hyland Division
Glendale, CA 91203, (818) 507-8394

Bechtel Group Inc.
San Francisco, CA 94119, (415) 768-4448

Bergen Brunswig Corp.
Orange, CA 92668-3502, (714) 385-4473

Berkeley (city)
Berkeley, CA 94704, (510) 644-6122

Biltmore Hotel
Los Angeles, CA 90071, (213) 612-1585

Biola University
La Mirada, CA 90639, (310) 903-4767

Blue Cross of California Inc.
Woodland Hills, CA 91367, (818) 703-3181

Brea (city)
Brea, CA 92621, (714) 671-4420

Buena Park (city)
90621, CA 90621, (714) 562-3519

Burbank (city)
Burbank, CA 91502, (818) 953-9724

Burlingame (city)
Burlingame, CA 94010, (415) 737-1238

Burlington Air Express Inc.
Irvine, CA 92715, (714) 752-1212

Butte County
Oroville, CA 95965, (916) 538-7653

CalFed Inc.
Los Angeles, CA 90036, (818) 312-6078

California (state)
Sacramento, CA 95814, (213) 620-6450, (619) 237-6163, (916) 445-0538

California (state) Conservation Department
Sacramento, CA 95814, (916) 327-2672

California (state) Corrections Department
Sacramento, CA 95814, (800) 622-9675

California (state) Department of Health Services
Sacramento, CA 95814, (916) 657-0141, (916) 657-2976

California (state) Department of Transporation
Los Angeles, CA 90012, (213) 897-3653
Oakland, CA 94612, (510) 286-6354
Redding, CA 96001, (916) 225-3000

California (state) Education Department
Sacramento, CA 95814, (916) 657-3821

California (state) Employment Development Department
San Jose, CA 95116, (408) 928-1308
Eureka, CA 95501, (707) 444-2222
Bakersfield, CA 93304, (805) 325-5627

California (state) Energy Commission
Sacramento, CA 95814, (916) 654-4316

California (state) Food and Agriculture Department
Sacramento, CA 95814, (916) 654-0441

California (state) Franchise Tax Board
Sacramento, CA 95812-0550, (916) 369-3624, (916) 369-3626

California (state) Highway Patrol
Golden Gate Division
Vallejo, CA 94951, (707) 648-4195

California (state) Lottery
Sacramento, CA 95814, (916) 322-0023

California (state) Motor Vehicles Department
Sacramento, CA 94232-3150, (916) 657-7713

California (state) Parks and Recreation Department
Sacramento, CA 95814, (916) 653-9903

California (state) Social Services Department
Sacramento, CA 95814, (916) 657-1696

California Institute of Technology
Pasadena, CA 91125, (818) 796-2229

California Polytechnic State University, San Luis Obispo
San Luis Obispo, CA 93407, (805) 756-1533

California State Polytechnic University, Pomona
Pomona, CA 91768-4019, (909) 869-2100

California State University, Fresno
Fresno, CA 93740, (209) 278-2360

California State University, Stanislaus
Turlock, CA 95380, (209) 667-3354

California State University, Los Angeles
Los Angeles, CA 90032, (213) 343-3678

California State University, Dominguez Hills
Carson, CA 90747, (310) 516-3840

California State University, Long Beach
Long Beach, CA 90840, (310) 985-5491

California State University, Hayward
Hayward, CA 94542, (510) 881-7474

California State University, Fullerton
Fullerton, CA 92634, (714) 773-3385

California State University, Northridge
Northridge, CA 91330, (818) 885-2087

California State University, San Bernardino
San Bernardino, CA 92407, (909) 880-5139

California State University, Sacramento
Sacramento, CA 95819, (916) 278-6704

California State University, Chico
Chico, CA 95929, (916) 898-6888

Capital Cities/ABC Inc.
Los Angeles, CA 90027, (310) 557-4222

Capitol-EMI Music Inc.
Hollywood, CA 90028, (213) 871-5763

Carlsbad (city)
Carlsbad, CA 92008, (619) 434-2940

CCH Computax Inc.
Torrance, CA 90503, (310) 543-8100

Century Plaza Hotel & Towers
Los Angeles, CA 90067, (310) 551-3390

Cerritos College
Norwalk, CA 90650, (310) 467-5042

Certified Grocers of California Limited
Los Angeles, CA 90040-1401, (213) 726-2601

Chaffey College
Rancho Cucamonga, CA 91701-3002, (909) 941-2750

Chevron Corp.
San Francisco, CA 94104, (415) 894-2552

Children's Hospital of Orange County
Orange, CA 92668, (714) 532-8500

Chino (city)
Chino, CA 91710, (909) 591-9808

Chula Vista (city)
Chula Vista, CA 91910, (619) 691-5095

Claremont (city)
Claremont, CA 91711, (909) 399-5351

Claremont Colleges
Claremont, CA 91711, (909) 621-9443

Claremont McKenna College
Claremont, CA 91711, (909) 621-8491

Clorox Co.
Oakland, CA 94612, (510) 271-7625

Clovis (city)
Clovis, CA 93612, (209) 297-2329

Coast Community College District
Costa Mesa, CA 92626, (714) 432-5586, (714) 432-5526

Coast Federal Bank
Los Angeles, CA 90017, (818) 366-8730

Coca Cola Bottling Co.
Los Angeles, CA 90021-2210, (213) 746-5555

Commerce (city)
Commerce, CA 90040, (213) 887-4415

Concord (city)
Concord, CA 94519, (510) 671-3151

Contra Costa Community College District
Martinez, CA 94553, (510) 229-1000

Contra Costa County
Martinez, CA 94553, (510) 646-4046

Costa Mesa (city)
Costa Mesa, CA 92627-1200, (714) 754-5070

Countrywide Mortgage Investments Inc.
Pasadena, CA 91109, (818) 304-5925

Covina (city)
Covina, CA 91723, (818) 858-7225

Cubic Corp.
San Diego, CA 92123-1515, (619) 277-6780

Culver City (city)
Culver City, CA 90232, (310) 202-5751

Daly City (city)
Daly City, CA 94105, (415) 991-8028

Daniel Freeman Memorial Hospital
Inglewood, CA 90301, (310) 419-8377, (310) 419-8373

Davis (city)
Davis, CA 95616, (916) 757-5645

Disneyland International
Anaheim, CA 92802, (714) 999-4343

Casting Center
Anaheim, CA 92806, (714) 999-4407

Doubletree Hotels
Marina del Rey, CA 90292, (310) 301-3000
Orange, CA 92668, (714) 634-4500
Pasadena, CA 91101, (818) 792-2727
San Francisco, CA 94010, (415) 348-4247

Downey Savings and Loan Association
Newport Beach, CA 92660, (714) 509-4310

El Cajon (city)
El Cajon, CA 92020, (619) 441-1671

El Dorado County
Placerville, CA 95667, (916) 621-5579

El Monte (city)
El Monte, CA 91731, (818) 580-2041

Elk Grove Unified School District
Sacramento, CA 95624, (916) 686-7781

Encinitas (city)
Encinitas, CA 92024, (619) 633-2726

Environmental Protection Agency
Region 9
San Francisco, CA 94105, (415) 744-1111

Escondido (city)
Escondido, CA 92025, (619) 432-4585

Eureka (city)
Eureka, CA 95501, (707) 441-4134

Fairfield (city)
Fairfield, CA 94533, (707) 428-7396

Fairmont Hotels
San Francisco, CA 94108, (415) 772-5139
San Jose, CA 95113, (408) 998-1900

Federal Express Corp.
Southern California District
Newport Beach, CA 92660, (714) 729-0330
Los Angeles Metro District, (818) 753-5552

Federal Reserve Bank of San Francisco
San Francisco, CA 94120, (415) 974-3330

First Interstate Bank NA
San Diego, CA 92101, (619) 557-3069

Fleetwood Enterprises Inc.
Riverside, CA 92513, (909) 788-5627

Fluor Daniel Inc.
Irvine, CA 92730-0001, (714) 975-5253

Fontana (city)
Fontana, CA 92335, (909) 350-7652

Foothill-De Anza Community College District
Los Altos Hills, CA 94022-4599, (415) 949-6218

Fountain Valley (city)
Fountain Valley, CA 92708, (714) 965-4409

Four Seasons Hotel
Los Angeles, CA 90048, (310) 276-0822
Newport Beach, CA 92660, (714) 854-9675

Fremont (city)
Fremont, CA 94538, (510) 494-4669

Fresno (city)
Fresno, CA 93721, (209) 498-1573

Fresno County
Fresno, CA 93721, (209) 488-3017

Frito-Lay Inc.
Rancho Cucamonga, CA 91730, (909) 948-3622

Fullerton (city)
Fullerton, CA 92632, (714) 738-6378

Gap Inc.
San Francisco, CA 94105, (415) 737-4495

Garden Grove (city)
Garden Grove, CA 92640, (714) 741-5016

Gardena (city)
Gardena, CA 90247, (310) 217-9515

General Services Administration
Region 9
San Francisco, CA 94105, (800) 347-3378

Glendale (city)
Glendale, CA 91206, (818) 548-2127

Glendora (city)
Glendora, CA 91741, (818) 914-8206

Golden 1 Credit Union
Sacramento, CA 95852, (916) 732-2844

Great Western Bank
Chatsworth, CA 91311, (800) 367-5545

Grossmont-Cuyamaca Community College District
El Cajon, CA 92020, (619) 589-7312

GTE California Inc.
Camarillo, CA 93011-6000, (800) 521-5749
Cerritos, CA 90701-5346, (800) 482-5627
Pomona, CA 91767, (800) 852-8884

Handlery Union Square
San Francisco, CA 94102, (415) 781-7922

Hanna-Barbera Productions Inc.
Hollywood, CA 90068, (213) 969-1262

Harrah's Lake Tahoe Casino Hotel
South Lake Tahoe, CA 89449, (702) 588-6611

Hayward (city)
Hayward, CA 94545, (510) 293-5313

Health Net
Van Nuys, CA 91409, (818) 593-7236

Hercules (city)
Hercules, CA 94547, (510) 799-8204

Hesperia (city)
Hesperia, CA 92345, (619) 261-3660

Hewlett-Packard Co.
Palo Alto, CA 94304-1112, (415) 857-2092
Roseville, CA 95747-6502, (916) 786-6662
San Diego, CA 92127-1801, (619) 592-8444

Sonoma County area
Rohnert Park, CA 94928-4902, (707) 794-3918

Southern California area
Fullerton, CA 92631-5221, (714) 758-5414

Hilton & Towers Hotels & Resorts
Anaheim, CA 92802, (714) 740-4319
Beverly Hills, CA 90210, (310) 285-1340
Burbank, CA 91501, (818) 840-6471
Long Beach, CA 90831, (310) 983-3445
Los Angeles, CA 90017, (213) 612-3990
Los Angeles, CA 90045, (310) 410-6111
Pasadena, CA 91101, (818) 577-1000
San Diego, CA 92108, (619) 543-9441
San Diego, CA 92109, (619) 275-8994
San Francisco, CA 94102, (415) 923-5068
San Francisco, CA 94128, (415) 875-3071
San Jose, CA 95110, (408) 947-4458

Holiday Inns
San Diego, CA 92101, (619) 232-3861
San Francisco, CA 94133, (415) 771-9000
San Francisco, CA 94108, (415) 398-8900

HomeFed Bank
San Diego, CA 92121, (800) 552-3638

Hospital of the Good Samaritan
Los Angeles, CA 90017, (213) 977-2300

Hotel del Coronado
Coronado, CA 92118, (619) 522-8158

Hotel Nikko at Beverly Hills
Los Angeles, CA 90048, (310) 246-2074

Hotel Sofitel
San Francisco, CA 94065, (415) 598-9000

Hotel Sofitel Ma Maison
Los Angeles, CA 90048, (310) 278-5444

Humboldt County
Eureka, CA 95501, (707) 445-7366

Humboldt State University
Arcata, CA 95521, (707) 826-4500

Huntington Beach (city)
Huntington Beach, CA 92648, (714) 374-1570

Huntington Memorial Hospital
Pasadena, CA 91109, (818) 397-8504

Huntington Park (city)
Huntington Park, CA 90255, (213) 584-6209

Hyatt/Regency/Grand Hotels
Burlingame, CA 94010, (415) 696-2625
Irvine, CA 92714, (714) 863-1818
Long Beach, CA 90802, (310) 432-7690
Los Angeles, CA 90017, (213) 683-1234
Monterey, CA 93940, (408) 372-1234
Sacramento, CA 95814, (916) 441-3111
San Diego, CA 92101, (619) 687-6000
San Diego, CA 92109, (619) 221-4888
San Diego, CA 92122, (619) 552-6058
San Francisco, CA 94108, (415) 398-1234
San Francisco, CA 94111, (415) 392-1234
San Francisco, CA 94111, (415) 788-1234
San Francisco, CA 94133, (415) 563-1234
San Jose, CA 95112, (408) 993-1234

Imperial County
El Centro, CA 92243, (619) 339-4577

Inglewood (city)
Inglewood, CA 90301, (310) 412-8888

Intel Corp.
Santa Clara, CA 95052, (408) 765-3981

Irvine (city)
Irvine, CA 92713, (714) 724-6096

Kaiser Foundation Health Plan Inc.
Oakland, CA 94612, (510) 271-6888

Kaiser Foundation Hospitals
Harbor City, CA 90710, (310) 517-3620
Los Angeles, CA 90027, (213) 667-6966
Los Angeles, CA 90034, (213) 857-2615

Kaiser Permanente
Regional Offices
Pasadena, CA 91101-5103, (818) 405-3280

KCET-TV
Los Angeles, CA 90027, (213) 953-5236

Kern County
Bakersfield, CA 93301, (805) 861-3712

KNBC-TV
Burbank, CA 91523, (818) 840-4397

L.A. Gear Inc.
Los Angeles, CA 90066, (310) 822-1995

Laguna Hills (city)
Laguna Hills, CA 92653, (714) 707-2628

Lancaster (city)
Lancaster, CA 93534, (805) 723-6200

Le Meridien Newport Beach
Newport Beach, CA 92660, (714) 955-5656

Levi Strauss Associates Inc.
San Francisco, CA 94111, (415) 544-7828

Livermore (city)
Livermore, CA 94550, (510) 866-3799

Lodi (city)
Lodi, CA 95240, (209) 333-6705

Loew's Coronado Bay Resort
San Diego, CA 92118, (619) 424-4480

Loew's Santa Monica Beach Hotel
Santa Monica, CA 90401, (310) 576-3121

Long Beach (city)
Long Beach, CA 90802, (310) 570-6201

Long Beach City College
Long Beach, CA 90808, (310) 420-4050

Long Beach Memorial Medical Center
Long Beach, CA 90801, (310) 933-2482

Long Beach Press-Telegram
Long Beach, CA 90844, (310) 435-1161

Long Beach Renaissance
Long Beach, CA 90804, (310) 499-2518

Los Angeles (city) City Attorney
Los Angeles, CA 90012, (213) 847-9424

Los Angeles Community College District
Los Angeles, CA 90017-3896, (213) 891-2099

Los Angeles County Department of Public Works
Alhambra, CA 91803, (818) 458-3926

Los Angeles County Metropolitan Transportation Authority
Los Angeles, CA 90017, (213) 972-6217

Los Angeles County Office of Education
Downey, CA 90242, (310) 803-8408

Los Angeles County Superior Court
Los Angeles, CA 90012, (213) 974-5357

Los Angeles County-University of Southern California Medical Center
Los Angeles, CA 90033, (213) 725-5083

Los Angeles Gay and Lesbian Community Services Center
West Hollywood, CA 90028, (213) 993-7687

Los Angeles Times
Los Angeles, CA 90053, (213) 237-5406, (213) 237-5407, (213) 237-5408

Los Gatos (city)
Los Gatos, CA 95032, (408) 354-6838

Los Rios Community College District
Sacramento, CA 95825, (916) 568-3011

Loyola Marymount University
Los Angeles, CA 90045, (310) 338-4488

Manteca Unified School District
Lathrop, CA 95330, (209) 825-3233

Marin Community College
Kentfield, CA 94904, (415) 485-9693

Marin County
San Rafael, CA 94903, (415) 472-2999

Marriott Hotels
Anaheim, CA 92802, (714) 748-2482
Berkeley, CA 94710, (510) 548-7920
Burlingame, CA 94010, (415) 692-9100
Irvine, CA 92715, (714) 724-3681
La Jolla, CA 92037, (619) 552-8578
Los Angeles, CA 90045, (310) 337-5327
Marina del Rey, CA 90291, (310) 822-8555
Monterey, CA 93940, (408) 647-4066
Newport Beach, CA 92660, (714) 640-4000
San Diego, CA 92101-7700, (619) 230-8901
San Diego, CA 92108, (619) 692-3800
Torrance, CA 90503-4897, (310) 316-3636
Woodland Hills, CA 91367, (818) 887-4800

Martinez (city)
Martinez, CA 94553, (510) 372-3513

Mattel Inc.
El Segundo, CA 90245, (310) 524-3535

MCA Inc.
MCA/Universal City Studios
Universal City, CA 91608, (818) 777-5627

McKesson Corp.
San Francisco, CA 94104, (415) 983-8409, (415) 983-8784

Mendocino County
Ukiah, CA 95482, (707) 463-5424

Merced County
Merced, CA 95340, (209) 385-7516

Methodist Hospital of Southern California
Arcadia, CA 91107, (818) 574-3760

Metropolitan Water District of Southern California
Los Angeles, CA 90012, (800) 540-6311

Micro Technology Inc.
Anaheim, CA 92807, (714) 970-0300

Milpitas (city)
Milpitas, CA 95035, (408) 262-5146

Mission Federal Credit Union
San Diego, CA 92191, (619) 546-2010

Modesto (city)
Modesto, CA 95354, (209) 577-5498

Montebello (city)
Montebello, CA 90640, (213) 887-1380

Monterey (city)
Monterey, CA 93940, (408) 646-3751

Monterey County
Salinas, CA 93901, (408) 647-7726

Morgan Hill (city)
Morgan Hill, CA 95037, (408) 779-7276

Morton Electronic Materials
Tustin, CA 92680, (714) 730-4200

Mountain View (city)
Mountain View, CA 94041, (415) 903-6310

Napa (city)
Napa, CA 94559, (707) 257-9542

Napa County
Napa, CA 94559, (707) 253-4808

National Aeronautics and Space Administration
Ames Research Center
Moffett Field, CA 94035-1000, (415) 604-8000

National City (city)
National City, CA 91320, (619) 336-4306

National Medical Enterprises Inc.
Santa Monica, CA 90404, (310) 998-8500

Neutrogena Corp.
Los Angeles, CA 90045, (310) 216-5238

Nevada County
Nevada City, CA 95959, (916) 265-1366

Nichols Institute
San Juan Capistrano, CA 92690-6130, (714) 728-4526

North Island Federal Credit Union
San Diego, CA 92186, (619) 656-6525

North Orange County Community College District
Fullerton, CA 92634, (714) 870-7371

Oakland (city)
Oakland, CA 94612, (510) 238-3111

Occidental College
Los Angeles, CA 90041, (213) 259-2615

Oceanside (city)
Oceanside, CA 92054, (619) 966-4499

Office of Personnel Management
Federal Job Information Center
San Diego, CA 92101-8821, (619) 557-6165
El Monte, CA 91731, (818) 575-6510
Sacramento, CA 95814, (916) 551-1464

Ontario (city)
Ontario, CA 91764, (909) 391-2580

Orange (city)
Orange, CA 92666, (714) 744-7262

Orange County
Santa Ana, CA 92701, (714) 834-5627

Orange County Register
Santa Ana, CA 92711, (714) 664-5099

Oxnard (city)
Oxnard, CA 93030, (805) 385-7580

Pacific Bell
San Francisco, CA 94105, (800) 255-7571, (415) 542-0817

Pacific Bell Directory
Los Angeles, CA 90010, (800) 559-7442

Pacific Gas and Electric Co.
San Francisco, CA 94105, (415) 973-5200

Palmdale (city)
Palmdale, CA 93550, (805) 267-5627

Palo Alto (city)
Palo Alto, CA 94301, (415) 329-2222

Palomar College
San Marcos, CA 92069-1487, (619) 744-1150

Pan Pacific
San Diego, CA 92101-3580, (619) 338-3659

Pan Pacific Hotel San Francisco
San Francisco, CA 94102, (415) 929-2011

Paramount (city)
Paramount, CA 90723, (310) 220-2080

Paramount Pictures Corp.
Los Angeles, CA 90038, (213) 956-5216

Parc Oakland
Oakland, CA 94607, (510) 451-4000

Pasadena (city)
Pasadena, CA 91104, (818) 405-4600

Pasadena City College
Pasadena, CA 91106, (818) 585-7257

Pepperdine University
Malibu, CA 90263, (310) 456-4776

Peralta Community College System
Oakland, CA 94606, (510) 466-7223

Pico Rivera (city)
Pico Rivera, CA 90660, (310) 801-4387

Pioneer Electronics USA Inc.
Long Beach, CA 90801-1639, (310) 835-6177

Placer County
Auburn, CA 95603, (916) 889-4070

Pleasant Hill (city)
Pleasant Hill, CA 94523, (510) 671-5255

Pleasant Valley Hospital
Camarillo, CA 93010, (805) 389-5198

Pleasanton (city)
Pleasanton, CA 94566, (510) 484-8356

Pomona (city)
Pomona, CA 91766, (909) 620-2290

Pomona College
Claremont, CA 91711-6312, (909) 621-8477

Poway (city)
Poway, CA 92064, (619) 679-4300

Radisson Plaza Hotel & Golf Course
Manhattan Beach, CA 90266, (310) 546-9933

Rancho Santiago College
Santa Ana, CA 92706, (714) 564-6499

Red Lion Hotels
Culver City, CA 90230, (310) 649-1776
Sacramento, CA 95815, (916) 922-8041
San Diego, CA 92108, (619) 688-4004
San Jose, CA 95110, (408) 437-2118

Redding (city)
Redding, CA 96001, (916) 225-4069

Redlands (city)
Redlands, CA 92373, (909) 798-7645

Redondo Beach (city)
Redondo Beach, CA 90277, (310) 318-0660

Redwood City (city)
Redwood City, CA 94063, (415) 364-4425

Regent Beverly Wilshire
Beverly Hills, CA 90212, (310) 288-0803

Renaissance Hotel Los Angeles
Los Angeles, CA 90045, (310) 337-4646

Rialto (city)
Rialto, CA 92376, (909) 820-2640

Richmond (city)
Richmond, CA 94804, (510) 620-6610

Ritz-Carlton Laguna Niguel
Dana Point, CA 92629, (714) 240-5037

Riverside (city)
Riverside, CA 92509, (909) 782-5492

Riverside County
Indio, CA 92201, (619) 863-8970
Riverside, CA 92501, (909) 275-3500

Rohr Industries Inc.
Chula Vista, CA 91912, (619) 691-2601

Roseville (city)
Roseville, CA 95678, (916) 782-8107

Sacramento (city)
Sacramento, CA 95814, (916) 443-9990

Sacramento County
Sacramento, CA 95814, (916) 440-6771

Saddleback Community College District
Mission Viejo, CA 92626, (714) 582-4852, (714) 582-4469

Safeway Inc.
Oakland, CA 94660, (800) 255-0812

Saint Mary Medical Center
Long Beach, CA 90801, (310) 491-9014, (310) 491-9844

Salinas (city)
Salinas, CA 93901, (408) 758-7246

San Bernardino (city)
San Bernardino, CA 92418, (909) 384-5376

San Bernardino Community College District
San Bernardino, CA 92410-3080, (909) 384-0853

San Bernardino County
San Bernardino, CA 92401, (909) 387-5611

San Clemente (city)
San Clemente, CA 92672, (714) 361-8294

San Diego (city)
San Diego, CA 92101, (619) 450-6210

San Diego Community College District
San Diego, CA 92108, (619) 584-6580

San Diego County
San Diego, CA 92101, (619) 531-5764

San Diego State University
San Diego, CA 92182-0771, (619) 594-5801, (619) 594-5850, (619) 594-5861

San Francisco (city and county)
San Francisco, CA 94103, (415) 557-4888

San Francisco (city and county) Department of Public Health
Central Office
San Francisco, CA 94102, (415) 206-5317

San Francisco Community College District
San Francisco, CA 94103, (415) 241-2349

San Francisco State University
San Francisco, CA 94132, (415) 338-1871

San Francisco Unified School District
San Francisco, CA 94102, (415) 241-6162

San Joaquin County
Stockton, CA 95202, (209) 468-3377

San Joaquin County Department of Health Care Services
French Camp, CA 95231, (209) 468-6034

San Joaquin Delta College
Stockton, CA 95207, (209) 474-5627

San Jose (city)
San Jose, CA 95110, (408) 277-5627

San Jose Evergreen Community College District
San Jose, CA 95135-1599, (408) 223-6707

San Jose State University
San Jose, CA 95192, (408) 924-1000

San Leandro (city)
San Leandro, CA 94577, (510) 577-3397

San Luis Obispo (city)
San Luis Obispo, CA 93403-8100, (805) 781-7153

San Luis Obispo County
San Luis Obispo, CA 93408, (805) 781-5958

San Mateo (city)
San Mateo, CA 94403, (415) 377-4797

San Mateo County
Redwood City, CA 94063, (415) 368-7214

San Mateo County Community College District
San Mateo, CA 94402, (415) 574-6111

San Ramon (city)
San Ramon, CA 94583, (510) 275-2338

Santa Ana (city)
Santa Ana, CA 92701, (714) 953-9675

Santa Barbara County
Santa Barbara, CA 93101, (805) 568-2820

Santa Clara (city)
Santa Clara, CA 95050, (408) 984-3150

Santa Clara County
San Jose, CA 95110, (408) 299-2856

Santa Clara University
Santa Clara, CA 95053, (408) 554-4030

Santa Clarita (city)
Santa Clarita, CA 91355, (805) 255-4392

Santa Cruz (city)
Santa Cruz, CA 95060, (408) 429-3040

Santa Cruz County
Santa Cruz, CA 95060, (408) 454-2151

Santa Monica (city)
Santa Monica, CA 90401, (310) 458-8697

Santa Monica Community College
Santa Monica, CA 90405-1628, (310) 450-5150

Santa Rosa (city)
Santa Rosa, CA 95404, (707) 543-3076

Santa Rosa Junior College
Santa Rosa, CA 95401-4395, (707) 527-4707

Santee (city)
Santee, CA 92071, (619) 258-4123

Sanwa Bank California
Los Angeles, CA 90017, (213) 896-7214

Science Applications International Corp.
San Diego, CA 92121, (619) 535-7536

Seagate Technology Inc.
Scotts Valley, CA 95066, (408) 439-5627

Sharp Healthcare
San Diego, CA 92123, (619) 450-6241

Shasta County
Redding, CA 96001, (916) 225-5078

Sheraton Hotels
La Jolla, CA 92037, (619) 558-8058
Long Beach, CA 90802, (310) 499-2056
Los Angeles, CA 90071, (213) 617-6088
San Diego, CA 92101-1092, (619) 692-2793
San Francisco, CA 94105, (415) 392-8600
Santa Monica, CA 90401, (310) 319-3145

Sierra College
Rocklin, CA 95677, (916) 781-0424

Signal Hill (city)
Signal Hill, CA 90806, (310) 989-7385

Sizzler International Inc.
Los Angeles, CA 90066, (310) 827-2300

Solano County
Fairfield, CA 94533, (707) 421-6174

Sonoma County
Santa Rosa, CA 95403, (707) 527-2803

Sonoma County Office of Education
Santa Rosa, CA 95403, (707) 524-2680

Sonoma State University
Rohnert Park, CA 94928, (707) 664-2168

Sony Pictures Entertainment Inc.
Culver City, CA 90232-3119, (310) 280-4436

South County Community College District
Hayward, CA 94545, (510) 786-6966

South San Francisco (city)
South San Francisco, CA 94080, (415) 877-3976

Southern California Edison Co.
Rosemead, CA 91770, (818) 302-9850

Southern California Gas Co.
Los Angeles, CA 90013, (213) 244-1234

Special Libraries Association
Southern California Chapter
Pasadena, CA 91106, (818) 795-2145

Stanford University
Stanford, CA 94305, (415) 725-5627

Hospital
Stanford, CA 94305, (415) 723-5140

Stanislaus County
Modesto, CA 95354-2379, (209) 525-4339

State Center Community College District
Fresno, CA 93704, (209) 226-5129

Stater Brothers
Colton, CA 92324, (909) 783-5031

Stockton (city)
Stockton, CA 95202, (209) 937-8523

Sutter County
Yuba City, CA 95993, (916) 671-1687

Syntex Laboratories
Palo Alto, CA 94304-1320, (415) 852-1800

Syva Co.
San Jose, CA 95161-9013, (408) 239-2725

Torrance (city)
Torrance, CA 90503, (310) 618-2969

Torrance Memorial Medical Center
Torrance, CA 90505, (310) 517-4790

Transamerica Life Companies
Los Angeles, CA 90015, (213) 741-7834

Tulare County
Visalia, CA 93291, (209) 733-6704

Tuolumne County
Sonora, CA 95370, (209) 533-5631

Twentieth Century-Fox Film Corp.
Beverly Hills, CA 90213, (310) 203-1360

Union Bank NA
San Diego, CA 92101, (619) 230-3371
San Francisco, CA 94104, (415) 705-7013

United States Department of the Air Force
McClellan Air Force Base
Sacramento, CA 95652, (916) 643-5911

United States Department of Health and Human Services
Region 9
San Francisco, CA 94102, (415) 556-1088

United States Department of the Interior
Bureau of Reclamation
Sacramento, CA 95825, (916) 978-4897

Geological Survey
Menlo Park, CA 94025, (415) 329-4122

National Park Service
San Francisco, CA 94107, (415) 744-3884
San Francisco, CA 94123, (415) 556-1839

United States Department of the Navy
Long Beach Naval Shipyard
Long Beach, CA 90822-5099, (310) 547-8277

Naval Medical Center
San Diego, CA 92134-5000, (619) 532-9325

Naval Weapon Station and Naval Warfare Assessment Center
Seal Beach, CA 90740, (310) 594-7881

North Island Naval Air Station
San Diego, CA 92135-7041, (619) 545-1620

United States Department of Veterans Affairs
Medical Center
Long Beach, CA 90822, (310) 494-5971

University of California, Los Angeles
Medical Center
Los Angeles, CA 90024, (310) 825-8320

University of California, Santa Cruz
Santa Cruz, CA 95064, (408) 459-2011

University of California, San Diego
San Diego, CA 92093, (619) 682-1000

University of California, Irvine
Medical Center
Orange, CA 92668, (714) 856-5850

University of California, Santa Barbara
Santa Barbara, CA 93106, (805) 893-3311

University of California, Davis
Davis, CA 95616, (916) 752-1760

University of LaVerne
LaVerne, CA 91750, (909) 593-3511

University of Redlands
Redlands, CA 92373-0999, (909) 798-7482

University of San Diego
San Diego, CA 92110, (619) 260-4626

University of San Francisco
San Francisco, CA 94117-1080, (415) 666-5600

University of Southern California
Los Angeles, CA 90089-0911, (213) 740-4728

University of the Pacific
Stockton, CA 95211, (209) 946-2621

Vacaville (city)
Vacaville, CA 95688, (707) 449-5113

Vallejo (city)
Vallejo, CA 94590, (707) 648-4364

Ventura (city)
Ventura, CA 93001, (805) 658-4777

Ventura County
Ventura, CA 93003, (805) 654-2847

Ventura County Health Care Agency
Ventura, CA 93003, (805) 652-6696

Viacom Productions Inc.
Universal City, CA 91608, (818) 505-7581

Victorville (city)
Victorville, CA 92392, (619) 245-7499

Visa International Service Association
San Mateo, CA 94402, (415) 432-8299

Visalia (city)
Visalia, CA 93291, (209) 730-7007

Vons Companies Inc.
Los Angeles, CA 91007, (800) 283-8667

Walnut Creek (city)
Walnut Creek, CA 94596, (510) 943-5817

Walt Disney Co.
Burbank, CA 91521, (818) 560-1811

Walt Disney Consumer Products
Burbank, CA 91521-6692, (818) 567-5800

Walt Disney Film Entertainment
Burbank, CA 91521, (818) 560-6335

Walt Disney Imagineering Inc.
Glendale, CA 91221-5020, (818) 544-5555

West Covina (city)
West Covina, CA 91790, (818) 814-8452

West Hollywood (city)
West Hollywood, CA 90069, (310) 854-7309

West Valley-Mission Community College District
Saratoga, CA 95070, (408) 867-3240

Westamerica Bancorporation
San Rafael, CA 94901, (415) 382-6400

Western Digital Corp.
Irvine, CA 92718, (714) 932-5766

Westin Hotels & Resorts
Los Angeles, CA 90071, (213) 612-4845
Los Angeles, CA 90045, (310) 417-4538
Millbrae, CA 94030, (415) 872-8158
Newport Beach, CA 92626-1988, (714) 540-2500
San Francisco, CA 94102, (415) 397-7000

Westmont College
Santa Barbara, CA 93108-1099, (805) 565-6100

Wherehouse Entertainment
Torrance, CA 90502, (310) 538-2314

White Memorial Medical Center
Los Angeles, CA 90033, (213) 343-1323

Whittier (city)
Whittier, CA 90602, (310) 945-8226

Woodland (city)
Woodland, CA 95695, (916) 661-5810

Yolo County
Woodland, CA 95695, (916) 666-8159

Yuba City (city)
Yuba City, CA 95993, (916) 741-4766

Yuba College
Marysville, CA 95901, (916) 634-7733

Colorado

Adams County
Brighton, CO 80601, (303) 654-6075

Adolph Coors Co.
Golden, CO 80401, (303) 277-2450

Arapahoe County
Littleton, CO 80120, (303) 795-4480

Arvada (city)
Arvada, CO 80002, (303) 431-3008

Aurora (city)
Aurora, CO 80012, (303) 695-7222

Boulder (city)
Boulder, CO 80302, (303) 441-3434

Boulder County
Boulder, CO 80304, (303) 441-4555

Broadmoor
Colorado Springs, CO 80906, (719) 577-5858

Broomfield (city)
Broomfield, CO 80020, (303) 438-6475

Colorado (state) Department of Education
State Library
Denver, CO 80203-1704, (303) 866-6741

Colorado (state) Department of Natural Resources
Division of Wildlife
Denver, CO 80216, (303) 291-7527

Colorado (state) Department of Transportation
Denver, CO 80222, (303) 757-9623

Colorado College
Colorado Springs, CO 80903, (719) 389-6888

Colorado National Bank of Denver
Denver, CO 80202, (303) 585-8600

Commerce City (city)
Commerce City, CO 80022, (303) 289-3618

Denver (city and county)
Denver, CO 80202-5206, (303) 640-1234

Denver (city and county) New Airport Employment Office
Denver, CO 80204, (800) 866-3382

Denver Convention Complex
Denver, CO 80202, (303) 640-8119

Denver Museum of Natural History
Denver, CO 80205, (303) 370-6437

Denver Regional Council of Governments
Denver, CO 80211, (303) 480-6714

Douglas County
Castle Rock, CO 80104, (303) 660-7420

El Paso County
Colorado Springs, CO 80903, (719) 520-7400

El Paso County Social Services Department
Colorado Springs, CO 80905, (719) 444-5663

Englewood (city)
Englewood, CO 80111, (303) 762-2304

Environmental Protection Agency
Region 8
Denver, CO 80202, (303) 293-1564

First Interstate Bank of Denver NA
Denver, CO 80270, (303) 293-5777

Gates Corp.
Denver, CO 80217, (303) 744-5900

Hewlett-Packard Co.
Colorado Networks Division
Fort Collins, CO 80525-9544, (800) 228-1399

Colorado Springs, CO 80907-3423, (719) 590-2014
Greeley, CO 80634-9776, (303) 350-4442

Hyatt Regency Tech Center Denver
Denver, CO 80906, (303) 779-1234

Jefferson County
Golden, CO 80401, (303) 271-8401

Lakewood (city)
Lakewood, CO 80226, (303) 987-7777

Littleton (city)
Littleton, CO 80120, (303) 795-3858

Marriott Hotels
Denver, CO 80202, (303) 291-3644
Denver, CO 80222, (303) 782-3214

Metropolitan State College of Denver
Denver, CO 80217-3362, (303) 556-8430

National Renewable Energy Laboratory
Golden, CO 80401, (303) 628-4650

North Colorado Medical Center
Greeley, CO 80631, (303) 350-6565, (303) 350-6397

Northglenn (city)
Northglenn, CO 80233, (303) 450-8789

Norwest Bank Denver NA
Denver, CO 80274, (303) 863-5627

Office of Personnel Management
Federal Job Information Center
Lakewood, CO 80225, (303) 969-7055
Denver, CO 80225, (303) 969-7052
Denver, CO 80225, (303) 969-7053

Public Service Company of Colorado
Denver, CO 80202, (303) 571-7563

Radisson Hotel Denver
Denver, CO 80202, (303) 893-0642

Sheraton Denver Tech Center Hotel
Denver, CO 80237, (303) 779-1100

Tele-Communications Inc.
Englewood, CO 80111, (303) 267-6650

Thornton (city)
Thornton, CO 80229, (303) 538-7629

United States Air Force Academy
Colorado Springs, CO 80840, (719) 472-2222

United States Department of the Army
Fort Carson
Colorado Springs, CO 80913, (719) 526-3307

United States Department of Commerce
National Oceanic and Atmospheric Administration
Boulder, CO 80303, (303) 497-6332

United States Department of Energy
Western Area Power Administration
Golden, CO 80401, (303) 275-1244

United States Department of Health and Human Services
Region 8
Denver, CO 80294-3538, (303) 844-6329

United States Department of Housing and Urban Development
Denver, CO 80202, (303) 672-5263

United States Department of the Interior
Geological Survey
Denver, CO 80225, (303) 236-5846

National Park Service
Lakewood, CO 80228, (303) 969-2010

University of Colorado, Boulder
Boulder, CO 80309, (303) 492-5442

University of Denver
Denver, CO 80208, (303) 871-3460

Vail Associates Inc.
Vail, CO 81658, (303) 479-3068

Westin Hotel Tabor Center Denver
Denver, CO 80202, (303) 572-9100

Westminster (city)
Westminster, CO 80030, (303) 650-0115

Wheat Ridge (city)
Wheat Ridge, CO 81008, (303) 234-5927

Connecticut

Bank of Boston Connecticut
Waterbury, CT 06702, (203) 574-7109

Connecticut College
New London, CT 06320-4196, (203) 439-2069

Duracell International Inc.
Bethel, CT 06801, (203) 796-4650

Hartford (city) courts
Hartford, CT 06106, (203) 566-1326

Hyatt Regency Greenwich
Greenwich, CT 06870, (203) 637-1234

New Haven (city)
New Haven, CT 06510, (203) 787-8265

Sheraton Hartford
Hartford, CT 06130, (203) 240-7255

Sheraton Stamford Hotel
Stamford, CT 06902, (203) 351-1897

Southern New England Telecommunications Corp.
New Haven, CT 06506, (800) 562-7006, (203) 771-5200

University of Connecticut
Storrs, CT 06268, (203) 486-2466

Delaware

Delaware (state) Employment and Training Department
Dover, DE 19903, (302) 739-4434
Georgetown, DE 19947, (302) 856-5625
Wilmington, DE 19805, (302) 577-2750

E.I. du Pont de Nemours and Company Inc.
Wilmington, DE 19898, (302) 992-6349

Hercules Inc.
Wilmington, DE 19894, (302) 594-6122

Milford Memorial Hospital
Milford, DE 19963, (302) 424-5519

University of Delaware
Newark, DE 19716, (302) 831-2100

Wilmington Trust Co.
Wilmington, DE 19890-0001, (302) 427-4555

District of Columbia

ACTION
Washington, DC 20525, (202) 606-5039

American University
Washington, DC 20016-8001, (202) 885-2639

Bureau of Broadcasting
Washington, DC 20547, (202) 619-0909

Capitol Hilton
Washington, DC 20036, (202) 639-5745

Catholic University of America
Washington, DC 20064, (202) 319-5263

Central Intelligence Agency
Washington, DC 20505, (703) 482-0677

Commodity Futures Trading Commission
Washington, DC 20581, (202) 254-3346

Corporation for Public Broadcasting
Washington, DC 20036, (202) 393-1045

Environmental Protection Agency
Washington, DC 20460, (202) 260-5055

Executive Office of the President
Washington, DC 20500, (202) 395-5892

Export-Import Bank
Washington, DC 20571, (202) 377-6396

Federal Communications Commission
Washington, DC 20554, (202) 632-0101

Federal Deposit Insurance Corp.
Washington, DC 20429, (800) 695-8052

Federal Emergency Management Agency
Washington, DC 20472, (202) 646-3244

Federal Reserve System
Board of Governors
Washington, DC 20551, (202) 452-3038

Federal Trade Commission
Washington, DC 20580, (202) 326-2020

GEICO Corp.
Washington, DC 20076, (800) 434-2655

General Accounting Office
Washington, DC 20548, (202) 512-6092

Georgetown University,
Washington, DC 20057, (202) 784-2683, (202) 687-2900, (202) 784-2370

Holiday Inn Crowne Plaza Metro Center
Washington, DC 20005, (202) 737-2200

Howard University
Washington, DC 20059, (202) 806-7711

Hyatt/Regency/Grand Hotels
Washington, DC 20001, (202) 942-1586
Washington, DC 20001, (202) 637-4946

Library of Congress
Washington, DC 20540, (202) 707-4315

Marriott Corp.
Washington, DC 20058, (301) 380-1202

Marriott Hotels
Washington D.C. and Virginia area
Washington, DC 20058, (703) 461-6100

MCI Communications Corp.
Washington, DC 20036, (800) 777-6063, (800) 289-0128, (800) 888-2413, (800) 234-5627, (800) 695-2380

Merit Systems Protection Board
Washington, DC 20419, (202) 254-8013

National Endowment for the Arts
Washington, DC 20506, (202) 682-5799

National Endowment for the Humanities
Washington, DC 20506, (202) 606-8281

National Railroad Passenger Corp. (Amtrak)
Washington, DC 20002, (202) 906-3866

National Science Foundation
Washington, DC 20550, (202) 357-7735

Office of Personnel Management
Federal Job Information Center
Washington, DC 20415, (202) 606-2700

Omni Shoreham Hotel
Washington, DC 20008, (202) 483-1119

Overseas Private Investment Corp.
Washington, DC 20527, (202) 336-8682

Peace Corps
Washington, DC 20526, (202) 606-3214

Pension Benefit Guarantee Corp.
Washington, DC 20006, (202) 326-4111

Ramada Renaissance Washington Tech World
Washington, DC 20001, (202) 682-3456

Sheraton Washington
Washington, DC 20008, (202) 328-2000

Smithsonian Institution
Washington, DC 20560, (202) 287-3102

United States Courts
Administrative Offices
Washington, DC 20544, (202) 273-2760

United States Department of Agriculture
Forest Service
Washington, DC 20090-6090, (703) 235-5627

United States Department of the Air Force
Washington, DC 20330-1000, (703) 693-6550

United States Department of the Army
Washington, DC 20310, (703) 695-2589

United States Department of Commerce
Washington, DC 20230, (202) 482-5138

Bureau of the Census
Washington, DC 20230, (301) 763-6064

Patent and Trademark Office
Washington, DC 20230, (703) 305-4221

United States Department of Defense
Defense Intelligence Agency
Washington, DC 20340-0001, (703) 284-1110

United States Department of Energy
Washington, DC 20585, (202) 586-4333

United States Department of Health and Human Services
Washington, DC 20201, (202) 619-2560

United States Department of Housing and Urban Development
Washington, DC 20410, (202) 708-3203

United States Department of the Interior
Washington, DC 20240, (800) 336-4562

Bureau of Indian Affairs
Washington, DC 20240, (202) 208-2682

Minerals Management Service
Washington, DC 20240, (703) 787-1402

National Park Service
Washington, DC 20240, (202) 619-7111

Office of the Secretary
Washington, DC 20240, (800) 822-5463

United States Fish and Wildlife Service
Washington, DC 20240, (703) 358-2120

United States Department of Justice
Bureau of Prisons
Washington, DC 20534, (800) 347-7744

Immigration and Naturalization Service
Washington, DC 20536, (202) 514-4301

United States Department of Labor
Washington, DC 20210, (202) 219-6646

United States Department of the Navy
Consolidated Civilian Personnel Office
Washington, DC 20374-5050, (202) 433-4930

United States Department of State
Washington, DC 20520, (202) 647-7284

Foreign Service
Washington, DC 20520, (703) 875-7490

United States Department of the Treasury
Bureau of Alcohol, Tobacco and Firearms
Washington, DC 20226, (202) 927-8423

United States Department of Transportation
Washington, DC 20590, (202) 366-9397

Federal Aviation Administration
Washington, DC 20591, (202) 267-3229

United States Department of Veterans Affairs
Medical Center
Washington, DC 20422, (202) 745-8000

United States Information Agency
Washington, DC 20547, (202) 619-4539

United States Marine Corps
Washington, DC 20380-0001, (703) 697-7474

United States Senate
Washington, DC 20510, (202) 228-5627

Washington Hilton & Towers
Washington, DC 20009, (202) 797-5818

Washington Post Co.
Washington, DC 20071, (202) 334-5350

Willard Inter-Continental
Washington, DC 20004, (202) 637-7445

Florida

American Savings of Florida FSB
Miami, FL 33169-5003, (305) 770-2019

Baptist Hospital of Miami
Miami, FL 33176, (305) 598-5999

Barnett Bank of Pinellas County
Clearwater, FL 34662, (813) 539-9300

Barnett Banks Inc.
Jacksonville, FL 32203-0789, (904) 464-2426

Barnett Banks of South Florida NA
Miami, FL 33131, (305) 374-4473

Barnett Banks of Southwest Florida
Sarasota, FL 34230, (813) 951-4753

Barnett Banks of Tampa NA
Tampa, FL 33630, (813) 225-8761

Bonaventure Resort & Spa
Fort Lauderdale, FL 33326, (305) 389-0185

Brevard Community College
Cocoa, FL 32922, (407) 632-1111

Broward Community College
Fort Lauderdale, FL 33301, (305) 761-7503

Broward County
Fort Lauderdale, FL 33301, (305) 357-6450

Buena Vista Palace at Walt Disney World
Walt Disney World, FL 32830, (407) 827-3255

Carnival Cruise Lines Inc.
Miami, FL 33178-2418, (305) 599-2600

Dade County
Miami, FL 33130, (305) 375-1871

Dade County Fire Department
Miami, FL 33173, (305) 596-8645

Doral Ocean Beach Resort
Miami Beach, FL 33140, (305) 535-2055

Doral Resort & Country Club
Miami, FL 33178, (305) 591-6424

Federal Reserve Bank of Miami
Miami, FL 33178, (305) 471-6480

First Union National Bank of Florida
Jacksonville, FL 32202, (904) 361-6971, (305) 467-5292

Florida (state) Agency for Health Care Administration
Tallahassee, FL 32308, (904) 488-8356

Florida (state) Attorney
Miami, FL 33136, (305) 547-0533

Florida (state) court system
Tallahassee, FL 32399-1900, (904) 488-2556

Florida (state) Department of Agriculture and Consumer Services
Tallahassee, FL 32399-0800, (904) 487-2474

Florida (state) Department of Business and Professional Regulation
Tallahassee, FL 32399-0750, (904) 488-4874

Florida (state) Department of Commerce
Tallahassee, FL 32399-2000, (904) 488-0869

Florida (state) Department of Community Affairs
Tallahassee, FL 32399-2100, (904) 488-4776

Florida (state) Department of Corrections
Lauderhill, FL 33319, (305) 497-3398
Orlando, FL 32801, (407) 423-6600
Tampa, FL 33609, (813) 871-7142
Marianna, FL 32446, (904) 482-3531
Gainesville, FL 32614-7007, (904) 334-1722

Florida (state) Department of Education
Tallahassee, FL 32399-0400, (904) 487-2367

Florida (state) Department of Environmental Protection
Tallahassee, FL 32399-3000, (904) 487-0436

Florida (state) Department of Health and Rehabilitative Services
Miami, FL 33128, (305) 377-5747
Fort Lauderdale, FL 33301-1885, (305) 467-4279
Orlando, FL 32801, (407) 423-6207
West Palm Beach, FL 33401, (407) 837-5014
Tampa, FL 33614, (813) 877-8349
Largo, FL 34648, (813) 588-6628
Jacksonville, FL 32211, (904) 723-2024
Tallahassee, FL 32399-0700, (904) 488-2255
Tallahassee, FL 32399-2949, (904) 488-0831
Pensacola, FL 32505-2949, (904) 444-8037
Gainesville, FL 32601, (904) 955-5190

Florida (state) Department of Highway Safety and Motor Vehicles
Tallahassee, FL 32399-0525, (904) 487-3669

Florida (state) Department of Insurance
Tallahassee, FL 32399-0300, (904) 487-2644

Florida (state) Department of Labor and Employment Security
Tallahassee, FL 32399-2166, (904) 487-5627

Florida (state) Department of Law Enforcement
Tallahassee, FL 32399-2166, (904) 488-0797

Florida (state) Department of Management Services
Tallahassee, FL 32399-0950, (904) 487-3988

Florida (state) Department of Revenue
Tallahassee, FL 32399-0100, (904) 488-3895

Florida (state) Department of State
Tallahassee, FL 32399-0252, (904) 488-1179

Division of Library and Information Services
Tallahassee, FL 32399-0250, (904) 488-5232

Florida (state) Department of Transportation
Miami, FL 33172, (305) 470-5128
Tallahassee, FL 32399-0450, (904) 922-9867

Florida (state) Game and Fresh Water Fish Commission
Tallahassee, FL 32399-1600, (904) 488-5805

Florida (state) Lottery
Tallahassee, FL 32399-4014, (904) 487-7731

Florida Agricultural and Mechanical University
Tallahassee, FL 32307, (904) 561-2436

Florida Atlantic University
Boca Raton, FL 33431-0991, (407) 367-3506

Florida Hospital Medical Center
Orlando, FL 32803, (407) 331-8000

Florida Institute of Technology
Melbourne, FL 32901, (407) 768-8000

Florida International University
Miami, FL 33199, (305) 348-2500

Florida State University
Tallahassee, FL 32306-1009, (904) 644-6066

Fontainebleau Hilton Resort
Miami Beach, FL 33140, (305) 538-2000

Greenlefe Resort
Haines City, FL 33844-9732, (813) 421-5027

Harcourt Brace and Co.
Orlando, FL 32821, (407) 345-3060

Hialeah (city)
Hialeah, FL 33010, (305) 883-8057

Hillsborough Community College
Tampa, FL 33631, (813) 253-7185

Hollywood (city)
Hollywood, FL 33020, (305) 921-3292

Home Shopping Network Inc.
Clearwater, FL 34618-9090, (813) 572-8585

Hyatt/Regency/Grand Hotels
Orlando, FL 32827, (407) 825-1342
Orlando, FL 32836, (407) 239-3899
Orlando, FL 34746, (407) 396-5001
Tampa, FL 33602, (813) 225-1234
Tampa, FL 33607, (813) 287-0666

Jack Eckerd Corp.
Largo, FL 34647, (813) 399-6443

Jacksonville (city)
Jacksonville, FL 32202, (904) 630-1144

Jacksonville (city) Port Authority
Jacksonville, FL 32206, (904) 630-3095

Leon County
Tallahassee, FL 32301, (904) 922-4944

Marriott Hotels
Miami, FL 33132, (305) 536-6320
Orlando, FL 32819, (407) 351-2420
Orlando, FL 32821, (407) 238-8822
Orlando, FL 32822, (407) 851-9000
Ponte Vedra Beach, FL 32082, (904) 285-7777

Memorial Medical Center of Jacksonville
Jacksonville, FL 32216, (904) 399-6702

Miami (city)
Miami, FL 33131, (305) 579-2400

Miami Herald Publishing Inc.
Miami, FL 33132, (305) 376-2880, (305) 376-8959

Miami-Dade Community College
Kendall and Homestead Campuses
Miami, FL 33176, (305) 237-0965, (305) 237-2925

Medical Center Campus
Miami, FL 33127, (305) 237-0985, (305) 237-2945

Mitchell Wolfson Campus
Miami, FL 33132, (305) 237-2935, (305) 237-0975

North Campus
Miami, FL 33167, (305) 237-2915, (305) 237-0955

Monroe County
Key West, FL 33040, (305) 292-4457

NationsBank of Florida NA
Tampa, FL 33602, (813) 224-5921

North Miami (city)
North Miami, FL 33161, (305) 895-8095

North Miami Beach (city)
North Miami Beach, FL 33162, (305) 947-7581

Omni International Hotel
Miami, FL 33132, (305) 374-8065

Orange Park Medical Center
Orange Park, FL 32073, (904) 276-8562

Palm Beach Community College
Lake Worth, FL 33461, (407) 439-8232

Parkway Regional Medical Center
North Miami Beach, FL 33169, (305) 651-1100

Peabody Orlando
Orlando, FL 32819, (407) 352-6481

Pembroke Pines (city)
Pembroke Pines, FL 33026, (305) 437-1108

Pier 66 Resort and Marina
Fort Lauderdale, FL 33316, (305) 728-3583

Pinellas Park (city)
Pinellas Park, FL 34665, (813) 541-0703

Registry Resort
Naples, FL 33940, (813) 597-6859

Republic National Bank of Miami
Miami, FL 33126, (305) 250-5051

Ryder System Inc.
Miami, FL 33166, (305) 593-3066

Saint Petersburg (city)
Saint Petersburg, FL 33701, (813) 893-7033

Saint Vincent's Health Systems
Jacksonville, FL 32203-9954, (904) 387-7363

Sea World of Florida Inc.
Orlando, FL 32821, (407) 363-2612

Sheraton Hotels
Miami Beach, FL 33154, (305) 865-7511
Orlando, FL 32821, (407) 354-5057

Stetson University
De Land, FL 32720, (904) 822-7562

SunBank NA
Orlando, FL 32801, (407) 237-6878

SunBank of Tampa Bay
Tampa, FL 33602, (813) 224-2002, (813) 224-2001

SunBank/Miami NA
Miami, FL 33131, (305) 579-7001

SunBank/South Florida NA
Fort Lauderdale, FL 33301, (305) 765-7100

Tallahassee (city)
Tallahassee, FL 32301, (904) 891-8219

United States Department of Veterans Affairs
Medical Center
Miami, FL 33125, (305) 324-3154
Bay Pines, FL 33504, (813) 398-9493

University of Central Florida
Orlando, FL 32816, (407) 823-2778

University of Florida
Gainesville, FL 32611-5002, (904) 392-4631

University of Miami
Coral Gables, FL 33124, (305) 284-6918, (305) 547-6999

University of South Florida
Tampa, FL 33620, (813) 974-2879

University of Tampa
Tampa, FL 33606, (813) 253-6254

University of West Florida
Pensacola, FL 32514, (904) 474-2842

Valencia Community College
Orlando, FL 32802, (407) 299-4943

Walt Disney World Co.
Lake Buena Vista, FL 32830-1000, (407) 345-5701

Walt Disney World Dolphin
Walt Disney World, FL 32830, (407) 934-4200

Walt Disney World Swan
Walt Disney World, FL 32830, (407) 934-1660

Georgia

Atlanta (city)
Atlanta, GA 30303, (404) 330-6456

Atlanta Renaissance Hotel
Atlanta, GA 30308, (404) 881-6000, (404) 762-7676

BellSouth Corp.
Atlanta, GA 30367-6000, (404) 329-9455

Callaway Gardens
Pine Mountain, GA 31822, (706) 663-5012

Charter Medical Corp.
Macon, GA 31298, (800) 633-2415

Chatham County
Savannah, GA 31401, (912) 652-7931

Clark Atlanta University
Atlanta, GA 30314, (404) 880-8368

Clayton County
Jonesboro, GA 30236, (404) 473-5800

Cobb County
Marietta, GA 30090-9679, (404) 528-2555

Columbus Bank and Trust Co.
Columbus, GA 31902, (706) 649-4758

Columbus Consolidated Government (city and county)
Columbus, GA 31993, (706) 571-4738

Dekalb County
Decatur, GA 30030, (404) 371-2331

Doubletree Hotel at Concourse
Atlanta, GA 30328, (404) 395-3900

Douglas County
Douglasville, GA 30134, (404) 920-7363

Environmental Protection Agency
Region 4
Atlanta, GA 30308, (800) 833-8130

Equifax Inc.
Atlanta, GA 30309, (404) 885-8550

Fayette County
Fayetteville, GA 30214, (404) 461-6041

Federal Reserve Bank of Atlanta
Atlanta, GA 30303-2706, (404) 521-8767

First Union National Bank of Georgia
Atlanta, GA 30374, (404) 827-7150

Fulton County
Atlanta, GA 30303, (404) 730-5627

General Services Administration
Region 4
Atlanta, GA 30303, (404) 331-5102

Georgia Institute of Technology
Atlanta, GA 30332, (404) 894-4592

Georgia Southern University
Statesboro, GA 30460-8024, (912) 681-0629

Georgia State University
Atlanta, GA 30303, (404) 651-4270

Hilton & Towers Hotels & Resorts
Atlanta, GA 30303, (404) 221-6807
Atlanta, GA 30354, (404) 559-6781

Holiday Inn Crowne Plaza Ravinia
Atlanta, GA 30346, (404) 395-7700

Home Depot Inc.
Atlanta, GA 30339, (404) 433-8211

Hyatt/Regency/Grand Hotels
Atlanta, GA 30371, (404) 588-3746
Savannah, GA 31401, (912) 944-3647

Kennesaw State College
Marietta, GA 30061, (404) 423-6031

Macon (city)
Macon, GA 31298, (912) 751-2733

Marietta (city)
Marietta, GA 30061, (404) 528-0593

Marriott Marquis
Atlanta, GA 30303, (404) 586-6240
Atlanta, GA 30326, (404) 262-3344

NationsBank of Georgia NA
Atlanta, GA 30303, (404) 491-4530

Office of Personnel Management
Career America Connection
Macon, GA 31298, (912) 757-3000

Federal Job Information Center
Atlanta, GA 30303, (404) 331-4315

Rockdale County
Conyers, GA 30207, (404) 929-4157

Savannah (city)
Savannah, GA 31401, (912) 651-6488

Sheraton Hotels
Atlanta, GA 30344, (404) 768-6660
Atlanta, GA 30361, (404) 892-6000

Southern Co.
Atlanta, GA 30346, (404) 668-3464

SouthTrust Bank of Georgia NA
Atlanta, GA 30303, (404) 951-4010

Spelman College
Atlanta, GA 30314, (404) 223-5627

Stouffer Waverly Hotel
Atlanta, GA 30339, (404) 953-4500

Trust Company Bank
Atlanta, GA 30302, (404) 588-7251

United Parcel Service of America Inc.
Atlanta, GA 30346, (404) 913-6800

United States Department of the Air Force
Dobbins Air Reserve Base
Atlanta, GA 30069-4916, (404) 421-4968

United States Department of the Army
Fort Benning
Fort Benning, GA 31905-5031, (706) 545-7084

United States Department of Health and Human Services
Centers for Disease Control
Atlanta, GA 30333, (404) 332-4577

United States Department of the Interior
Geological Survey
Atlanta, GA 30303, (404) 448-5320

National Park Service
Atlanta, GA 30303, (404) 331-5189

United States Department of the Treasury
Internal Revenue Service
Chamblee, GA 30341, (404) 455-2455

University of Georgia
Athens, GA 30602, (706) 542-8722, (706) 542-5781,
  (706) 542-5720, (706) 542-5769

Wachovia Bank of Georgia
Atlanta, GA 30302, (404) 841-7050

Westin Peachtree Plaza
Atlanta, GA 30343-9986, (404) 659-1400

Hawaii

First Hawaiian Bank
Honolulu, HI 96847, (808) 525-5627

Hawaii (state)
Honolulu, HI 96813, (808) 587-0977

Honolulu (city and county)
Honolulu, HI 96813, (808) 523-4303

HTH Corp.
Honolulu, HI 96814, (808) 921-6110

Office of Personnel Management
Federal Job Information Center
Honolulu, HI 96850, (808) 541-2791, (808) 541-2784

Idaho

Ada County
Boise, ID 83702, (208) 364-2562

Ada County Sheriff's Department
Boise, ID 83704, (208) 377-6707

Albertson's Inc.
Boise, ID 83726, (208) 385-6422

Boise (city)
Boise, ID 83702, (208) 384-3855

Boise Cascade Corp.
Boise, ID 83728, (208) 384-4900

First Security Bank of Idaho NA
Boise, ID 83730, (208) 393-2453

Hewlett-Packard Co.
Boise Division
Boise, ID 83714-1021, (208) 396-5200

Idaho (state)
Boise, ID 83702, (208) 334-2568

Idaho (state) Department of Employment
Boise, ID 83702, (208) 334-6457

JR Simplot Co.
Boise, ID 83707, (208) 389-7510, (208) 384-8002

Red Lion Hotel/Riverside
Boise, ID 83714, (208) 386-9254

United States Department of the Interior
Bureau of Reclamation
Boise, ID 83724, (208) 378-5144

University of Idaho
Moscow, ID 83843, (208) 885-5702

West One Bank Idaho NA
Boise, ID 83733, (208) 383-5400

Illinois

Abbott Laboratories
Abbott Park, IL 60064, (708) 938-6295

Ameritech Corp.
Chicago, IL 60606, (800) 808-5627

Amoco Corp.
Chicago, IL 60601, (312) 856-5551

Baxter International Inc.
Deerfield, IL 60015-4625, (800) 322-9837

Chicago (city)
Chicago, IL 60602, (312) 744-1369

College of DuPage
Glen Ellyn, IL 60137, (708) 858-2800

DePaul University
Chicago, IL 60604, (312) 362-6803

Drake City Center
Chicago, IL 60611, (312) 787-2200

Environmental Protection Agency
Region 5
Chicago, IL 60604, (312) 353-2026

Harris Trust and Savings Bank
Chicago, IL 60690, (312) 461-6900

Hewlett-Packard Co.
Mid-America Sales Region
Rolling Meadows, IL 60008-3700, (708) 245-3909

Hilton & Towers Hotels & Resorts
Chicago, IL 60603, (312) 726-7500
Chicago, IL 60605, (312) 922-4400
Chicago, IL 60666, (312) 601-2800

Hotel Inter-Continental Chicago
Chicago, IL 60611, (312) 321-8819

Hyatt/Regency/Grand Hotels
Chicago, IL 60601, (312) 565-1234
Schaumburg, IL 60173, (708) 605-1234

Illinois (state)
Chicago, IL 60601, (312) 814-2390

Illinois Institute of Technology
Chicago, IL 60616, (312) 567-5703

Loyola University, Chicago
Chicago, IL 60611, (312) 508-3400

Marriott Chicago Downtown
Chicago, IL 60611, (312) 245-6909

Motorola Inc.
Schaumburg, IL 60196, (708) 576-2551

Northern Illinois University
DeKalb, IL 60115, (815) 753-1051

Office of Personnel Management
Federal Job Information Center
Chicago, IL 60604, (312) 353-6192, (312) 353-6189

Peoria County
Peoria, IL 61602, (309) 672-6943

Quaker Oats Co.
Chicago, IL 60610, (312) 222-7744

Ritz-Carlton
Chicago, IL 60611, (312) 266-1000

Riverside Medical Center
Kankakee, IL 60901, (815) 937-7969

ServiceMaster Limited Partnership
Downer's Grove, IL 60515, (800) 999-6678

Sheraton Chicago Hotel & Towers
Chicago, IL 60611, (312) 464-1000

Southern Illinois University at Carbondale
Carbondale, IL 62901, (618) 536-2116

Southern Illinois University at Edwardsville
Edwardsville, IL 62026-1001, (618) 692-2420

Springfield (city)
Springfield, IL 62701, (217) 789-2440

Stouffer Riviere Hotel
Chicago, IL 60601, (312) 372-2022

Sundstrand Corp.
Rockford, IL 61125, (815) 226-6269

Swissotel Chicago
Chicago, IL 60601, (312) 565-0565

UAL Corp.
Chicago, IL 60666, (708) 952-4000

United States Department of the Army
Rock Island Arsenal
Rock Island, IL 61299-5000, (309) 782-2214

Westin Hotels & Resorts
Chicago, IL 60611, (312) 943-7200
Rosemont, IL 60018, (708) 698-6000

Indiana

Allen County   449-
Fort Wayne, IN 46802, (219) 428-7510

Ball State University
Muncie, IN 47306, (317) 285-8565

Butler University
Indianapolis, IN 46208, (317) 283-9984

Eli Lilly and Co.
Indianapolis, IN 46285, (317) 276-7472

Fort Wayne (city)
Fort Wayne, IN 46802, (219) 427-1186

Fort Wayne National Bank Inc.
Fort Wayne, IN 46802-2304, (219) 461-6200

INB National Bank
Indianapolis, IN 46266, (317) 266-7788

Indiana State University
Terre Haute, IN 477809, (812) 237-4122

Indiana University at South Bend
South Bend, IN 46634, (219) 237-4182

Indiana University Bloomington
Bloomington, IN 47401, (812) 855-9102

Indiana University-Purdue University at Fort Wayne
Fort Wayne, IN 46805-1499, (219) 481-6971

Indiana University-Purdue University at Indianapolis
Indianapolis, IN 46202, (317) 274-2255

Mayflower Group Inc.
Carmel, IN 46032, (317) 875-1599

National City Bank, Indiana
Indianapolis, IN 46255, (317) 267-7700

Norwest Bank Fort Wayne NA
Fort Wayne, IN 46801, (219) 461-6318

Purdue University
West Lafayette, IN 47907, (317) 494-7417, (317) 494-7418, (317) 494-7419, (317) 494-6957

Society National Bank, Indiana
South Bend, IN 46601, (219) 239-4865

United States Department of the Army
Fort Benjamin Harrison
Indianapolis, IN 46249, (317) 542-2454

University of Notre Dame
Notre Dame, IN 46556, (219) 631-4663

Westin Hotel Indianapolis
Indianapolis, IN 46204, (317) 231-3996

Iowa

Des Moines (city)
Des Moines, IA 50309, (515) 283-4115

Drake University
Des Moines, IA 50311, (515) 271-4144

Iowa (state)
Des Moines, IA 50319-0150, (515) 281-5820

Iowa (state) Workforce Center
Cedar Rapids, IA 52406, (319) 365-9474

Iowa State University
Ames, IA 50011, (515) 294-0146

Marriott Hotel
Des Moines, IA 50309, (515) 245-5544

Mercy Hospital Medical Center
Des Moines, IA 50314, (515) 247-3105

Principal Mutual Life Insurance Co.
Principal Financial Group Division
Des Moines, IA 50392-0001, (800) 525-2593

University of Iowa
Iowa City, IA 52242, (319) 335-2684, (319) 335-2686, (319) 335-2685

University of Northern Iowa
Cedar Falls, IA 50614, (319) 273-2421

Kansas

Cessna Aircraft Co.
Wichita, KS 67215, (316) 941-6155

Environmental Protection Agency
Region 7
Kansas City, KS 66101, (913) 551-7068

Intrust Bank NA
Wichita, KS 67201, (316) 383-1155

Johnson County
Olathe, KS 66061-3441, (913) 780-2929

Kansas (state)
Topeka, KS 66612, (913) 296-2208

Kansas City (city)
Kansas City, KS 66105, (913) 573-5688

Kansas State University
Manhattan, KS 66506, (913) 532-6271

Marriott Overland Park
Overland Park, KS 66210, (913) 451-0259

Office of Personnel Management
Federal Job Information Center
Wichita, KS 67202, (816) 426-7820

Sedgwick County
Wichita, KS 67203, (316) 383-7633

Shawnee County
Topeka, KS 66603, (913) 233-8200

University of Kansas
Lawrence, KS 66045, (913) 864-4623

Wichita (city)
Wichita, KS 67202, (316) 268-4537

Yellow Freight System Inc.
Overland Park, KS 66211, (913) 344-3900

Kentucky

Alliant Health System
Louisville, KY 40201, (800) 789-5627

Ashland Oil Inc.
Ashland, KY 41114, (606) 329-4328

Bank One Lexington NA
Lexington, KY 40507, (606) 231-2760

Humana Inc.
Louisville, KY 40202, (502) 580-3450

Jefferson County
Louisville, KY 40202, (502) 574-6182

Liberty National Bank and Trust Company of Louisville
Louisville, KY 40232, (502) 566-1629

Louisville (city)
Louisville, KY 40202, (502) 574-3355

Morehead State University
Morehead, KY 40351, (606) 783-2101

National City Bank, Kentucky
Louisville, KY 40233, (502) 581-5627, (502) 581-7678

National Processing Center
Louisville, KY 40217, (502) 364-2381

Northern Kentucky University
Highland Heights, KY 41076, (606) 572-5201

United States Department of the Treasury
Internal Revenue Service
Covington, KY 41011, (606) 292-5304

University of Kentucky
Lexington, KY 40506, (606) 257-3841

University of Louisville
Louisville, KY 40292, (502) 852-5627

Louisiana

Baton Rouge (city)
Baton Rouge, LA 70802, (504) 389-4980

Clarion Hotel New Orleans
New Orleans, LA 70112, (504) 522-4500

Commercial National Bank
Shreveport, LA 71152, (318) 429-1803

Fairmont Hotel
New Orleans, LA 70140, (504) 529-7111

First National Bank of Commerce
New Orleans, LA 70112, (504) 582-7500

Hibernia National Bank
New Orleans, LA 70161, (504) 586-5518

Hotel Inter-Continental New Orleans
New Orleans, LA 70130, (504) 525-5566

Hyatt Regency New Orleans at Superdome
New Orleans, LA 70140, (504) 561-1234

Louisiana State University and Agricultural and Mechanical College
Baton Rouge, LA 70803-2750, (504) 388-1101, (504) 388-1201

Loyola University
New Orleans, LA 70118, (504) 865-3400

Premier Bank NA
Baton Rouge, LA 70821, (504) 332-3512

Royal Sonesta Hotel
New Orleans, LA 70140, (504) 553-2336

Sheraton New Orleans Hotel
New Orleans, LA 70130, (504) 525-2500

Shreveport (city)
Shreveport, LA 71130, (318) 226-3564

Tulane University
New Orleans, LA 70118, (504) 865-5627

Westin Canal Place
New Orleans, LA 70130, (504) 553-5059

Whitney National Bank
New Orleans, LA 70161, (504) 586-3482

Maine

Fleet Bank of Maine
Portland, ME 04104, (207) 874-5000

Key Bank of Maine
Portland, ME 04112, (207) 623-7000

Maryland

Anne Arundel County
Annapolis, MD 21401, (410) 222-1170

Baltimore (city)
Baltimore, MD 21202, (410) 576-9675

Baltimore County
Towson, MD 21204, (410) 887-5627

Baltimore County Public Schools
Towson, MD 21204, (410) 887-4080

Enoch Pratt Free Library
Baltimore, MD 21201, (410) 396-5353

First National Bank of Maryland
Baltimore, MD 21201, (410) 347-6562

Harford County
Bel Air, MD 21014, (410) 638-4473

Hechinger Co.
Landover, MD 20785, (301) 341-0526

Holiday Inn Crowne Plaza
Rockville, MD 20852, (301) 230-6770

Howard County
Ellicott City, MD 21043, (410) 313-4460

Hyatt/Regency/Grand Hotels
Baltimore, MD 21202, (410) 528-1234
Bethesda, MD 20814, (301) 657-1234

Johns Hopkins University
Baltimore, MD 21218, (410) 516-8022

Loyola College
Baltimore, MD 21210, (410) 617-5037

Manor Care Inc.
Silver Spring, MD 20901, (800) 348-2041

Marriott Hotels
Baltimore, MD 21201, (410) 962-0202
Hunt Valley, MD 21031, (410) 637-5574

Maryland (state)
Baltimore, MD 21201, (410) 333-7510

McCormick and Co.
Sparks, MD 21152-6000, (410) 527-6969

Montgomery College
Rockville, MD 20850, (301) 279-5373, (301) 279-5374

National Aeronautics and Space Administration
Goddard Space Flight Center
Greenbelt, MD 20771, (301) 286-5326

NationsBank of Maryland NA
Bethesda, MD 20817, (301) 897-0547

Office of Personnel Management
Federal Job Information Center
Baltimore, MD 21201, (410) 962-3822

Omni Inner Harbor Hotel
Baltimore, MD 21201, (410) 385-6442

Provident Bank of Maryland
Baltimore, MD 21244, (410) 281-7263

Sheraton Inner Harbor Hotel
Baltimore, MD 21201, (410) 347-1808

Signet Bank/Maryland
Baltimore, MD 21202, (410) 332-5627

Stouffer Harborplace Hotel
Baltimore, MD 21202, (410) 752-1920

United States Department of Agriculture
Agricultural Research Service
Beltsville, MD 20705, (301) 344-2288

United States Department of Commerce
National Institute of Standards and Technology
Gaithersburg, MD 20899, (301) 926-4851

United States Department of Health and Human Services
Food and Drug Administration
Rockville, MD 20857, (301) 443-1969

Health Resources and Services Administration
Rockville, MD 20857, (301) 443-1230

Office of the Assistant Secretary for Health
Rockville, MD 20857, (301) 443-1986

Substance Abuse and Mental Health Services
Administration
Rockville, MD 20857, (301) 443-2282

National Institutes of Health
Bethesda, MD 20892, (301) 496-2403

United States Department of the Navy
Naval Air Station
Patuxent River, MD 20670, (301) 826-4801

United States Naval Academy
Annapolis, MD 21402-5018, (410) 293-3021

University of Maryland at College Park
College Park, MD 20742, (301) 405-5677

University of Maryland Baltimore County
Baltimore, MD 21228, (410) 455-1100

University of Maryland Eastern Shore
Princess Anne, MD 21853, (410) 651-6000

Massachusetts

Bank of Boston Corp.
Boston, MA 02210, (617) 434-0165

Boston Park Plaza Hotel & Towers
Boston, MA 02117, (617) 457-2452

Brandeis University
Waltham, MA 02254-9110, (617) 736-5627

Copley Plaza
Boston, MA 02116, (617) 421-9478

Emerson College
Boston, MA 02116, (617) 578-8578

First National Bank of Boston
Boston, MA 02110, (617) 434-0165

Gillette Co.
Boston, MA 02199-8001, (617) 421-7567

Hewlett-Packard Co.
Medical Products Group Division
Andover, MA 01810-1099, (508) 659-3012

Hyatt Regency Cambridge Overlooking Boston
Boston, MA 02139, (617) 492-1234

Marriott Hotels
Boston, MA 02109, (617) 227-0800
Boston, MA 02116, (617) 578-0686
Cambridge, MA 02142, (617) 494-6600
Newton, MA 02166, (617) 969-1000

Massachusetts (state)
Boston, MA 02108, (617) 727-9244

Massachusetts Water Resources Authority
Boston, MA 02129, (617) 241-6400

Merrimack College
North Andover, MA 01845, (508) 837-5315

Mount Holyoke College
South Hadley, MA 01075-1497, (413) 538-2024

Northeastern University
Boston, MA 02115, (617) 373-5373

Office of Personnel Management
Federal Job Information Center
Boston, MA 02222-1031, (617) 565-5900

Omni Parker House
Boston, MA 02108, (617) 725-1623

Sheraton Hotels
Braintree, MA 02184, (617) 848-0600
Danvers, MA 01923, (508) 777-2500

Smith College
Northampton, MA 01063, (413) 585-2278

Suffolk University
Boston, MA 02108, (617) 573-8055

Swissotel Boston
Boston, MA 02111, (617) 422-5425

United States Department of the Interior
National Park Service
Boston, MA 02109, (617) 223-5200

Westin Hotel Copley Place
Boston, MA 02116, (617) 351-7337

Williams College
Williamstown, MA 01267, (413) 597-2679

Worcester Polytechnic Institute
Worcester, MA 01609, (508) 831-5860

Michigan

Central Michigan University
Mount Pleasant, MI 48859, (517) 774-7195

Comerica Inc.
Detroit, MI 48226, (313) 222-6266

Detroit (city)
Detroit, MI 48226, (313) 224-6928

Detroit Edison Co.
Detroit, MI 48226-1203, (313) 237-6600

Dow Chemical Co.
Midland, MI 48674, (517) 636-6100

Eastern Michigan University
Ypsilanti, MI 48197, (313) 487-2462

Eaton County
Charlotte, MI 48813, (517) 543-2452

Ferris State University
Big Rapids, MI 49307, (616) 592-5627

Ingham County
Lansing, MI 48911, (517) 887-4329

Metpath of Michigan
Auburn Hills, MI 48326, (810) 373-9120

Michigan (state) Department of Corrections
Lansing, MI 48933, (517) 373-4246

Michigan (state) Public Health Department
Lansing, MI 48409, (517) 335-8797

Michigan National Bank
Farmington Hills, MI 48333-9065, (810) 473-4328

Michigan State University
East Lansing, MI 48824-1046, (517) 355-9518

Michigan Technological University
Houghton, MI 49931, (906) 487-2895

Munson Medical Center
Traverse City, MI 49684, (616) 935-7390

Oakland University
Rochester, MI 48309, (810) 370-4500

Office of Personnel Management
Federal Job Information Center
Detroit, MI 48226, (313) 226-6950

Radisson Hotels
Detroit, MI 48226, (313) 965-0200
Southfield, MI 48075, (810) 827-4000

Sinai Hospital
Detroit, MI 48235, (313) 493-6161

University of Michigan, Dearborn
Dearborn, MI 43128-1491, (313) 593-5517

University of Michigan, Ann Arbor
Ann Arbor, MI 48109-1316, (313) 764-7292, (313) 747-2375

Upjohn Co.
Kalamazoo, MI 49001, (616) 329-5550

Wayne County
Detroit, MI 48226, (313) 224-5900

Western Michigan University
Kalamazoo, MI 49008, (616) 387-3669

Minnesota

Anoka County
Anoka, MN 55303, (612) 422-7498

Bethel College
Saint Paul, MN 55112-6999, (612) 635-8633

Burnsville (city)
Burnsville, MN 55337, (612) 895-4475

Carver County
Chaska, MN 55318, (612) 361-1522

Dakota County
Hastings, MN 55033, (612) 438-4473

Dayton Hudson Corp.
Minneapolis, MN 55402, (612) 375-2200

Deluxe Corp.
Shoreview, MN 55126, (612) 481-4100

General Mills Inc.
Minneapolis, MN 55426, (612) 540-2334

Hennepin County
Minneapolis, MN 55487-0040, (612) 348-4698

Honeywell Inc.
Minneapolis, MN 55440, (612) 951-2914

Hyatt Regency Minneapolis Nicollet Mall
Minneapolis, MN 55403, (612) 370-1202

International MultiFoods Corp.
Minneapolis, MN 55402, (612) 340-3923

Land O'Lakes Inc.
Minneapolis, MN 55440, (612) 481-2250

Macalester College
Saint Paul, MN 55105, (612) 696-6400

Marriott Hotels
Minneapolis, MN 55403, (612) 349-4077
Minneapolis, MN 55425, (612) 854-3809

Minneapolis (city)
Minneapolis, MN 55415, (612) 673-2666, (612) 673-2999

Minneapolis Cityline
Saint Paul, MN 55114, (612) 645-6060

Minnesota (state)
Minneapolis, MN 55416, (612) 296-2616

Norwest Corp.
Minneapolis, MN 55479, (612) 667-5627

Office of Personnel Management
Federal Job Information Center
Twin Cities, MN 55111, (612) 725-3430

Radisson Hotel South
Minneapolis, MN 55435, (612) 835-7800

Ramsey County
Saint Paul, MN 55102, (612) 266-2666

Saint Paul (city)
Saint Paul, MN 55110, (612) 266-6502

Scott County
Shakopee, MN 55379, (612) 496-8598

University of Minnesota, Duluth
Duluth, MN 55812, (218) 726-6506

University of Minnesota, Twin Cities
Minneapolis, MN 55455, (612) 645-6060

University of Saint Thomas
Saint Paul, MN 55105, (612) 962-6520

Washington County
Stillwater, MN 55082, (612) 430-6084

Mississippi

Jackson (city)
Jackson, MS 39201, (601) 960-1003

Mississippi State University
Mississippi State, MS 39762, (601) 325-4132

Trustmark National Bank
Jackson, MS 39201, (601) 949-2337

University of Mississippi
University, MS 38677, (601) 232-7666

Missouri

Anheuser-Busch Companies Inc.
Saint Louis, MO 63118, (314) 577-2392

Blue Springs (city)
Blue Springs, MO 64015, (816) 228-0290

Boatmen's Bancshares Inc.
Saint Louis, MO 63101, (314) 466-4473

Boatmen's First National Bank of Kansas City
Kansas City, MO 64183, (816) 691-7000

Brown Group Inc.
Saint Louis, MO 63105, (314) 854-2434

Central Missouri State University
Warrensburg, MO 64093, (816) 543-8300

Commerce Bank of Kansas City NA
Kansas City, MO 64106, (816) 234-2139

Commerce Bank of Saint Louis NA
Clayton, MO 63105, (314) 746-7382

Electronics and Space Corp.
Saint Louis, MO 63136, (314) 553-2485

Farmland Industries Inc.
Kansas City, MO 64116, (816) 459-5056

General Services Administration
Region 6
Kansas City, MO 64131, (816) 926-7804

Hyatt Regency Crown Center Kansas City
Kansas City, MO 64108, (816) 283-4473

Independence (city)
Independence, MO 64050, (816) 325-7394

Jackson County
Kansas City, MO 64106, (816) 881-3134

Jackson County Circuit Court
Kansas City, MO 64106, (816) 881-3470

Kansas City (city)
Kansas City, MO 64106, (816) 274-1127

Marriott Hotels
Osage Beach, MO 65065, (314) 348-8429
Saint Louis, MO 63102, (314) 259-3381

McDonnell Douglas Corp.
Saint Louis, MO 63166, (314) 232-4222

Medical Center of Independence
Independence, MO 64057, (816) 373-7373

Office of Personnel Management
Federal Job Information Center
Saint Louis, MO 63101, (314) 539-2285
Kansas City, MO 64106, (816) 426-5702, (816) 426-7819

Ralston Purina Co.
Saint Louis, MO 63134, (314) 982-2962

Ritz-Carlton Kansas City
Kansas City, MO 64112, (816) 756-1500

Saint Louis Community College
Saint Louis, MO 63102, (314) 539-5200

Saint Louis County
Saint Louis, MO 63105, (314) 889-3665

Saint Louis University
Saint Louis, MO 63103, (314) 658-2265

Schnuck Markets Inc.
Saint Louis, MO 63146, (314) 344-9292

Southwestern Bell Corp.
Saint Louis, MO 63101, (314) 235-9800

United States Department of Agriculture
Farmers Home Administration
Saint Louis, MO 63103, (314) 539-2830

United States Department of the Army
Corps of Engineers
Saint Louis, MO 63103, (314) 331-8550

United States Department of Commerce
Central Administrative Support Center
Kansas City, MO 64106, (816) 426-7463

United States Department of the Interior
Geological Survey
Rolla, MO 65401, (314) 341-0909

University of Missouri, Saint Louis
Saint Louis, MO 63121, (314) 553-5926

University of Missouri, Columbia
Columbia, MO 65211, (314) 882-8800

University of Missouri, Rolla
Rolla, MO 65401, (314) 341-4242

University of Missouri, Kansas City
Kansas City, MO 64110, (816) 235-1627

Westin Crown Center
Kansas City, MO 64108, (816) 474-4400

Montana

Eastern Montana College
Billings, MT 59101, (406) 657-2116

Helena (city)
Helena, MT 59623, (406) 447-8444

Montana State University
Bozeman, MT 59717, (406) 994-3343

United States Department of Agriculture
Forest Service
Helena, MT 59601, (406) 449-5419

Nebraska

ConAgra Inc.
Omaha, NE 68102-1826, (402) 595-4499

Creighton University
Omaha, NE 68178, (402) 280-2943

Douglas County
Omaha, NE 68183, (402) 444-6270

FirsTier Bank NA Lincoln
Lincoln, NE 68501, (402) 434-1426

FirsTier Bank NA Omaha
Omaha, NE 68102, (402) 348-6400

Lincoln (city) and Lancaster County
Lincoln, NE 68508, (402) 441-7736

Mutual of Omaha Insurance Co.
Omaha, NE 68175, (402) 978-2040

Nebraska (state)
Lincoln, NE 68508, (402) 471-2200

Nebraska (state) Job Service
Lincoln, NE 68508, (402) 471-3607

Omaha (city)
Omaha, NE 68183, (402) 444-5302

Red Lion Hotel Omaha
Omaha, NE 68102, (402) 346-1250

Union Pacific Railroad Co.
Omaha, NE 68179, (402) 271-5000

United States Department of the Interior
National Park Service
Omaha, NE 68102, (402) 221-3434

University of Nebraska, Omaha
Omaha, NE 68182-0005, (402) 554-2959

University of Nebraska, Lincoln
Lincoln, NE 68588, (402) 472-2303

Nevada

Aladdin Hotel & Casino
Las Vegas, NV 89109, (702) 736-0190

Bank of America Nevada
Las Vegas, NV 89193-8600, (800) 288-3162

Boulder City (city)
Boulder City, NV 89005, (702) 293-9430

Caesars Palace
Las Vegas, NV 89109, (702) 731-7386

Carson City (city)
Carson City, NV 89706, (702) 887-2240

Circus Circus Enterprises Inc.
Las Vegas, NV 89109, (702) 794-3732

Clark County
Las Vegas, NV 89101, (702) 455-3174

First Interstate Bank of Nevada NA
Reno, NV 89520, (702) 334-5666

Harrah's Las Vegas
Las Vegas, NV 89109, (702) 369-5050

Harvey's Resort Hotel & Casino
Stateline, NV 89449, (702) 588-2411

Henderson (city)
Henderson, NV 89015, (702) 565-2318

Hilton & Towers Hotels & Resorts
Reno, NV 89501, (702) 785-7006
Reno, NV 89595, (702) 789-2223

Hyatt Regency Lake Tahoe Resort & Casino
Incline Village, NV 89450, (702) 832-3274

Imperial Palace Hotel
Las Vegas, NV 89109, (702) 794-3191

Las Vegas (city)
Las Vegas, NV 89101, (702) 229-6346

Mirage
Las Vegas, NV 89109, (702) 791-7111

Nevada (state)
Carson City, NV 89701, (702) 687-4160
Las Vegas, NV 89104, (702) 486-4020

Nevada Power Co.
Las Vegas, NV 89102, (702) 367-5200

North Las Vegas (city)
North Las Vegas, NV 89030, (702) 642-9266

Palace Station
Las Vegas, NV 89102, (702) 253-2950

Primerit Bank
Las Vegas, NV 89102, (702) 226-0466

Reno (city)
Reno, NV 89505, (702) 334-2287

Sparks (city)
Sparks, NV 89431, (702) 353-2444

U.S. Bank Nevada
Reno, NV 89501, (800) 366-6698

Universities and Community Colleges of Nevada
Reno, NV 89557-0055, (702) 784-1464

Washoe County
Reno, NV 89520, (800) 473-2091

Westward Ho Hotel & Casino
Las Vegas, NV 89109, (702) 731-6374

New Hampshire

Dartmouth College
Hanover, NH 03755, (603) 646-3328

University of New Hampshire
Durham, NH 03824, (603) 862-4473

New Jersey

Bally's Park Palace Casino Hotel & Tower and Grand Casino Hotel
Atlantic City, NJ 08401, (609) 340-2211

Caesars Atlantic City Hotel Casino
Atlantic City, NJ 08401, (609) 343-2660

Claridge Casino & Hotel
Atlantic City, NJ 08401, (609) 340-3604

Drew University
Madison, NJ 07940, (201) 408-5555

Ethicon Inc.
Somerville, NJ 08876, (800) 642-9534

Harrah's Marina Hotel Casino
Atlantic City, NJ 08401, (609) 441-5681

Johnson and Johnson Inc.
New Brunswick, NJ 08933, (908) 524-2086

Merck and Co.
Rahway, NJ 07065, (908) 423-7820

Merv Griffin's Resorts Casino Hotel
Atlantic City, NJ 08404, (609) 340-6297

Metpath Inc.
Teterboro, NJ 07608, (201) 393-6161

Midlantic National Bank
Edison, NJ 08818, (908) 321-2562

New Jersey (state) Corrections Department
Trenton, NJ 08625, (609) 633-0496

New Jersey (state) Personnel Department
Trenton, NJ 08609, (609) 292-8668

Ortho Diagnostic Systems Inc.
Raritan, NJ 08869-0606, (908) 218-8808

Ortho McNeil Pharmaceutical Corp.
Raritan, NJ 08869-0602, (908) 218-6200

Personal Products Co.
Milltown, NJ 08850, (908) 524-0257

Princeton University
Princeton, NJ 08544, (609) 258-6130

Prudential Insurance Company of America
Newark, NJ 07102, (201) 802-8494

Rowan College of New Jersey
Glassboro, NJ 08028, (609) 863-5329

Rutgers, the State University of New Jersey
New Brunswick, NJ 08903-2101, (908) 445-2720, (908) 445-3045, (908) 445-3031

Sands Hotel & Casino
Atlantic City, NJ 08401, (609) 441-4525

Tropworld Casino & Entertainment Resort
Atlantic City, NJ 08401-6390, (609) 340-4261

Trump Plaza Hotel & Casino
Atlantic City, NJ 08401, (800) 677-5627

Trump Taj Mahal
Atlantic City, NJ 08401, (609) 449-5627

Trump's Castle Casino Resort by the Bay
Atlantic City, NJ 08401, (609) 441-8464

New Mexico

Albuquerque (city)
Albuquerque, NM 87102, (505) 768-4636

Bernalillo County
Albuquerque, NM 87102, (505) 768-4887

Eastern New Mexico University
Portales, NM 88130, (505) 562-2411

Hyatt Regency Albuquerque
Albuquerque, NM 87102, (505) 766-6730

Marriott Hotel Albuquerque
Albuquerque, NM 87110, (505) 881-6800

New Mexico State University
Las Cruces, NM 88003, (505) 646-1900

Office of Personnel Management
Federal Job Information Center
Albuquerque, NM 87102, (505) 766-5583

Sante Fe (city)
Santa Fe, NM 87501, (505) 984-6742

University of New Mexico
Albuquerque, NM 87131, (505) 272-5627

New York

American Telephone and Telegraph Co.
New York, NY 10013, (800) 562-7288, (800) 348-4313

Anchor Savings Bank
Hewlett, NY 11557, (800) 932-2995

Avis Inc.
Garden City, NY 11530, (516) 222-3399

Bankers Trust New York Corp.
New York, NY 10017, (212) 250-9955

Bausch and Lomb Inc.
Rochester, NY 14601, (716) 338-8265

Chase Manhattan Bank NA
Rochester, NY 14643, (716) 258-5000

Chase Manhattan Corp.
New York, NY 10081, (718) 242-7537

Citibank NA
New York, NY 10022, (718) 248-7072

College of Saint Rose
Albany, NY 12203, (518) 458-5475

Columbia University
Columbia College
New York, NY 10027, (212) 854-5804

Corning Inc.
Corning, NY 14831, (607) 974-2393

Eastman Kodak Co.
Rochester, NY 14650, (716) 724-4609

Fleet Bank
Syracuse, NY 13221, (315) 798-2680

Grand Hyatt New York Park Avenue at Grand Central
New York, NY 10017, (212) 850-5942

Holiday Inn Crowne Plaza
White Plains, NY 10601, (914) 682-0050

Hotel Macklowe
New York, NY 10036, (212) 789-7600

Hotel Parker Meridien
New York, NY 10019, (212) 708-7351

ITT Corp.
New York, NY 10019, (212) 258-1768

Key Services Corp.
Albany, NY 12211, (518) 436-2533

Marriott Hotels
Hauppauge, NY 11788, (516) 232-9800
New York, NY 10036, (212) 704-8959
Uniondale, NY 11553, (516) 794-3800

Metropolitan Life Insurance Co.
New York, NY 10010, (212) 578-4111

New York Hilton & Towers
New York, NY 10019, (212) 586-7000

Newsday Inc.
Melville, NY 11747, (516) 843-2076, (718) 575-2498

NYNEX Corp.
New York, NY 10017, (212) 395-2800

Office of Personnel Management
Federal Job Information Center
New York, NY 10278, (212) 264-0422
Syracuse, NY 13260, (315) 423-5660

Pfizer Inc.
New York, NY 10017, (212) 573-3000

Sheraton New York Hotel & Towers
New York, NY 10019, (212) 581-3300

State University of New York at Albany
Albany, NY 12222, (518) 442-3151

State University of New York at Stony Brook
Stony Brook, NY 11794, (516) 632-9222

Hospital
Stony Brook, NY 11794, (516) 444-7710

Waldorf-Astoria
New York, NY 10022, (212) 872-4717

North Carolina

Appalachian State University
Boone, NC 28608, (704) 262-6488

Cary (city)
Cary, NC 27512-1147, (919) 460-4905

Central Piedmont Community College
Charlotte, NC 28235, (704) 342-6400

Charlotte (city and county)
Charlotte, NC 28202, (704) 336-3968

Duke Power Co.
Charlotte, NC 28242-0001, (800) 726-6736

Duke University
Durham, NC 27706, (919) 684-8895, (919) 684-8896,
(919) 684-8897, (919) 684-8898, (919) 684-8899

Elon College
Elon College, NC 27244, (910) 584-2255

Environmental Protection Agency
Region 4 (satellite office)
Research Triangle Park, NC 27711, (919) 541-3014

Food Lion Inc.
Salisbury, NC 28145-1330, (704) 633-8250

Forsyth County
Winston Salem, NC 27101, (910) 631-6333

Greensboro (city)
Greensboro, NC 27402-3136, (910) 373-2080

Guilford County
Greensboro, NC 27401, (910) 373-3600

Marriott Hotels
Charlotte area
Charlotte, NC 28202, (704) 551-8000

North Carolina (state) Office of the Controller
Raleigh, NC 27609, (919) 715-5627

North Carolina State University
Raleigh, NC 27695-7103, (919) 515-3737

Office of Personnel Management
Federal Job Information Center
Raleigh, NC 27609-6296, (919) 790-2822

Omni Charlotte
Charlotte, NC 28202, (704) 377-6664

Pembroke State University
Pembroke, NC 28372, (910) 521-6532

Raleigh (city)
Raleigh, NC 27602, (919) 890-3305

Roche Biomedical Laboratories Inc.
Burlington, NC 27216, (910) 229-1127

University of North Carolina at Chapel Hill
Chapel Hill, NC 27514, (919) 990-3000

University of North Carolina at Charlotte
Charlotte, NC 28223, (704) 547-2075

University of North Carolina at Greensboro
Greensboro, NC 27412, (910) 334-5023

University of North Carolina at Wilmington
Wilmington, NC 28403, (910) 395-3791

Wachovia Corp.
Winston Salem, NC 27150, (910) 770-5520

Wake County
Raleigh, NC 27602, (919) 856-6115

Wake Forest University
Winston Salem, NC 27109, (910) 759-4448

Winston Salem (city)
Winston Salem, NC 27101, (910) 631-6496

North Dakota

North Dakota (state) Job Service
Bismarck, ND 58502, (701) 221-5049

North Dakota State University
Fargo, ND 58105, (701) 237-8273

Ohio

Banc One Corp.
Columbus, OH 43271, (614) 248-0779

Bank One Akron NA
Akron, OH 44309, (216) 972-1810

Bank One Columbus NA
Columbus, OH 43271, (614) 248-0779

Bank One Dayton NA
Dayton, OH 45401, (513) 449-7446

Bowling Green State University
Bowling Green, OH 43403, (419) 372-8522, (419) 372-8669

Case Western Reserve University
Cleveland, OH 44106, (216) 368-4500

Cincinnati (city)
Cincinnati, OH 45202, (513) 352-2489

Cincinnati Bell Inc.
Cincinnati, OH 45202, (513) 397-9900

Clermont County
Batavia, OH 45103, (513) 732-7853

Cleveland (city)
Cleveland, OH 44114, (216) 664-2420

Cleveland State University
Cleveland, OH 44115, (216) 687-9300

Columbus (city)
Columbus, OH 43215, (614) 645-7667

Columbus State Community College
Columbus, OH 43216, (800) 621-6407

Cuyahoga County
Cleveland, OH 44113, (216) 443-2039

Dayton (city)
Dayton, OH 45402, (513) 443-3719

Deaconess Hospital of Cleveland
Cleveland, OH 44109, (216) 459-6560

Environmental Protection Agency
Andrew Breidenbach Center
Cincinnati, OH 45268, (513) 569-7840

Fifth Third Bank
Cincinnati, OH 45263, (513) 579-5627

Fifth Third Bank of Toledo NA
Toledo, OH 43604, (419) 259-7694

Grandview Hospital and Medical Center
Dayton, OH 45405, (513) 226-2675

Hamilton County
Cincinnati, OH 45202, (513) 763-4900

Huntington Bank
Columbus, OH 43215, (614) 463-4305

Kent State University
Kent, OH 44242, (216) 672-2103

Miami University
Oxford, OH 45056, (513) 529-6400

Montgomery County
Dayton, OH 45402, (513) 225-6128

National City Bank, Northeast
Akron, OH 44308, (216) 375-8685

National City Bank, Northwest
Toledo, OH 43603, (419) 259-6710

National City Bank, Columbus
Columbus, OH 43251, (614) 463-6736

Nationwide Mutual Insurance Co.
Columbus, OH 43216, (614) 249-5725

Office of Personnel Management
Federal Job Information Center
Dayton, OH 45402, (513) 225-2720

Ohio (state) Environmental Protection Agency
Columbus, OH 43215, (614) 644-2102

Ohio State University, Columbus
Columbus, OH 43210, (614) 292-1212

Ohio University
Athena, OH 45701, (614) 593-4080

Proctor and Gamble Co.
Cincinnati, OH 45202, (513) 983-2125, (513) 983-7494

Public Utilities Commission of Ohio
Columbus, OH 43215, (614) 644-5656

Sherwin-Williams Co.
Cleveland, OH 44115, (216) 566-2120

Society Bank NA
Dayton, OH 45402, (513) 226-6388

Society Corp.
Cleveland, OH 44114, (216) 689-5153

Southern Ohio Medical Center
Portsmouth, OH 45662, (614) 354-7644

University of Akron
Akron, OH 44325, (216) 972-7091

University of Dayton
Dayton, OH 45469-0001, (513) 229-3377

University of Toledo
Toledo, OH 43606, (419) 537-2020

Wright State University
Dayton, OH 45435, (513) 873-4562

Oklahoma

Bank of Oklahoma NA
Tulsa, OK 74192, (918) 588-6828

Cameron University
Lawton, OK 73505, (405) 581-2501

Edmond (city)
Edmond, OK 73083, (405) 840-8000

Liberty National Bank and Trust Company of Tulsa
Tulsa, OK 74193, (918) 586-5818

Mapco Inc.
Tulsa, OK 74119, (918) 586-7178

Midwest City (city)
Midwest City, OK 73110, (405) 739-1236

Norman (city)
Norman, OK 73069, (405) 366-5321

Oklahoma City (city)
Oklahoma City, OK 73102, (405) 297-2419

Oklahoma State University
Stillwater, OK 74078, (405) 744-7692

Phillips Petroleum Co.
Bartlesville, OK 74004, (918) 661-5547

Tulsa (city)
Tulsa, OK 74103, (918) 596-7444

Tulsa Junior College
Tulsa, OK 74135, (918) 631-7854

United States Department of the Air Force
Tinker Air Force Base
Tinker Air Force Base, OK 73150, (405) 739-3271

University of Central Oklahoma
Edmond, OK 73034, (405) 341-2980

University of Oklahoma
Norman, OK 73019, (405) 325-2711, (405) 325-4343

University of Tulsa
Tulsa, OK 74104, (918) 631-4000

Oregon

Bank of America Oregon
Portland, OR 97204, (503) 275-1390

Beaverton (city)
Beaverton, OR 97005, (503) 526-2299

Beaverton School District No. 48J
Beaverton, OR 97075, (503) 591-4600

Benton County
Corvallis, OR 97330, (503) 757-6755

Clackamas County
Oregon City, OR 97045, (503) 655-8894

Corvallis (city)
Corvallis, OR 97333, (503) 757-6955

Douglas County
Roseburg, OR 97470, (503) 440-6291

Eugene (city)
Eugene, OR 97401, (503) 687-5060

Eugene (city) Water and Electric Board
Eugene, OR 97401, (503) 484-3769

Eugene School District No. 4J
Eugene, OR 97402, (503) 687-3344

Far West Federal Savings Bank
Portland, OR 97204, (503) 323-6467

First Interstate Bank of Oregon NA
Portland, OR 97208, (503) 340-8888

Fred Meyer Inc.
Portland, OR 97202-2918, (800) 401-5627

Freightliner Corp.
Portland, OR 97217, (503) 735-8657, (503) 735-7091

Gresham (city)
Gresham, OR 97030, (503) 669-2309

Hewlett-Packard Co.
Corvallis Division
Corvallis, OR 97330-4239, (503) 754-0919

Key Bank of Oregon
Portland, OR 97204, (503) 598-3573

Klamath County
Klamath Falls, OR 97601, (503) 883-4188

Lake Oswego (city)
Lake Oswego, OR 97034, (503) 635-0256

Lake Oswego School District No. 7J
Lake Oswego, OR 97034, (503) 635-0342

Lane County
Eugene, OR 97401, (503) 687-4473

Lewis and Clark College
Portland, OR 97219, (503) 768-7840

Linn-Benton Community College
Albany, OR 97321, (503) 926-8800

Marion County
Salem, OR 97301, (503) 588-5589

Marriott Hotel Portland
Portland, OR 97201, (503) 499-6334

Metropolitan Service District
Portland, OR 97232, (503) 797-1777

Multnomah County
Portland, OR 97204, (503) 248-5035

Multnomah Education Service District
Portland, OR 97220, (503) 257-1510

Nike Inc.
Beaverton, OR 97005, (503) 644-4224

Office of Personnel Management
Federal Job Information Center
Portland, OR 97204, (503) 326-3141

Oregon (state)
Salem, OR 97301, (503) 378-8344

Oregon (state) Department of Environmental Quality
Portland, OR 97204, (503) 229-5785

Oregon (state) Employment Division
Astoria, OR 97103, (503) 325-7856
Eugene, OR 97401, (503) 686-7652
Newport, OR 97365, (503) 265-5627

Oregon City School District No. 62
Oregon City, OR 97045, (503) 657-2465

Oregon State University
Corvallis, OR 97331, (503) 737-0554

PacifiCorp
Portland, OR 97204, (503) 464-6848

Portland (city)
Portland, OR 97204, (503) 823-4573

Portland Community College
Portland, OR 97219, (503) 273-2826

Portland Hilton
Portland, OR 97204, (503) 220-2560

Portland School District No. 1J
Portland, OR 97227, (503) 331-3102

Red Lion Hotels
Portland, OR 97232, (503) 978-4515

Salem (city)
Salem, OR 97301, (503) 588-6162

Salem-Keizer School District No. 24J
Salem, OR 97301, (503) 399-3404

Springfield (city)
Springfield, OR 97477, (503) 726-3648

Springfield School District No. 19
Springfield, OR 97477, (503) 726-3364

Tigard (city)
Tigard, OR 97223, (503) 624-9471

Tri-County Metropolitan Transportation District of Oregon
Portland, OR 97202, (503) 238-4840

United States Department of Agriculture
Forest Service
Grants Pass, OR 97526, (503) 471-6715

United States Department of Veterans Affairs
Medical Center
Portland, OR 97207, (503) 273-5249

University of Portland
Portland, OR 97203-5798, (503) 283-7536

Washington County
Hillsboro, OR 97124, (503) 648-8607

Pennsylvania

Adam's Mark Philadelphia
Philadelphia, PA 19131, (215) 581-5074

Armstrong World Industries Inc.
Lancaster, PA 17604, (717) 396-3441

Bell Atlantic Corp.
Philadelphia, PA 19103, (800) 967-5422

Bloomsburg University of Pennsylvania
Bloomsburg, PA 17815, (717) 389-2093

Bucknell University
Lewisburg, PA 17837, (717) 524-1635

Carnegie Mellon University
Pittsburgh, PA 15213, (412) 268-8545

Clarion University of Pennsylvania
Clarion, PA 16214, (814) 226-2045

Continental Bank
Philadelphia, PA 19102, (215) 564-7678

CoreStates Bank NA
Philadelphia, PA 19101, (215) 973-4556

Dauphin Deposit Bank and Trust Co.
Harrisburg, PA 17105, (717) 255-2121

Doubletree Philadelphia
Philadelphia, PA 19107, (215) 893-1600

Drexel University
Philadelphia, PA 19104, (215) 895-2562

East Stroudsburg University of Pennsylvania
East Stroudsburg, PA 18301, (717) 424-3280

Germantown Savings Bank
Bala-Cynwyd, PA 19004, (610) 660-8451

Hamot Medical Center
Erie, PA 16550, (814) 877-5627

Intelligent Electronics Inc.
Exton, PA 19341, (610) 458-6793

Kutztown University
Kutztown, PA 19530, (610) 683-4130

Lehigh County
Allentown, PA 18101, (610) 820-3386

Lehigh University
Bethlehem, PA 18015-3035, (610) 758-5627

Mellon PSFS
Philadelphia, PA 19101-7899, (215) 553-3213

Meridian Bancorp Inc.
Reading, PA 19603, (800) 321-5627

Pennsylvania State University
University Park, PA 16802, (814) 865-5627

Philadelphia Electric Co.
Philadelphia, PA 19101, (215) 841-4340

Pittsburgh (city)
Pittsburgh, PA 15219, (412) 255-2388

PNC Bank
Philadelphia, PA 19101, (800) 762-5627

PPG Industries Inc.
Pittsburgh, PA 15272, (412) 434-2002

Scott Paper Co.
Philadelphia, PA 19113, (215) 522-5885

University of Pennsylvania
Philadelphia, PA 19104, (215) 898-5627

University of Pittsburgh, Pittsburgh Campus
Pittsburgh, PA 15260, (412) 624-8040

Puerto Rico

Office of Personnel Management
Federal Job Information Center
San Juan, PR 00918-1710, (809) 766-5242, (809) 774-8790

Rhode Island

Brown University
Providence, RI 02912, (401) 863-9675

Landmark Medical Center
Woonsocket and Fogarty Units
Woonsocket, RI 02895, (401) 769-4100

South Carolina

Charleston (city)
Charleston, SC 29403, (803) 720-3907

Charleston County
Charleston, SC 29401, (803) 724-0694

Clemson University
Clemson, SC 29634-4024, (803) 656-2228

College of Charleston
Charleston, SC 29424, (803) 953-5419

Columbia (city)
Columbia, SC 29201, (803) 733-8478

Lexington County
Lexington, SC 29072, (803) 359-8562

Richland County
Columbia, SC 29202, (803) 748-4832

South Carolina (state)
Columbia, SC 29205, (803) 734-9333, (803) 734-9334

South Carolina (state) Department of Corrections
Columbia, SC 29210, (803) 896-8524, (803) 896-1201, (803) 896-1202

South Carolina (state) Department of Juvenile Justice
Columbia, SC 29210, (803) 737-4293

South Carolina (state) Department of Mental Health
Columbia, SC 29201, (803) 734-7674

South Carolina (state) Educational Television Commission
Columbia, SC 29201, (803) 737-3320

United States Department of the Air Force
Charleston Air Force Base
Charleston Air Force Base, SC 29404-5021, (803) 566-4490

University of South Carolina, Columbia
Columbia, SC 29208, (803) 777-2100

Westin Resort
Hilton Head Island, SC 29928, (803) 681-4000

South Dakota

Black Hills State University
Spearfish, SD 57799, (605) 642-6511

Pennington County
Rapid City, SD 57701, (605) 394-8090

Rapid City (city)
Rapid City, SD 57701, (605) 394-5329

South Dakota (state)
Pierre, SD 57501-5070, (605) 773-3326

Tennessee

Comdata Holdings Corp.
Brentwood, TN 37027, (615) 370-7747

Federal Express Corp.
Memphis, TN 38132, (901) 797-6830, (901) 535-9555

First American Corp.
Nashville, TN 37211-7115, (615) 781-7400

First Tennessee Bank NA
Memphis, TN 38101-8416, (901) 523-5090, (901) 523-5056, (901) 523-5033

First Union National Bank of Tennessee
Nashville, TN 37219, (615) 251-9238

Gaylord Entertainment Co.
Broadcast Division
Nashville, TN 37214, (615) 871-5920

Holiday Inn Briley Parkway
Nashville, TN 37210, (615) 885-4491

Jackson-Madison County General Hospital
Jackson, TN 38301, (901) 425-6759

Knoxville (city)
Knoxville, TN 37902, (615) 521-2562

Loew's Vanderbilt Plaza Hotel
Nashville, TN 37203, (615) 321-1908

Memphis (city)
Memphis, TN 38103, (901) 576-6548

Memphis (city) Light Gas and Water Division
Memphis, TN 38103, (901) 528-4241

Nashville (city) and Davidson County
Nashville, TN 37201, (615) 862-6660

Nashville Airport Marriott
Nashville, TN 37210, (615) 872-2952

NationsBank of Tennessee NA
Nashville, TN 37239, (615) 749-3900

Promus Companies Inc.
Memphis, TN 38117, (901) 748-7626

Regional Medical Center
Memphis, TN 38103, (901) 575-8432

Service Merchandise Company Inc.
Brentwood, TN 37027, (615) 660-3199

Shelby County
Memphis, TN 38103, (901) 576-4434

Union Planters National Bank
Cordova, TN 38018, (901) 383-6663

United States Department of Defense
Defense Logistics Agency
Memphis, TN 38114, (901) 775-4933

University of Tennessee at Chattanooga
Chattanooga, TN 37403, (615) 755-4473

University of Tennessee at Knoxville
Knoxville, TN 37996, (615) 974-6644

University of Tennessee at Martin
Martin, TN 38238, (901) 587-7848

Vanderbilt University
Nashville, TN 37212-2099, (615) 322-8383

Texas

Adam's Mark Houston
Houston, TX 77042, (713) 735-2775

Addison (city)
Addison, TX 75240, (214) 450-2815

Alamo Community College District
San Antonio, TX 78207, (210) 220-1600

Amarillo (city)
Amarillo, TX 79101, (806) 378-4205

American General Corp.
Houston, TX 77019, (713) 831-3100

American Medical International Inc.
Dallas, TX 75225, (214) 360-6373

AMR Corp.
Dallas/Fort Worth Airport, TX 75261, (817) 963-1234, (817) 963-1110

Arlington (city)
Arlington, TX 76010, (817) 265-7938

Austin (city)
Austin, TX 78701, (512) 499-3201, (512) 499-3203,
(512) 499-3202, (512) 499-3204

Austin Community College
Austin, TX 78714, (512) 483-7648

Bank of America Texas NA
Irving, TX 75063, (214) 444-6970

Bank One Texas NA
Arlington, TX 76013, (817) 459-9910
Dallas, TX 75265-5415, (214) 290-3637
Fort Worth, TX 76113, (817) 884-6709

Processing Center
Bedford, TX 76021, (817) 884-6761

Baylor University
Waco, TX 76798, (817) 755-3675

Beaumont (city)
Beaumont, TX 77704, (409) 838-5627

Bexar County
San Antonio, TX 78205, (210) 270-6333

Brinker International Inc.
Dallas, TX 75240, (214) 770-9463

Camino Real Paso del Norte
El Paso, TX 79901, (915) 534-3067

Central and South West Corp.
Dallas, TX 75266-0164, (214) 777-1877

Clubcorp International
Dallas, TX 75234, (214) 888-7599

Coastal Corp.
Houston, TX 77046, (713) 877-6978

Comerica Bank Texas
Dallas, TX 75201, (214) 969-6177

Continental Airlines Holdings Inc.
Houston, TX 77210-4330, (713) 834-5300

Corpus Christi (city)
Corpus Christi, TX 78401, (512) 880-3333

Dallas (city)
Dallas, TX 75201, (214) 670-3552

Dallas County
Dallas, TX 75202, (214) 653-7637

Dallas County Community College District
Dallas, TX 75202, (214) 746-2438

De Soto (city)
De Soto, TX 75115, (214) 230-9698

Diamond Shamrock Inc.
San Antonio, TX 78269, (210) 641-2387

Doctors Hospital
Houston, TX 77076, (713) 696-4488

Doubletree Hotels
Austin, TX 78752, (512) 454-4107
Dallas, TX 75240, (214) 701-5279
Houston, TX 77056, (713) 961-9300

El Paso (city)
El Paso, TX 79901, (915) 541-4094

El Paso County
El Paso, TX 79901, (915) 546-2039

Enron Corp.
Houston, TX 77002-7337, (713) 853-5884

Environmental Protection Agency
Region 6
Dallas, TX 75202, (214) 655-6560

Euless (city)
Euless, TX 76039, (817) 685-1456

Fairmont Hotel Dallas Arts District
Dallas, TX 75201, (214) 720-5311

Farmers Branch (city)
Farmers Branch, TX 75234, (214) 919-2559

First Interstate Bank of Texas NA
Houston, TX 77002, (713) 250-7356

Fort Worth (city)
Fort Worth, TX 76102, (817) 871-7760

Four Seasons Hotel Houston
Houston, TX 77010, (713) 650-3437

Frost National Bank
San Antonio, TX 78205, (210) 220-5627

Grand Prairie (city)
Grand Prairie, TX 75050, (214) 660-8190

Harvey Hotel Dallas-Fort Worth
Irving, TX 75063, (214) 929-4500

Hilton & Towers Hotels & Resorts
San Antonio, TX 78205, (210) 222-1400
San Antonio, TX 78216, (210) 340-6060

Holiday Inns
Houston, TX 77027, (713) 961-7272
Houston, TX 77079, (713) 558-5580

Houston Community College System
Houston, TX 77007, (713) 868-0711, (713) 866-8369

Houston Lighting and Power Co.
Houston, TX 77251, (713) 238-5854

Houston Medallion
Houston, TX 77092, (713) 688-0100

Houston Northwest Medical Center
Houston, TX 77090, (713) 440-6321

Hyatt/Regency/Grand Hotels
Austin, TX 78704, (512) 477-1234
Dallas, TX 75207, (214) 712-7018
Dallas-Fort Worth Airport, TX 75261, (214) 615-6809
Houston, TX 77002, (713) 646-6912
San Antonio, TX 78205, (210) 531-2396

JC Penney Co.
Dallas, TX 75301, (214) 431-2300

Jefferson County
Beaumont, TX 77704, (409) 839-2384

Lamar University
Beaumont, TX 77710, (409) 880-8371

Loew's Anatole Dallas
Dallas, TX 75207, (214) 761-7333

Lubbock (city)
Lubbock, TX 79457, (806) 762-2444

Lyondell Petrochemical Co.
Houston, TX 77010, (713) 652-4562

Marriott Hotels
Austin, TX 78701, (512) 478-1111
Houston, TX 77030, (713) 796-2218
Houston, TX 77056, (713) 961-1500
San Antonio, TX 78205, (210) 299-6518
San Antonio, TX 78205, (210) 554-6289

MCI Communications Corp.
Richardson, TX 75082, (800) 456-5243

Mesquite (city)
Mesquite, TX 75149, (214) 216-6484

NationsBank of Texas NA
Dallas, TX 75202, (214) 712-2103

North Harris Montgomery Community College District
Houston, TX 77060, (713) 591-3534

Nueces County
Corpus Christi, TX 78401, (512) 888-0563

Office of Personnel Management
Federal Job Information Center
San Antonio, TX 78217, (210) 805-2406, (210) 805-2402
Dallas, TX 75242, (214) 767-8035

Omni Houston Hotel
Houston, TX 77056, (713) 624-4823

Oryx Energy Co.
Dallas, TX 75240, (214) 715-8200

Owen Healthcare Inc.
Houston, TX 77036, (713) 777-8173

Pennzoil Co.
Houston, TX 77252, (713) 546-6630

Radisson Plaza Fort Worth
Fort Worth, TX 76102, (817) 870-2100

Ramada Hotels
Houston, TX 77030, (713) 797-9000
Richardson, TX 75081, (214) 231-9600

Rice University
Houston, TX 77251, (713) 527-6080

Richardson (city)
Richardson, TX 75080, (214) 238-4151

S and A Restaurant Corp.
Dallas, TX 75251, (214) 404-5622

Saint Anthony
San Antonio, TX 78205, (210) 227-4392

Saint David's Hospital
Austin, TX 78765-4039, (512) 397-4000

Saint Mary's University
San Antonio, TX 78284-0400, (210) 436-3343

Sam Houston State University
Huntsville, TX 77341, (409) 294-1067

San Antonio (city)
San Antonio, TX 78205, (210) 299-7280

San Antonio (city) Water System
San Antonio, TX 78205, (210) 704-7280

Santa Rosa Health Care Corp.
San Antonio, TX 78207, (210) 228-2343

Sheraton Hotels
Dallas, TX 75251, (214) 385-3000
Houston, TX 77032, (713) 442-5100
San Antonio, TX 78205, (210) 227-3241

Southern Methodist University
Dallas, TX 75275, (214) 768-1111

Southland Corp.
Dallas, TX 75204, (214) 841-6758

Southwest Airlines Co.
Dallas, TX 75235, (214) 904-4803

Southwest Texas State University
San Marcos, TX 78666, (512) 245-2619

State National Bank
El Paso, TX 79958, (915) 546-4335

Stephen F. Austin State University
Nacogdoches, TX 75962-3051, (409) 568-3003

Stouffer Hotels
Austin, TX 78759, (512) 343-2626
Dallas, TX 75207, (214) 631-2222

Tandy Corp.
Fort Worth, TX 76102, (817) 390-2949

Tarleton State University
Stephenville, TX 76402, (817) 968-9750

Tarrant County Junior College
Fort Worth, TX 76102, (817) 335-6721

Tenneco Inc.
Houston, TX 77252-2511, (713) 757-4193

Texas (state)
Austin, TX 78701, (512) 463-3433

Texas (state) Auditor
Austin, TX 78701, (512) 479-3055

Texas (state) Department of Insurance
Austin, TX 78701, (512) 463-6170

Texas (state) Department of Protective and Regulatory Services
San Antonio, TX 78223, (210) 337-3234
Austin, TX 78751, (512) 450-3600
El Paso, TX 79925, (915) 599-3635

Texas (state) Department of Transportation
Austin, TX 78704, (512) 416-3000

Texas (state) Higher Education Coordinating Board
Austin, TX 78711, (512) 483-6574

Texas (state) Library and Archives
Austin, TX 78701, (512) 463-5470

Texas (state) Natural Resource Conservation Commission
Austin, TX 78711-3087, (512) 239-0100

Texas (state) Rehabilitation Commission
Austin, TX 78751, (512) 483-4880

Texas A&I University
Kingsville, TX 78363, (512) 595-3004

Texas A&M University, College Station
College Station, TX 77843, (409) 845-4444

Texas Christian University
Fort Worth, TX 76129, (817) 921-7791

Texas Commerce Bank Dallas NA
Dallas, TX 75266-0197, (214) 922-2224

Texas Commerce Bank El Paso NA
El Paso, TX 79980, (915) 546-6540

Texas Commerce Bank Houston NA
Houston, TX 77002, (713) 216-4541

Texas Instruments Inc.
Dallas, TX 75251, (214) 995-6666

Texas Southern University
Houston, TX 77004, (713) 527-7011

Texas Tech University
Lubbock, TX 79409, (806) 742-2211

Texas Woman's University
Denton, TX 76204, (817) 898-3565

Travis County
Austin, TX 78767, (512) 473-9675

Trinity University
San Antonio, TX 78212, (210) 736-7510

United States Department of the Army
Fort Bliss and William Beaumont Army Medical Center
Fort Bliss, TX 79916-5803, (915) 568-4755

United States Department of Health and Human Services
Region 6
Dallas, TX 75202, (214) 767-3124

United States Department of the Treasury
Internal Revenue Service
Austin, TX 78741, (512) 477-5627, (512) 462-8115

United States Department of Veterans Affairs
Medical Center
Amarillo, TX 79106, (806) 354-7828

University of Houston, Downtown
Houston, TX 77002, (713) 221-8609

University of Houston
Houston, TX 77204-2161, (713) 743-5788

University of North Texas
Denton, TX 76203-3797, (817) 565-4070

University of Texas at Arlington
Arlington, TX 76019, (817) 273-3455

University of Texas at Austin
Austin, TX 78712-1159, (512) 471-4295

University of Texas at El Paso
El Paso, TX 79968, (915) 747-8837

University of Texas at San Antonio
San Antonio, TX 78285, (210) 691-4650

University Park (city)
University Park, TX 75205, (214) 653-3175

West Texas State University
Canyon, TX 79016, (806) 656-4636

Westin Galleria Hotel and Westin Oaks Hotel
Houston, TX 77056, (713) 960-6520

Wichita County
Wichita Falls, TX 76301, (817) 766-8129

Wyndham Greenspoint
Houston, TX 77060, (713) 875-4506

Zale Corp.
Irving, TX 75038, (214) 580-5408

Utah

American Stores Co.
Salt Lake City, UT 84102, (800) 284-5560

Brigham Young University
Provo, UT 84602, (801) 378-4357

Davis County
Farmington, UT 84025, (801) 451-3484

Doubletree Hotel
Salt Lake City, UT 84101, (801) 531-7500

First Interstate Bank of Utah NA
Salt Lake City, UT 84101, (801) 350-7070

First Security Bank of Utah NA
Salt Lake City, UT 84111, (801) 246-1885

Intermountain Health Care Inc.
Salt Lake City, UT 84111, (801) 533-3654

Key Bank of Utah
Salt Lake City, UT 84144, (801) 535-1117

Marriott Salt Lake City
Salt Lake City, UT 84101, (801) 537-6050

Murray (city)
Murray, UT 84157, (801) 264-2525

Red Lion Hotel/Salt Lake
Salt Lake City, UT 84101, (801) 328-7082

Salt Lake City (city)
Salt Lake City, UT 84111, (801) 535-6625

Salt Lake County
Salt Lake City, UT 84115, (801) 468-2390

Sandy (city)
Sandy, UT 84070, (801) 561-7009

University of Utah
Salt Lake City, UT 84112, (801) 581-5627

Utah (state)
Salt Lake City, UT 84114, (801) 538-3118

Utah State University
Logan, UT 84322-1600, (801) 797-1819

West Jordan (city)
West Jordan, UT 84088, (801) 569-5045

Vermont

Burlington (city)
Burlington, VT 05401, (802) 865-7147

Middlebury College
Middlebury, VT 05753, (802) 388-3711

University of Vermont
Burlington, VT 05405-3596, (802) 656-2248

Vermont (state)
Montpelier, VT 05602, (802) 828-3484

Vermont (state) Employment and Training Department
Jobsline
Montpelier, VT 05602, (802) 828-3939

Virginia

Alexandria (city)
Alexandria, VA 22314, (703) 838-4422

American Medical Laboratories Inc.
Chantilly, VA 22021, (703) 802-7282

Arlington County
Arlington, VA 22201, (703) 358-3363

Chesapeake (city)
Chesapeake, VA 23328, (804) 547-6416

Circuit City Stores Inc.
Richmond, VA 23233, (804) 527-4094

College of William and Mary in Virginia
Williamsburg, VA 23185, (804) 221-3167

Crestar Bank
Richmond, VA 23219-4625, (804) 270-8572

Dominion First Union Bank of Virginia
Roanoke, VA 24019, (703) 563-7907

Fairfax (city)
Fairfax, VA 22030, (703) 385-7861

Fairfax County
Fairfax, VA 22030, (703) 324-5627

Falls Church (city)
Falls Church, VA 22046, (703) 241-5163

First Union National Bank of Virginia
McLean, VA 22102, (703) 903-7777

Gannett Company Inc.
Arlington, VA 22234, (703) 284-6054

George Mason University
Fairfax, VA 22030, (703) 993-8799

Hampton (city)
Hampton, VA 23669, (804) 727-6406

Hampton University
Hampton, VA 23368, (804) 727-5954

Herndon (city)
Herndon, VA 22070, (703) 481-3892

Hyatt Regency Crystal City-National Airport
Arlington, VA 22202, (703) 418-7228

Inova Health Systems Inc.
Springfield, VA 22151, (800) 854-6682

James Madison University
Harrisonburg, VA 22807, (703) 568-3561

Loudoun County
Leesburg, VA 22075, (703) 777-0536

Marriott Hotels
Norfolk, VA 23510, (804) 628-6491
Richmond, VA 23219, (804) 643-3400

Mary Washington College
Fredericksburg, VA 22401-5358, (703) 899-4624

McLean Hilton at Tysons Corner
McLean, VA 22102, (703) 761-5155

Mobil Corp.
Fairfax, VA 22037, (703) 846-2777, (703) 849-6005

NationsBank of Virginia NA
Norfolk, VA 23510, (804) 441-4451

Navy Federal Credit Union
Merrifield, VA 22119, (703) 255-8800

Newport News (city)
Newport News, VA 23607, (804) 928-9281

Norfolk (city)
Norfolk, VA 25301, (804) 627-8768

Norfolk State University
Norfolk, VA 23504, (804) 683-8184

Northern Virginia Community College
Annandale, VA 22003, (703) 323-3444

Old Dominion University
Norfolk, VA 23529-0050, (804) 683-3066, (804) 683-4011

Portsmouth (city)
Portsmouth, VA 23704, (804) 398-0682

Radford University
Radford, VA 24142, (703) 831-5825

Radisson Plaza Hotel at Mark Center
Alexandria, VA 22311, (703) 845-7654

Ramada Hotel Tyson's
Falls Church, VA 22043, (703) 821-3161

Sheraton Premiere at Tyson's Corner
Vienna, VA 22182, (703) 506-2518

Suffolk (city)
Suffolk, VA 23434, (804) 925-6435

United States Department of the Army
Peninsula Job Information Center
Newport News, VA 23606, (804) 873-3160

United States Department of Commerce
National Oceanic and Atmospheric Administration
Norfolk, VA 23510-2314, (804) 441-3720

United States Department of Defense
Defense Contract Audit Agency
Alexandria, VA 22304-6178, (703) 274-4068

Defense Logistics Agency
Alexandria, VA 22304-6100, (703) 274-7372

United States Department of the Interior
Geological Survey
Reston, VA 22092, (703) 648-7676

United States Department of Justice
United States Marshals Service
Arlington, VA 22202-4210, (202) 307-9400

United States Department of the Navy
Little Creek Amphibious Base and Oceana Naval Air Station
Norfolk, VA 23511-3997, (804) 444-7541

Norfolk Naval Shipyard
Portsmouth, VA 23709-5000, (804) 396-5657

University of Richmond
Richmond, VA 23173, (804) 287-6001

University of Virginia
Charlottesville, VA 22903, (804) 924-4400

USAir Group Inc.
Arlington, VA 22227, (703) 418-7499

Virginia Beach (city)
Virginia Beach, VA 23456, (804) 427-3580

Virginia Commonwealth University
Richmond, VA 23298, (804) 278-0266

Virginia Polytechnic Institute and State University
Blacksburg, VA 24061, (703) 231-6196, (703) 231-6176, (703) 231-6160, (703) 231-4649

Virginia State University
Petersburg, VA 23803, (804) 524-5627

Washington

Airborne Freight Corp.
Seattle, WA 98111, (800) 426-2323

Alaska Air Group Inc.
Seattle, WA 98168, (206) 433-3230

Auburn (city)
Auburn, WA 98001, (206) 931-3077

Bainbridge School District
Bainbridge Island, WA 98110, (206) 842-2920

Battle Ground Public Schools
Battle Ground, WA 98604, (206) 256-5385

Bethel School District
Spanaway, WA 98387, (206) 536-7270

Boeing Co.
Seattle, WA 98108-4002, (206) 965-3111

Central Kitsap School District
Silverdale, WA 93838, (206) 698-3470

Central Washington University
Ellensburg, WA 98926, (509) 963-1562

Clark County
Vancouver, WA 98660, (206) 737-6018

Clover Park School District
Tacoma, WA 98499, (206) 589-7436

Eastern Washington University
Cheney, WA 99004, (509) 359-6200

Edmonds School District
Lynnwood, WA 98036, (206) 670-7021

Everett (city)
Everett, WA 98201, (206) 259-8768

Everett School District
Everett, WA 98203, (206) 259-2935

Evergreen School District
Vancouver, WA 98686, (206) 254-7403

Evergreen State College
Olympia, WA 98505, (206) 866-6000

Federal Way (city)
Federal Way, WA 98003, (206) 661-4089

Federal Way School District
Federal Way, WA 98003, (206) 941-2273, (206) 941-2058

First Interstate Bank of Washington NA
Seattle, WA 98111, (206) 292-3551

Four Seasons Olympic Hotel
Seattle, WA 98101, (206) 682-9164

Franklin Pierce School District
Tacoma, WA 98444, (206) 535-8829

Gonzaga University
Spokane, WA 99258-0001, (509) 484-6816

Hewlett-Packard Co.
Spokane Division
Spokane, WA 99220, (509) 921-4888

Vancouver Division
Camas, WA 98607-9410, (206) 944-2493

Highline School District
Seattle, WA 98166, (206) 433-6339

Kent (city)
Kent, WA 98032, (206) 859-3375

Kent (city) Civil Service Commission
Kent, WA 98032-5895, (206) 859-2876

Kent School District
Kent, WA 98031, (206) 859-7508

Key Bank of Washington
Tacoma, WA 98411-5500, (800) 677-6150

King County
Seattle, WA 98104, (206) 296-5209

King County Metropolitan Services
Seattle, WA 98104, (206) 684-1313

Kitsap County
Port Orchard, WA 98366, (206) 876-7169

Lacey (city)
Lacey, WA 98503, (206) 491-3213

Marysville School District
Marysville, WA 98270, (206) 653-0807

McCaw Communication Co.
Kirkland, WA 98033, (206) 828-8484

Mead School District
Mead, WA 99021, (509) 468-3193

Mercer Island (city)
Mercer Island, WA 98040, (206) 236-5326

Mercer Island School District
Mercer Island, WA 98040, (206) 236-3302

Metropolitan Park District of Tacoma
Tacoma, WA 98405, (206) 305-1009

Office of Personnel Management
Federal Job Information Center
Seattle, WA 98174, (206) 220-6400

Olympia (city)
Olympia, WA 98501, (206) 753-8383

PACCAR Inc.
Bellevue, WA 98004, (206) 637-5011

Pacific Lutheran University
Tacoma, WA 98447, (206) 535-8598

Pierce College
Tacoma, WA 98498, (206) 964-7341

Pierce County
Tacoma, WA 98405, (206) 591-7466

Port of Seattle
Seattle, WA 98121, (206) 728-3290

Red Lion Hotels
Bellevue, WA 98004, (206) 455-1300
Seattle, WA 98188, (206) 246-8600

Renton (city)
Renton, WA 98055, (206) 235-2514

Renton School District
Renton, WA 98055, (206) 235-5826

Richland (city)
Richland, WA 99352, (509) 943-7399

Sacred Heart Medical Center
Spokane, WA 99220-2550, (509) 455-3192

SAFECO Corp.
Seattle, WA 98185, (206) 545-3233

Seafirst Corp.
Seattle, WA 98124, (206) 358-7523

SeaTac (city)
SeaTac, WA 98188, (206) 878-6190

Seattle (city)
Seattle, WA 98104, (206) 684-7999

Seattle (city) Public Safety Civil Service Commission
Seattle, WA 98104, (206) 386-1303

Seattle Center
Seattle, WA 98109, (206) 684-7218

Seattle Community College District
Seattle, WA 98122, (206) 587-5454

Seattle Marriott SeaTac Airport
Seattle, WA 98188, (206) 241-2421

Seattle Pacific University
Seattle, WA 98119, (206) 281-2065

Seattle School District
Seattle, WA 98109, (206) 298-7382

Seattle Sheraton Hotel & Towers
Seattle, WA 98101, (206) 287-5505

Seattle University
Seattle, WA 98122, (206) 296-6363

Snohomish County
Everett, WA 98201-4046, (206) 388-3686, (206) 738-4550

South Kitsap School District
Port Orchard, WA 98366, (206) 876-7389

Spokane (city)
Spokane, WA 99201, (509) 625-6161

Spokane School District
Spokane, WA 99201, (509) 353-5459, (509) 353-7639

Stouffer Madison Hotel
Seattle, WA 98104, (206) 583-0300

Tacoma (city)
Tacoma, WA 98402, (206) 591-5795

Tacoma School District
Tacoma, WA 98405, (206) 596-1265

Thurston County
Olympia, WA 98502, (206) 786-5499

U.S. Bank of Washington NA
Seattle, WA 98111, (206) 344-5656

United States Department of the Army
Corps of Engineers
Seattle, WA 98134, (206) 764-3739

United States Department of Commerce
National Oceanic and Atmospheric Administration
Seattle, WA 98115, (206) 526-6294, (206) 526-6051

United States Department of Energy
Bonneville Power Administration
Seattle, WA 98109, (206) 553-7564

Richland Field Office
Richland, WA 99352, (800) 695-4363

United States Department of Health and Human Services
Region 10
Seattle, WA 98121, (206) 615-2036

United States Department of the Interior
National Park Service
Seattle, WA 98104, (206) 220-4053
Port Angeles, WA 98362, (206) 452-0308

United States Department of the Treasury
Internal Revenue Service
Seattle, WA 98104, (206) 220-5757

United States Department of Transportation
Federal Aviation Administration
Renton, WA 98055, (206) 227-2014

University of Washington
Medical Center
Seattle, WA 98195, (800) 685-4899

Vancouver (city)
Vancouver, WA 98668-1995, (206) 696-8128

Vancouver School District
Vancouver, WA 98661, (206) 696-7023

Washington (state)
Olympia, WA 98501, (206) 586-0545, (206) 464-7378, (509) 456-2889

Washington (state) Department of Employment Security
Job Service
Wenatchee, WA 98801, (509) 662-1811
Walla Walla, WA 99362, (509) 527-4346

Washington Mutual Savings Bank
Seattle, WA 98101, (206) 461-8787

Washington State University
Pullman, WA 99164-1036, (509) 335-7637

Western Washington University
Bellingham, WA 98225, (206) 650-3776

Westin Hotel Seattle
Seattle, WA 98101, (206) 727-5766

Whatcom County
Bellingham, WA 98225, (206) 738-4550

Yakima (city)
Yakima, WA 98901, (509) 575-6089

Yakima School District
Yakima, WA 98902, (509) 575-2988

West Virginia

Kanawha County Board of Education
Charleston, WV 25311, (304) 348-6193

Marshall University
Huntington, WV 25755-2020, (304) 696-3644

Putnam County Board of Education
Winfield, WV 25213, (304) 586-0555

Weirton Steel Corp.
Weirton, WV 26062, (304) 797-4668

West Virginia University
Morgantown, WV 26506-6009, (304) 293-7234

Wisconsin

American Family Mutual Insurance Co.
Madison, WI 53783, (608) 242-4100

Bank One Milwaukee NA
Milwaukee, WI 53202, (414) 765-2677

Cuna Mutual Insurance Group
Madison, WI 53705, (800) 562-2862

Dane County
Madison, WI 53710, (608) 266-4123

Firstar Corp.
Milwaukee, WI 53202, (414) 765-5627

Harnischfeger Corp.
Brookfield, WI 53201, (414) 671-7528

M and I Data Services Inc.
Milwaukee, WI 53223-2422, (414) 357-5627

Madison (city)
Madison, WI 53710, (608) 266-6500

Marquette University
Milwaukee, WI 53233, (414) 288-7000

Marshall and Ilsley Corp.
Milwaukee, WI 53202, (414) 765-8300

Milwaukee (city)
Milwaukee, WI 53202, (414) 286-5555

Milwaukee County
Milwaukee, WI 53233, (414) 278-5321

Saint Luke's Medical Center
Milwaukee, WI 53201, (414) 649-6378

Unicare Health Facilities Inc.
Milwaukee, WI 53203, (414) 347-4343, (414) 347-4636

University of Wisconsin, Milwaukee
Milwaukee, WI 53201, (414) 229-6629

University of Wisconsin, Stevens Point
Milwaukee, WI 54481, (715) 346-2606

Waukesha County
Waukesha, WI 53188, (414) 548-7059

Wyoming

University of Wyoming
Laramie, WY 82071, (307) 766-5602

Joblines by Industry

Administration of Economic Programs
Administration of Environmental Quality & Housing Programs
Administration of Human Resource Programs
Amusement & Recreation Services
Apparel & Accessory Stores
Automotive Repair, Services & Parking
Building Materials, Hardware, Garden Supply, & Mobile Home Dealers
Business Services
Chemicals & Allied Products
Communications
Depository Institutions
Eating & Drinking Places
Educational Services
Electric, Gas & Sanitary Services
Electronic & Other Electrical Equipment & Components Except Computer Equipment
Engineering, Accounting, Research, Management & Related Services
Executive, Legislative, & General Government, Except Finance
Fabricated Metal Products, Except Machinery & Transportation Equipment
Food & Kindred Products
Food Stores
General Merchandise Stores
Health Services
Heavy Construction Other than Building Construction—Contractors
Holding & Other Investment Offices
Home Furniture, Furnishings & Equipment Stores
Hotels, Rooming Houses, Camps & Other Lodging Places
Industrial & Commercial Machinery & Computer Equipment
Insurance Agents, Brokers & Service

Insurance Carriers
Justice, Public Order & Safety
Leather & Leather Products
Lumber & Wood Products, Except Furniture
Measuring, Analyzing & Controlling Instruments; Photographic, Medical & Optical Goods; Watches & Clocks
Membership Organizations
Metal Mining
Mining & Quarrying of Nonmetallic Minerals, Except Fuels
Miscellaneous Manufacturing Industries
Miscellaneous Retail
Motion Pictures
Motor Freight Transportation & Warehousing
Museums, Art Galleries & Botanical & Zoological Gardens
National Security & International Affairs
Nondepository Credit Institutions
Oil & Gas Extraction
Paper & Allied Products
Petroleum Refining & Related Industries
Primary Metal Industrials
Printing, Publishing & Allied Industries
Public Finance, Taxation & Monetary Policy
Railroad Transportation
Real Estate
Rubber & Miscellaneous Plastic Products
Services, Not Elsewhere Classified
Social Services
Stone, Clay, Glass, & Concrete Products
Transportation by Air
Transportation Equipment
Transportation Services
Water Transportation
Wholesale Trade—Durable Goods
Wholesale Trade—Nondurable Goods

Administration of Economic Programs

California (state) Department of Transporation
Los Angeles, CA 90012, (213) 897-3653
Oakland, CA 94612, (510) 286-6354
Redding, CA 96001, (916) 225-3000

California (state) Energy Commission
Sacramento, CA 95814, (916) 654-4316

California (state) Food and Agriculture Department
Sacramento, CA 95814, (916) 654-0441

California (state) Motor Vehicles Department
Sacramento, CA 94232-3150, (916) 657-7713

Colorado (state) Department of Transportation
Denver, CO 80222, (303) 757-9623

Commodity Futures Trading Commission
Washington, DC 20581, (202) 254-3346

Export-Import Bank
Washington, DC 20571, (202) 377-6396

Federal Communications Commission
Washington, DC 20554, (202) 632-0101

Federal Trade Commission
Washington, DC 20580, (202) 326-2020

Florida (state) Department of Agriculture and Consumer Services
Tallahassee, FL 32399-0800, (904) 487-2474

Florida (state) Department of Business and Professional Regulation
Tallahassee, FL 32399-0750, (904) 488-4874

Florida (state) Department of Commerce
Tallahassee, FL 32399-2000, (904) 488-0869

Florida (state) Department of Highway Safety and Motor Vehicles
Tallahassee, FL 32399-0525, (904) 487-3669

Florida (state) Department of Insurance
Tallahassee, FL 32399-0300, (904) 487-2644

Florida (state) Department of Transportation
Tallahassee, FL 32399-0450, (904) 922-9867
Miami, FL 33172, (305) 470-5128

Jacksonville (city) Port Authority
Jacksonville, FL 32206, (904) 630-3095

King County Metropolitan Services
Seattle, WA 98104, (206) 684-1313

Los Angeles County Metropolitan Transportation Authority
Los Angeles, CA 90017, (213) 972-6217

National Aeronautics and Space Administration
Ames Research Center
Moffett Field, CA 94035-1000, (415) 604-8000

Goddard Space Flight Center
Greenbelt, MD 20771, (301) 286-5326

Overseas Private Investment Corp.
Washington, DC 20527, (202) 336-8682

Port of Seattle
Seattle, WA 98121, (206) 728-3290

Public Utilities Commission of Ohio
Columbus, OH 43215, (614) 644-5656

Texas (state) Department of Insurance
Austin, TX 78701, (512) 463-6170

Texas (state) Department of Transportation
Austin, TX 78704, (512) 416-3000

Tri-County Metropolitan Transportation District of Oregon
Portland, OR 97202, (503) 238-4840

United States Department of Agriculture
Agricultural Research Service
Beltsville, MD 20705, (301) 344-2288

Farmers Home Administration
Saint Louis, MO 63103, (314) 539-2830

United States Department of Commerce
Washington, DC 20230, (202) 482-5138

Bureau of the Census
Washington, DC 20230, (301) 763-6064

Central Administrative Support Center
Kansas City, MO 64106, (816) 426-7463

National Institute of Standards and Technology
Gaithersburg, MD 20899, (301) 926-4851

Patent and Trademark Office
Washington, DC 20230, (703) 305-4221

United States Department of Energy
Washington, DC 20585, (202) 586-4333
Richland, WA 99352, (800) 695-4363

United States Department of the Treasury
Bureau of Alcohol, Tobacco and Firearms
Washington, DC 20226, (202) 927-8423

United States Department of Transportation
Washington, DC 20590, (202) 366-9397

Federal Aviation Administration
Washington, DC 20591, (202) 267-3229
Renton, WA 98055, (206) 227-2014

Administration of Environmental Quality & Housing Programs

Arkansas (state) Game and Fish Commission
Little Rock, AR 72205, (501) 377-6600

California (state) Conservation Department
Sacramento, CA 95814, (916) 327-2672

California (state) Parks and Recreation Department
Sacramento, CA 95814, (916) 653-9903

Colorado (state) Department of Natural Resources
Division of Wildlife
Denver, CO 80216, (303) 291-7527

Environmental Protection Agency
Atlanta, GA 30308, (800) 833-8130
Chicago, IL 60604, (312) 353-2026
Dallas, TX 75202, (214) 655-6560
Denver, CO 80202, (303) 293-1564
Kansas City, KS 66101, (913) 551-7068
Research Triangle Park, NC 27711, (919) 541-3014
San Francisco, CA 94105, (415) 744-1111
Washington, DC 20460, (202) 260-5055

Florida (state) Department of Environmental Protection
Tallahassee, FL 32399-3000, (904) 487-0436

Florida (state) Game and Fresh Water Fish Commission
Tallahassee, FL 32399-1600, (904) 488-5805

Los Angeles County Department of Public Works
Alhambra, CA 91803, (818) 458-3926

Metropolitan Park District of Tacoma
Tacoma, WA 98405, (206) 305-1009

Metropolitan Service District
Portland, OR 97232, (503) 797-1777

Ohio (state) Environmental Protection Agency
Columbus, OH 43215, (614) 644-2102

Oregon (state) Department of Environmental Quality
Portland, OR 97204, (503) 229-5785

Texas (state) Natural Resource Conservation Commission
Austin, TX 78711-3087, (512) 239-0100

United States Department of Agriculture
Forest Service
Grants Pass, OR 97526, (503) 471-6715
Helena, MT 59601, (406) 449-5419
Phoenix, AZ 85010, (602) 225-5382
Washington, DC 20090-6090, (703) 235-5627

United States Department of Commerce
National Oceanic and Atmospheric Administration
Boulder, CO 80303, (303) 497-6332
Norfolk, VA 23510-2314, (804) 441-3720
Seattle, WA 98115, (206) 526-6051, (206) 526-6294

United States Department of Housing and Urban Development
Denver, CO 80202, (303) 672-5263
Washington, DC 20410, (202) 708-3203

United States Department of the Interior
Washington, DC 20240, (800) 336-4562

Bureau of Indian Affairs
Washington, DC 20240, (202) 208-2682

Bureau of Reclamation
Boise, ID 83724, (208) 378-5144
Sacramento, CA 95825, (916) 978-4897

Geological Survey
Atlanta, GA 30303, (404) 448-5320
Denver, CO 80225, (303) 236-5846
Menlo Park, CA 94025, (415) 329-4122
Reston, VA 22092, (703) 648-7676
Rolla, MO 65401, (314) 341-0909

Minerals Management Service
Washington, DC 20240, (703) 787-1402

National Park Service
Atlanta, GA 30303, (404) 331-5189
Boston, MA 02109, (617) 223-5200
Lakewood, CO 80228, (303) 969-2010
Omaha, NE 68102, (402) 221-3434
Port Angeles, WA 98362, (206) 452-0308
San Francisco, CA 94123, (415) 556-1839, (415) 744-3884
Seattle, WA 98104, (206) 220-4053
Washington, DC 20240, (202) 619-7111

Office of the Secretary
Washington, DC 20240, (800) 822-5463

United States Fish and Wildlife Service
Washington, DC 20240, (703) 358-2120

Virginia Beach (city)
Virginia Beach, VA 23456, (804) 427-3580

Administration of Human Resource Programs

California (state) Department of Health Services
Sacramento, CA 95814, (916) 657-0141, (916) 657-2976

California (state) Education Department
Sacramento, CA 95814, (916) 657-3821

California (state) Social Services Department
Sacramento, CA 95814, (916) 657-1696

Colorado (state) Department of Education
State Library
Denver, CO 80203-1704, (303) 866-6741

El Paso County Social Services Department
Colorado Springs, CO 80905, (719) 444-5663

Florida (state) Agency for Health Care Administration
Tallahassee, FL 32308, (904) 488-8356

Florida (state) Department of Community Affairs
Tallahassee, FL 32399-2100, (904) 488-4776

Florida (state) Department of Education
Tallahassee, FL 32399-0400, (904) 487-2367

Florida (state) Department of Health and Rehabilitative Services
Fort Lauderdale, FL 33301-1885, (305) 467-4279
Gainesville, FL 32601, (904) 955-5190
Jacksonville, FL 32211, (904) 723-2024
Largo, FL 34648, (813) 588-6628
Miami, FL 33128, (305) 377-5747
Orlando, FL 32801, (407) 423-6207
Pensacola, FL 32505-2949, (904) 444-8037
Tallahassee, FL 32399-2949, (904) 488-0831
Tallahassee, FL 32399-0700, (904) 488-2255
Tampa, FL 33614, (813) 877-8349
West Palm Beach, FL 33401, (407) 837-5014

Florida (state) Department of Labor and Employment Security
Tallahassee, FL 32399-2166, (904) 487-5627

Michigan (state) Public Health Department
Lansing, MI 48409, (517) 335-8797

San Francisco (city and county) Department of Public Health
Central Office
San Francisco, CA 94102, (415) 206-5317

San Joaquin County Department of Health Care Services
French Camp, CA 95231, (209) 468-6034

South Carolina (state) Department of Mental Health
Columbia, SC 29201, (803) 734-7674

Texas (state) Department of Protective and Regulatory Services
Austin, TX 78751, (512) 450-3600
El Paso, TX 79925, (915) 599-3635
San Antonio, TX 78223, (210) 337-3234

Texas (state) Higher Education Coordinating Board
Austin, TX 78711, (512) 483-6574

Texas (state) Rehabilitation Commission
Austin, TX 78751, (512) 483-4880

United States Department of Health and Human Services
Dallas, TX 75202, (214) 767-3124
Denver, CO 80294-3538, (303) 844-6329
San Francisco, CA 94102, (415) 556-1088
Seattle, WA 98121, (206) 615-2036
Washington, DC 20201, (202) 619-2560

Centers for Disease Control
Atlanta, GA 30333, (404) 332-4577

Food and Drug Administration
Rockville, MD 20857, (301) 443-1969

Health Resources and Services Administration
Rockville, MD 20857, (301) 443-1230

National Institutes of Health
Bethesda, MD 20892, (301) 496-2403

Office of the Assistant Secretary for Health
Rockville, MD 20857, (301) 443-1986

Substance Abuse and Mental Health Services
   Administration
Rockville, MD 20857, (301) 443-2282

United States Department of Labor
Washington, DC 20210, (202) 219-6646

Ventura County Health Care Agency
Ventura, CA 93003, (805) 652-6696

Virginia Beach (city)
Virginia Beach, VA 23456, (804) 427-3580

Amusement & Recreation Services

Disneyland International
Anaheim, CA 92802, (714) 999-4343

MCA Inc.
MCA/Universal City Studios
Universal City, CA 91608, (818) 777-5627

Seattle Center
Seattle, WA 98109, (206) 684-7218

Sea World of Florida Inc.
Orlando, FL 32821, (407) 363-2612

Vail Associates Inc.
Vail, CO 81658, (303) 479-3068

Walt Disney World Co.
Lake Buena Vista, FL 32830-1000, (407) 345-5701

Apparel & Accessory Stores

Brown Group Inc.
Saint Louis, MO 63105, (314) 854-2434

Gap Inc.
San Francisco, CA 94105, (415) 737-4495

Apparel & Other Finished Products made from Fabrics and Similar Materials

Levi Strauss Associates Inc.
San Francisco, CA 94111, (415) 544-7828

Automotive Repair, Services & Parking

Avis Inc.
Garden City, NY 11530, (516) 222-3399

Ryder System Inc.
Miami, FL 33166, (305) 593-3066

Building Materials, Hardware, Garden Supply, & Mobile Home Dealers

Hechinger Co.
Landover, MD 20785, (301) 341-0526

Home Depot Inc.
Atlanta, GA 30339, (404) 433-8211

Business Services

Alabama (state) Industrial Relations Department
Employment Service Division
Birmingham, AL 35222, (205) 254-1389

Alaska (state) Department of Labor
Employment Service
Anchorage, AK 99510, (907) 269-4725, (907) 269-4730, (907) 269-4735, (907) 269-4740, (907) 269-4750, (907) 269-4770, (907) 269-4865
Fairbanks, AK 99701, (907) 451-2875
Wasilla, AK 99654, (907) 376-8860

Arizona (state) Department of Economic Security
Job Service
Flagstaff, AZ 86001, (602) 526-1800

Arkansas (state) Department of Computer Services
Little Rock, AR 72203, (501) 682-9500

California (state) Employment Development Department
Bakersfield, CA 93304, (805) 325-5627
Eureka, CA 95501, (707) 444-2222
San Jose, CA 95116, (408) 928-1308

CCH Computax Inc.
Torrance, CA 90503, (310) 543-8100

Delaware (state) Employment and Training Department
Dover, DE 19903, (302) 739-4434
Georgetown, DE 19947, (302) 856-5625
Wilmington, DE 19805, (302) 577-2750

Hewlett-Packard Co.
Colorado Networks Division
Fort Collins, CO 80525-9544, (800) 228-1399

Idaho (state) Department of Employment
Boise, ID 83702, (208) 334-6457

Iowa (state) Workforce Center
Cedar Rapids, IA 52406, (319) 365-9474

Key Services Corp.
Albany, NY 12211, (518) 436-2533

M and I Data Services Inc.
Milwaukee, WI 53223-2422, (414) 357-5627

Nebraska (state) Job Service
Lincoln, NE 68508, (402) 471-3607

North Dakota (state) Job Service
Bismarck, ND 58502, (701) 221-5049

Oregon (state) Employment Division
Astoria, OR 97103, (503) 325-7856
Eugene, OR 97401, (503) 686-7652
Newport, OR 97365, (503) 265-5627

Vermont (state) Employment and Training Department
Jobsline
Montpelier, VT 05602, (802) 828-3939

Virginia Beach (city)
Virginia Beach, VA 23456, (804) 427-3580

Walt Disney Imagineering Inc.
Glendale, CA 91221-5020, (818) 544-5555

Washington (state) Department of Employment Security
Job Service
Walla Walla, WA 99362, (509) 527-4346
Wenatchee, WA 98801, (509) 662-1811

Chemicals & Allied Products

Abbott Laboratories
Abbott Park, IL 60064, (708) 938-6295

Alcon Surgical Inc.
Fort Worth, TX 76134-2001, (714) 753-6585

Baxter HealthCare Corp.
Hyland Division
Glendale, CA 91203, (818) 507-8394

Clorox Co.
Oakland, CA 94612, (510) 271-7625

Dow Chemical Co.
Midland, MI 48674, (517) 636-6100

Eli Lilly and Co.
Indianapolis, IN 46285, (317) 276-7472

Hercules Inc.
Wilmington, DE 19894, (302) 594-6122

Johnson and Johnson Inc.
New Brunswick, NJ 08933, (908) 524-2086

Lyondell Petrochemical Co.
Houston, TX 77010, (713) 652-4562

Merck and Co.
Rahway, NJ 07065, (908) 423-7820

Neutrogena Corp.
Los Angeles, CA 90045, (310) 216-5238

Ortho Diagnostic Systems Inc.
Raritan, NJ 08869-0606, (908) 218-8808

Ortho McNeil Pharmaceutical Corp.
Raritan, NJ 08869-0602, (908) 218-6200

Pfizer Inc.
New York, NY 10017, (212) 573-3000

Proctor and Gamble Co.
Cincinnati, OH 45202, (513) 983-2125, (513) 983-7494

Sherwin-Williams Co.
Cleveland, OH 44115, (216) 566-2120

Syntex Laboratories
Palo Alto, CA 94304-1320, (415) 852-1800

Syva Co.
San Jose, CA 95161-9013, (408) 239-2725

Upjohn Co.
Kalamazoo, MI 49001, (616) 329-5550

Communications

American Telephone and Telegraph Co.
New York, NY 10013, (800) 562-7288, (800) 348-4313

Ameritech Corp.
Chicago, IL 60606, (800) 808-5627

Bell Atlantic Corp.
Philadelphia, PA 19103, (800) 967-5422

BellSouth Corp.
Atlanta, GA 30367-6000, (404) 329-9455

Bureau of Broadcasting
Washington, DC 20547, (202) 619-0909

Capital Cities/ABC Inc.
Los Angeles, CA 90027, (310) 557-4222

Cincinnati Bell Inc.
Cincinnati, OH 45202, (513) 397-9900

GTE California Inc.
Cerritos, CA 90701-5346, (800) 482-5627
Camarillo, CA 93011-6000, (800) 521-5749
Pomona, CA 91767, (800) 852-8884

KCET-TV
Los Angeles, CA 90027, (213) 953-5236

KNBC-TV
Burbank, CA 91523, (818) 840-4397

McCaw Communication Co.
Kirkland, WA 98033, (206) 828-8484

MCI Communications Corp.
Washington, DC 20036, (800) 234-5627, (800)
  289-0128, (800) 695-2380, (800) 777-6063, (800)
  888-2413
Richardson, TX 75082, (800) 456-5243

NYNEX Corp.
New York, NY 10017, (212) 395-2800

Pacific Bell
San Francisco, CA 94105, (415) 542-0817, (800)
  255-7571

South Carolina (state) Educational Television Commission
Columbia, SC 29201, (803) 737-3320

Southern New England Telecommunications Corp.
New Haven, CT 06506, (203) 771-5200, (800) 562-7006

Southwestern Bell Corp.
Saint Louis, MO 63101, (314) 235-9800

Tele-Communications Inc.
Englewood, CO 80111, (303) 267-6650

United States Information Agency
Washington, DC 20547, (202) 619-4539

Depository Institutions

American Savings of Florida FSB
Miami, FL 33169-5003, (305) 770-2019

Anchor Savings Bank
Hewlett, NY 11557, (800) 932-2995

Bank of America Arizona
Phoenix, AZ 85011, (602) 594-2500

Bank of America Nevada
Las Vegas, NV 89193-8600, (800) 288-3162

Bank of America Oregon
Portland, OR 97204, (503) 275-1390

Bank of America Texas NA
Irving, TX 75063, (214) 444-6970

Bank of Boston Connecticut
Waterbury, CT 06702, (203) 574-7109

Bank of California NA
Los Angeles, CA 90071, (213) 243-3333
San Francisco, CA 94104, (415) 765-3535

Bank of Oklahoma NA
Tulsa, OK 74192, (918) 588-6828

Bank One Akron NA
Akron, OH 44309, (216) 972-1810

Bank One Arizona NA
Phoenix, AZ 85001, (602) 221-2441

Bank One Columbus NA
Columbus, OH 43271, (614) 248-0779

Bank One Dayton NA
Dayton, OH 45401, (513) 449-7446

Bank One Lexington NA
Lexington, KY 40507, (606) 231-2760

Bank One Milwaukee NA
Milwaukee, WI 53202, (414) 765-2677

Bank One Texas NA
Arlington, TX 76013, (817) 459-9910
Dallas, TX 75265-5415, (214) 290-3637
Fort Worth, TX 76113, (817) 884-6709

Processing Center
Bedford, TX 76021, (817) 884-6761

Barnett Bank of Pinellas County
Clearwater, FL 34662, (813) 539-9300

Barnett Banks of South Florida NA
Miami, FL 33131, (305) 374-4473

Barnett Banks of Southwest Florida
Sarasota, FL 34230, (813) 951-4753

Barnett Banks of Tampa NA
Tampa, FL 33630, (813) 225-8761

Boatmen's First National Bank of Kansas City
Kansas City, MO 64183, (816) 691-7000

CalFed Inc.
Los Angeles, CA 90036, (818) 312-6078

Chase Manhattan Bank NA
Rochester, NY 14643, (716) 258-5000

Citibank NA
New York, NY 10022, (718) 248-7072

Coast Federal Bank
Los Angeles, CA 90017, (818) 366-8730

Colorado National Bank of Denver
Denver, CO 80202, (303) 585-8600

Comdata Holdings Corp.
Brentwood, TN 37027, (615) 370-7747

Comerica Bank Texas
Dallas, TX 75201, (214) 969-6177

Commerce Bank of Kansas City NA
Kansas City, MO 64106, (816) 234-2139

Commerce Bank of Saint Louis NA
Clayton, MO 63105, (314) 746-7382

Commercial National Bank
Shreveport, LA 71152, (318) 429-1803

Continental Bank
Philadelphia, PA 19102, (215) 564-7678

CoreStates Bank NA
Philadelphia, PA 19101, (215) 973-4556

Crestar Bank
Richmond, VA 23219-4625, (804) 270-8572

Dauphin Deposit Bank and Trust Co.
Harrisburg, PA 17105, (717) 255-2121

Dominion First Union Bank of Virginia
Roanoke, VA 24019, (703) 563-7907

Downey Savings and Loan Association
Newport Beach, CA 92660, (714) 509-4310

Far West Federal Savings Bank
Portland, OR 97204, (503) 323-6467

Federal Reserve Bank of —
Atlanta, GA 30303-2706, (404) 521-8767
Miami, FL 33178, (305) 471-6480
San Francisco, CA 94120, (415) 974-3330

Federal Reserve System
Board of Governors
Washington, DC 20551, (202) 452-3038

Fifth Third Bank
Cincinnati, OH 45263, (513) 579-5627

Fifth Third Bank of Toledo NA
Toledo, OH 43604, (419) 259-7694

First Hawaiian Bank
Honolulu, HI 96847, (808) 525-5627

First Interstate Bank NA
San Diego, CA 92101, (619) 557-3069

First Interstate Bank of Arizona NA
Phoenix, AZ 85072, (602) 528-1199

First Interstate Bank of Denver NA
Denver, CO 80270, (303) 293-5777

First Interstate Bank of Nevada NA
Reno, NV 89520, (702) 334-5666

First Interstate Bank of Oregon NA
Portland, OR 97208, (503) 340-8888

First Interstate Bank of Texas NA
Houston, TX 77002, (713) 250-7356

First Interstate Bank of Utah NA
Salt Lake City, UT 84101, (801) 350-7070

First Interstate Bank of Washington NA
Seattle, WA 98111, (206) 292-3551

First National Bank of Anchorage
Anchorage, AK 99510-0720, (907) 265-3027

First National Bank of Boston
Boston, MA 02110, (617) 434-0165

First National Bank of Commerce
New Orleans, LA 70112, (504) 582-7500

First National Bank of Maryland
Baltimore, MD 21201, (410) 347-6562

First Security Bank of Idaho NA
Boise, ID 83730, (208) 393-2453

First Security Bank of Utah NA
Salt Lake City, UT 84111, (801) 246-1885

First Tennessee Bank NA
Memphis, TN 38101-8416, (901) 523-5033, (901) 523-5056, (901) 523-5090

First Union National Bank of Florida
Miami, FL 33131, (305) 467-5292
Jacksonville, FL 32202, (904) 361-6971

First Union National Bank of Georgia
Atlanta, GA 30374, (404) 827-7150

First Union National Bank of Tennessee
Nashville, TN 37219, (615) 251-9238

First Union National Bank of Virginia
McLean, VA 22102, (703) 903-7777

FirsTier Bank NA Lincoln
Lincoln, NE 68501, (402) 434-1426

FirsTier Bank NA Omaha
Omaha, NE 68102, (402) 348-6400

Fleet Bank
Syracuse, NY 13221, (315) 798-2680

Fleet Bank of Maine
Portland, ME 04104, (207) 874-5000

Fort Wayne National Bank Inc.
Fort Wayne, IN 46802-2304, (219) 461-6200

Frost National Bank
San Antonio, TX 78205, (210) 220-5627

Germantown Savings Bank
Bala-Cynwyd, PA 19004, (610) 660-8451

Golden 1 Credit Union
Sacramento, CA 95852, (916) 732-2844

Great Western Bank
Chatsworth, CA 91311, (800) 367-5545

Harris Trust and Savings Bank
Chicago, IL 60690, (312) 461-6900

Hibernia National Bank
New Orleans, LA 70161, (504) 586-5518

HomeFed Bank
San Diego, CA 92121, (800) 552-3638

Huntington Bank
Columbus, OH 43215, (614) 463-4305

INB National Bank
Indianapolis, IN 46266, (317) 266-7788

Intrust Bank NA
Wichita, KS 67201, (316) 383-1155

Key Bank of Maine
Portland, ME 04112, (207) 623-7000

Key Bank of Oregon
Portland, OR 97204, (503) 598-3573

Key Bank of Utah
Salt Lake City, UT 84144, (801) 535-1117

Key Bank of Washington
Tacoma, WA 98411-5500, (800) 677-6150

Liberty National Bank and Trust Company of Louisville
Louisville, KY 40232, (502) 566-1629

Liberty National Bank and Trust Company of Tulsa
Tulsa, OK 74193, (918) 586-5818

Mellon PSFS
Philadelphia, PA 19101-7899, (215) 553-3213

Michigan National Bank
Farmington Hills, MI 48333-9065, (810) 473-4328

Midlantic National Bank
Edison, NJ 08818, (908) 321-2562

Mission Federal Credit Union
San Diego, CA 92191, (619) 546-2010

National Bank of Alaska
Anchorage, AK 99503, (907) 265-2197

National City Bank, Columbus
Columbus, OH 43251, (614) 463-6736

National City Bank, Indiana
Indianapolis, IN 46255, (317) 267-7700

National City Bank, Kentucky
Louisville, KY 40233, (502) 581-5627, (502) 581-7678

National Processing Center
Louisville, KY 40217, (502) 364-2381

National City Bank, Northeast
Akron, OH 44308, (216) 375-8685

National City Bank, Northwest
Toledo, OH 43603, (419) 259-6710

NationsBank of Florida NA
Tampa, FL 33602, (813) 224-5921

NationsBank of Georgia NA
Atlanta, GA 30303, (404) 491-4530

NationsBank of Maryland NA
Bethesda, MD 20817, (301) 897-0547

NationsBank of Tennessee NA
Nashville, TN 37239, (615) 749-3900

NationsBank of Texas NA
Dallas, TX 75202, (214) 712-2103

NationsBank of Virginia NA
Norfolk, VA 23510, (804) 441-4451

Navy Federal Credit Union
Merrifield, VA 22119, (703) 255-8800

North Island Federal Credit Union
San Diego, CA 92186, (619) 656-6525

Norwest Bank Arizona NA
Phoenix, AZ 85012, (602) 248-1283

Norwest Bank Denver NA
Denver, CO 80274, (303) 863-5627

Norwest Bank Fort Wayne NA
Fort Wayne, IN 46801, (219) 461-6318

PNC Bank
Philadelphia, PA 19101, (800) 762-5627

Premier Bank NA
Baton Rouge, LA 70821, (504) 332-3512

Primerit Bank
Las Vegas, NV 89102, (702) 226-0466

Provident Bank of Maryland
Baltimore, MD 21244, (410) 281-7263

Republic National Bank of Miami
Miami, FL 33126, (305) 250-5051

Sanwa Bank California
Los Angeles, CA 90017, (213) 896-7214

Signet Bank/Maryland
Baltimore, MD 21202, (410) 332-5627

Society Bank NA
Dayton, OH 45402, (513) 226-6388

Society National Bank, Indiana
South Bend, IN 46601, (219) 239-4865

SouthTrust Bank of Georgia NA
Atlanta, GA 30303, (404) 951-4010

State National Bank
El Paso, TX 79958, (915) 546-4335

SunBank NA
Orlando, FL 32801, (407) 237-6878

SunBank of Tampa Bay
Tampa, FL 33602, (813) 224-2001, (813) 224-2002

SunBank/Miami NA
Miami, FL 33131, (305) 579-7001

SunBank/South Florida NA
Fort Lauderdale, FL 33301, (305) 765-7100

Texas Commerce Bank Dallas NA
Dallas, TX 75266-0197, (214) 922-2224

Texas Commerce Bank El Paso NA
El Paso, TX 79980, (915) 546-6540

Texas Commerce Bank Houston NA
Houston, TX 77002, (713) 216-4541

Trust Company Bank
Atlanta, GA 30302, (404) 588-7251

Trustmark National Bank
Jackson, MS 39201, (601) 949-2337

U.S. Bank Nevada
Reno, NV 89501, (800) 366-6698

U.S. Bank of Washington NA
Seattle, WA 98111, (206) 344-5656

Union Bank NA
San Francisco, CA 94104, (415) 705-7013
San Diego, CA 92101, (619) 230-3371

Union Planters National Bank
Cordova, TN 38018, (901) 383-6663

Wachovia Bank of Georgia
Atlanta, GA 30302, (404) 841-7050

Washington Mutual Savings Bank
Seattle, WA 98101, (206) 461-8787

West One Bank Idaho NA
Boise, ID 83733, (208) 383-5400

Westamerica Bancorporation
San Rafael, CA 94901, (415) 382-6400

Whitney National Bank
New Orleans, LA 70161, (504) 586-3482

Wilmington Trust Co.
Wilmington, DE 19890-0001, (302) 427-4555

Eating & Drinking Places

Brinker International Inc.
Dallas, TX 75240, (214) 770-9463

General Mills Inc.
Minneapolis, MN 55426, (612) 540-2334

S and A Restaurant Corp.
Dallas, TX 75251, (214) 404-5622

Sizzler International Inc.
Los Angeles, CA 90066, (310) 827-2300

Educational Services

Alamo Community College District
San Antonio, TX 78207, (210) 220-1600

American University
Washington, DC 20016-8001, (202) 885-2639

Appalachian State University
Boone, NC 28608, (704) 262-6488

Arizona State University, West
Phoenix, AZ 85069-7100, (602) 543-5627

Arizona State University
Tempe, AZ 85287, (602) 965-5627

Auburn University
Auburn University, AL 36849, (205) 844-4336

Auburn University at Montgomery
Montgomery, AL 36117-3596, (205) 244-3218

Austin Community College
Austin, TX 78714, (512) 483-7648

Bainbridge School District
Bainbridge Island, WA 98110, (206) 842-2920

Ball State University
Muncie, IN 47306, (317) 285-8565

Baltimore County Public Schools
Towson, MD 21204, (410) 887-4080

Battle Ground Public Schools
Battle Ground, WA 98604, (206) 256-5385

Baylor University
Waco, TX 76798, (817) 755-3675

Beaverton School District No. 48J
Beaverton, OR 97075, (503) 591-4600

Bethel College
Saint Paul, MN 55112-6999, (612) 635-8633

Bethel School District
Spanaway, WA 98387, (206) 536-7270

Biola University
La Mirada, CA 90639, (310) 903-4767

Black Hills State University
Spearfish, SD 57799, (605) 642-6511

Bloomsburg University of Pennsylvania
Bloomsburg, PA 17815, (717) 389-2093

Bowling Green State University
Bowling Green, OH 43403, (419) 372-8522, (419) 372-8669

Brandeis University
Waltham, MA 02254-9110, (617) 736-5627

Brevard Community College
Cocoa, FL 32922, (407) 632-1111

Brigham Young University
Provo, UT 84602, (801) 378-4357

Broward Community College
Fort Lauderdale, FL 33301, (305) 761-7503

Brown University
Providence, RI 02912, (401) 863-9675

Bucknell University
Lewisburg, PA 17837, (717) 524-1635

Butler University
Indianapolis, IN 46208, (317) 283-9984

California Institute of Technology
Pasadena, CA 91125, (818) 796-2229

California Polytechnic State University, San Luis Obispo
San Luis Obispo, CA 93407, (805) 756-1533

California State Polytechnic University, Pomona
Pomona, CA 91768-4019, (909) 869-2100

California State University, Chico
Chico, CA 95929, (916) 898-6888

California State University, Dominguez Hills
Carson, CA 90747, (310) 516-3840

California State University, Fresno
Fresno, CA 93740, (209) 278-2360

California State University, Fullerton
Fullerton, CA 92634, (714) 773-3385

California State University, Hayward
Hayward, CA 94542, (510) 881-7474

California State University, Long Beach
Long Beach, CA 90840, (310) 985-5491

California State University, Los Angeles
Los Angeles, CA 90032, (213) 343-3678

California State University, Northridge
Northridge, CA 91330, (818) 885-2087

California State University, Sacramento
Sacramento, CA 95819, (916) 278-6704

California State University, San Bernardino
San Bernardino, CA 92407, (909) 880-5139

California State University, Stanislaus
Turlock, CA 95380, (209) 667-3354

Cameron University
Lawton, OK 73505, (405) 581-2501

Carnegie Mellon University
Pittsburgh, PA 15213, (412) 268-8545

Case Western Reserve University
Cleveland, OH 44106, (216) 368-4500

Catholic University of America
Washington, DC 20064, (202) 319-5263

Central Kitsap School District
Silverdale, WA 93838, (206) 698-3470

Central Michigan University
Mount Pleasant, MI 48859, (517) 774-7195

Central Missouri State University
Warrensburg, MO 64093, (816) 543-8300

Central Piedmont Community College
Charlotte, NC 28235, (704) 342-6400

Central Washington University
Ellensburg, WA 98926, (509) 963-1562

Cerritos College
Norwalk, CA 90650, (310) 467-5042

Chaffey College
Rancho Cucamonga, CA 91701-3002, (909) 941-2750

Claremont Colleges
Claremont, CA 91711, (909) 621-9443

Claremont McKenna College
Claremont, CA 91711, (909) 621-8491

Clarion University of Pennsylvania
Clarion, PA 16214, (814) 226-2045

Clark Atlanta University
Atlanta, GA 30314, (404) 880-8368

Clemson University
Clemson, SC 29634-4024, (803) 656-2228

Cleveland State University
Cleveland, OH 44115, (216) 687-9300

Clover Park School District
Tacoma, WA 98499, (206) 589-7436

Coast Community College District
Costa Mesa, CA 92626, (714) 432-5526, (714) 432-5586

College of Charleston
Charleston, SC 29424, (803) 953-5419

College of DuPage
Glen Ellyn, IL 60137, (708) 858-2800

College of Saint Rose
Albany, NY 12203, (518) 458-5475

College of William and Mary in Virginia
Williamsburg, VA 23185, (804) 221-3167

Colorado College
Colorado Springs, CO 80903, (719) 389-6888

Columbia University
Columbia College
New York, NY 10027, (212) 854-5804

Columbus State Community College
Columbus, OH 43216, (800) 621-6407

Connecticut College
New London, CT 06320-4196, (203) 439-2069

Contra Costa Community College District
Martinez, CA 94553, (510) 229-1000

Creighton University
Omaha, NE 68178, (402) 280-2943

Dallas County Community College District
Dallas, TX 75202, (214) 746-2438

Dartmouth College
Hanover, NH 03755, (603) 646-3328

DePaul University
Chicago, IL 60604, (312) 362-6803

Drake University
Des Moines, IA 50311, (515) 271-4144

Drew University
Madison, NJ 07940, (201) 408-5555

Drexel University
Philadelphia, PA 19104, (215) 895-2562

Duke University
Durham, NC 27706, (919) 684-8895, (919) 684-8896, (919) 684-8897, (919) 684-8898, (919) 684-8899

East Stroudsburg University of Pennsylvania
East Stroudsburg, PA 18301, (717) 424-3280

Eastern Michigan University
Ypsilanti, MI 48197, (313) 487-2462

Eastern Montana College
Billings, MT 59101, (406) 657-2116

Eastern New Mexico University
Portales, NM 88130, (505) 562-2411

Eastern Washington University
Cheney, WA 99004, (509) 359-6200

Edmonds School District
Lynnwood, WA 98036, (206) 670-7021

Elk Grove Unified School District
Sacramento, CA 95624, (916) 686-7781

Elon College
Elon College, NC 27244, (910) 584-2255

Emerson College
Boston, MA 02116, (617) 578-8578

Enoch Pratt Free Library
Baltimore, MD 21201, (410) 396-5353

Eugene School District No. 4J
Eugene, OR 97402, (503) 687-3344

Everett School District
Everett, WA 98203, (206) 259-2935

Evergreen School District
Vancouver, WA 98686, (206) 254-7403

Evergreen State College
Olympia, WA 98505, (206) 866-6000

Federal Way School District
Federal Way, WA 98003, (206) 941-2058, (206) 941-2273

Ferris State University
Big Rapids, MI 49307, (616) 592-5627

Florida (state) Department of State
Division of Library and Information Services
Tallahassee, FL 32399-0250, (904) 488-5232

Florida Agricultural and Mechanical University
Tallahassee, FL 32307, (904) 561-2436

Florida Atlantic University
Boca Raton, FL 33431-0991, (407) 367-3506

Florida Institute of Technology
Melbourne, FL 32901, (407) 768-8000

Florida International University
Miami, FL 33199, (305) 348-2500

Florida State University
Tallahassee, FL 32306-1009, (904) 644-6066

Foothill-De Anza Community College District
Los Altos Hills, CA 94022-4599, (415) 949-6218

Franklin Pierce School District
Tacoma, WA 98444, (206) 535-8829

George Mason University
Fairfax, VA 22030, (703) 993-8799

Georgetown University
Washington, DC 20057, (202) 687-2900, (202) 784-2370, (202) 784-2683

Georgia Institute of Technology
Atlanta, GA 30332, (404) 894-4592

Georgia Southern University
Statesboro, GA 30460-8024, (912) 681-0629

Georgia State University
Atlanta, GA 30303, (404) 651-4270

Gonzaga University
Spokane, WA 99258-0001, (509) 484-6816

Grossmont-Cuyamaca Community College District
El Cajon, CA 92020, (619) 589-7312

Hampton University
Hampton, VA 23368, (804) 727-5954

Highline School District
Seattle, WA 98166, (206) 433-6339

Hillsborough Community College
Tampa, FL 33631, (813) 253-7185

Houston Community College System
Houston, TX 77007, (713) 866-8369, (713) 868-0711

Howard University
Washington, DC 20059, (202) 806-7711

Humboldt State University
Arcata, CA 95521, (707) 826-4500

Huntsville (city) Schools
Huntsville, AL 35807, (205) 532-4746

Illinois Institute of Technology
Chicago, IL 60616, (312) 567-5703

Indiana State University
Terre Haute, IN 477809, (812) 237-4122

Indiana University at South Bend
South Bend, IN 46634, (219) 237-4182

Indiana University Bloomington
Bloomington, IN 47401, (812) 855-9102

Indiana University-Purdue University at Fort Wayne
Fort Wayne, IN 46805-1499, (219) 481-6971

Indiana University-Purdue University at Indianapolis
Indianapolis, IN 46202, (317) 274-2255

Iowa State University
Ames, IA 50011, (515) 294-0146

Jacksonville State University
Jacksonville, AL 36265, (205) 782-5578

James Madison University
Harrisonburg, VA 22807, (703) 568-3561

Jefferson County Board of Education
Birmingham, AL 35233, (205) 325-5107

Johns Hopkins University
Baltimore, MD 21218, (410) 516-8022

Kanawha County Board of Education
Charleston, WV 25311, (304) 348-6193

Kansas State University
Manhattan, KS 66506, (913) 532-6271

Kennesaw State College
Marietta, GA 30061, (404) 423-6031

Kent School District
Kent, WA 98031, (206) 859-7508

Kent State University
Kent, OH 44242, (216) 672-2103

Kutztown University
Kutztown, PA 19530, (610) 683-4130

Lake Oswego School District No. 7J
Lake Oswego, OR 97034, (503) 635-0342

Lamar University
Beaumont, TX 77710, (409) 880-8371

Lehigh University
Bethlehem, PA 18015-3035, (610) 758-5627

Lewis and Clark College
Portland, OR 97219, (503) 768-7840

Library of Congress
Washington, DC 20540, (202) 707-4315

Linn-Benton Community College
Albany, OR 97321, (503) 926-8800

Long Beach City College
Long Beach, CA 90808, (310) 420-4050

Los Angeles Community College District
Los Angeles, CA 90017-3896, (213) 891-2099

Los Angeles County Office of Education
Downey, CA 90242, (310) 803-8408

Los Rios Community College District
Sacramento, CA 95825, (916) 568-3011

Louisiana State University and Agricultural and Mechanical College
Baton Rouge, LA 70803-2750, (504) 388-1101, (504) 388-1201

Loyola College
Baltimore, MD 21210, (410) 617-5037

Loyola Marymount University
Los Angeles, CA 90045, (310) 338-4488

Loyola University, Chicago
Chicago, IL 60611, (312) 508-3400

Loyola University
New Orleans, LA 70118, (504) 865-3400

Macalester College
Saint Paul, MN 55105, (612) 696-6400

Madison County Board of Education
Huntsville, AL 35804, (205) 532-2851

Manteca Unified School District
Lathrop, CA 95330, (209) 825-3233

Maricopa County Community College District
Tempe, AZ 85281, (602) 731-8444

Marin Community College
Kentfield, CA 94904, (415) 485-9693

Marquette University
Milwaukee, WI 53233, (414) 288-7000

Marshall University
Huntington, WV 25755-2020, (304) 696-3644

Mary Washington College
Fredericksburg, VA 22401-5358, (703) 899-4624

Marysville School District
Marysville, WA 98270, (206) 653-0807

Mead School District
Mead, WA 99021, (509) 468-3193

Mercer Island School District
Mercer Island, WA 98040, (206) 236-3302

Merrimack College
North Andover, MA 01845, (508) 837-5315

Metropolitan State College of Denver
Denver, CO 80217-3362, (303) 556-8430

Miami University
Oxford, OH 45056, (513) 529-6400

Miami-Dade Community College
Kendall and Homestead Campuses
Miami, FL 33176, (305) 237-0965, (305) 237-2925

Medical Center Campus
Miami, FL 33127, (305) 237-0985, (305) 237-2945

Mitchell Wolfson Campus
Miami, FL 33132, (305) 237-0975, (305) 237-2935

North Campus
Miami, FL 33167, (305) 237-0955, (305) 237-2915

Michigan State University
East Lansing, MI 48824-1046, (517) 355-9518

Michigan Technological University
Houghton, MI 49931, (906) 487-2895

Middlebury College
Middlebury, VT 05753, (802) 388-3711

Mississippi State University
Mississippi State, MS 39762, (601) 325-4132

Mobile County school board
Mobile, AL 36633, (205) 690-8394

Montana State University
Bozeman, MT 59717, (406) 994-3343

Montgomery College
Rockville, MD 20850, (301) 279-5373, (301) 279-5374

Morehead State University
Morehead, KY 40351, (606) 783-2101

Mount Holyoke College
South Hadley, MA 01075-1497, (413) 538-2024

Multnomah Education Service District
Portland, OR 97220, (503) 257-1510

New Mexico State University
Las Cruces, NM 88003, (505) 646-1900

Norfolk State University
Norfolk, VA 23504, (804) 683-8184

North Carolina State University
Raleigh, NC 27695-7103, (919) 515-3737

North Dakota State University
Fargo, ND 58105, (701) 237-8273

North Harris Montgomery Community College District
Houston, TX 77060, (713) 591-3534

North Orange County Community College District
Fullerton, CA 92634, (714) 870-7371

Northeastern University
Boston, MA 02115, (617) 373-5373

Northern Arizona University
Flagstaff, AZ 86011, (602) 523-5627

Northern Illinois University
DeKalb, IL 60115, (815) 753-1051

Northern Kentucky University
Highland Heights, KY 41076, (606) 572-5201

Northern Virginia Community College
Annandale, VA 22003, (703) 323-3444

Oakland University
Rochester, MI 48309, (810) 370-4500

Occidental College
Los Angeles, CA 90041, (213) 259-2615

Ohio State University, Columbus
Columbus, OH 43210, (614) 292-1212

Ohio University
Athena, OH 45701, (614) 593-4080

Oklahoma State University
Stillwater, OK 74078, (405) 744-7692

Old Dominion University
Norfolk, VA 23529-0050, (804) 683-3066, (804) 683-4011

Oregon City School District No. 62
Oregon City, OR 97045, (503) 657-2465

Oregon State University
Corvallis, OR 97331, (503) 737-0554

Pacific Lutheran University
Tacoma, WA 98447, (206) 535-8598

Palm Beach Community College
Lake Worth, FL 33461, (407) 439-8232

Palomar College
San Marcos, CA 92069-1487, (619) 744-1150

Pasadena City College
Pasadena, CA 91106, (818) 585-7257

Pembroke State University
Pembroke, NC 28372, (910) 521-6532

Pennsylvania State University
University Park, PA 16802, (814) 865-5627

Pepperdine University
Malibu, CA 90263, (310) 456-4776

Peralta Community College System
Oakland, CA 94606, (510) 466-7223

Pierce College
Tacoma, WA 98498, (206) 964-7341

Pima Community College District
Tucson, AZ 85709, (602) 748-4623

Pomona College
Claremont, CA 91711-6312, (909) 621-8477

Portland Community College
Portland, OR 97219, (503) 273-2826

Portland School District No. 1J
Portland, OR 97227, (503) 331-3102

Princeton University
Princeton, NJ 08544, (609) 258-6130

Purdue University
West Lafayette, IN 47907, (317) 494-6957, (317) 494-7417, (317) 494-7418, (317) 494-7419

Putnam County Board of Education
Winfield, WV 25213, (304) 586-0555

Radford University
Radford, VA 24142, (703) 831-5825

Rancho Santiago College
Santa Ana, CA 92706, (714) 564-6499

Renton School District
Renton, WA 98055, (206) 235-5826

Rice University
Houston, TX 77251, (713) 527-6080

Rowan College of New Jersey
Glassboro, NJ 08028, (609) 863-5329

Rutgers, the State University of New Jersey
New Brunswick, NJ 08903-2101, (908) 445-2720, (908) 445-3031, (908) 445-3045

Saddleback Community College District
Mission Viejo, CA 92626, (714) 582-4469, (714) 582-4852

Saint Louis Community College
Saint Louis, MO 63102, (314) 539-5200

Saint Louis University
Saint Louis, MO 63103, (314) 658-2265

Saint Mary's University
San Antonio, TX 78284-0400, (210) 436-3343

Salem-Keizer School District No. 24J
Salem, OR 97301, (503) 399-3404

Sam Houston State University
Huntsville, TX 77341, (409) 294-1067

San Bernardino Community College District
San Bernardino, CA 92410-3080, (909) 384-0853

San Diego Community College District
San Diego, CA 92108, (619) 584-6580

San Diego State University
San Diego, CA 92182-0771, (619) 594-5801, (619) 594-5850, (619) 594-5861

San Francisco Community College District
San Francisco, CA 94103, (415) 241-2349

San Francisco State University
San Francisco, CA 94132, (415) 338-1871

San Francisco Unified School District
San Francisco, CA 94102, (415) 241-6162

San Joaquin Delta College
Stockton, CA 95207, (209) 474-5627

San Jose Evergreen Community College District
San Jose, CA 95135-1599, (408) 223-6707

San Jose State University
San Jose, CA 95192, (408) 924-1000

San Mateo County Community College District
San Mateo, CA 94402, (415) 574-6111

Santa Clara University
Santa Clara, CA 95053, (408) 554-4030

Santa Monica Community College
Santa Monica, CA 90405-1628, (310) 450-5150

Santa Rosa Junior College
Santa Rosa, CA 95401-4395, (707) 527-4707

Scottsdale Unified School District No. 48
Phoenix, AZ 85018, (602) 952-6296

Seattle Community College District
Seattle, WA 98122, (206) 587-5454

Seattle Pacific University
Seattle, WA 98119, (206) 281-2065

Seattle School District
Seattle, WA 98109, (206) 298-7382

Seattle University
Seattle, WA 98122, (206) 296-6363

Sierra College
Rocklin, CA 95677, (916) 781-0424

Smith College
Northampton, MA 01063, (413) 585-2278

Sonoma County Office of Education
Santa Rosa, CA 95403, (707) 524-2680

Sonoma State University
Rohnert Park, CA 94928, (707) 664-2168

South County Community College District
Hayward, CA 94545, (510) 786-6966

South Kitsap School District
Port Orchard, WA 98366, (206) 876-7389

Southern Illinois University at Carbondale
Carbondale, IL 62901, (618) 536-2116

Southern Illinois University at Edwardsville
Edwardsville, IL 62026-1001, (618) 692-2420

Southern Methodist University
Dallas, TX 75275, (214) 768-1111

Southwest Texas State University
San Marcos, TX 78666, (512) 245-2619

Spelman College
Atlanta, GA 30314, (404) 223-5627

Spokane School District
Spokane, WA 99201, (509) 353-5459, (509) 353-7639

Springfield School District No. 19
Springfield, OR 97477, (503) 726-3364

Stanford University
Stanford, CA 94305, (415) 725-5627

State Center Community College District
Fresno, CA 93704, (209) 226-5129

State University of New York at Albany
Albany, NY 12222, (518) 442-3151

State University of New York at Stony Brook
Stony Brook, NY 11794, (516) 632-9222

Hospital
Stony Brook, NY 11794, (516) 444-7710

Stephen F. Austin State University
Nacogdoches, TX 75962-3051, (409) 568-3003

Stetson University
De Land, FL 32720, (904) 822-7562

Suffolk University
Boston, MA 02108, (617) 573-8055

Tacoma School District
Tacoma, WA 98405, (206) 596-1265

Tarleton State University
Stephenville, TX 76402, (817) 968-9750

Tarrant County Junior College
Fort Worth, TX 76102, (817) 335-6721

Texas (state) Library and Archives
Austin, TX 78701, (512) 463-5470

Texas A&I University
Kingsville, TX 78363, (512) 595-3004

Texas A&M University, College Station
College Station, TX 77843, (409) 845-4444

Texas Christian University
Fort Worth, TX 76129, (817) 921-7791

Texas Southern University
Houston, TX 77004, (713) 527-7011

Texas Tech University
Lubbock, TX 79409, (806) 742-2211

Texas Woman's University
Denton, TX 76204, (817) 898-3565

Trinity University
San Antonio, TX 78212, (210) 736-7510

Tulane University
New Orleans, LA 70118, (504) 865-5627

Tulsa Junior College
Tulsa, OK 74135, (918) 631-7854

United States Air Force Academy
Colorado Springs, CO 80840, (719) 472-2222

United States Naval Academy
Annapolis, MD 21402-5018, (410) 293-3821

Universities and Community Colleges of Nevada
Reno, NV 89557-0055, (702) 784-1404

University of Akron
Akron, OH 44325, (216) 972-7091

University of Alabama, Tuscaloosa
Tuscaloosa, AL 35487-0132, (205) 348-7780

University of Alabama at Birmingham
Birmingham, AL 35294, (205) 934-2611

University of Alabama in Huntsville
Huntsville, AL 35899, (205) 895-6105

University of Alaska Anchorage
Anchorage, AK 99508, (907) 786-4887

University of Arizona
Tucson, AZ 85721-0007, (602) 621-3087

University of Arkansas, Fayetteville
Fayetteville, AR 72701, (501) 575-5627

University of Arkansas at Little Rock
Little Rock, AR 72204, (501) 569-3038

University of California, Davis
Davis, CA 95616, (916) 752-1760

University of California, San Diego
San Diego, CA 92093, (619) 682-1000

University of California, Santa Barbara
Santa Barbara, CA 93106, (805) 893-3311

University of California, Santa Cruz
Santa Cruz, CA 95064, (408) 459-2011

University of Central Florida
Orlando, FL 32816, (407) 823-2778

University of Central Oklahoma
Edmond, OK 73034, (405) 341-2980

University of Colorado, Boulder
Boulder, CO 80309, (303) 492-5442

University of Connecticut
Storrs, CT 06268, (203) 486-2466

University of Dayton
Dayton, OH 45469-0001, (513) 229-3377

University of Delaware
Newark, DE 19716, (302) 831-2100

University of Denver
Denver, CO 80208, (303) 871-3460

University of Florida
Gainesville, FL 32611-5002, (904) 392-4631

University of Georgia
Athens, GA 30602, (706) 542-5720, (706) 542-5769, (706) 542-5781, (706) 542-8722

University of Houston, Downtown
Houston, TX 77002, (713) 221-8609

University of Houston
Houston, TX 77204-2161, (713) 743-5788

University of Idaho
Moscow, ID 83843, (208) 885-5702

University of Iowa
Iowa City, IA 52242, (319) 335-2684, (319) 335-2685, (319) 335-2686

University of Kansas
Lawrence, KS 66045, (913) 864-4623

University of Kentucky
Lexington, KY 40506, (606) 257-3841

University of LaVerne
LaVerne, CA 91750, (909) 593-3511

University of Louisville
Louisville, KY 40292, (502) 852-5627

University of Maryland at College Park
College Park, MD 20742, (301) 405-5677

University of Maryland Baltimore County
Baltimore, MD 21228, (410) 455-1100

University of Maryland Eastern Shore
Princess Anne, MD 21853, (410) 651-6000

University of Miami
Coral Gables, FL 33124, (305) 284-6918, (305) 547-6999

University of Michigan, Ann Arbor
Ann Arbor, MI 48109-1316, (313) 747-2375, (313) 764-7292

University of Michigan, Dearborn
Dearborn, MI 43128-1491, (313) 593-5517

University of Minnesota, Duluth
Duluth, MN 55812, (218) 726-6506

University of Minnesota, Twin Cities
Minneapolis, MN 55455, (612) 645-6060

University of Mississippi
University, MS 38677, (601) 232-7666

University of Missouri, Columbia
Columbia, MO 65211, (314) 882-8800

University of Missouri, Kansas City
Kansas City, MO 64110, (816) 235-1627

University of Missouri, Rolla
Rolla, MO 65401, (314) 341-4242

University of Missouri, Saint Louis
Saint Louis, MO 63121, (314) 553-5926

University of Montevallo
Montevallo, AL 35115-6000, (205) 665-8050

University of Nebraska, Lincoln
Lincoln, NE 68588, (402) 472-2303

University of Nebraska, Omaha
Omaha, NE 68182-0005, (402) 554-2959

University of New Hampshire
Durham, NH 03824, (603) 862-4473

University of New Mexico
Albuquerque, NM 87131, (505) 272-5627

University of North Carolina at Chapel Hill
Chapel Hill, NC 27514, (919) 990-3000

University of North Carolina at Charlotte
Charlotte, NC 28223, (704) 547-2075

University of North Carolina at Greensboro
Greensboro, NC 27412, (910) 334-5023

University of North Carolina at Wilmington
Wilmington, NC 28403, (910) 395-3791

University of North Texas
Denton, TX 76203-3797, (817) 565-4070

University of Northern Iowa
Cedar Falls, IA 50614, (319) 273-2421

University of Notre Dame
Notre Dame, IN 46556, (219) 631-4663

University of Oklahoma
Norman, OK 73019, (405) 325-2711, (405) 325-4343

University of Pennsylvania
Philadelphia, PA 19104, (215) 898-5627

University of Pittsburgh, Pittsburgh Campus
Pittsburgh, PA 15260, (412) 624-8040

University of Portland
Portland, OR 97203-5798, (503) 283-7536

University of Redlands
Redlands, CA 92373-0999, (909) 798-7482

University of Richmond
Richmond, VA 23173, (804) 287-6001

University of Saint Thomas
Saint Paul, MN 55105, (612) 962-6520

University of San Diego
San Diego, CA 92110, (619) 260-4626

University of San Francisco
San Francisco, CA 94117-1080, (415) 666-5600

University of South Carolina, Columbia
Columbia, SC 29208, (803) 777-2100

University of South Florida
Tampa, FL 33620, (813) 974-2879

University of Southern California
Los Angeles, CA 90089-0911, (213) 740-4728

University of Tampa
Tampa, FL 33606, (813) 253-6254

University of Tennessee at Chattanooga
Chattanooga, TN 37403, (615) 755-4473

University of Tennessee at Knoxville
Knoxville, TN 37996, (615) 974-6644

University of Tennessee at Martin
Martin, TN 38238, (901) 587-7848

University of Texas at Arlington
Arlington, TX 76019, (817) 273-3455

University of Texas at Austin
Austin, TX 78712-1159, (512) 471-4295

University of Texas at El Paso
El Paso, TX 79968, (915) 747-8837

University of Texas at San Antonio
San Antonio, TX 78285, (210) 691-4650

University of the Pacific
Stockton, CA 95211, (209) 946-2621

University of Toledo
Toledo, OH 43606, (419) 537-2020

University of Tulsa
Tulsa, OK 74104, (918) 631-4000

University of Utah
Salt Lake City, UT 84112, (801) 581-5627

University of Vermont
Burlington, VT 05405-3596, (802) 656-2248

University of Virginia
Charlottesville, VA 22903, (804) 924-4400

University of West Florida
Pensacola, FL 32514, (904) 474-2842

University of Wisconsin, Milwaukee
Milwaukee, WI 53201, (414) 229-6629

University of Wisconsin, Stevens Point
Milwaukee, WI 54481, (715) 346-2606

University of Wyoming
Laramie, WY 82071, (307) 766-5602

Utah State University
Logan, UT 84322-1600, (801) 797-1819

Valencia Community College
Orlando, FL 32802, (407) 299-4943

Vancouver School District
Vancouver, WA 98661, (206) 696-7023

Vanderbilt University
Nashville, TN 37212-2099, (615) 322-8383

Virginia Commonwealth University
Richmond, VA 23298, (804) 278-0266

Virginia Polytechnic Institute and State University
Blacksburg, VA 24061, (703) 231-4649, (703) 231-6160, (703) 231-6176, (703) 231-6196

Virginia State University
Petersburg, VA 23803, (804) 524-5627

Wake Forest University
Winston Salem, NC 27109, (910) 759-4448

Washington State University
Pullman, WA 99164-1036, (509) 335-7637

West Texas State University
Canyon, TX 79016, (806) 656-4636

West Valley-Mission Community College District
Saratoga, CA 95070, (408) 867-3240

West Virginia University
Morgantown, WV 26506-6009, (304) 293-7234

Western Michigan University
Kalamazoo, MI 49008, (616) 387-3669

Western Washington University
Bellingham, WA 98225, (206) 650-3776

Westmont College
Santa Barbara, CA 93108-1099, (805) 565-6100

Williams College
Williamstown, MA 01267, (413) 597-2679

Worcester Polytechnic Institute
Worcester, MA 01609, (508) 831-5860

Wright State University
Dayton, OH 45435, (513) 873-4562

Yakima School District
Yakima, WA 98902, (509) 575-2988

Yuba College
Marysville, CA 95901, (916) 634-7733

Electric, Gas & Sanitary Services

Central and South West Corp.
Dallas, TX 75266-0164, (214) 777-1877

Coastal Corp.
Houston, TX 77046, (713) 877-6978

Detroit Edison Co.
Detroit, MI 48226-1203, (313) 237-6600

Duke Power Co.
Charlotte, NC 28242-0001, (800) 726-6736

Eugene (city) Water and Electric Board
Eugene, OR 97401, (503) 484-3769

Houston Lighting and Power Co.
Houston, TX 77251, (713) 238-5854

Little Rock (city) Water Works
Little Rock, AR 72203, (501) 377-7919

Massachusetts Water Resources Authority
Boston, MA 02129, (617) 241-6400

Memphis (city) Light Gas and Water Division
Memphis, TN 38103, (901) 528-4241

Metropolitan Water District of Southern California
Los Angeles, CA 90012, (800) 540-6311

Nevada Power Co.
Las Vegas, NV 89102, (702) 367-5200

Pacific Gas and Electric Co.
San Francisco, CA 94105, (415) 973-5200

PacifiCorp
Portland, OR 97204, (503) 464-6848

Philadelphia Electric Co.
Philadelphia, PA 19101, (215) 841-4340

Public Service Company of Colorado
Denver, CO 80202, (303) 571-7563

San Antonio (city) Water System
San Antonio, TX 78205, (210) 704-7280

Southern California Edison Co.
Rosemead, CA 91770, (818) 302-9850

Southern California Gas Co.
Los Angeles, CA 90013, (213) 244-1234

Southern Co.
Atlanta, GA 30346, (404) 668-3464

United States Department of Energy
Bonneville Power Administration
Seattle, WA 98109, (206) 553-7564

Western Area Power Administration
Golden, CO 80401, (303) 275-1244

Electronic & Other Electrical Equipment & Components Except Computer Equipment

Capitol-EMI Music Inc.
Hollywood, CA 90028, (213) 871-5763

Duracell International Inc.
Bethel, CT 06801, (203) 796-4650

Hewlett-Packard Co.
San Diego, CA 92127-1801, (619) 592-8444

Intel Corp.
Santa Clara, CA 95052, (408) 765-3981

Motorola Inc.
Schaumburg, IL 60196, (708) 576-2551

Texas Instruments Inc.
Dallas, TX 75251, (214) 995-6666

Engineering, Accounting, Research, Management & Related Services

Arkansas (state) Department of Finance and Administration
Little Rock, AR 72203, (501) 682-5627

Bechtel Group Inc.
San Francisco, CA 94119, (415) 768-4448

Environmental Protection Agency
Andrew Breidenbach Center
Cincinnati, OH 45268, (513) 569-7840

Fluor Daniel Inc.
Irvine, CA 92730-0001, (714) 975-5253

Metpath Inc.
Teterboro, NJ 07608, (201) 393-6161

National Renewable Energy Laboratory
Golden, CO 80401, (303) 628-4650

Science Applications International Corp.
San Diego, CA 92121, (619) 535-7536

ServiceMaster Limited Partnership
Downer's Grove, IL 60515, (800) 999-6678

Executive, Legislative, & General Government, Except Finance

Ada County
Boise, ID 83702, (208) 364-2562

Adams County
Brighton, CO 80601, (303) 654-6075

Addison (city)
Addison, TX 75240, (214) 450-2815

Alameda (city)
Alameda, CA 94501, (510) 748-4635

Alaska (state)
Juneau, AK 99811, (907) 465-8910
Anchorage, AK 99503, (907) 563-0200

Albuquerque (city)
Albuquerque, NM 87102, (505) 768-4636

Alexandria (city)
Alexandria, VA 22314, (703) 838-4422

Allen County
Fort Wayne, IN 46802, (219) 428-7510

Amarillo (city)
Amarillo, TX 79101, (806) 378-4205

Anaheim (city)
Anaheim, CA 92805, (714) 254-5197

Anchorage (city)
Anchorage, AK 99519-6650, (907) 343-4451

Anne Arundel County
Annapolis, MD 21401, (410) 222-1170

Anoka County
Anoka, MN 55303, (612) 422-7498

Antioch (city)
Antioch, CA 94509, (510) 779-7022

Arapahoe County
Littleton, CO 80120, (303) 795-4480

Arizona (state)
Phoenix, AZ 85003, (602) 542-4966
Tucson, AZ 85701, (602) 792-2853

Arlington (city)
Arlington, TX 76010, (817) 265-7938

Arlington County
Arlington, VA 22201, (703) 358-3363

Arvada (city)
Arvada, CO 80002, (303) 431-3008

Atlanta (city)
Atlanta, GA 30303, (404) 330-6456

Auburn (city)
Auburn, WA 98001, (206) 931-3077

Aurora (city)
Aurora, CO 80012, (303) 695-7222

Austin (city)
Austin, TX 78701, (512) 499-3201, (512) 499-3202,
(512) 499-3203, (512) 499-3204

Baldwin Park (city)
Baldwin Park, CA 91706, (818) 813-5206

Baltimore (city)
Baltimore, MD 21202, (410) 576-9675

Baltimore County
Towson, MD 21204, (410) 887-5627

Baton Rouge (city)
Baton Rouge, LA 70802, (504) 389-4980

Beaumont (city)
Beaumont, TX 77704, (409) 838-5627

Beaverton (city)
Beaverton, OR 97005, (503) 526-2299

Benton County
Corvallis, OR 97330, (503) 757-6755

Berkeley (city)
Berkeley, CA 94704, (510) 644-6122

Bernalillo County
Albuquerque, NM 87102, (505) 768-4887

Bexar County
San Antonio, TX 78205, (210) 270-6333

Blue Springs (city)
Blue Springs, MO 64015, (816) 228-0290

Boise (city)
Boise, ID 83702, (208) 384-3855

Boulder (city)
Boulder, CO 80302, (303) 441-3434

Boulder City (city)
Boulder City, NV 89005, (702) 293-9430

Boulder County
Boulder, CO 80304, (303) 441-4555

Brea (city)
Brea, CA 92621, (714) 671-4420

Broomfield (city)
Broomfield, CO 80020, (303) 438-6475

Broward County
Fort Lauderdale, FL 33301, (305) 357-6450

Buena Park (city)
90621, CA 90621, (714) 562-3519

Burbank (city)
Burbank, CA 91502, (818) 953-9724

Burlingame (city)
Burlingame, CA 94010, (415) 737-1238

Burlington (city)
Burlington, VT 05401, (802) 865-7147

Burnsville (city)
Burnsville, MN 55337, (612) 895-4475

Butte County
Oroville, CA 95965, (916) 538-7653

California (state)
Sacramento, CA 95814, (213) 620-6450, (619)
237-6163, (916) 445-0538

Carlsbad (city)
Carlsbad, CA 92008, (619) 434-2940

Carson City (city)
Carson City, NV 89706, (702) 887-2240

Carver County
Chaska, MN 55318, (612) 361-1522

Cary (city)
Cary, NC 27512-1147, (919) 460-4905

Central Intelligence Agency
Washington, DC 20505, (703) 482-0677

Chandler (city)
Chandler, AZ 85224, (602) 786-2294

Charleston (city)
Charleston, SC 29403, (803) 720-3907

Charleston County
Charleston, SC 29401, (803) 724-0694

Charlotte (city and county)
Charlotte, NC 28202, (704) 336-3968

Chatham County
Savannah, GA 31401, (912) 652-7931

Chesapeake (city)
Chesapeake, VA 23328, (804) 547-6416

Chicago (city)
Chicago, IL 60602, (312) 744-1369

Chino (city)
Chino, CA 91710, (909) 591-9808

Chula Vista (city)
Chula Vista, CA 91910, (619) 691-5095

Cincinnati (city)
Cincinnati, OH 45202, (513) 352-2489

Clackamas County
Oregon City, OR 97045, (503) 655-8894

Claremont (city)
Claremont, CA 91711, (909) 399-5351

Clark County
Las Vegas, NV 89101, (702) 455-3174

Clark County
Vancouver, WA 98660, (206) 737-6018

Clayton County
Jonesboro, GA 30236, (404) 473-5800

Clermont County
Batavia, OH 45103, (513) 732-7853

Cleveland (city)
Cleveland, OH 44114, (216) 664-2420

Clovis (city)
Clovis, CA 93612, (209) 297-2329

Cobb County
Marietta, GA 30090-9679, (404) 528-2555

Columbia (city)
Columbia, SC 29201, (803) 733-8478

Columbus (city)
Columbus, OH 43215, (614) 645-7667

Columbus Consolidated Government (city and county)
Columbus, GA 31993, (706) 571-4738

Commerce (city)
Commerce, CA 90040, (213) 887-4415

Commerce City (city)
Commerce City, CO 80022, (303) 289-3618

Concord (city)
Concord, CA 94519, (510) 671-3151

Contra Costa County
Martinez, CA 94553, (510) 646-4046

Corpus Christi (city)
Corpus Christi, TX 78401, (512) 880-3333

Corvallis (city)
Corvallis, OR 97333, (503) 757-6955

Costa Mesa (city)
Costa Mesa, CA 92627-1200, (714) 754-5070

Covina (city)
Covina, CA 91723, (818) 858-7225

Culver City (city)
Culver City, CA 90232, (310) 202-5751

Cuyahoga County
Cleveland, OH 44113, (216) 443-2039

Dade County
Miami, FL 33130, (305) 375-1871

Dakota County
Hastings, MN 55033, (612) 438-4473

Dallas (city)
Dallas, TX 75201, (214) 670-3552

Dallas County
Dallas, TX 75202, (214) 653-7637

Daly City (city)
Daly City, CA 94105, (415) 991-8028

Dane County
Madison, WI 53710, (608) 266-4123

Davis (city)
Davis, CA 95616, (916) 757-5645

Davis County
Farmington, UT 84025, (801) 451-3484

Dayton (city)
Dayton, OH 45402, (513) 443-3719

De Soto (city)
De Soto, TX 75115, (214) 230-9698

Dekalb County
Decatur, GA 30030, (404) 371-2331

Denver (city and county)
Denver, CO 80202-5206, (303) 640-1234

Denver Regional Council of Governments
Denver, CO 80211, (303) 480-6714

Des Moines (city)
Des Moines, IA 50309, (515) 283-4115

Detroit (city)
Detroit, MI 48226, (313) 224-6928

Douglas County
Castle Rock, CO 80104, (303) 660-7420

Douglas County
Douglasville, GA 30134, (404) 920-7363

Douglas County
Omaha, NE 68183, (402) 444-6270

Douglas County
Roseburg, OR 97470, (503) 440-6291

Eaton County
Charlotte, MI 48813, (517) 543-2452

Edmond (city)
Edmond, OK 73083, (405) 840-8000

El Cajon (city)
El Cajon, CA 92020, (619) 441-1671

El Dorado County
Placerville, CA 95667, (916) 621-5579

El Monte (city)
El Monte, CA 91731, (818) 580-2041

El Paso (city)
El Paso, TX 79901, (915) 541-4094

El Paso County
Colorado Springs, CO 80903, (719) 520-7400

El Paso County
El Paso, TX 79901, (915) 546-2039

Encinitas (city)
Encinitas, CA 92024, (619) 633-2726

Englewood (city)
Englewood, CO 80111, (303) 762-2304

Escondido (city)
Escondido, CA 92025, (619) 432-4585

Eugene (city)
Eugene, OR 97401, (503) 687-5060

Euless (city)
Euless, TX 76039, (817) 685-1456

Eureka (city)
Eureka, CA 95501, (707) 441-4134

Everett (city)
Everett, WA 98201, (206) 259-8768

Executive Office of the President
Washington, DC 20500, (202) 395-5892

Fairbanks North Star Borough
Fairbanks, AK 99707, (907) 459-1206

Fairfax (city)
Fairfax, VA 22030, (703) 385-7861

Fairfax County
Fairfax, VA 22030, (703) 324-5627

Fairfield (city)
Fairfield, CA 94533, (707) 428-7396

Falls Church (city)
Falls Church, VA 22046, (703) 241-5163

Farmers Branch (city)
Farmers Branch, TX 75234, (214) 919-2559

Fayette County
Fayetteville, GA 30214, (404) 461 6041

Federal Way (city)
Federal Way, WA 98003, (206) 661-4089

Florida (state) Department of Management Services
Tallahassee, FL 32399-0950, (904) 487-3988

Florida (state) Department of State
Tallahassee, FL 32399-0252, (904) 488-1179

Fontana (city)
Fontana, CA 92335, (909) 350-7652

Forsyth County
Winston Salem, NC 27101, (910) 631-6333

Fort Wayne (city)
Fort Wayne, IN 46802, (219) 427-1186

Fort Worth (city)
Fort Worth, TX 76102, (817) 871-7760

Fountain Valley (city)
Fountain Valley, CA 92708, (714) 965-4409

Fremont (city)
Fremont, CA 94538, (510) 494-4669

Fresno (city)
Fresno, CA 93721, (209) 498-1573

Fresno County
Fresno, CA 93721, (209) 488-3017

Fullerton (city)
Fullerton, CA 92632, (714) 738-6378

Fulton County
Atlanta, GA 30303, (404) 730-5627

Garden Grove (city)
Garden Grove, CA 92640, (714) 741-5016

Gardena (city)
Gardena, CA 90247, (310) 217-9515

General Accounting Office
Washington, DC 20548, (202) 512-6092

General Services Administration
Atlanta, GA 30303, (404) 331-5102
Kansas City, MO 64131, (816) 926-7804
San Francisco, CA 94105, (800) 347-3378

Gilbert (city)
Gilbert, AZ 85296, (602) 497-4950

Glendale (city)
Glendale, AZ 85301, (602) 435-4402

Glendale (city)
Glendale, CA 91206, (818) 548-2127

Glendora (city)
Glendora, CA 91741, (818) 914-8206

Grand Prairie (city)
Grand Prairie, TX 75050, (214) 660-8190

Greensboro (city)
Greensboro, NC 27402-3136, (910) 373-2080

Gresham (city)
Gresham, OR 97030, (503) 669-2309

Guilford County
Greensboro, NC 27401, (910) 373-3600

Hamilton County
Cincinnati, OH 45202, (513) 763-4900

Hampton (city)
Hampton, VA 23669, (804) 727-6406

Harford County
Bel Air, MD 21014, (410) 638-4473

Hawaii (state)
Honolulu, HI 96813, (808) 587-0977

Hayward (city)
Hayward, CA 94545, (510) 293-5313

Helena (city)
Helena, MT 59623, (406) 447-8444

Henderson (city)
Henderson, NV 89015, (702) 565-2318

Hennepin County
Minneapolis, MN 55487-0040, (612) 348-4698

Hercules (city)
Hercules, CA 94547, (510) 799-8204

Herndon (city)
Herndon, VA 22070, (703) 481-3892

Hesperia (city)
Hesperia, CA 92345, (619) 261-3660

Hialeah (city)
Hialeah, FL 33010, (305) 883-8057

Hollywood (city)
Hollywood, FL 33020, (305) 921-3292

Honolulu (city and county)
Honolulu, HI 96813, (808) 523-4303

Howard County
Ellicott City, MD 21043, (410) 313-4460

Humboldt County
Eureka, CA 95501, (707) 445-7366

Huntington Beach (city)
Huntington Beach, CA 92648, (714) 374-1570

Huntington Park (city)
Huntington Park, CA 90255, (213) 584-6209

Huntsville (city)
Huntsville, AL 35804, (205) 535-4942

Idaho (state)
Boise, ID 83702, (208) 334-2568

Illinois (state)
Chicago, IL 60601, (312) 814-2390

Imperial County
El Centro, CA 92243, (619) 339-4577

Independence (city)
Independence, MO 64050, (816) 325-7394

Ingham County
Lansing, MI 48911, (517) 887-4329

Inglewood (city)
Inglewood, CA 90301, (310) 412-8888

Iowa (state)
Des Moines, IA 50319-0150, (515) 281-5820

Irvine (city)
Irvine, CA 92713, (714) 724-6096

Jackson (city)
Jackson, MS 39201, (601) 960-1003

Jackson County
Kansas City, MO 64106, (816) 881-3134

Jacksonville (city)
Jacksonville, FL 32202, (904) 630-1144

Jefferson County
Beaumont, TX 77704, (409) 839-2384

Jefferson County
Golden, CO 80401, (303) 271-8401

Jefferson County
Louisville, KY 40202, (502) 574-6182

Johnson County
Olathe, KS 66061-3441, (913) 780-2929

Kansas (state)
Topeka, KS 66612, (913) 296-2208

Kansas City (city)
Kansas City, KS 66105, (913) 573-5688

Kansas City (city)
Kansas City, MO 64106, (816) 274-1127

Kent (city)
Kent, WA 98032, (206) 859-3375

Kern County
Bakersfield, CA 93301, (805) 861-3712

King County
Seattle, WA 98104, (206) 296-5209

Kitsap County
Port Orchard, WA 98366, (206) 876-7169

Klamath County
Klamath Falls, OR 97601, (503) 883-4188

Knoxville (city)
Knoxville, TN 37902, (615) 521-2562

Lacey (city)
Lacey, WA 98503, (206) 491-3213

Laguna Hills (city)
Laguna Hills, CA 92653, (714) 707-2628

Lake Oswego (city)
Lake Oswego, OR 97034, (503) 635-0256

Lakewood (city)
Lakewood, CO 80226, (303) 987-7777

Lancaster (city)
Lancaster, CA 93534, (805) 723-6200

Lane County
Eugene, OR 97401, (503) 687-4473

Las Vegas (city)
Las Vegas, NV 89101, (702) 229-6346

Lehigh County
Allentown, PA 18101, (610) 820-3386

Leon County
Tallahassee, FL 32301, (904) 922-4944

Lexington County
Lexington, SC 29072, (803) 359-8562

Lincoln (city) and Lancaster County
Lincoln, NE 68508, (402) 441-7736

Little Rock (city)
Little Rock, AR 72201, (501) 371-4505

Littleton (city)
Littleton, CO 80120, (303) 795-3858

Livermore (city)
Livermore, CA 94550, (510) 866-3799

Lodi (city)
Lodi, CA 95240, (209) 333-6705

Long Beach (city)
Long Beach, CA 90802, (310) 570-6201

Los Gatos (city)
Los Gatos, CA 95032, (408) 354-6838

Loudoun County
Leesburg, VA 22075, (703) 777-0536

Louisville (city)
Louisville, KY 40202, (502) 574-3355

Lubbock (city)
Lubbock, TX 79457, (806) 762-2444

Macon (city)
Macon, GA 31298, (912) 751-2733

Madison (city)
Madison, WI 53710, (608) 266-6500

Madison County
Huntsville, AL 35801, (205) 532-6906

Maricopa County
Phoenix, AZ 85003, (602) 506-3329

Marietta (city)
Marietta, GA 30061, (404) 528-0593

Marin County
San Rafael, CA 94903, (415) 472-2999

Marion County
Salem, OR 97301, (503) 588-5589

Martinez (city)
Martinez, CA 94553, (510) 372-3513

Maryland (state)
Baltimore, MD 21201, (410) 333-7510

Massachusetts (state)
Boston, MA 02108, (617) 727-9244

Memphis (city)
Memphis, TN 38103, (901) 576-6548

Mendocino County
Ukiah, CA 95482, (707) 463-5424

Merced County
Merced, CA 95340, (209) 385-7516

Mercer Island (city)
Mercer Island, WA 98040, (206) 236-5326

Merit Systems Protection Board
Washington, DC 20419, (202) 254-8013

Mesa (city)
Mesa, AZ 85211-1466, (602) 644-2759

Mesquite (city)
Mesquite, TX 75149, (214) 216-6484

Miami (city)
Miami, FL 33131, (305) 579-2400

Midwest City (city)
Midwest City, OK 73110, (405) 739-1236

Milpitas (city)
Milpitas, CA 95035, (408) 262-5146

Milwaukee (city)
Milwaukee, WI 53202, (414) 286-5555

Milwaukee County
Milwaukee, WI 53233, (414) 278-5321

Minneapolis (city)
Minneapolis, MN 55415, (612) 673-2666, (612) 673-2999

Minnesota (state)
Minneapolis, MN 55416, (612) 296-2616

Modesto (city)
Modesto, CA 95354, (209) 577-5498

Monroe County
Key West, FL 33040, (305) 292-4457

Montebello (city)
Montebello, CA 90640, (213) 887-1380

Monterey (city)
Monterey, CA 93940, (408) 646-3751

Monterey County
Salinas, CA 93901, (408) 647-7726

Montgomery (city and county)
Montgomery, AL 36101-1111, (205) 241-2217

Montgomery County
Dayton, OH 45402, (513) 225-6128

Morgan Hill (city)
Morgan Hill, CA 95037, (408) 779-7276

Mountain View (city)
Mountain View, CA 94041, (415) 903-6310

Multnomah County
Portland, OR 97204, (503) 248-5035

Murray (city)
Murray, UT 84157, (801) 264-2525

Napa (city)
Napa, CA 94559, (707) 257-9542

Napa County
Napa, CA 94559, (707) 253-4808

Nashville (city) and Davidson County
Nashville, TN 37201, (615) 862-6660

National City (city)
National City, CA 91320, (619) 336-4306

Nebraska (state)
Lincoln, NE 68508, (402) 471-2200

Nevada (state)
Las Vegas, NV 89104, (702) 486-4020
Carson City, NV 89701, (702) 687-4160

Nevada County
Nevada City, CA 95959, (916) 265-1366

New Haven (city)
New Haven, CT 06510, (203) 787-8265

Newport News (city)
Newport News, VA 23607, (804) 928-9281

Norfolk (city)
Norfolk, VA 25301, (804) 627-8768

Norman (city)
Norman, OK 73069, (405) 366-5321

North Las Vegas (city)
North Las Vegas, NV 89030, (702) 642-9266

North Miami (city)
North Miami, FL 33161, (305) 895-8095

North Miami Beach (city)
North Miami Beach, FL 33162, (305) 947-7581

Northglenn (city)
Northglenn, CO 80233, (303) 450-8789

Nueces County
Corpus Christi, TX 78401, (512) 888-0563

Oakland (city)
Oakland, CA 94612, (510) 238-3111

Oceanside (city)
Oceanside, CA 92054, (619) 966-4499

Office of Personnel Management
Career America Connection
Macon, GA 31298, (912) 757-3000

Federal Job Information Center
Albuquerque, NM 87102, (505) 766-5583
Anchorage, AK 99513-7572, (907) 271-5821
Atlanta, GA 30303, (404) 331-4315
Baltimore, MD 21201, (410) 962-3822
Boston, MA 02222-1031, (617) 565-5900
Chicago, IL 60604, (312) 353-6189, (312) 353-6192
Dallas, TX 75242, (214) 767-8035
Dayton, OH 45402, (513) 225-2720
Denver, CO 80225, (303) 969-7052, (303) 969-7053
Detroit, MI 48226, (313) 226-6950
El Monte, CA 91731, (818) 575-6510
Honolulu, HI 96850, (808) 541-2784, (808) 541-2791
Kansas City, MO 64106, (816) 426-5702, (816) 426-7819
Lakewood, CO 80225, (303) 969-7055
New York, NY 10278, (212) 264-0422
Phoenix, AZ 85012, (602) 640-4800
Portland, OR 97204, (503) 326-3141
Raleigh, NC 27609-6296, (919) 790-2822
Sacramento, CA 95814, (916) 551-1464
Saint Louis, MO 63101, (314) 539-2285
San Antonio, TX 78217, (210) 805-2402, (210) 805-2406
San Diego, CA 92101-8821, (619) 557-6165
San Francisco, CA 94120, (415) 744-5627
San Juan, PR 00918-1710, (809) 766-5242, (809) 774-8790
Seattle, WA 98174, (206) 220-6400

Office of Personnel Management (cont.)
Syracuse, NY 13260, (315) 423-5660
Twin Cities, MN 55111, (612) 725-3430
Washington, DC 20415, (202) 606-2700
Wichita, KS 67202, (816) 426-7820

Oklahoma City (city)
Oklahoma City, OK 73102, (405) 297-2419

Olympia (city)
Olympia, WA 98501, (206) 753-8383

Omaha (city)
Omaha, NE 68183, (402) 444-5302

Ontario (city)
Ontario, CA 91764, (909) 391-2580

Orange (city)
Orange, CA 92666, (714) 744-7262

Orange County
Santa Ana, CA 92701, (714) 834-5627

Oregon (state)
Salem, OR 97301, (503) 378-8344

Oxnard (city)
Oxnard, CA 93030, (805) 385-7580

Palmdale (city)
Palmdale, CA 93550, (805) 267-5627

Palo Alto (city)
Palo Alto, CA 94301, (415) 329-2222

Paramount (city)
Paramount, CA 90723, (310) 220-2080

Pasadena (city)
Pasadena, CA 91104, (818) 405-4600

Pembroke Pines (city)
Pembroke Pines, FL 33026, (305) 437-1108

Pennington County
Rapid City, SD 57701, (605) 394-8090

Peoria (city)
Peoria, AZ 85345, (602) 412-7105

Peoria County
Peoria, IL 61602, (309) 672-6943

Phoenix (city)
Phoenix, AZ 85004, (602) 252-5627

Pico Rivera (city)
Pico Rivera, CA 90660, (310) 801-4387

Pierce County
Tacoma, WA 98405, (206) 591-7466

Pima County
Tucson, AZ 85701, (602) 740-3530

Pinellas Park (city)
Pinellas Park, FL 34665, (813) 541-0703

Pittsburgh (city)
Pittsburgh, PA 15219, (412) 255-2388

Placer County
Auburn, CA 95603, (916) 889-4070

Pleasant Hill (city)
Pleasant Hill, CA 94523, (510) 671-5255

Pleasanton (city)
Pleasanton, CA 94566, (510) 484-8356

Pomona (city)
Pomona, CA 91766, (909) 620-2290

Portland (city)
Portland, OR 97204, (503) 823-4573

Portsmouth (city)
Portsmouth, VA 23704, (804) 398-0682

Poway (city)
Poway, CA 92064, (619) 679-4300

Prescott (city)
Prescott, AZ 86302, (602) 776-6280

Raleigh (city)
Raleigh, NC 27602, (919) 890-3305

Ramsey County
Saint Paul, MN 55102, (612) 266-2666

Rapid City (city)
Rapid City, SD 57701, (605) 394-5329

Redding (city)
Redding, CA 96001, (916) 225-4069

Redlands (city)
Redlands, CA 92373, (909) 798-7645

Redondo Beach (city)
Redondo Beach, CA 90277, (310) 318-0660

Redwood City (city)
Redwood City, CA 94063, (415) 364-4425

Reno (city)
Reno, NV 89505, (702) 334-2287

Renton (city)
Renton, WA 98055, (206) 235-2514

Rialto (city)
Rialto, CA 92376, (909) 820-2640

Richardson (city)
Richardson, TX 75080, (214) 238-4151

Richland (city)
Richland, WA 99352, (509) 943-7399

Richland County
Columbia, SC 29202, (803) 748-4832

Richmond (city)
Richmond, CA 94804, (510) 620-6610

Riverside (city)
Riverside, CA 92509, (909) 782-5492

Riverside County
Indio, CA 92201, (619) 863-8970
Riverside, CA 92501, (909) 275-3500

Rockdale County
Conyers, GA 30207, (404) 929-4157

Roseville (city)
Roseville, CA 95678, (916) 782-8107

Sacramento (city)
Sacramento, CA 95814, (916) 443-9990

Sacramento County
Sacramento, CA 95814, (916) 440-6771

Saint Louis County
Saint Louis, MO 63105, (314) 889-3665

Saint Paul (city)
Saint Paul, MN 55110, (612) 266-6502

Saint Petersburg (city)
Saint Petersburg, FL 33701, (813) 893-7033

Salem (city)
Salem, OR 97301, (503) 588-6162

Salinas (city)
Salinas, CA 93901, (408) 758-7246

Salt Lake City (city)
Salt Lake City, UT 84111, (801) 535-6625

Salt Lake County
Salt Lake City, UT 84115, (801) 468-2390

San Antonio (city)
San Antonio, TX 78205, (210) 299-7280

San Bernardino (city)
San Bernardino, CA 92418, (909) 384-5376

San Bernardino County
San Bernardino, CA 92401, (909) 387-5611

San Clemente (city)
San Clemente, CA 92672, (714) 361-8294

San Diego (city)
San Diego, CA 92101, (619) 450-6210

San Diego County
San Diego, CA 92101, (619) 531-5764

San Francisco (city and county)
San Francisco, CA 94103, (415) 557-4888

San Joaquin County
Stockton, CA 95202, (209) 468-3377

San Jose (city)
San Jose, CA 95110, (408) 277-5627

San Leandro (city)
San Leandro, CA 94577, (510) 577-3397

San Luis Obispo (city)
San Luis Obispo, CA 93403-8100, (805) 781-7153

San Luis Obispo County
San Luis Obispo, CA 93408, (805) 781-5958

San Mateo (city)
San Mateo, CA 94403, (415) 377-4797

San Mateo County
Redwood City, CA 94063, (415) 368-7214

San Ramon (city)
San Ramon, CA 94583, (510) 275-2338

Sandy (city)
Sandy, UT 84070, (801) 561-7009

Santa Ana (city)
Santa Ana, CA 92701, (714) 953-9675

Santa Barbara County
Santa Barbara, CA 93101, (805) 568-2820

Santa Clara (city)
Santa Clara, CA 95050, (408) 984-3150

Santa Clara County
San Jose, CA 95110, (408) 299-2856

Santa Clarita (city)
Santa Clarita, CA 91355, (805) 255-4392

Santa Cruz (city)
Santa Cruz, CA 95060, (408) 429-3040

Santa Cruz County
Santa Cruz, CA 95060, (408) 454-2151

Santa Monica (city)
Santa Monica, CA 90401, (310) 458-8697

Santa Rosa (city)
Santa Rosa, CA 95404, (707) 543-3076

Sante Fe (city)
Santa Fe, NM 87501, (505) 984-6742

Santee (city)
Santee, CA 92071, (619) 258-4123

Savannah (city)
Savannah, GA 31401, (912) 651-6488

Scott County
Shakopee, MN 55379, (612) 496-8598

Scottsdale (city)
Scottsdale, AZ 85251, (602) 994-2395

SeaTac (city)
SeaTac, WA 98188, (206) 878-6190

Seattle (city)
Seattle, WA 98104, (206) 684-7999

Sedgwick County
Wichita, KS 67203, (316) 383-7633

Shasta County
Redding, CA 96001, (916) 225-5078

Shawnee County
Topeka, KS 66603, (913) 233-8200

Shelby County
Memphis, TN 38103, (901) 576-4434

Shreveport (city)
Shreveport, LA 71130, (318) 226-3564

Signal Hill (city)
Signal Hill, CA 90806, (310) 989-7385

Snohomish County
Everett, WA 98201-4046, (206) 388-3686

Solano County
Fairfield, CA 94533, (707) 421-6174

Sonoma County
Santa Rosa, CA 95403, (707) 527-2803

South Carolina (state)
Columbia, SC 29205, (803) 734-9333, (803) 734-9334

South Dakota (state)
Pierre, SD 57501-5070, (605) 773-3326

South San Francisco (city)
South San Francisco, CA 94080, (415) 877-3976

Sparks (city)
Sparks, NV 89431, (702) 353-2444

Spokane (city)
Spokane, WA 99201, (509) 625-6161

Springfield (city)
Springfield, IL 62701, (217) 789-2440

Springfield (city)
Springfield, OR 97477, (503) 726-3648

Stanislaus County
Modesto, CA 95354-2379, (209) 525-4339

Stockton (city)
Stockton, CA 95202, (209) 937-8523

Suffolk (city)
Suffolk, VA 23434, (804) 925-6435

Sutter County
Yuba City, CA 95993, (916) 671-1687

Tacoma (city)
Tacoma, WA 98402, (206) 591-5795

Tallahassee (city)
Tallahassee, FL 32301, (904) 891-8219

Tempe (city)
Tempe, AZ 85281, (602) 350-8217

Texas (state)
Austin, TX 78701, (512) 463-3433

Thornton (city)
Thornton, CO 80229, (303) 538-7629

Thurston County
Olympia, WA 98502, (206) 786-5499

Tigard (city)
Tigard, OR 97223, (503) 624-9471

Torrance (city)
Torrance, CA 90503, (310) 618-2969

Travis County
Austin, TX 78767, (512) 473-9675

Tucson (city)
Tucson, AZ 85701, (602) 791-5068

Tulare County
Visalia, CA 93291, (209) 733-6704

Tulsa (city)
Tulsa, OK 74103, (918) 596-7444

Tuolumne County
Sonora, CA 95370, (209) 533-5631

United States Senate
Washington, DC 20510, (202) 228-5627

University Park (city)
University Park, TX 75205, (214) 653-3175

Utah (state)
Salt Lake City, UT 84114, (801) 538-3118

Vacaville (city)
Vacaville, CA 95688, (707) 449-5113

Vallejo (city)
Vallejo, CA 94590, (707) 648-4364

Vancouver (city)
Vancouver, WA 98668-1995, (206) 696-8128

Ventura (city)
Ventura, CA 93001, (805) 658-4777

Ventura County
Ventura, CA 93003, (805) 654-2847

Vermont (state)
Montpelier, VT 05602, (802) 828-3484

Victorville (city)
Victorville, CA 92392, (619) 245-7499

Virginia Beach (city)
Virginia Beach, VA 23456, (804) 427-3580, (804) 427-3580

Visalia (city)
Visalia, CA 93291, (209) 730-7007

Wake County
Raleigh, NC 27602, (919) 856-6115

Walnut Creek (city)
Walnut Creek, CA 94596, (510) 943-5817

Washington (state)
Olympia, WA 98501, (206) 464-7378, (206) 586-0545, (509) 456-2889

Washington County
Hillsboro, OR 97124, (503) 648-8607

Washington County
Stillwater, MN 55082, (612) 430-6084

Washoe County
Reno, NV 89520, (800) 473-2091

Waukesha County
Waukesha, WI 53188, (414) 548-7059

Wayne County
Detroit, MI 48226, (313) 224-5900

West Covina (city)
West Covina, CA 91790, (818) 814-8452

West Hollywood (city)
West Hollywood, CA 90069, (310) 854-7309

West Jordan (city)
West Jordan, UT 84088, (801) 569-5045

Westminster (city)
Westminster, CO 80030, (303) 650-0115

Whatcom County
Bellingham, WA 98225, (206) 738-4550

Wheat Ridge (city)
Wheat Ridge, CO 81008, (303) 234-5927

Whittier (city)
Whittier, CA 90602, (310) 945-8226

Wichita (city)
Wichita, KS 67202, (316) 268-4537

Wichita County
Wichita Falls, TX 76301, (817) 766-8129

Winston Salem (city)
Winston Salem, NC 27101, (910) 631-6496

Woodland (city)
Woodland, CA 95695, (916) 661-5810

Yakima (city)
Yakima, WA 98901, (509) 575-6089

Yavapai County
Prescott, AZ 86301, (602) 771-3171

Yolo County
Woodland, CA 95695, (916) 666-8159

Yuba City (city)
Yuba City, CA 95993, (916) 741-4766

Fabricated Metal Products, Except Machinery & Transportation Equipment

Gillette Co.
Boston, MA 02199-8001, (617) 421-7567

United States Department of the Army
Rock Island Arsenal
Rock Island, IL 61299-5000, (309) 782-2214

Food & Kindred Products

Adolph Coors Co.
Golden, CO 80401, (303) 277-2450

Anheuser-Busch Companies Inc.
Saint Louis, MO 63118, (314) 577-2392

Coca Cola Bottling Co.
Los Angeles, CA 90021-2210, (213) 746-5555

ConAgra Inc.
Omaha, NE 68102-1826, (402) 595-4499

Frito-Lay Inc.
Rancho Cucamonga, CA 91730, (909) 948-3622

General Mills Inc.
Minneapolis, MN 55426, (612) 540-2334

International MultiFoods Corp.
Minneapolis, MN 55402, (612) 340-3923

JR Simplot Co.
Boise, ID 83707, (208) 384-8002, (208) 389-7510

Land O'Lakes Inc.
Minneapolis, MN 55440, (612) 481-2250

McCormick and Co.
Sparks, MD 21152-6000, (410) 527-6969

Quaker Oats Co.
Chicago, IL 60610, (312) 222-7744

Ralston Purina Co.
Saint Louis, MO 63134, (314) 982-2962

Food Stores

Albertson's Inc.
Boise, ID 83726, (208) 385-6422

American Stores Co.
Salt Lake City, UT 84102, (800) 284-5560

Food Lion Inc.
Salisbury, NC 28145-1330, (704) 633-8250

Safeway Inc.
Oakland, CA 94660, (800) 255-0812

Schnuck Markets Inc.
Saint Louis, MO 63146, (314) 344-9292

Southland Corp.
Dallas, TX 75204, (214) 841-6758

Stater Brothers
Colton, CA 92324, (909) 783-5031

Vons Companies Inc.
Los Angeles, CA 91007, (800) 283-8667

General Merchandise Stores

Dayton Hudson Corp.
Minneapolis, MN 55402, (612) 375-2200

JC Penney Co.
Dallas, TX 75301, (214) 431-2300

Fred Meyer Inc.
Portland, OR 97202-2918, (800) 401-5627

Service Merchandise Company Inc.
Brentwood, TN 37027, (615) 660-3199

Health Services

Alliant Health System
Louisville, KY 40201, (800) 789-5627

American Medical International Inc.
Dallas, TX 75225, (214) 360-6373

American Medical Laboratories Inc.
Chantilly, VA 22021, (703) 802-7282

American Red Cross
Los Angeles Chapter
Los Angeles, CA 90057, (213) 739-4596

AMI Brookwood Medical Center
Birmingham, AL 35209, (205) 877-1910

Baptist Hospital of Miami
Miami, FL 33176, (305) 598-5999

Baptist Hospitals & Health Systems Inc.
Phoenix, AZ 85021, (602) 246-5627

Charter Medical Corp.
Macon, GA 31298, (800) 633-2415

Children's Hospital of Orange County
Orange, CA 92668, (714) 532-8500

Daniel Freeman Memorial Hospital
Inglewood, CA 90301, (310) 419-8373, (310) 419-8377

Deaconess Hospital of Cleveland
Cleveland, OH 44109, (216) 459-6560

Doctors Hospital
Houston, TX 77076, (713) 696-4488

Florida Hospital Medical Center
Orlando, FL 32803, (407) 331-8000

Grandview Hospital and Medical Center
Dayton, OH 45405, (513) 226-2675

Hamot Medical Center
Erie, PA 16550, (814) 877-5627

Hospital of the Good Samaritan
Los Angeles, CA 90017, (213) 977-2300

Houston Northwest Medical Center
Houston, TX 77090, (713) 440-6321

Huntington Memorial Hospital
Pasadena, CA 91109, (818) 397-8504

Inova Health Systems Inc.
Springfield, VA 22151, (800) 854-6682

Intermountain Health Care Inc.
Salt Lake City, UT 84111, (801) 533-3654

Jackson-Madison County General Hospital
Jackson, TN 38301, (901) 425-6759

Kaiser Foundation Hospitals
Los Angeles, CA 90027, (213) 667-6966, (213) 857-2615
Harbor City, CA 90710, (310) 517-3620

Landmark Medical Center
Woonsocket and Fogarty Units
Woonsocket, RI 02895, (401) 769-4100

Long Beach Memorial Medical Center
Long Beach, CA 90801, (310) 933-2482

Los Angeles County-University of Southern California Medical Center
Los Angeles, CA 90033, (213) 725-5083

Manor Care Inc.
Silver Spring, MD 20901, (800) 348-2041

Medical Center of Independence
Independence, MO 64057, (816) 373-7373

Memorial Medical Center of Jacksonville
Jacksonville, FL 32216, (904) 399-6702

Mercy Hospital Medical Center
Des Moines, IA 50314, (515) 247-3105

Methodist Hospital of Southern California
Arcadia, CA 91107, (818) 574-3760

Metpath of Michigan
Auburn Hills, MI 48326, (810) 373-9120

Milford Memorial Hospital
Milford, DE 19963, (302) 424-5519

Munson Medical Center
Traverse City, MI 49684, (616) 935-7390

National Medical Enterprises Inc.
Santa Monica, CA 90404, (310) 998-8500

Nichols Institute
San Juan Capistrano, CA 92690-6130, (714) 728-4526

North Colorado Medical Center
Greeley, CO 80631, (303) 350-6397, (303) 350-6565

Orange Park Medical Center
Orange Park, FL 32073, (904) 276-8562

Parkway Regional Medical Center
North Miami Beach, FL 33169, (305) 651-1100

Pleasant Valley Hospital
Camarillo, CA 93010, (805) 389-5198

Regional Medical Center
Memphis, TN 38103, (901) 575-8432

Riverside Medical Center
Kankakee, IL 60901, (815) 937-7969

Roche Biomedical Laboratories Inc.
Burlington, NC 27216, (910) 229-1127

Sacred Heart Medical Center
Spokane, WA 99220-2550, (509) 455-3192

Saint David's Hospital
Austin, TX 78765-4039, (512) 397-4000

Saint Luke's Medical Center
Milwaukee, WI 53201, (414) 649-6378

Saint Mary Medical Center
Long Beach, CA 90801, (310) 491-9014, (310) 491-9844

Saint Vincent's Health Systems
Jacksonville, FL 32203-9954, (904) 387-7363

Santa Rosa Health Care Corp.
San Antonio, TX 78207, (210) 228-2343

Scottsdale Memorial Health Systems Inc.
Scottsdale, AZ 85251, (602) 941-5221

Sharp Healthcare
San Diego, CA 92123, (619) 450-6241

Sinai Hospital
Detroit, MI 48235, (313) 493-6161

Southern Ohio Medical Center
Portsmouth, OH 45662, (614) 354-7644

Stanford University Hospital
Stanford, CA 94305, (415) 723-5140

SunHealth Corp.
Sun City, AZ 85372, (602) 974-7984

Torrance Memorial Medical Center
Torrance, CA 90505, (310) 517-4790

Unicare Health Facilities Inc.
Milwaukee, WI 53203, (414) 347-4343, (414) 347-4636

United States Department of the Navy
Naval Medical Center
San Diego, CA 92134-5000, (619) 532-9325

United States Department of Veterans Affairs
Medical Center
Amarillo, TX 79106, (806) 354-7828
Bay Pines, FL 33504, (813) 398-9493

Long Beach, CA 90822, (310) 494-5971
Miami, FL 33125, (305) 324-3154
Portland, OR 97207, (503) 273-5249
Washington, DC 20422, (202) 745-8000

University of California, Irvine
Medical Center
Orange, CA 92668, (714) 856-5850

University of California, Los Angeles
Medical Center
Los Angeles, CA 90024, (310) 825-8320

University of Washington
Medical Center
Seattle, WA 98195, (800) 685-4899

White Memorial Medical Center
Los Angeles, CA 90033, (213) 343-1323

Heavy Construction Other than Building Construction—Contractors

United States Department of the Army
Corps of Engineers
Little Rock, AR 72201, (501) 324-5660
Saint Louis, MO 63103, (314) 331-8550
Seattle, WA 98134, (206) 764-3739

Holding & Other Investment Offices

Banc One Corp.
Columbus, OH 43271, (614) 248-0779

Bank of Boston Corp.
Boston, MA 02210, (617) 434-0165

Bankers Trust New York Corp.
New York, NY 10017, (212) 250-9955

Barnett Banks Inc.
Jacksonville, FL 32203-0789, (904) 464-2426

Boatmen's Bancshares Inc.
Saint Louis, MO 63101, (314) 466-4473

Chase Manhattan Corp.
New York, NY 10081, (718) 242-7537

Columbus Bank and Trust Co.
Columbus, GA 31902, (706) 649-4758

Comerica Inc.
Detroit, MI 48226, (313) 222-6266

Corporation for Public Broadcasting
Washington, DC 20036, (202) 393-1045

Countrywide Mortgage Investments Inc.
Pasadena, CA 91109, (818) 304-5925

First American Corp.
Nashville, TN 37211-7115, (615) 781-7400

First Commercial Corp.
Little Rock, AR 72203, (501) 371-3310

Firstar Corp.
Milwaukee, WI 53202, (414) 765-5627

Marshall and Ilsley Corp.
Milwaukee, WI 53202, (414) 765-8300

Meridian Bancorp Inc.
Reading, PA 19603, (800) 321-5627

National Endowment for the Arts
Washington, DC 20506, (202) 682-5799

National Endowment for the Humanities
Washington, DC 20506, (202) 606-8281

National Science Foundation
Washington, DC 20550, (202) 357-7735

Norwest Corp.
Minneapolis, MN 55479, (612) 667-5627

Seafirst Corp.
Seattle, WA 98124, (206) 350-7523

Society Corp.
Cleveland, OH 44114, (216) 689-5153

Wachovia Corp.
Winston Salem, NC 27150, (910) 770-5520

Worthen Banking Corp.
Little Rock, AR 72201, (501) 377-1445

Home Furniture, Furnishings & Equipment Stores

Circuit City Stores Inc.
Richmond, VA 23233, (804) 527-4094

Tandy Corp.
Fort Worth, TX 76102, (817) 390-2949

Wherehouse Entertainment
Torrance, CA 90502, (310) 538-2314

Hotels, Rooming Houses, Camps & Other Lodging Places

Adam's Mark Hotels
Houston, TX 77042, (713) 735-2775
Philadelphia, PA 19131, (215) 581-5074

Aladdin Hotel & Casino
Las Vegas, NV 89109, (702) 736-0190

Atlanta Renaissance Hotel
Atlanta, GA 30337, (404) 762-7676, (404) 881-6000

Atlas Hotels Inc.
San Diego, CA 92108, (619) 299-2254

Bahia Hotel and Catamaran Resort Hotel
San Diego, CA 92109, (619) 539-7733

Bally's Park Palace Casino Hotel & Tower and Grand Casino Hotel
Atlantic City, NJ 08401, (609) 340-2211

Biltmore Hotel
Los Angeles, CA 90071, (213) 612-1585

Bonaventure Resort & Spa
Fort Lauderdale, FL 33326, (305) 389-0185

Boston Park Plaza Hotel & Towers
Boston, MA 02117, (617) 457-2452

Broadmoor
Colorado Springs, CO 80906, (719) 577-5858

Buena Vista Palace at Walt Disney World
Walt Disney World, FL 32830, (407) 827-3255

Caesars Atlantic City Hotel Casino
Atlantic City, NJ 08401, (609) 343-2660

Caesars Palace
Las Vegas, NV 89109, (702) 731-7386

Callaway Gardens
Pine Mountain, GA 31822, (706) 663-5012

Camino Real Paso del Norte
El Paso, TX 79901, (915) 534-3067

Captain Cook Hotel
Anchorage, AK 99501, (907) 276-6000

Century Plaza Hotel & Towers
Los Angeles, CA 90067, (310) 551-3390

Circus Circus Enterprises Inc.
Las Vegas, NV 89109, (702) 794-3732

Claridge Casino & Hotel
Atlantic City, NJ 08401, (609) 340-3604

Clarion Hotel New Orleans
New Orleans, LA 70112, (504) 522-4500

Clubcorp International
Dallas, TX 75234, (214) 888-7599

Copley Plaza
Boston, MA 02116, (617) 421-9478

Disneyland International
Casting Center
Anaheim, CA 92806, (714) 999-4407

Doral Ocean Beach Resort
Miami Beach, FL 33140, (305) 535-2055

Doral Resort & Country Club
Miami, FL 33178, (305) 591-6424

Doubletree Hotels
Atlanta, GA 30328, (404) 395-3900
Austin, TX 78752, (512) 454-4107
Dallas, TX 75240, (214) 701-5279
Houston, TX 77056, (713) 961-9300
Marina del Rey, CA 90292, (310) 301-3000
Orange, CA 92668, (714) 634-4500

Doubletree Hotels (cont.)
Pasadena, CA 91101, (818) 792-2727
Philadelphia, PA 19107, (215) 893-1600
Salt Lake City, UT 84101, (801) 531-7500
San Francisco, CA 94010, (415) 348-4247

Drake City Center
Chicago, IL 60611, (312) 787-2200

Fairmont Hotels
Dallas, TX 75201, (214) 720-5311
New Orleans, LA 70140, (504) 529-7111
San Francisco, CA 94108, (415) 772-5139
San Jose, CA 95113, (408) 998-1900

Four Seasons Hotels
Houston, TX 77010, (713) 650-3437
Los Angeles, CA 90048, (310) 276-0822
Newport Beach, CA 92660, (714) 854-9675
Seattle, WA 98101, (206) 682-9164

Greenlefe Resort
Haines City, FL 33844-9732, (813) 421-5027

Handlery Union Square
San Francisco, CA 94102, (415) 781-7922

Harrah's Lake Tahoe Casino Hotel
South Lake Tahoe, CA 89449, (702) 588-6611

Harrah's Las Vegas
Las Vegas, NV 89109, (702) 369-5050

Harrah's Marina Hotel Casino
Atlantic City, NJ 08401, (609) 441-5681

Harvey Hotel Dallas-Fort Worth
Irving, TX 75063, (214) 929-4500

Harvey's Resort Hotel & Casino
Stateline, NV 89449, (702) 588-2411

Hilton & Towers Hotels & Resorts
Anaheim, CA 92802, (714) 740-4319
Anchorage, AK 99501, (907) 265-7124
Atlanta, GA 30303, (404) 221-6807
Atlanta, GA 30354, (404) 559-6781
Beverly Hills, CA 90210, (310) 285-1340
Burbank, CA 91501, (818) 840-6471
Chicago, IL 60603, (312) 726-7500
Chicago, IL 60605, (312) 922-4400
Chicago, IL 60666, (312) 601-2800
Long Beach, CA 90831, (310) 983-3445
Los Angeles, CA 90017, (213) 612-3990
Los Angeles, CA 90045, (310) 410-6111
McLean, VA 22102, (703) 761-5155
Miami Beach, FL 33140, (305) 538-2000
New York, NY 10019, (212) 586-7000
Pasadena, CA 91101, (818) 577-1000
Phoenix, AZ 85020, (602) 861-9505
Phoenix, AZ 85044, (602) 438-9303
Portland, OR 97204, (503) 220-2560
Reno, NV 89501, (702) 785-7006
Reno, NV 89595, (702) 789-2223
San Antonio, TX 78205, (210) 222-1400
San Antonio, TX 78216, (210) 340-6060
San Diego, CA 92108, (619) 543-9441
San Diego, CA 92109, (619) 275-8994

San Francisco, CA 94102, (415) 923-5068
San Francisco, CA 94128, (415) 875-3071
San Jose, CA 95110, (408) 947-4458
Washington, DC 20009, (202) 797-5818
Washington, DC 20036, (202) 639-5745

Holiday Inns
Atlanta, GA 30346, (404) 395-7700
Houston, TX 77027, (713) 961-7272
Houston, TX 77079, (713) 558-5580
Nashville, TN 37210, (615) 885-4491
Rockville, MD 20852, (301) 230-6770
San Diego, CA 92101, (619) 232-3861
San Francisco, CA 94108, (415) 398-8900
San Francisco, CA 94133, (415) 771-9000
Washington, DC 20005, (202) 737-2200
White Plains, NY 10601, (914) 682-0050

Hotel del Coronado
Coronado, CA 92118, (619) 522-8158

Hotel Inter-Continental
Chicago, IL 60611, (312) 321-8819
New Orleans, LA 70130, (504) 525-5566

Hotel Macklowe
New York, NY 10036, (212) 789-7600

Hotel Nikko at Beverly Hills
Los Angeles, CA 90048, (310) 246-2074

Hotel Parker Meridien
New York, NY 10019, (212) 708-7351

Hotel Sofitel
San Francisco, CA 94065, (415) 598-9000

Hotel Sofitel Ma Maison
Los Angeles, CA 90048, (310) 278-5444

Houston Medallion
Houston, TX 77092, (713) 688-0100

Hyatt/Regency/Grand Hotels
Albuquerque, NM 87102, (505) 766-6730
Arlington, VA 22202, (703) 418-7228
Atlanta, GA 30371, (404) 588-3746
Austin, TX 78704, (512) 477-1234
Baltimore, MD 21202, (410) 528-1234
Bethesda, MD 20814, (301) 657-1234
Boston, MA 02139, (617) 492-1234
Burlingame, CA 94010, (415) 696-2625
Chicago, IL 60601, (312) 565-1234
Dallas, TX 75207, (214) 712-7018
Dallas-Fort Worth Airport, TX 75261, (214) 615-6809
Denver, CO 80206, (303) 779-1234
Greenwich, CT 06870, (203) 637-1234
Houston, TX 77002, (713) 646-6912
Incline Village, NV 89450, (702) 832-3274
Irvine, CA 92714, (714) 863-1818
Kansas City, MO 64108, (816) 283-4473
Long Beach, CA 90802, (310) 432-7690
Los Angeles, CA 90017, (213) 683-1234
Minneapolis, MN 55403, (612) 370-1202
Monterey, CA 93940, (408) 372-1234
New Orleans, LA 70140, (504) 561-1234
New York, NY 10017, (212) 850-5942
Orlando, FL 32827, (407) 825-1342

Hyatt/Regency/Grand Hotels (cont.)
Orlando, FL 32836, (407) 239-3899
Orlando, FL 34746, (407) 396-5001
Phoenix, AZ 85004, (602) 252-1234
Sacramento, CA 95814, (916) 441-3111
San Antonio, TX 78205, (210) 531-2396
San Diego, CA 92101, (619) 687-6000
San Diego, CA 92109, (619) 221-4888
San Diego, CA 92122, (619) 552-6058
San Francisco, CA 94108, (415) 398-1234
San Francisco, CA 94111, (415) 392-1234
San Francisco, CA 94111, (415) 788-1234
San Francisco, CA 94133, (415) 563-1234
San Jose, CA 95112, (408) 993-1234
Savannah, GA 31401, (912) 944-3647
Schaumburg, IL 60173, (708) 605-1234
Tampa, FL 33602, (813) 225-1234
Tampa, FL 33607, (813) 287-0666
Washington, DC 20001, (202) 942-1586
Washington, DC 20001, (202) 637-4946

Imperial Palace Hotel
Las Vegas, NV 89109, (702) 794-3191

Le Meridien Newport Beach
Newport Beach, CA 92660, (714) 955-5656

Loew's Anatole Dallas
Dallas, TX 75207, (214) 761-7333

Loew's Coronado Bay Resort
San Diego, CA 92118, (619) 424-4480

Loew's Santa Monica Beach Hotel
Santa Monica, CA 90401, (310) 576-3121

Loew's Vanderbilt Plaza Hotel
Nashville, TN 37203, (615) 321-1908

Long Beach Renaissance
Long Beach, CA 90804, (310) 499-2518

Marriott Corp.
Washington, DC 20058, (301) 380-1202

Marriott Hotels
Albuquerque, NM 87110, (505) 881-6800
Anaheim, CA 92802, (714) 748-2482
Atlanta, GA 30303, (404) 586-6240
Atlanta, GA 30326, (404) 262-3344
Austin, TX 78701, (512) 478-1111
Baltimore, MD 21201, (410) 962-0202
Berkeley, CA 94710, (510) 548-7920
Boston, MA 02109, (617) 227-0800
Boston, MA 02116, (617) 578-0686
Burlingame, CA 94010, (415) 692-9100
Cambridge, MA 02142, (617) 494-6600
Charlotte, NC 28202, (704) 551-8000
Chicago, IL 60611, (312) 245-6909
Denver, CO 80202, (303) 291-3644
Denver, CO 80222, (303) 782-3214
Des Moines, IA 50309, (515) 245-5544
Hauppauge, NY 11788, (516) 232-9800
Houston, TX 77030, (713) 796-2218
Houston, TX 77056, (713) 961-1500
Hunt Valley, MD 21031, (410) 637-5574
Irvine, CA 92715, (714) 724-3681
La Jolla, CA 92037, (619) 552-8578

Los Angeles, CA 90045, (310) 337-5327
Marina del Rey, CA 90291, (310) 822-8555
Miami, FL 33132, (305) 536-6320
Minneapolis, MN 55403, (612) 349-4077
Minneapolis, MN 55425, (612) 854-3809
Monterey, CA 93940, (408) 647-4066
Nashville, TN 37210, (615) 872-2952
New York, NY 10036, (212) 704-8959
Newport Beach, CA 92660, (714) 640-4000
Newton, MA 02166, (617) 969-1000
Norfolk, VA 23510, (804) 628-6491
Orlando, FL 32819, (407) 351-2420
Orlando, FL 32822, (407) 851-9000
Orlando, FL 32821, (407) 238-8822
Osage Beach, MO 65065, (314) 348-8429
Overland Park, KS 66210, (913) 451-0259
Ponte Vedra Beach, FL 32082, (904) 285-7777
Portland, OR 97201, (503) 499-6334
Richmond, VA 23219, (804) 643-3400
Saint Louis, MO 63102, (314) 259-3381
Salt Lake City, UT 84101, (801) 537-6050
San Antonio, TX 78205, (210) 299-6518
San Antonio, TX 78205, (210) 554-6289
San Diego, CA 92101-7700, (619) 230-8901
San Diego, CA 92108, (619) 692-3800
Seattle, WA 98188, (206) 241-2421
Torrance, CA 90503-4897, (310) 316-3636
Uniondale, NY 11553, (516) 794-3800
Washington, DC 20058, (703) 461-6100
Woodland Hills, CA 91367, (818) 887-4800

Merv Griffin's Resorts Casino Hotel
Atlantic City, NJ 08404, (609) 340-6297

Mirage
Las Vegas, NV 89109, (702) 791-7111

Omni Hotels
Baltimore, MD 21201, (410) 385-6442
Boston, MA 02108, (617) 725-1623
Charlotte, NC 28202, (704) 377-6664
Houston, TX 77056, (713) 624-4823
Miami, FL 33132, (305) 374-8065
Washington, DC 20008, (202) 483-1119

Palace Station
Las Vegas, NV 89102, (702) 253-2950

Pan Pacific Hotel
San Diego, CA 92101-3580, (619) 338-3659
San Francisco, CA 94102, (415) 929-2011

Parc Oakland
Oakland, CA 94607, (510) 451-4000

Peabody Orlando
Orlando, FL 32819, (407) 352-6481

Phoenician
Scottsdale, AZ 85251, (602) 941-8200

Pier 66 Resort and Marina
Fort Lauderdale, FL 33316, (305) 728-3583

Promus Companies Inc.
Memphis, TN 38117, (901) 748-7626

Radisson Hotels
Alexandria, VA 22311, (703) 845-7654
Denver, CO 80202, (303) 893-0642
Detroit, MI 48226, (313) 965-0200
Fort Worth, TX 76102, (817) 870-2100
Manhattan Beach, CA 90266, (310) 546-9933
Minneapolis, MN 55435, (612) 835-7800
Southfield, MI 48075, (810) 827-4000

Ramada Hotels
Falls Church, VA 22043, (703) 821-3161
Houston, TX 77030, (713) 797-9000
Richardson, TX 75081, (214) 231-9600
Washington, DC 20001, (202) 682-3456

Red Lion Hotels
Bellevue, WA 98004, (206) 455-1300
Boise, ID 83714, (208) 386-9254
Culver City, CA 90230, (310) 649-1776
Omaha, NE 68102, (402) 346-1250
Portland, OR 97232, (503) 978-4515
Sacramento, CA 95815, (916) 922-8041
Salt Lake City, UT 84101, (801) 328-7082
San Diego, CA 92108, (619) 688-4004
San Jose, CA 95110, (408) 437-2118
Seattle, WA 98188, (206) 246-8600

Regent Beverly Wilshire
Beverly Hills, CA 90212, (310) 288-0803

Registry Resort
Naples, FL 33940, (813) 597-6859

Renaissance Hotel Los Angeles
Los Angeles, CA 90045, (310) 337-4646

Ritz-Carlton Hotels
Chicago, IL 60611, (312) 266-1000
Dana Point, CA 92629, (714) 240-5037
Kansas City, MO 64112, (816) 756-1500

Royal Sonesta Hotel
New Orleans, LA 70140, (504) 553-2336

Saint Anthony
San Antonio, TX 78205, (210) 227-4392

Sands Hotel & Casino
Atlantic City, NJ 08401, (609) 441-4525

Scottsdale Princess
Scottsdale, AZ 85255, (602) 585-2756

Sheraton Hotels
Atlanta, GA 30344, (404) 768-6660
Atlanta, GA 30361, (404) 892-6000
Baltimore, MD 21201, (410) 347-1808
Birmingham, AL 35203, (205) 307-3016
Braintree, MA 02184, (617) 848-0600
Chicago, IL 60611, (312) 464-1000
Dallas, TX 75251, (214) 385-3000
Danvers, MA 01923, (508) 777-2500
Denver, CO 80237, (303) 779-1100
Hartford, CT 06130, (203) 240-7255
Houston, TX 77032, (713) 442-5100
La Jolla, CA 92037, (619) 558-8058
Long Beach, CA 90802, (310) 499-2056
Los Angeles, CA 90071, (213) 617-6088

Miami Beach, FL 33154, (305) 865-7511
New Orleans, LA 70130, (504) 525-2500
New York, NY 10019, (212) 581-3300
Orlando, FL 32821, (407) 354-5057
San Antonio, TX 78205, (210) 227-3241
San Diego, CA 92101-1092, (619) 692-2793
San Francisco, CA 94105, (415) 392-8600
Santa Monica, CA 90401, (310) 319-3145
Seattle, WA 98101, (206) 287-5505
Stamford, CT 06902, (203) 351-1897
Tucson, AZ 85737, (602) 544-1240
Vienna, VA 22182, (703) 506-2518
Washington, DC 20008, (202) 328-2000

Stouffer Hotels
Atlanta, GA 30339, (404) 953-4500
Austin, TX 78759, (512) 343-2626
Baltimore, MD 21202, (410) 752-1920
Chicago, IL 60601, (312) 372-2022
Dallas, TX 75207, (214) 631-2222
Seattle, WA 98104, (206) 583-0300

Swissotel Hotels
Boston, MA 02111, (617) 422-5425
Chicago, IL 60601, (312) 565-0565

Tropworld Casino & Entertainment Resort
Atlantic City, NJ 08401-6390, (609) 340-4261

Trump Plaza Hotel & Casino
Atlantic City, NJ 08401, (800) 677-5627

Trump Taj Mahal
Atlantic City, NJ 08401, (609) 449-5627

Trump's Castle Casino Resort by the Bay
Atlantic City, NJ 08401, (609) 441-8464

Waldorf-Astoria
New York, NY 10022, (212) 872-4717

Walt Disney World Dolphin
Walt Disney World, FL 32830, (407) 934-4200

Walt Disney World Swan
Walt Disney World, FL 32830, (407) 934-1660

Westin Hotels & Resorts
Atlanta, GA 30343-9986, (404) 659-1400
Boston, MA 02116, (617) 351-7337
Chicago, IL 60611, (312) 943-7200
Denver, CO 80202, (303) 572-9100
Hilton Head Island, SC 29928, (803) 681-4000
Houston, TX 77056, (713) 960-6520
Indianapolis, IN 46204, (317) 231-3996
Kansas City, MO 64108, (816) 474-4400
Los Angeles, CA 90045, (310) 417-4538
Los Angeles, CA 90071, (213) 612-4845
Millbrae, CA 94030, (415) 872-8158
New Orleans, LA 70130, (504) 553-5059
Newport Beach, CA 92626-1988, (714) 540-2500
Rosemont, IL 60018, (708) 698-6000
San Francisco, CA 94102, (415) 397-7000
Seattle, WA 98101, (206) 727-5766
Tucson, AZ 85718, (602) 577-5850

Westward Ho Hotel & Casino
Las Vegas, NV 89109, (702) 731-6374

Willard Inter-Continental
Washington, DC 20004, (202) 637-7445

Wyndham Greenspoint
Houston, TX 77060, (713) 875-4506

Industrial & Commercial Machinery & Computer Equipment

Applied Magnetics Corp.
Goleta, CA 93117, (805) 683-5353

AST Research Inc.
Irvine, CA 92718, (714) 727-4141

Harnischfeger Corp.
Brookfield, WI 53201, (414) 671-7528

Hewlett-Packard Co.
Boise, ID 83714-1021, (208) 396-5200
Camas, WA 98607-9410, (206) 944-2493
Corvallis, OR 97330-4239, (503) 754-0919
Greeley, CO 80634-9776, (303) 350-4442
Palo Alto, CA 94304-1112, (415) 857-2092
Roseville, CA 95747-6502, (916) 786-6662

Micro Technology Inc.
Anaheim, CA 92807, (714) 970-0300

Seagate Technology Inc.
Scotts Valley, CA 95066, (408) 439-5627

Tenneco Inc.
Houston, TX 77252-2511, (713) 757-4193

Western Digital Corp.
Irvine, CA 92718, (714) 932-5766

Insurance Agents, Brokers & Service

Equifax Inc.
Atlanta, GA 30309, (404) 885-8550

Insurance Carriers

American Family Mutual Insurance Co.
Madison, WI 53783, (608) 242-4100

American General Corp.
Houston, TX 77019, (713) 831-3100

Blue Cross of California Inc.
Woodland Hills, CA 91367, (818) 703-3181

Cuna Mutual Insurance Group
Madison, WI 53705, (800) 562-2862

Federal Deposit Insurance Corp.
Washington, DC 20429, (800) 695-8052

GEICO Corp.
Washington, DC 20076, (800) 434-2655

Health Net
Van Nuys, CA 91409, (818) 593-7236

Humana Inc.
Louisville, KY 40202, (502) 580-3450

ITT Corp.
New York, NY 10019, (212) 258-1768

Kaiser Foundation Health Plan Inc.
Oakland, CA 94612, (510) 271-6888

Kaiser Permanente
Regional Offices
Pasadena, CA 91101-5103, (818) 405-3280

Metropolitan Life Insurance Co.
New York, NY 10010, (212) 578-4111

Mutual of Omaha Insurance Co.
Omaha, NE 68175, (402) 978-2040

Nationwide Mutual Insurance Co.
Columbus, OH 43216, (614) 249-5725

Principal Mutual Life Insurance Co.
Principal Financial Group Division
Des Moines, IA 50392-0001, (800) 525-2593

Prudential Insurance Company of America
Newark, NJ 07102, (201) 802-8494

SAFECO Corp.
Seattle, WA 98185, (206) 545-3233

Transamerica Life Companies
Los Angeles, CA 90015, (213) 741-7834

Justice, Public Order & Safety

Ada County Sheriff's Department
Boise, ID 83704, (208) 377-6707

Arizona (state) Department of Public Safety
Phoenix, AZ 85009, (602) 223-2148

California (state) Corrections Department
Sacramento, CA 95814, (800) 622-9675

California (state) Highway Patrol
Golden Gate Division
Vallejo, CA 94951, (707) 648-4195

Dade County Fire Department
Miami, FL 33173, (305) 596-8645

Federal Emergency Management Agency
Washington, DC 20472, (202) 646-3244

Florida (state) Attorney
Miami, FL 33136, (305) 547-0533

Florida (state) court system
Tallahassee, FL 32399-1900, (904) 488-2556

Florida (state) Department of Corrections
Gainesville, FL 32614-7007, (904) 334-1722
Lauderhill, FL 33319, (305) 497-3398
Marianna, FL 32446, (904) 482-3531
Orlando, FL 32801, (407) 423-6600
Tampa, FL 33609, (813) 871-7142

Florida (state) Department of Law Enforcement
Tallahassee, FL 32399-2166, (904) 488-0797

Hartford (city) courts
Hartford, CT 06106, (203) 566-1326

Jackson County Circuit Court
Kansas City, MO 64106, (816) 881-3470

Kent (city) Civil Service Commission
Kent, WA 98032-5895, (206) 859-2876

Los Angeles (city) City Attorney
Los Angeles, CA 90012, (213) 847-9424

Los Angeles County Superior Court
Los Angeles, CA 90012, (213) 974-5357

Michigan (state) Department of Corrections
Lansing, MI 48933, (517) 373-4246

New Jersey (state) Corrections Department
Trenton, NJ 08625, (609) 633-0496

New Jersey (state) Personnel Department
Trenton, NJ 08609, (609) 292-8668

Phoenix (city)
Phoenix, AZ 85004, (602) 262-7356

Portsmouth (city)
Portsmouth, VA 23704, (804) 398-0682

Seattle (city) Public Safety Civil Service Commission
Seattle, WA 98104, (206) 386-1303

South Carolina (state) Department of Corrections
Columbia, SC 29210, (803) 896-1201, (803) 896-1202, (803) 896-8524

South Carolina (state) Department of Juvenile Justice
Columbia, SC 29210, (803) 737-4293

United States Courts
Administrative Offices
Washington, DC 20544, (202) 273-2760

United States Department of Justice
Bureau of Prisons
Washington, DC 20534, (800) 347-7744

United States Marshals Service
Arlington, VA 22202-4210, (202) 307-9400

Virginia Beach (city)
Virginia Beach, VA 23456, (804) 427-3580

Leather & Leather Products

L.A. Gear Inc.
Los Angeles, CA 90066, (310) 822-1995

Nike Inc.
Beaverton, OR 97005, (503) 644-4224

Lumber & Wood Products, Except Furniture

Fleetwood Enterprises Inc.
Riverside, CA 92513, (909) 788-5627

Measuring, Analyzing & Controlling Instruments; Photographic, Medical & Optical Goods; Watches & Clocks

Bausch and Lomb Inc.
Rochester, NY 14601, (716) 338-8265

Baxter International Inc.
Deerfield, IL 60015-4625, (800) 322-9837

Cubic Corp.
San Diego, CA 92123-1515, (619) 277-6780

Eastman Kodak Co.
Rochester, NY 14650, (716) 724-4609

Electronics and Space Corp.
Saint Louis, MO 63136, (314) 553-2485

Ethicon Inc.
Somerville, NJ 08876, (800) 642-9534

Hewlett-Packard Co.
Colorado Springs, CO 80907-3423, (719) 590-2014
Rohnert Park, CA 94928-4902, (707) 794-3918
Spokane, WA 99220, (509) 921-4888

Honeywell Inc.
Minneapolis, MN 55440, (612) 951-2914

Morton Electronic Materials
Tustin, CA 92680, (714) 730-4200

Membership Organizations

American Marketing Association
Southern California Chapter
Northridge, CA 91325, (818) 363-4127

Special Libraries Association
Southern California Chapter
Pasadena, CA 91106, (818) 795-2145

Metal Mining

Phelps Dodge Corp.
Phoenix, AZ 85004, (602) 234-8281

Mining & Quarrying of Nonmetallic Minerals, Except Fuels

Vulcan Materials Co.
Birmingham, AL 35209, (205) 877-3986

Miscellaneous Manufacturing Industries

Armstrong World Industries Inc.
Lancaster, PA 17604, (717) 396-3441

Mattel Inc.
El Segundo, CA 90245, (310) 524-3535

Miscellaneous Retail

Hewlett-Packard Co.
Medical Products Group Division
Andover, MA 01810-1099, (508) 659-3012

Home Shopping Network Inc.
Clearwater, FL 34618-9090, (813) 572-8585

Jack Eckerd Corp.
Largo, FL 34647, (813) 399-6443

Owen Healthcare Inc.
Houston, TX 77036, (713) 777-8173

Walt Disney Consumer Products
Burbank, CA 91521-6692, (818) 567-5800

Zale Corp.
Irving, TX 75038, (214) 580-5408

Motion Pictures

Gaylord Entertainment Co.
Broadcast Division
Nashville, TN 37214, (615) 871-5920

Hanna-Barbera Productions Inc.
Hollywood, CA 90068, (213) 969-1262

Paramount Pictures Corp.
Los Angeles, CA 90038, (213) 956-5216

Sony Pictures Entertainment Inc.
Culver City, CA 90232-3119, (310) 280-4436

Twentieth Century-Fox Film Corp.
Beverly Hills, CA 90213, (310) 203-1360

Viacom Productions Inc.
Universal City, CA 91608, (818) 505-7581

Walt Disney Co.
Burbank, CA 91521, (818) 560-1811

Walt Disney Film Entertainment
Burbank, CA 91521, (818) 560-6335

Motor Freight Transportation & Warehousing

Mayflower Group Inc.
Carmel, IN 46032, (317) 875-1599

United Parcel Service of America Inc.
Atlanta, GA 30346, (404) 913-6800

Yellow Freight System Inc.
Overland Park, KS 66211, (913) 344-3900

Museums, Art Galleries & Botanical & Zoological Gardens

Denver Museum of Natural History
Denver, CO 80205, (303) 370-6437

Smithsonian Institution
Washington, DC 20560, (202) 287-3102

National Security & International Affairs

United States Department of the Air Force
The Pentagon
Washington, DC 20330-1000, (703) 693-6550

Charleston Air Force Base
Charleston Air Force Base, SC 29404-5021, (803) 566-4490

Dobbins AirReserve Base
Atlanta, GA 30069-4916, (404) 421-4968

McClellan AirForce Base
Sacramento, CA 95652, (916) 643-5911

Tinker Air Force Base
Tinker Air Force Base, OK 73150, (405) 739-3271

United States Department of the Army
The Pentagon
Washington, DC 20310, (703) 695-2589

Fort Benjamin Harrison
Indianapolis, IN 46249, (317) 542-2454

Fort Benning
Fort Benning, GA 31905-5031, (706) 545-7084

Fort Bliss
Fort Bliss, TX 79916-5803, (915) 568-4755

Fort Carson
Colorado Springs, CO 80913, (719) 526-3307

Peninsula Job Information Center
Newport News, VA 23606, (804) 873-3160

United States Department of Defense
Defense Contract Audit Agency
Alexandria, VA 22304-6178, (703) 274-4068

Defense Intelligence Agency
Washington, DC 20340-0001, (703) 284-1110

Defense Logistics Agency
Memphis, TN 38114, (901) 775-4933
Alexandria, VA 22304-6100, (703) 274-7372

United States Department of Justice
Immigration and Naturalization Service
Washington, DC 20536, (202) 514-4301

United States Department of State
Washington, DC 20520, (202) 647-7284

Foreign Service
Washington, DC 20520, (703) 875-7490

United States Department of the Navy
Consolidated Civilian Personnel Office
Washington, DC 20374-5050, (202) 433-4930

Little Creek Amphibious Base and Oceana Naval Air
  Station
Norfolk, VA 23511-3997, (804) 444-7541

Long Beach Naval Shipyard
Long Beach, CA 90822-5099, (310) 547-8277

Naval Air Station
Patuxent River, MD 20670, (301) 826-4801

Naval Weapon Station and Naval Warfare Assessment
  Center
Seal Beach, CA 90740, (310) 594-7881

Norfolk Naval Shipyard
Portsmouth, VA 23709-5000, (804) 396-5657

North Island Naval Air Station
San Diego, CA 92135-7041, (619) 545-1620

United States Marine Corps
Washington, DC 20380-0001, (703) 697-7474

Nondepository Credit Institutions

Visa International Service Association
San Mateo, CA 94402, (415) 432-8299

Oil & Gas Extraction

Amoco Corp.
Chicago, IL 60601, (312) 856-5551

Enron Corp.
Houston, TX 77002-7337, (713) 853-5884

Oryx Energy Co.
Dallas, TX 75240, (214) 715-8200

Pennzoil Co.
Houston, TX 77252, (713) 546-6630

Phillips Petroleum Co.
Bartlesville, OK 74004, (918) 661-5547

Paper & Allied Products

Avery Dennison Corp.
Pasadena, CA 91103, (800) 456-2751

Boise Cascade Corp.
Boise, ID 83728, (208) 384-4900

Personal Products Co.
Milltown, NJ 08850, (908) 524-0257

Scott Paper Co.
Philadelphia, PA 19113, (215) 522-5885

Petroleum Refining & Related Industries

Ashland Oil Inc.
Ashland, KY 41114, (606) 329-4328

Chevron Corp.
San Francisco, CA 94104, (415) 894-2552

Diamond Shamrock Inc.
San Antonio, TX 78269, (210) 641-2387

E.I. du Pont de Nemours and Company Inc.
Wilmington, DE 19898, (302) 992-6349

Farmland Industries Inc.
Kansas City, MO 64116, (816) 459-5056

Mapco Inc.
Tulsa, OK 74119, (918) 586-7178

Mobil Corp.
Fairfax, VA 22037, (703) 846-2777, (703) 849-6005

Primary Metal Industries

Weirton Steel Corp.
Weirton, WV 26062, (304) 797-4668

Printing, Publishing & Allied Industries

Deluxe Corp.
Shoreview, MN 55126, (612) 481-4100

Gannett Company Inc.
Arlington, VA 22234, (703) 284-6054

Harcourt Brace and Co.
Orlando, FL 32821, (407) 345-3060

Long Beach Press-Telegram
Long Beach, CA 90844, (310) 435-1161

Los Angeles Times
Los Angeles, CA 90053, (213) 237-5406, (213)
237-5407, (213) 237-5408

Miami Herald Publishing Inc.
Miami, FL 33132, (305) 376-2880, (305) 376-8959

Newsday Inc.
Melville, NY 11747, (516) 843-2076, (718) 575-2498

Orange County Register
Santa Ana, CA 92711, (714) 664-5099

Pacific Bell Directory
Los Angeles, CA 90010, (800) 559-7442

Washington Post Co.
Washington, DC 20071, (202) 334-5350

Public Finance, Taxation & Monetary Policy

California (state) Franchise Tax Board
Sacramento, CA 95812-0550, (916) 369-3624, (916)
369-3626

California (state) Lottery
Sacramento, CA 95814, (916) 322-0023

Florida (state) Department of Revenue
Tallahassee, FL 32399-0100, (904) 488-3895

Florida (state) Lottery
Tallahassee, FL 32399-4014, (904) 487-7731

North Carolina (state) Office of the Controller
Raleigh, NC 27609, (919) 715-5627

Pension Benefit Guarantee Corp.
Washington, DC 20006, (202) 326-4111

Texas (state) Auditor
Austin, TX 78701, (512) 479-3055

United States Department of the Treasury
Internal Revenue Service
Austin, TX 78741, (512) 462-8115, (512) 477-5627
Chamblee, GA 30341, (404) 455-2455
Covington, KY 41011, (606) 292-5304
Seattle, WA 98104, (206) 220-5757

Railroad Transportation

Consolidated Rail Corp.
Philadelphia, PA 19101, (609) 231-2165

National Railroad Passenger Corp. (Amtrak)
Washington, DC 20002, (202) 906-3866

Union Pacific Railroad Co.
Omaha, NE 68179, (402) 271-5000

Real Estate

Denver Convention Complex
Denver, CO 80202, (303) 640-8119

HTH Corp.
Honolulu, HI 96814, (808) 921-6110

Rubber & Miscellaneous Plastic Products

Gates Corp.
Denver, CO 80217, (303) 744-5900

Services, Not Elsewhere Classified

Minneapolis Cityline
Saint Paul, MN 55114, (612) 645-6060

Social Services

ACTION
Washington, DC 20525, (202) 606-5039

Los Angeles Gay and Lesbian Community Services Center
West Hollywood, CA 90028, (213) 993-7687

Peace Corps
Washington, DC 20526, (202) 606-3214

Stone, Clay, Glass, & Concrete Products

Corning Inc.
Corning, NY 14831, (607) 974-2393

PPG Industries Inc.
Pittsburgh, PA 15272, (412) 434-2002

Transportation by Air

Alaska Air Group Inc.
Seattle, WA 98168, (206) 433-3230

America West Airlines Inc.
Phoenix, AZ 85034, (602) 693-8650

AMR Corp.
Dallas/Fort Worth Airport, TX 75261, (817) 963-1110,
(817) 963-1234

Continental Airlines Holdings Inc.
Houston, TX 77210-4330, (713) 834-5300

Denver (city and county) New Airport Employment Office
Denver, CO 80204, (800) 866-3382

Federal Express Corp.
Memphis, TN 38132, (901) 535-9555, (901) 797-6830
Newport Beach, CA 92660, (818) 753-5552, (714)
729-0330

Southwest Airlines Co.
Dallas, TX 75235, (214) 904-4803

UAL Corp.
Chicago, IL 60666, (708) 952-4000

USAir Group Inc.
Arlington, VA 22227, (703) 418-7499

Transportation Equipment

Boeing Co.
Seattle, WA 98108-4002, (206) 965-3111

Cessna Aircraft Co.
Wichita, KS 67215, (316) 941-6155

Freightliner Corp.
Portland, OR 97217, (503) 735-7091, (503) 735-8657

McDonnell Douglas Corp.
Saint Louis, MO 63166, (314) 232-4222

PACCAR Inc.
Bellevue, WA 98004, (206) 637-5011

Rohr Industries Inc.
Chula Vista, CA 91912, (619) 691-2601

Sundstrand Corp.
Rockford, IL 61125, (815) 226-6269

Transportation Services

Airborne Freight Corp.
Seattle, WA 98111, (800) 426-2323

Burlington Air Express Inc.
Irvine, CA 92715, (714) 752-1212

Water Transportation

American President Companies Ltd.
Oakland, CA 94607, (510) 272-8082

Carnival Cruise Lines Inc.
Miami, FL 33178-2418, (305) 599-2600

Wholesale Trade—Durable Goods

Hewlett-Packard Co.
Southern California area
Fullerton, CA 92631-5221, (714) 758-5414

Mid-America Sales Region
Rolling Meadows, IL 60008-3700, (708) 245-3909

Intelligent Electronics Inc.
Exton, PA 19341, (610) 458-6793

Pioneer Electronics USA Inc.
Long Beach, CA 90801-1639, (310) 835-6177

Wholesale Trade—Nondurable Goods

Bergen Brunswig Corp.
Orange, CA 92668-3502, (714) 385-4473

Certified Grocers of California Limited
Los Angeles, CA 90040-1401, (213) 726-2601

McKesson Corp.
San Francisco, CA 94104, (415) 983-8409, (415) 983-8784